Practical Ethics

Third Edition

PETER SINGER

Princeton University and the University of Melbourne

CAMBRIDGE
UNIVERSITY PRESS

CAMBRIDGE UNIVERSITY PRESS
Cambridge, New York, Melbourne, Madrid, Cape Town, Singapore,
São Paulo, Delhi, Dubai, Tokyo, Mexico City

Cambridge University Press
32 Avenue of the Americas, New York, NY 10013-2473, USA

www.cambridge.org
Information on this title: www.cambridge.org/9780521707688

First edition published 1980
Second edition published 1993
Third edition published 2011

Printed in Great Britain by Clays Ltd, St Ives plc

A catalog record for this publication is available from the British Library.

Library of Congress Cataloging in Publication data

Singer, Peter, 1946–
Practical ethics / Peter Singer. – 3rd ed.
   p. cm.
Includes bibliographical references and index.
ISBN 978-0-521-88141-8 (hardback) – ISBN 978-0-521-70768-8 (paperback)
1. Ethics.   2. Social ethics.   I. Title.
BJ1012.S49   2011
170–dc22   2010043690

ISBN 978-0-521-88141-8 Hardback
ISBN 978-0-521-70768-8 Paperback

Practical Ethics

Third Edition

For thirty years, Peter Singer's *Practical Ethics* has been the classic
introduction to applied ethics. For this third edition, the author
has revised and updated all the chapters and added a new chapter
addressing climate change, one of the most important ethical challenges of our generation.

Some of the questions discussed in this book concern our daily
lives. Is it ethical to buy luxuries when others do not have enough to
eat? Should we buy meat produced from intensively reared animals?
Am I doing something wrong if my carbon footprint is above the
global average? Other questions confront us as concerned citizens:
equality and discrimination on the grounds of race or sex; abortion,
the use of embryos for research, and euthanasia; political violence
and terrorism; and the preservation of our planet's environment.

This book's lucid style and provocative arguments make it an ideal
text for university courses and for anyone willing to think about how
she or he ought to live.

Peter Singer is currently Ira W. DeCamp Professor of Bioethics at
the University Center for Human Values at Princeton University and
Laureate Professor at the Centre for Applied Philosophy and Public
Ethics at the University of Melbourne. He is the author or editor of
more than forty books, including *Animal Liberation* (1975), *Rethinking
Life and Death* (1996) and, most recently, *The Life You Can Save* (2009).
In 2005, he was named one of the 100 most influential people in the
world by *Time* magazine.

Contents

Preface

Practical ethics covers a wide area. We can find ethical ramifications in most of our choices, if we look hard enough. This book does not attempt to cover the whole area. The problems it deals with have been selected on two grounds: relevance and the extent to which philosophical reasoning can contribute to discussion of them.

The most relevant ethical issues are those that confront us daily: is it right to spend money on entertaining ourselves when we could use it to help people living in extreme poverty? Are we justified in treating animals as nothing more than machines producing flesh for us to eat? Should we drive a car – thus emitting greenhouse gases that warm the planet – if we could walk, cycle or use public transport? Other problems, like abortion and euthanasia, fortunately are not everyday decisions for most of us; but they are still relevant because they can arise at some time in our lives. They are also issues of current concern about which any active participant in a democratic society should have informed and considered opinions.

The extent to which an issue can be usefully discussed philosophically depends on the kind of issue it is. Some issues are controversial largely because there are facts in dispute. Should we build nuclear power stations to replace the coal-fired ones that are a major cause of global warming? The answer to that question seems to hang largely on whether it is possible to make the nuclear fuel cycle safe, both against accidental release of radioactive materials and against terrorist attacks. Philosophers are unlikely to have the expertise to answer this question. (That does not mean that they can have nothing to say about it – for instance, they may still be able to say something useful about whether it is acceptable to run a given risk.) In other cases, however, the facts are clear and accepted by both sides, and it is conflicting ethical views that give rise to disagreement over what to do. The important facts about abortion are not really in dispute – as we shall see in Chapter 6, when does a human life begin? is really a question of values rather than of facts – but the ethics of abortion is hotly disputed. With questions of this kind, the methods of reasoning and analysis in which philosophers engage really can make a difference. The issues discussed in this book are ones in which ethical, rather than factual, disagreement plays a major role. Thinking about them philosophically should enable us to reach better-justified conclusions.

Practical Ethics, first published in 1980, has been widely read, used in many courses at universities and colleges and translated into fifteen languages. I always expected that many readers would disagree with the conclusions I defend. What I did not expect was that some would try to prevent the book's arguments being discussed. Yet in the late 1980s and early 1990s, in Germany, Austria and Switzerland, opposition to the views on euthanasia contained in this book reached such a peak that conferences or lectures at which I was invited to speak were cancelled, and courses taught by professors at German universities in which the book was to be used were subjected to such repeated disruption that they had to be abandoned. In Zurich in 1991, when I was attempting to lecture, a protester leapt onto the stage, tore my glasses from my face, threw them down on the floor and stamped on them. Less violent protests took place at Princeton University in 1999, when I was appointed to a chair of bioethics. People objecting to my views barred the entrance to the central administrative building of the university, demanding that my appointment be rescinded. Steve Forbes, a trustee of the university and at the time a candidate for the Republican nomination for the President of the United States, announced that as long as I was at the university, he would withhold further donations to it. Both the university president and I received death threats. To its great credit, the university stood firm in its defence of academic freedom.

The protests led me to reflect on whether the views defended in this book really are so erroneous or so dangerous that they would be better left unsaid. Although many of the protesters were simply misinformed about what I am saying, there is an underlying truth to the claim that the book breaks a taboo – or perhaps more than one taboo. In Germany since the Nazi era, for many years it was impossible to discuss openly the question of euthanasia or whether a human life may be so full of misery as not to be worth living. More fundamental still, and not limited to Germany, is the taboo on comparing the value of human and nonhuman lives. In the commotion that followed the cancellation of a conference in Germany at which I had been invited to speak, the German sponsoring organization, to disassociate itself from my views, passed a series of motions, one of which read: 'The uniqueness of human life forbids any comparison – or more specifically, equation – of human existence with other living beings, with their forms of life or interests.' Comparing, and in some cases equating, the lives of humans and animals is exactly what some chapters of this book are about; in fact, it could be said that if there is any single aspect of this book that distinguishes it from other approaches to such issues as human equality, abortion, euthanasia and the environment, it is the fact that these topics are approached with a conscious disavowal of any assumption that all members of our own species have, merely because they are members of our species, any distinctive worth or inherent value that puts them above members of other species. The belief in human superiority is a very fundamental one, and it underlies our thinking in many sensitive areas. To challenge it is no trivial matter, and that such a challenge should provoke a strong reaction ought not to surprise us. Nevertheless, once we have understood that the breaching of this taboo on comparing humans and animals is partially responsible for the protests, it becomes clear that there is no going back. For reasons that are developed in subsequent chapters, to prohibit any cross-species comparisons would be philosophically indefensible. It would also make it impossible to overcome the wrongs we are now doing to nonhuman animals and would reinforce attitudes that have done irreparable damage to the environment of our planet.

So I have not backed away from the views that have caused so much controversy. If these views have their dangers, the danger of attempting to continue to silence criticism of widely accepted ideas is greater still. Since the days of Plato, philosophy has advanced dialectically as philosophers have offered reasons for disagreeing with the views of other philosophers. Learning from disagreement leads us to a more defensible position and is one reason why, even if the views I hold are mistaken, they should be discussed.

Though I have not changed my views on those topics – euthanasia and abortion – against which most of the protests were directed, this third edition is significantly different from the first and second editions. Every chapter has been reworked, factual material has been updated, and where my position has been misunderstood by my critics, I have tried to make it clearer. On some issues, new questions and new arguments relevant to old questions have emerged. In the discussion of the moral status of early human life, for instance, scientific advances have led to a new debate about the destruction of human embryos to obtain stem cells. The developing scientific understanding of early human life has not only given rise to hopes of major gains in treating disease; it has also demonstrated that many cells – not only the fertilized egg – contain the potential to start a new human life. We need to ask whether this changes the arguments about the moral status of human embryos and, if so, in what way.

The sections of the book that have left me in the greatest philosophical uncertainty are those parts of Chapters 4 and 5 that discuss whether there is some sense in which bringing into existence a new being – whether a human being or a nonhuman animal – can compensate for the death of a similar being who has been killed. That issue in turn leads to questions about the optimum population size and whether the existence of more sentient beings enjoying their lives would, other things being equal, be a good thing. These questions may seem arcane and far removed from the 'practical ethics' promised by the title of this book, but they have important ethical implications. As we shall see, they can serve as an example of how our judgments of what is right and wrong need to be informed by investigations into deep and difficult philosophical issues. In revising these sections for this edition, I have found myself unable to maintain with any confidence that the position I took in the previous edition – based solely on preference utilitarianism – offers a satisfactory answer to these quandaries.

That reconsideration of my earlier position is the most significant philosophical change to this edition. The addition with the greatest practical importance, however, is a new chapter that deals with the great moral challenge of our time – climate change. Too often, we fail to see climate change as an ethical issue. I hope this chapter will show clearly that it is. The number of chapters in this edition remains the same as it was for the second edition because a chapter that I added to that edition, on our obligation to accept refugees, does not appear in this edition. This is not because the issue of admitting refugees has become any less important than it was in 1993. On the contrary, it is probably more significant now and will become more significant still, in coming decades, as we begin to see increasing numbers of 'climate refugees' – people who can no longer live where their parents and grandparents lived, because rainfall patterns have changed or sea levels have risen. But I had become dissatisfied with the chapter as it stood. This is partly because the issue is one to which the facts – for example, about the possibility of a country taking in large numbers of refugees without this leading to a racist backlash that would harm minority groups within the country – are highly relevant. I had also become more aware of differences between countries that are relevant to this issue, and so I reluctantly concluded that any attempt to deal with the issue in a single chapter of a volume such as this, aimed at an international audience, is bound to be superficial. If the issue cannot be treated adequately and in a properly nuanced way, I decided, it would be better not to include it in this book, especially as it is one of those issues on which governments must set policy rather than one on which individuals actions can make a significant difference.

In writing and revising this book, I have made extensive use of my own previously published articles and books. Chapter 3 is based on my book, *Animal Liberation* (2nd edition, New York Review/Random House, 1990), although it also takes account of objections made since the book first appeared in 1975. The sections of Chapter 6 on such topics as in vitro fertilization, the argument from potential, embryo experimentation and the use of fetal tissue, all draw on work I wrote jointly with Karen Dawson, which was published as "IVF and the Argument from Potential", in *Philosophy and Public Affairs*, vol. 17 (1988) and in Peter Singer, Helga Kuhse and others, *Embryo Experimentation* (Cambridge University Press, 1990). In the third edition, this chapter includes material responding to the arguments of Patrick Lee and Robert George that first appeared in Agata Sagan and Peter Singer, "The Moral Status of Stem Cells", *Metaphilosophy*, 38 (2007). Chapter 7 contains material from the much fuller treatment of the issue of euthanasia for severely disabled infants that Helga Kuhse and I provided in *Should the Baby Live?* (Oxford University Press, 1985). Chapter 8 restates arguments from "Famine, Affluence and Morality", *Philosophy and Public Affairs*, vol. 1 (1972), and for this edition, I drew on my much more recent and comprehensive account of the issue in *The Life You Can Save* (Random House, 2009). The new Chapter 9 draws on material first published in *One World* (Yale University Press, 2002) and from "Climate Change as an Ethical Issue", in Jeremy Moss (ed.), *Climate Change and Social Justice* (Melbourne University Press, 2009). Chapter 10 is based on "Environmental Values", a chapter I contributed to Ian Marsh (ed.), *The Environmental Challenge* (Longman Cheshire, Melbourne, 1991). Portions of Chapter 11 draw on my first book, *Democracy and Disobedience* (Oxford, Clarendon Press, 1973). The revisions for the third edition also include passages from my responses to critics in *Peter Singer Under Fire,* edited by Jeff Schaler (Open Court, Chicago, 2009).

H. J. McCloskey, Derek Parfit and Robert Young provided useful comments on a draft version of the first edition of this book. Robert Young's ideas also entered into my thinking at an earlier stage, when we jointly taught a course on these topics at La Trobe University. The chapter on euthanasia, in particular, owes much to his ideas, though he may not agree with everything in it. Going back further still, my interest in ethics was stimulated by H. J. McCloskey, whom I was fortunate to have as a teacher during my undergraduate years; and the mark left by R. M. Hare, who taught me at Oxford, is apparent in the ethical foundations underlying the positions taken in this book. Jeremy Mynott of Cambridge University Press encouraged me to write the book and helped to shape and improve it as it went along. The second edition of the book benefited from work I did with Karen Dawson, Paola Cavalieri, Renata Singer and especially Helga Kuhse. For this third edition, I must give what are, sadly, posthumous thanks to Brent Howard, a gifted thinker who several years ago sent me extensive notes for a possible revision of the second edition. I am also most grateful to Agata Sagan for suggestions and research assistance throughout the revision of the book. Her contribution is most evident in the discussion of the moral status of embryos and stem cells, but her ideas and suggestions have improved the book in several other areas as well.

There are, of course, many others with whom I have discussed the issues that are the subject of this book. Back in 1984, Dale Jamieson made me aware of the significance of climate change as an ethical issue, and I continue to check my thoughts on that topic and on many others with him. I have learned a lot from Jeff McMahan, from personal contact, from a graduate seminar we co-taught on issues of life and death and from his many writings. At Princeton University, I have often benefited from comments on my work from my colleagues, from visiting Fellows at the University Center for Human Values and from students, both graduate and undergraduate. Don Marquis and David Benatar each spent a year at the Center, and those visits provided opportunities for many good discussions. I also thank my colleagues and the graduate students at the Centre for Applied Philosophy and Public Ethics at the University of Melbourne for their comments at occasional lectures and seminars at which I have presented my work.

Harriet McBryde Johnson and I disagreed vehemently about euthanasia for infants with severe disabilities, but there was never any acrimony between us, and she always presented my views with scrupulous fairness. Sadly, our exchanges ended with her death in 2008, and I miss her critical presence.

The astute reader who compares this edition with the previous one may notice that I am now more ready to entertain – although not yet embrace – the idea that there are objective ethical truths that are independent of what anyone desires. I owe that shift – which could not be adequately explored in a book of this nature – to my reading of a draft of Derek Parfit's immensely impressive forthcoming book, *On What Matters*. I hope to write more about this question on another occasion.

Peter Singer
Princeton and Melbourne, 2010

Note to the reader. To avoid cluttering the text, notes, references and suggested further reading are grouped together at the end of the book.

1

About Ethics

This book is about practical ethics, that is, about the application of ethics or morality – I shall use the words interchangeably – to practical issues. Though the reader may be impatient to get to these issues without delay, if we are to have a useful discussion within ethics, it is necessary to say a little *about* ethics so that we have a clear understanding of what we are doing when we discuss ethical questions. This first chapter, therefore, sets the stage for the remainder of the book. To prevent it from growing into an entire volume itself, it is brief and at times dogmatic. I cannot take the space properly to consider all the different conceptions of ethics that might be opposed to the one I shall defend, but this chapter will at least serve to reveal the assumptions on which the remainder of the book is based.

WHAT ETHICS IS NOT

Ethics is not Primarily About Sex

There was a time, around the 1950s, when if you saw a newspaper headline reading RELIGIOUS LEADER ATTACKS DECLINING MORAL STANDARDS, you would expect to read yet again about promiscuity, homosexuality and pornography, and not about the puny amounts we give as overseas aid to poorer nations or the damage we are causing to our planet's environment. As a reaction to the dominance of this narrow sense of morality, it became popular to regard morality as a system of nasty puritanical prohibitions, mainly designed to stop people from having fun.

Fortunately, this era has passed. We no longer think that morality, or ethics, is a set of prohibitions particularly concerned with sex. Even religious leaders talk more about global poverty and climate change and less about promiscuity and pornography. Decisions about sex may involve considerations of honesty, concern for others, prudence, avoidance of harm to others and so on, but the same could be said of decisions about driving a car. (In fact, the moral issues raised by driving a car, both from an environmental and from a safety point of view, are much more serious than those raised by safe sex.) Accordingly, this book contains no discussion of sexual morality. There are more important ethical issues to be considered.

Ethics is not 'Good in Theory but not in Practice'

The second thing that ethics is not is an ideal system that is all very noble in theory but no good in practice. The reverse of this is closer to the truth: an ethical judgment that is no good in practice must suffer from a theoretical defect as well, for the whole point of ethical judgments is to guide practice.

People sometimes believe that ethics is inapplicable to the real world because they assume that ethics is a system of short and simple rules like 'Do not lie', 'Do not steal' and 'Do not kill'. It is not surprising that those who hold this model of ethics should also believe that ethics is not suited to life's complexities. In unusual situations, simple rules conflict; and even when they do not, following a rule can lead to disaster. It may normally be wrong to lie, but if you were living in Nazi Germany and the Gestapo came to your door looking for Jews, it would surely be right to deny the existence of the Jewish family hiding in your attic.

Like the failure of a morality focused on restricting our sexual behavior, the failure of an ethic of simple rules must not be taken as a failure of ethics as a whole. It is only a failure of one view of ethics, and not even an irremediable failure of that view. Those who think that ethics is a system of rules – the deontologists – can rescue their position by finding more complicated and more specific rules that do not conflict with each other, or by ranking the rules in some hierarchical structure to resolve conflicts between them. Moreover, there is a long-standing approach to ethics that is quite untouched by the complexities that make simple rules difficult to apply. This is the consequentialist view. Consequentialists start not with moral rules but with goals. They assess actions by the extent to which they further these goals. The best-known, though not the only, consequentialist theory is utilitarianism. The classical utilitarian regards an action as right if it produces more happiness for all affected by it than any alternative action and wrong if it does not. Two qualifications to that statement are necessary: 'more happiness' here means net happiness, after deducting any suffering or misery that may also have been caused by the action; and if two different actions tie for the title of producing the greatest amount of happiness, either of them is right.

The consequences of an action vary according to the circumstances in which it is performed. Hence, a utilitarian can never properly be accused of a lack of realism or of a rigid adherence to ideals in defiance of practical experience. The utilitarian will judge lying as bad in some circumstances and good in others, depending on its consequences.

Ethics is not Based on Religion

The third thing ethics is not is something intelligible only in the context of religion. I shall treat ethics as entirely independent of religion.

Some theists say that ethics cannot do without religion because the very meaning of 'good' is nothing other than 'what God approves'. Plato refuted a similar claim more than two thousand years ago by arguing that if the gods approve of some actions it must be because those actions are good, in which case it cannot be the gods' approval that makes them good. The alternative view makes divine approval entirely arbitrary: if the gods had happened to approve of torture and disapprove of helping our neighbours, torture would have been good and helping our neighbours bad. Some theists have attempted to extricate themselves from this dilemma by maintaining that God is good and so could not possibly approve of torture; but if these theists want to maintain that good means what God approves, they are caught in a trap of their own making, for what can they possibly mean by the assertion that God is good – that God is approved of by God?

Traditionally, the more important link between religion and ethics was that religion was thought to provide a reason for doing what is right, the reason being that those who are virtuous will be rewarded by an eternity of bliss while the rest roast in hell. Not all religious thinkers have accepted this: Immanuel Kant, a most pious Christian, scorned anything that smacked of a self-interested motive for obeying the moral law. We must obey it, he said, for its own sake. Nor do we have to be Kantians to dispense with the motivation offered by traditional religion. There is a long line of thought that finds the source of ethics in our benevolent inclinations and the sympathy most of us have for others. This is, however, a complex topic, and I shall not pursue it here because it is the subject of the final chapter of this book. It is enough to say that our everyday observation of our fellows clearly shows that ethical behaviour does not require belief in heaven and hell and, conversely, that belief in heaven and hell does not always lead to ethical behaviour.

If morality was not given to us by a divine creator, from where did it come? We know that, like our close relatives the chimpanzees and bonobos, we have evolved from social mammals. It seems that during this long period of evolution, we developed a moral faculty that generates intuitions about right and wrong. Some of these we share with our primate relatives – they too have a strong sense of reciprocity; and in their sometimes outraged responses to a flagrant failure to repay a good turn, we can see the beginnings of our own sense of justice. Observing a group of chimps living together, Frans de Waal noticed that after one chimp, Puist, had supported another, Luit, in fending off an attack from a third, Nikkie, Nikkie subsequently attacked Puist. Puist beckoned to Luit for support, but Luit did nothing. When the attack from Nikkie was over, Puist furiously attacked Luit. De Waal comments: 'If her fury was in fact the result of Luit's failure to help her after she had helped him, this would suggest that reciprocity among chimpanzees is governed by the same sense of moral rightness and justice as it is among humans.'

From these intuitive responses, shared with other social mammals, morality has developed under the influence of our acquisition of language. It has taken distinct forms in different human cultures, but there is still a surprisingly large common ground which you, the reader, will most probably share. It is vital for everything that follows in this book that we should understand that these evolved intuitions do not necessarily give us the right answers to moral questions. What was good for our ancestors may not be good for human beings as a whole today, let alone for our planet and all the other beings living on it. No doubt small human communities on a lightly populated planet were more likely to survive if they had an ethic that said 'Be fruitful and multiply' and, consistently with this, favoured large families and condemned homosexuality. Today, we can and should critically examine any intuitive reactions we may have to such practices and take account of the consequences of having large families or of homosexuality, for the world in which we live.

Many people assume that anything natural is good. They are likely to think that if our moral intuitions are natural, we ought to follow them, but this would be a mistake. As John Stuart Mill pointed out in his essay *On Nature*, the word 'nature' either means everything that exists in the universe, including human beings and all that they create, or it means the world as it would be, apart from human beings and what humans bring about. In the first sense, nothing that humans do can be 'unnatural.' In the second sense, the claim that something humans do is 'unnatural' is no objection at all to doing it, for everything that we do is an interference with nature, and obviously much of that interference – like treating disease – is highly desirable.

Understanding the origins of morality, therefore, frees us from two putative masters, God and nature. We have inherited a set of moral intuitions from our ancestors. Now we need to work out which of them should be changed.

Ethics is not Relative to the Society in which You Live

The most philosophically challenging view about ethics that I shall deny in this opening chapter is that ethics is relative or subjective. At least, I shall deny this view in some of the senses in which it is often asserted. This point requires a more extended discussion than the other three.

Let us take first the oft-asserted idea that ethics is relative to the society one happens to live in. This is true in one sense and false in another. It is true that, as we have already seen in discussing consequentialism, actions that are right in one situation because of their good consequences may be wrong in another situation because of their bad consequences. Thus, casual sexual intercourse may be wrong when it leads to the existence of children who cannot be adequately cared for and not wrong when, because of the existence of effective contraception, it does not lead to reproduction at all. This is only a superficial form of relativism. It suggests that a specific principle like 'Casual sex is wrong' may be relative to time and place, but it is compatible with such a principle being objectively false when it is stated to apply to all instances of casual sex, no matter what the circumstances. Nor does this form of relativism give us any reason to reject the universal applicability of a more general principle like 'Do what increases happiness and reduces suffering.'

A more fundamental form of relativism became popular in the nineteenth century when data on the moral beliefs and practices of far-flung societies began pouring in. The knowledge that there were places where sexual relations between unmarried people were regarded as perfectly wholesome brought the seeds of a revolution in sexual attitudes to the strict reign of Victorian prudery. It is not surprising that to some the new knowledge suggested, not merely that the moral code of nineteenth-century Europe was not objectively valid, but that no moral judgment can do more than reflect the customs of the society in which it is made.

Marxists adapted this form of relativism to their own theories. The ruling ideas of each period, they said, are the ideas of its ruling class, and so the morality of a society is relative to its dominant economic class, and thus indirectly relative to its economic basis. This enabled them, they thought, to triumphantly refute the claims of feudal and bourgeois morality to objective, universal validity. Then some Marxists noticed that this raises a problem: if all morality is relative, what is so special about communism? Why side with the proletariat rather than the bourgeoisie?

Friedrich Engels, Marx's co-author, dealt with this problem in the only way possible: by abandoning relativism in favour of the more limited descriptive claim that the morality of a society divided into classes will always reflect the interests of the ruling class. In contrast, the morality of a society without class antagonisms would, Engels wrote, be a 'really human' morality. This is no longer normative relativism – that is, relativism about what we ought to do – at all, but Marxism still, in a confused sort of way, provides the impetus for a lot of woolly relativist ideas, often dressed up as 'postmodernism'.

The problem that led Engels to abandon relativism defeats ordinary ethical relativism as well. Anyone who has thought about a difficult ethical decision knows that being told what our society thinks we ought to do does not settle the quandary. We have to reach our own decision. The beliefs and customs we were brought up with may exercise great influence on us, but once we start to reflect on them, we can decide whether to act in accordance with them or go against them.

The opposite view – that ethics is and can only be relative to a particular society – has most implausible consequences. If our society disapproves of slavery while another society approves of it, this kind of relativism gives us no basis for choosing between these conflicting views. Indeed, on a relativist analysis, there is no conflict – when I say slavery is wrong, I am really only saying that my society disapproves of slavery, and when the slave owners from the other society say that slavery is right, they are only saying that their society approves of it. Why argue? Most likely, we are both speaking the truth.

Worse still, the relativist cannot satisfactorily account for the non-conformist. If 'slavery is wrong' means 'my society disapproves of slavery', then someone who lives in a society that does not disapprove of slavery is, in claiming that slavery is wrong, making a simple factual error. An opinion poll could demonstrate the error of an ethical judgment. Would-be reformers are therefore in a parlous situation: when they set out to change the ethical views of their fellow citizens, they are *necessarily* mistaken; it is only when they succeed in winning most of the society over to their own views that those views become right.

Ethics is not Merely a Matter of Subjective Taste or Opinion

These difficulties are enough to sink ethical relativism; ethical subject-ivism at least avoids making nonsense of the valiant efforts of would-be moral reformers, for it makes ethical judgments depend on the approval or disapproval of the individual making the judgment, rather than that person's society. There are other difficulties, though, that at least some forms of ethical subjectivism cannot overcome.

If those who say that ethics is subjective mean by this that when I say that cruelty to animals is wrong I am really only saying that I disapprove of cruelty to animals, they are faced with an aggravated form of one of the difficulties of relativism: the inability to account for ethical disagreement. What was true for the relativist in the case of disagreement between people from different societies is for the subjectivist true of all ethical disagreement. I say cruelty to animals is wrong; you say it is not wrong. If this means that I disapprove of cruelty to animals and you do not, both statements may be true and there is nothing to argue about.

Other theories that can be regarded as falling under the broad label of 'subjectivism' are not open to this objection. Suppose someone main-tains that ethical judgments are neither true nor false because they do not describe anything – neither objective moral facts nor one's own subject-ive states of mind. This theory might hold that ethical judgments express emotional attitudes rather than describe them, and we disagree about ethics because we try, by expressing our own attitude, to bring our listen-ers to a similar attitude. This view, first developed by C. L. Stevenson, is known as emotivism. Or it might be, as R. M. Hare has urged, that ethical judgments are prescriptions and therefore more closely related to com-mands than to statements of fact. On this view – Hare calls it universal prescriptivism, and we shall look at it more closely later in this chapter – we disagree because we care about what people do. A third view, defen-ded by J. L. Mackie, grants that many aspects of the way we think and talk about ethics imply the existence of objective moral standards, but asserts that these features of our thought and talk involve us in some kind of error – perhaps the legacy of the belief that ethics is a God-given system of law, or perhaps just another example of our tendency to objectify our personal wants and preferences.

These are plausible accounts of ethics, as long as they are carefully distinguished from the crude form of subjectivism that sees ethical judgments as descriptions of the speaker's attitudes. In their denial of a realm of ethical facts that is part of the real world, existing quite independently of us, they may be correct. Suppose that they are correct: does it follow from this that ethical judgments are immune from criticism, that there is no role for reason or argument in ethics and that, from the standpoint of reason, any ethical judgment is as good as any other? I do not think it does, and advocates of the three positions referred to in the previous paragraph do not deny reason and argument a role in ethics, though they disagree as to the significance of this role.

This issue of the role that reason can play in ethics is the crucial point raised by the claim that ethics is subjective. To put practical ethics on a sound basis, it has to be shown that ethical reasoning is possible. The denial of objective ethical facts does not imply the rejection of ethical reasoning. Here the temptation is to say simply that the proof of the pudding lies in the eating, and the proof that reasoning is possible in ethics is to be found in the remaining chapters of this book; but this is not entirely satisfactory. From a theoretical point of view, it is unsatisfactory because we might find ourselves reasoning about ethics without really understanding how this can happen; and from a practical point of view, it is unsatisfactory because our reasoning is more likely to go astray if we lack a grasp of its foundations. I shall therefore attempt to say something about how we can reason in ethics.

WHAT ETHICS IS: ONE VIEW

What follows is a sketch of a view of ethics that allows reason to play an important role in ethical decisions. It is not the only possible view of ethics, but it is a plausible view. Once again, however, I shall have to pass over qualifications and objections worth a chapter to themselves. To those who think there are objections that defeat the position I am advancing, I can only say, again, that this entire chapter may be treated as no more than a statement of the assumptions on which this book is based. In that way, it will at least assist in giving a clear view of what I take ethics to be.

What is it to make a moral judgment, or to argue about an ethical issue, or to live according to ethical standards? How do moral judgments differ from other practical judgments? What is the difference between a person who lives by ethical standards and one who doesn't?

All these questions are related, so we only need to consider one of them; but to do this, we need to say something about the nature of ethics. Suppose that we have studied the lives of several people, and we know a lot about what they do, what they believe and so on. Can we then decide which of them are living by ethical standards and which are not?

We might think that the way to proceed here is to find out who believes it wrong to lie, cheat, steal and so on, and does not do any of these things, and who has no such beliefs, and shows no such restraint in their actions. Then those in the first group would be living according to ethical standards, and those in the second group would not be. But this procedure runs together two distinctions: the first is the distinction between living according to (what we judge to be) the right ethical standards and living according to (what we judge to be) mistaken ethical standards; the second is the distinction between living according to some ethical standards and living according to no ethical standards at all. Those who lie and cheat, but do not believe what they are doing to be wrong, may be living according to ethical standards. They may believe, for any of a number of possible reasons, that it is right to lie, cheat, steal and so on. They are not living according to conventional ethical standards, but they may be living according to some other ethical standards.

This first attempt to distinguish the ethical from the non-ethical was mistaken, but we can learn from our mistakes. We found that we must concede that those who hold unconventional ethical beliefs are still living according to ethical standards *if they believe, for some reason, that it is right to do as they are doing.* The italicized condition gives us a clue to the answer we are seeking. The notion of living according to ethical standards is tied up with the notion of defending the way one is living, of giving a reason for it, of justifying it. Thus, people may do all kinds of things we regard as wrong, yet still be living according to ethical standards if they are prepared to defend and justify what they do. We may find the justification inadequate and may hold that the actions are wrong, but the attempt at justification, whether successful or not, is sufficient to bring the person's conduct within the domain of the ethical as opposed to the non-ethical. When, on the other hand, people cannot put forward any justification for what they do, we may reject their claim to be living according to ethical standards, even if what they do is in accordance with conventional moral principles.

We can go further. If we are to accept that a person is living according to ethical standards, the justification must be of a certain kind. For instance, a justification in terms of self-interest alone will not do. When Macbeth, contemplating the murder of Duncan, admits that only 'vaulting ambition' drives him to do it, he is admitting that the act cannot be justified ethically. 'So that I can be king in his place' is not a weak attempt at an ethical justification for assassination; it is not the sort of reason that counts as an ethical justification at all. Self-interested acts must be shown to be compatible with more broadly based ethical principles if they are to be ethically defensible, for the notion of ethics carries with it the idea of something bigger than the individual. If I am to defend my conduct on ethical grounds, I cannot point only to the benefits it brings me. I must address myself to a larger audience. 'So that I can end the reign of a cruel tyrant' would at least have been an attempt at an ethical justification of murdering the king, although as Shakespeare portrays the 'gentle Duncan', it would have been false.

From ancient times, philosophers and moralists have expressed the idea that ethical conduct is acceptable from a point of view that is somehow *universal*. The 'Golden Rule' attributed to Moses, to be found in the book of Leviticus and subsequently reiterated by Jesus, tells us to go beyond our own personal interests and 'Do unto others as you would have them do unto you' – in other words, give the same weight to the interests of others as you give to your own interests. The same idea of putting oneself in the position of another is involved in the other Christian formulation, that we love our neighbours as ourselves (at least, if we interpret 'neighbour' sufficiently broadly). It was commonly expressed by ancient Greek philosophers and by the Stoics in the Roman era. The Stoics held that ethics derives from a universal natural law, an idea that Kant developed into his famous formula: 'Act only on that maxim through which you can at the same time will that it should become a universal law.' Kant's theory received further development in the work of R. M. Hare, who saw 'universalizability' as a logical feature of moral judgments. The eighteenth-century British philosophers Hutcheson, Hume and Adam Smith appealed to an imaginary 'impartial spectator' as the test of a moral judgment. Utilitarians, from Jeremy Bentham to the present, take it as axiomatic that in deciding moral issues, 'each counts for one and none for more than one'; and John Rawls incorporated essentially the same axiom into his own theory by deriving basic ethical principles from an imaginary choice behind a 'veil of ignorance' that prevents those choosing from knowing whether they will be the ones who gain or lose by the principles they select. Even Continental philo-sophers like the existentialist Jean-Paul Sartre and the critical theorist Jürgen Habermas, who differ in many ways from their English-speaking colleagues – and from one another – agree that ethics is in some sense universal.

One could argue endlessly about the merits of each of these character-izations of the ethical, but what they have in common is more important than their differences. They agree that the justification of an ethical prin-ciple cannot be in terms of any partial or sectional group. Ethics takes a universal point of view. This does not mean that a particular ethical judgment must be universally applicable. Circumstances alter cases, as we have seen. What it does mean is that in making ethical judgments, we go beyond our own likes and dislikes. From an ethical perspective, it is irrelevant that it is I who benefit from cheating you and you who lose by it. Ethics goes beyond 'I' and 'you' to the universal law, the universalizable judgment, the standpoint of the impartial spectator or ideal observer, or whatever we choose to call it.

Can we use this universal aspect of ethics to derive an ethical theory that will give us guidance about right and wrong? Philosophers from the Stoics to Hare and Rawls have attempted this. No attempt has met with general acceptance. The problem is that if we describe the universal aspect of ethics in bare, formal terms, a wide range of ethical theories, including quite irreconcilable ones, are compatible with this notion of universality; if, on the other hand, we build up our description of the universal aspect of ethics so that it leads us ineluctably to one particular ethical theory, we shall be accused of smuggling our own ethical beliefs into our definition of the ethical – and this definition was supposed to be broad enough, and neutral enough, to encompass all serious candidates for the status of 'ethical theory'. Because so many others have failed to overcome this obstacle to deducing an ethical theory from the universal aspect of ethics, it would be foolish to attempt to do so in a brief intro-duction to a work with a quite different aim. Instead, I shall propose something less ambitious. The universal aspect of ethics, I suggest, does provide a ground for at least starting with a broadly utilitarian position. If we are going to move beyond utilitarianism, we need to be given good reasons why we should do so.

My reason for suggesting this is as follows. In accepting that ethical judgments must be made from a universal point of view, I am accepting that my own needs, wants and desires cannot, simply because they are my preferences, count more than the wants, needs and desires of anyone else.

Thus, my very natural concern that my own wants, needs and desires –
henceforth I shall refer to them as 'preferences' – be looked after must,
when I think ethically, be extended to the preferences of others. Now,
imagine that I am one of a group of people who live by gathering food
from the forest in which we live. When I am alone, I find a particularly
good fruit tree and face the choice of whether to eat all the fruit myself
or to share it with others. Imagine, too, that I am deciding in a complete
ethical vacuum and that I know nothing of any ethical considerations – I
am, we might say, in a pre-ethical stage of thinking. How would I make up
my mind? One thing – perhaps at this pre-ethical stage, the *only* thing –
that would be relevant would be how the choice I make will affect my
preferences.

Suppose I then begin to think ethically, to the extent of putting myself
in the position of others affected by my decision. To know what it is like
to be in their position, I must take on their preferences – I must imagine
how hungry they are, how much they will enjoy the fruit and so on.
Once I have done that, I must recognize that as I am thinking ethically,
I cannot give my own preferences greater weight, simply because they
are my own, than I give to the preferences of others. Hence, in place of
my own preferences, I now have to take account of the preferences of
all those affected by my decision. Unless there are some other ethically
relevant considerations, this will lead me to weigh all these preferences
and adopt the course of action most likely to maximize the preferences of
those affected. Thus, at least at some level in my moral reasoning, ethics
points towards the course of action that has the best consequences, on
balance, for all affected.

In the previous paragraph, I wrote 'points towards' because, as we
shall see in a moment, there could be other considerations that point
in a different direction. I wrote 'at some level in my moral reasoning'
because, as we shall see later, there are utilitarian reasons for believing
that we ought not to try to calculate these consequences for every ethical
decision we make in our daily lives, but only in very unusual circumstances
or when we are reflecting on our choice of general principles to guide us
in the future. In other words, in the specific example given, one might
at first think it obvious that sharing the fruits that I have gathered has
better consequences for all affected than not sharing them. This may
in the end also be the best general principle for us all to adopt, but
before we can have grounds for believing this to be the case, we must
also consider whether the effect of a general practice of sharing gathered
fruits will benefit all those affected or will harm them by reducing the

amount of food gathered, because some will cease to gather anything if they know that they will get sufficient food from their share of what others gather.

The way of thinking I have outlined is a form of utilitarianism, but not the version of utilitarianism defended by classical utilitarians like Jeremy Bentham, John Stuart Mill and Henry Sidgwick. They held that we should always do what will maximize pleasure, or happiness, and minimize pain, or unhappiness. This is 'hedonistic utilitarianism' – the term 'hedonist' comes from the Greek word for pleasure. In contrast, the view we have reached is known as 'preference utilitarianism' because it holds that we should do what, on balance, furthers the preferences of those affected. Some scholars think that Bentham and Mill may have used 'pleasure' and 'pain' in a broad sense that allowed them to include achieving what one desires as a 'pleasure' and the reverse as a 'pain'. If this interpretation is correct, the difference between preference utilitarianism and the utilitarianism of Bentham and Mill disappears. (Sidgwick, as always, was more precise: in *The Methods of Ethics,* he carefully distinguishes the preference view from the hedonistic one and opts for the latter.)

I am not claiming that preference utilitarianism can be deduced from the universal aspect of ethics. Instead of universalizing my preferences, I could base my ethical views on something completely distinct from preferences. Hedonistic utilitarianism, like preference utilitarianism, is fully impartial between individuals and satisfies the requirement of universalizability; so too are other ethical ideals, like individual rights, fairness, the sanctity of life, justice, purity and so on. They are, at least in some versions, incompatible with any form of utilitarianism. So – to return to the situation of the finder of abundant fruit, who is deciding whether to share it with others – I might hold that I have a right to the fruit, because I found it. Or I might claim that it is fair that I should get the fruit, because I did the hard work of finding the tree. Alternatively, I could hold that everyone has an equal right to the abundance nature provides, and so I am required to share the fruit equally.

If I take one of these views but can offer no reason for holding it, other than the fact that *I* prefer it – I prefer a society in which those who find natural objects have a right to them, or I prefer a society with a sense of fairness that rewards effort, or I prefer a society in which everything is shared equally – then my preference must be weighed against the contrary preferences of others. Perhaps, though, I want to maintain that this view is not just my preference, but I *really* have a right to the fruit I found, or everyone *really* is entitled to an equal share of nature's abundance. If so, then that claim needs to be defended by some kind of ethical theory. Where are we to get such a theory? Some substantial moral argument is needed.

What this shows is that we very swiftly arrive at an initially preference utilitarian position once we apply the universal aspect of ethics to simple, pre-ethical decision making. The preference utilitarian position is a minimal one, a first base that we reach by universalizing self-interested decision making. We cannot, if we are to think ethically, refuse to take this step. To go beyond preference utilitarianism we need to produce something more. We cannot just rely on our intuitions, even those that are very widely shared, since these could, as we have seen, be the result of our evolutionary heritage and therefore an unreliable guide to what is right.

One way of arguing would be to hold up to critical reflection and scrutiny the claim that the satisfaction of preferences should be our ultimate end. People have very strong preferences for winning lotteries, although researchers have shown that those who win major lotteries are not, once the initial elation has passed, significantly happier than they were before. Is it nevertheless good that they got what they wanted? Faced with such reports, preference utilitarians are likely to grant that people often form preferences on the basis of misinformation about what it would be like to have their preference satisfied. The preferences that should be counted, the preference utilitarians may say, are those that we would have if we were fully informed, in a calm frame of mind and thinking clearly. On the other hand, hedonistic utilitarians would say that the fact that we would abandon many of our preferences, if we knew that their satisfaction would not bring us happiness, shows that it is happiness we really care about, not the satisfaction of our preferences. To this the preference utilitarians may reply that a would-be poet may choose a life with less happiness, if she thinks it will enable her to write great poetry. These are the kinds of argument we need to sort through in order to decide which is the more defensible form of utilitarianism. Then we also have to consider arguments against any kind of utilitarianism and in favor of quite different moral theories. That, however, is a topic for a different book.

This book can be read as an attempt to indicate how a consistent preference utilitarian would deal with a number of controversial problems. Despite the difficulties just mentioned, preference utilitarianism is a straightforward ethical theory that requires minimal metaphysical presuppositions. We all know what preferences are, whereas claims that something is intrinsically morally wrong, or violates a natural right, or is contrary to human dignity invoke less tangible concepts that make their truth more difficult to assess. But because preference utilitarianism may, in the end, prove not to be the best approach to ethical issues, I'll also consider, at various points, how hedonistic utilitarianism, theories of rights, of justice, of absolute moral rules and so on, bear on the problems discussed. In this way, you will be able to come to your own conclusions about the possibility of reason and argument in ethics and about the merits of utilitarian and non-utilitarian approaches to ethics.

2

Equality and Its Implications

THE BASIS OF EQUALITY

The period since the end of World War II has seen dramatic shifts in moral attitudes on issues like abortion, sex outside marriage, same-sex relationships, pornography, euthanasia and suicide. Great as the changes have been, no new consensus has been reached. The issues remain controversial, and the traditional views still have respected defenders.

Equality seems to be different. The change in attitudes towards inequality – especially racial inequality – has been no less sudden and dramatic than the change in attitudes towards sex, but it has been more complete. Racist assumptions shared by most Europeans at the beginning of the twentieth century have become totally unacceptable, at least in public life. A poet could not now write of 'lesser breeds without the law', and retain – indeed enhance – his reputation, as Rudyard Kipling did in 1897. This does not mean that there are no longer any racists, but only that they must disguise their racism if their views and policies are to have any chance of general acceptance. The principle that all humans are equal is now part of the prevailing political and ethical orthodoxy. But what, exactly, does it mean and why do we accept it?

Once we go beyond the agreement that blatant forms of racial discrimination are wrong and raise questions about the basis of the principle that all humans are equal, the consensus starts to weaken. It weakens even more if we seek to apply the principle of equality to particular cases. One sign of this was the controversy that occurred during the 1970s over the claims made by Arthur Jensen, professor of Educational Psychology at the University of California, Berkeley, and H. J. Eysenck, professor of

Psychology at the University of London, that genetic differences lie behind variations in intelligence between different races. The issue was revived in 1994 by the publication of *The Bell Curve* by Richard Herrnstein and Charles Murray. Many of the most forceful opponents of Jensen, Eysenck, Herrnstein and Murray assumed that these claims would, if sound, justify racial discrimination. Are they right? A similar question can be asked about the speculation by Lawrence Summers in 2005, when he was president of Harvard University, that biological differences between men and women could be a factor in the difficulty the university was having in appointing more women to chairs in math and science. The ensuing row was widely seen as a factor in Summers' subsequent resignation as Harvard's president. Was he being sexist?

Another issue requiring us to reconsider our understanding of equality is whether members of disadvantaged minorities should be given preferential treatment in employment or university admission. Some philosophers and lawyers argue that equality requires affirmative action, whereas others contend that equality rules out any discrimination on grounds of race, ethnicity or sex, whether for or against members of a disadvantaged group.

To answer these questions, we need to be clear about what it is we can justifiably say when we assert that all humans are equal. We can start by inquiring into the ethical foundations of the principle of equality.

When we say that all humans are equal, irrespective of race or sex, what exactly are we claiming? Racists, sexists and other opponents of equality have often pointed out that, by whatever test we choose, it simply is not true that all humans are equal. Some are tall, some are short; some are brilliant at mathematics, others can barely add; some can run 100 metres in ten seconds, some can't run at all; some would never intentionally hurt another being, others would kill a stranger for $100 if they could get away with it; some have emotional lives that reach the heights of ecstasy and the depths of despair, whereas others live on a more even plane, relatively untouched by what goes on around them . . . and this list of differences could be continued for many more lines. The plain fact is that humans differ, and the differences apply to so many characteristics that the search for a factual basis on which to erect the principle of equality seems hopeless.

John Rawls suggested, in his influential book *A Theory of Justice*, that equality can be founded on the natural characteristics of human beings, provided we select what he calls a 'range property'. Suppose we draw a circle on a piece of paper. Then all points within the circle – this is the 'range' – have the property of being within the circle, and they have this property equally. Some points may be closer to the centre and others nearer the edge, but all are, equally, points inside the circle. Similarly, Rawls suggests, the property of 'moral personality' is a property that virtually all humans possess, and all humans who possess this property possess it equally. By 'moral personality' Rawls does not mean 'morally good personality'; he is using 'moral' in contrast to 'amoral'. A moral person, Rawls says, must have a sense of justice. More broadly, one might say that to be a moral person is to be the kind of person to whom one can make moral appeals with some prospect that the appeal will be heeded.

Rawls maintains that moral personality is the basis of human equality, a view that derives from his adherence to an approach to justice that stems from the social contract tradition. That tradition sees ethics as a kind of mutually beneficial agreement: 'Don't hit me, and I won't hit you.' (That is far too crude but gives you the general idea.) Hence, only those capable of appreciating that they are not being hit, and of restraining their own hitting accordingly, are within the sphere of ethics.

There are problems with using moral personality as the basis of equality. One objection is that having a moral personality is a matter of degree. Some people are highly sensitive to issues of justice and ethics generally; others, for a variety of reasons, have only a very limited awareness of such principles. The suggestion that being a moral person is the minimum necessary for coming within the scope of the principle of equality still leaves it open as to where this minimal line is to be drawn. Nor is it intuitively obvious why, if moral personality is so important, we should not have grades of moral status, with rights and duties corresponding to the degree of refinement of one's sense of justice.

Still more serious is the objection that not all humans are moral persons, even in the most minimal sense. Infants and small children, along with humans with profound intellectual disabilities, lack the required sense of justice. Shall we then say that all humans are equal, except for very young or intellectually disabled ones? This is certainly not what we ordinarily understand by the principle of equality. If this revised principle implies that we may disregard the interests of very young or intellectually disabled humans in ways that would be wrong if they were older or more intelligent, we would need far stronger arguments to induce us to accept it. (Rawls deals with infants and children by including *potential* moral persons along with actual ones within the scope of the principle of equality. This is an ad hoc device, confessedly designed to square his theory with our ordinary moral intuitions, rather than something for which independent arguments can be produced. Moreover, although Rawls admits that those with irreparable intellectual disabilities 'may present a difficulty', he offers no suggestions towards the solution of this difficulty.)

So the possession of 'moral personality' does not provide a satisfactory basis for the principle that all humans are equal. I doubt that any natural characteristic, whether a 'range property' or not, can fulfil this function, for I doubt that there is any morally significant property that all humans possess equally.

There is another possible line of defence for the belief that there is a factual basis for a principle of equality that prohibits racism and sexism. We can admit that humans differ as individuals and yet insist that there are no morally significant differences between the races and sexes. Knowing that someone is of African or European descent, female or male, does not enable us to draw conclusions about her or his intelligence, sense of justice, depth of feelings or anything else that would entitle us to treat her or him as less than equal. The racist claim that people of European descent are superior to those of other races in these capacities is false. The differences between individuals in these respects are not captured by racial boundaries. The same is true of the sexist stereotype that sees women as emotionally deeper and more caring, but also less aggressive and less enterprising, than men. Obviously, this is not true of women as a whole. Some women are emotionally shallower, less caring and more aggressive and more enterprising than some men.

The fact that humans differ as individuals, not as races or sexes, is important, and we shall return to it when we come to discuss the implications of the claims made by Jensen, Eysenck and others; yet it provides neither a satisfactory principle of equality nor an adequate defence against a more sophisticated opponent of equality than the blatant racist or sexist. Suppose that someone proposes that people should be given intelligence tests and then classified into higher or lower status categories on the basis of the results. Perhaps those scoring higher than 125 would be a slave-owning class; those scoring between 100 and 125 would be free citizens but lack the right to own slaves; whereas those scoring less than 100 would be the slaves of those scoring higher than 125. A hierarchical society of this sort seems as abhorrent as one based on race or sex; but if we base our support for equality on the factual claim that differences between individuals cut across racial and sexual boundaries, we have no grounds for opposing this kind of hierarchical society, for it would be based on real differences between people.

We can reject this 'hierarchy of intelligence' and similar fantastic schemes only if we are clear that the claim to equality does not rest on the possession of intelligence, moral personality, rationality or similar matters of fact. There is no logically compelling reason for assuming that a difference in ability between two people justifies any difference in the amount of consideration we give to their interests. Equality is a basic ethical principle, not an assertion of fact. We can see this if we return to our earlier discussion of the universal aspect of ethical judgments.

We saw in the previous chapter that when we make ethical judgments, we must go beyond a personal or sectional point of view and take into account the interests of all those affected, unless we have sound ethical grounds for doing otherwise. This means that we weigh interests, considered simply as interests and not as my interests, or the interests of people of European descent, or of people with IQs higher than 100. This provides us with a basic principle of equality: the principle of equal consideration of interests.

The essence of the principle of equal consideration of interests is that we give equal weight in our moral deliberations to the like interests of all those affected by our actions. This means that if only X and Y would be affected by a possible act, and if X stands to lose more than Y stands to gain, it is better not to do the act. We cannot, if we accept the principle of equal consideration of interests, say that doing the act is better, despite the facts described, because we are more concerned about Y than we are about X. What the principle really amounts to is: an interest is an interest, whoever's interest it may be.

We can make this more concrete by considering a particular interest, say the interest we have in the relief of pain. Then the principle says that the ultimate moral reason for relieving pain is simply the undesirability of pain as such, and not the undesirability of X's pain, which might be different from the undesirability of Y's pain. Of course, X's pain might be more undesirable than Y's pain because it is more painful, and then the principle of equal consideration would give greater weight to the relief of X's pain. Again, even where the pains are equal, other factors might be relevant, especially if others are affected. If there has been an earthquake, we might give priority to the relief of a doctor's pain so she can treat other victims. But the doctor's pain itself counts only once and with no added weighting. The principle of equal consideration of interests acts like a pair of scales, weighing interests impartially. True scales favour the side where the interest is stronger or where several interests combine to outweigh a smaller number of similar interests, but they take no account of whose interests they are weighing.

From this point of view, race is irrelevant to the consideration of interests; for all that counts are the interests themselves. To give less consideration to a specified amount of pain because that pain was experienced by a member of a particular race would be to make an arbitrary distinction. Why pick on race? Why not on whether a person was born in a leap year? Or whether there is more than one vowel in her surname? All these characteristics are equally irrelevant to the undesirability of pain from the universal point of view. Hence, the principle of equal consideration of interests shows straightforwardly why the most blatant forms of racism, like that of the Nazis, are wrong: the Nazis based their policies only on what would be good for the 'Aryan' race, and the sufferings of Jews, Gypsies and Slavs were of no concern to them.

The principle of equal consideration of interests is sometimes thought to be a purely formal principle, lacking in substance and too weak to exclude any inegalitarian practice. We have already seen, however, that it does exclude racism and sexism, at least in their most blatant forms. If we look at the impact of the principle on the imaginary hierarchical society based on intelligence tests, we can see that it is strong enough to provide a basis for rejecting this more sophisticated form of inegalitarianism too.

The principle of equal consideration of interests prohibits making our readiness to consider the interests of others depend on their abilities or other characteristics, apart from the characteristic of having interests. It is true that we cannot know where equal consideration of interests will lead us until we know what interests people have, and this may vary according to their abilities or other characteristics. Consideration of the interests of mathematically gifted children may lead us to teach them advanced mathematics at an early age, which for different children might be entirely pointless or positively harmful. The basic element, the taking into account of the person's interests, whatever they may be, must apply to everyone, irrespective of race, sex or scores on an intelligence test. Enslaving those who score below a certain line on an intelligence test would not – barring extraordinary and implausible beliefs about human nature – be compatible with equal consideration. Intelligence has nothing to do with many important interests that humans have, like the interest in avoiding pain, in satisfying basic needs for food and shelter, to love and care for any children one may have, to enjoy friendly and loving relations with others and to be free to pursue one's projects without unnecessary interference from others. Slavery prevents the slaves from satisfying these interests as they would want to, and the benefits it confers on the slave owners are hardly comparable in importance to the harm it does to the slaves.

So the principle of equal consideration of interests is strong enough to rule out an intelligence-based slave society as well as cruder forms of racism and sexism. It also rules out discrimination on the grounds of disability, whether intellectual or physical, insofar as the disability is not relevant to the interests under consideration (as, for example, severe intellectual disability might be if we are considering a person's interest in voting in an election). The principle of equal consideration of interests, therefore, may be a defensible form of the principle that all humans are equal, a form that we can use in discussing more controversial issues about equality. Before we go on to these topics, however, it will be useful to say a little more about the nature of the principle.

Equal consideration of interests is a minimal principle of equality in the sense that it does not dictate equal treatment. Take a relatively straightforward example of an interest, the interest in relief of physical pain. Imagine that after an earthquake I come across two victims: one with a crushed leg, in agony, and one with a gashed thigh, in slight pain. I have only two shots of morphine left. Equal treatment would suggest that I give one to each injured person, but one shot would not do much to relieve the pain of the person with the crushed leg. She would still be in much more pain than the other victim, and even after I have given her one shot, giving her the second shot would achieve a more marked reduction in her pain than giving one shot to the person in slight pain would do for that person. Hence, equal consideration of interests in this situation leads to what some may consider an inegalitarian result: two shots of morphine for one person and none for the other.

There is a still more controversial inegalitarian implication of the principle of equal consideration of interests. In the example involving earthquake victims, although equal consideration of interests leads to unequal treatment, this unequal treatment produces a more egalitarian result. By giving the double dose to the more seriously injured person, we bring about a situation in which there is less difference in the degree of suffering felt by the two victims than there would be if we gave one dose to each. Instead of ending up with one person in considerable pain and one in no pain, we end up with two people in slight pain. This is in line with the principle of declining marginal utility, a principle well-known to economists, which states that the more someone has of something, the less she will gain from an additional quantity of it. If I am struggling to survive on 200 grams of rice a day, and you provide me with an extra 50 grams per day, you have improved my position significantly; but if I already have a kilo of rice per day, I won't care much about the extra 50 grams. The same is true of money: $100 means a lot to someone for whom it is equivalent to his weekly income, but it means very little to a billionaire. When marginal utility is taken into account, the principle of equal consideration of interests inclines us towards an equal distribution of income – disincentive effects aside – and to that extent the egalitarian will endorse its conclusions. What is likely to trouble the egalitarian about the principle of equal consideration of interests is that there are circumstances in which the principle of declining marginal utility does not hold or is overridden by countervailing factors.

We can vary the example of the earthquake victims to illustrate this. Let us say, again, that there are two victims, one more severely injured than the other, but this time we shall say that the more severely injured victim, A, has lost a leg and is in danger of losing a toe from her remaining leg; while the less severely injured victim, B, has an injury that threatens her leg. We have medical supplies for only one person. If we use them on A, the more severely injured victim, the most we can do is save her toe; whereas if we use them on B, the less severely injured victim, we can save her leg. In other words, we assume that the situation is: without medical treatment, A loses a leg and a toe, while B loses a leg; if we give the treatment to A, then A loses a leg and B also loses a leg; if we give the treatment to B, A loses a leg and a toe, while B loses nothing.

Assuming that it is much worse to lose a leg than it is to lose a toe (even when that toe is on one's sole remaining foot), the principle of declining marginal utility does not suffice to give us the right answer in this situation. We will do more to further the interests, impartially considered, of those affected by our actions if we use our limited resources on the less seriously injured victim than on the more seriously injured one. Therefore, this is what the principle of equal consideration of interests leads us to do. Thus, equal consideration of interests can, in special cases, widen rather than narrow the gap between two people at different levels of welfare. It is for this reason that the principle is a minimal principle of equality, rather than a thorough-going egalitarian principle. A more thorough-going form of egalitarianism would, however, be difficult to justify, both in general terms and in its application to special cases of the kind just described.

Minimal as it is, the principle of equal consideration of interests can seem too demanding in some cases. Can any of us really give equal consideration to the welfare of our family and that of strangers? This question will be dealt with in Chapter 8, when we consider our obligations to assist those in need in poorer parts of the world. I shall try to show, then, that although the principle of equal consideration of interests may clash with some widely held views about what it is to live ethically, it is these other views we should reject, not the principle of equal consideration of interests. Meanwhile, we shall see how the principle assists us in discussing some of the controversial issues raised by demands for equality.

EQUALITY AND GENETIC DIVERSITY

In 1969, Arthur Jensen published a long article in the *Harvard Educational Review* entitled 'How Much Can We Boost IQ and Scholastic Achievement?' One short section of the article discussed the probable causes of the undisputed fact that – on average – African Americans do not score as well as other Americans in standard IQ tests. Jensen summarized the upshot of this section as follows:

all we are left with are various lines of evidence, no one of which is definitive alone, but which, viewed altogether, make it a not unreasonable hypothesis that genetic factors are strongly implicated in the average negro-white intelligence difference. The preponderance of evidence is, in my opinion, less consistent with a strictly environmental hypothesis than with a genetic hypothesis, which, of course, does not exclude the influence of environment or its interaction with genetic factors.

This heavily qualified statement comes in the midst of a detailed review of a complex scientific subject, published in a scholarly journal. It would hardly have been surprising if it passed unnoticed by anyone but scientists working in the area of psychology or genetics. Instead, it was widely reported in the popular press as an attempt to defend racism on scientific grounds. Jensen was accused of spreading racist propaganda and was likened to Hitler. His lectures were shouted down, and students demanded that he be dismissed from his university post. H. J. Eysenck, a British professor of psychology who supported Jensen's theories received similar treatment, in Britain and Australia as well as in the United States. Interestingly, Eysenck did not suggest that those of European descent have the highest average intelligence among Americans; instead, he noted some evidence that Americans of Japanese and Chinese descent do better on tests of abstract reasoning (despite coming from back-grounds lower on the socioeconomic scale) than Americans of European descent.

The opposition to genetic explanations of alleged racial differences in intelligence is only one manifestation of a more general opposition to genetic explanations in other socially sensitive areas. It closely parallels, for instance, the hostility of 1970s feminists to the idea that there are bio-logical factors behind male dominance in politics and business. (Today's feminists are more willing to entertain the idea that biological differences between the sexes are influential in, for example, greater male aggres-sion and stronger female caring behaviour.) The opposition to genetic explanations also has obvious links with the intensity of feelings aroused by evolutionary explanations of human behaviour. The worry here is that if human social behaviour is seen as having evolved over millions of years and having links with the behaviour of other social mammals, we shall come to think of hierarchy, male dominance and inequality as part of our evolved nature, and thus unchangeable. Nevertheless, evolutionary explanations of human behaviour are now much more widely accepted than they were in the 1970s. The mapping of the human genome, which is part of the larger scientific undertaking of achieving greater under-standing of the nature and function of the human genetic code, has also given rise to concern over what such a map might reveal about genetic differences among humans and the uses to which such information might be put.

It would be inappropriate for me to attempt to assess the scientific merits of biological explanations of human behaviour in general, or of racial or sexual differences in particular. My concern is rather with the implications of these theories for the ideal of equality. For this purpose, it is not necessary for us to establish whether the theories are right. All we have to ask is: suppose that one ethnic group does turn out to have a higher average IQ than another, and that part of this difference has a genetic basis; would this mean that racism is defensible and that we have to reject the principle of equality? A similar question can be asked about the impact of theories of biological differences between the sexes. In neither case does the question assume that the theories are sound. Suppose that our scepticism about such theories led us to neglect these questions, and then unexpected evidence turned up giving support to the theories. A confused and unprepared public might then take the theories to have implications for the principle of equality that they do not have.

I shall begin by considering the implications of the view that there is
a difference in the average IQ of two different ethnic groups, and that
genetic factors are responsible for at least a part of this difference. I shall
then consider the impact of alleged differences in temperament and
ability between the sexes.

Racial Differences and Racial Equality

Let us suppose, just for the sake of exploring the consequences, that evidence accumulates supporting the hypothesis that there are differences in
intelligence between the different ethnic groups of human beings. (We
should not assume that this would mean that Europeans come out on
top. As we have already seen, there is some evidence to the contrary.)
What significance would this have for our views about racial equality?

First, a word of caution. When people talk of differences in intelligence
between ethnic groups, they are usually referring to differences in scores
on standard IQ tests. 'IQ' stands for 'Intelligence Quotient', but this does
not mean that an IQ test really measures what we mean by 'intelligence'
in ordinary contexts. Obviously there is some correlation between the
two: if schoolchildren regarded by their teachers as highly intelligent did
not generally score better on IQ tests than schoolchildren regarded as
below normal intelligence, the tests would have to be changed – as indeed
they have been changed in the past. This does not show how close the
correlation is, however, and because our ordinary concept of intelligence
is vague, there is no way of telling. Some psychologists have attempted
to overcome this difficulty by defining 'intelligence' as 'what intelligence
tests measure', but this merely introduces a new concept of 'intelligence',
which is easier to measure than our ordinary notion but may be quite
different in meaning. Because 'intelligence' is a word in everyday use, to
use the same word in a different sense is a sure path to confusion. What
we should talk about, then, is differences in IQ rather than differences in
intelligence, because this is all that the available evidence could support.

The distinction between intelligence and scores on IQ tests has led
some to conclude that IQ is of no importance; this is the opposite, but
equally erroneous, extreme to the view that IQ is identical with intelligence. IQ is important in our society. One's IQ is a factor in one's
prospects of improving one's occupational status, income or social class.
If there are genetic factors in racial differences in IQ, there are likely
to be genetic factors in racial differences in occupational status, income
and social class. So if we are interested in equality, we cannot ignore IQ.

When people of different racial origin are given IQ tests, there tend to be differences in the average scores they get. The existence of such differences is not seriously disputed, even by those who most vigorously opposed the views put forward by Jensen and Eysenck and by the authors of *The Bell Curve*. What is hotly disputed is whether the differences are primarily to be explained by heredity or by environment – in other words, whether they reflect innate differences between different groups of human beings or whether they are due to the different social and educational situations in which these groups find themselves. Almost everyone accepts that environmental factors do play a role in IQ differences between groups; the debate is over whether these environmental factors can explain all or virtually all of the differences.

Let us suppose that the genetic hypothesis turns out to be correct (making this supposition, as I have said, not because we believe it *is* correct but in order to explore its implications). What would be the implications of genetically based differences in IQ between different races? For three reasons, the implications of this supposition are less drastic than they are often supposed to be, and they give no comfort to racists.

First, the genetic hypothesis does not imply that we should reduce our efforts to overcome other causes of inequality between people; for example, in the quality of housing and schooling available to less well-off people. Admittedly, if the genetic hypothesis is correct, these efforts will not bring about a situation in which different racial groups have equal IQs. But this is no reason for accepting a situation in which any people are hindered by their environment from doing as well as they can. Perhaps we should put extra efforts into helping those who start from a position of disadvantage so that we end with a more egalitarian result.

Second, the fact that the average IQ of one racial group is a few points higher than that of another does not allow anyone to say that all members of the group with the higher average IQ have IQs above all members of the group with the lower average – this is clearly false for any racial group – or that a randomly selected individual from the group with the higher average IQ group will have a higher IQ than a randomly selected individual from the group with the lower average IQ – this will often be false. The point is that these figures are averages and say nothing about individuals. There will be a substantial overlap in IQ scores between the two groups. So whatever the cause of the difference in average IQs, it will provide no justification for racial segregation in education or any other field. It remains true that members of different racial groups must be treated as individuals, irrespective of their race.

The third reason why the genetic hypothesis gives no support for racism is the most fundamental of the three. It is simply that, as we saw earlier, the principle of equality is not based on a claim about people being equal in any nonmoral characteristic. I have argued that the only defensible basis for the principle of equality is equal consideration of interests, and I have also suggested that the most important human interests – like the interest in avoiding pain, in satisfying basic needs for food and shelter, in enjoying warm personal relationships, in being free to pursue one's projects without interference, and many others – are not affected by differences in intelligence. Thomas Jefferson, who drafted the ringing assertion of equality with which the American Declaration of Independence begins, knew this. In reply to an author who had endeavoured to refute the then common view that Africans lack intelligence, he wrote:

Be assured that no person living wishes more sincerely than I do, to see a complete refutation of the doubts I have myself entertained and expressed on the grade of understanding allotted to them by nature, and to find that they are on a par with ourselves . . . but whatever be their degree of talent, it is no measure of their rights. Because Sir Isaac Newton was superior to others in understanding, he was not therefore lord of the property or person of others.

Jefferson was right. Equal status does not depend on intelligence. Racists who maintain the contrary are in peril of being forced to kneel before the next genius they encounter.

These three reasons suffice to show that claims that there is a genetic basis for differences between racial groups on IQ tests do not provide grounds for denying the moral principle that all humans are equal. The third reason, however, has further ramifications that we shall follow up after discussing differences between the sexes.

Sexual Differences and Sexual Equality

The debates over psychological differences between females and males are not about IQ in general, but about the distinct abilities measured by different questions in the IQ test. There is some evidence suggesting that females have greater verbal ability than males. This involves being better able to understand complex pieces of writing and being more creative with words. Males, on the other hand, do better on tests involving what is known as 'visual-spatial' ability. Reading a map and using it to navigate involves visual-spatial ability, although the sex differences are most clearly shown on the mental rotation test, in which subjects are shown two three-dimensional shapes and asked whether the shapes are identical but have been rotated or are mirror images of each other.

Girls score higher than boys on tests requiring them to recognize the emotional states of others and to predict other people's behaviour from an awareness of their emotional states. Although it is commonly believed that boys do better than girls in mathematics, the average scores of girls and boys differ little and the difference sometimes favours girls. The boys' scores tend to be more spread out, at both ends of the scale, whereas the girls' scores are clustered around the middle. This means that boys are more likely to finish at both top and bottom of the math class.

We shall discuss the significance of these relatively minor differences in intellectual abilities shortly. There is also one major nonintellectual characteristic in respect of which there is a marked difference between the sexes: aggression. Studies conducted on children in several different cultures have borne out what parents have long suspected: boys are more likely to play roughly, attack each other and fight back when attacked, than girls. Males are readier to hurt others than females, a tendency reflected in the fact that almost all violent criminals are male. It has been suggested that aggression is associated with competitiveness, and the drive to dominate others and get to the top of whatever pyramid one is a part of. In contrast, females are readier to adopt a role that involves caring for others.

These are the major psychological differences that have repeatedly been observed in many studies of females and males. They emerge, of course, only when averages are taken; there is a substantial overlap between the sexes. What is the origin of these differences? Once again, the rival explanations are environmental versus biological. Although this question of origin is important in some special contexts, it was given too much weight by the 1970s feminists who assumed that the case for women's liberation rested on acceptance of the environmentalist view. What is true of racial discrimination holds here too: discrimination can be shown to be wrong whatever the origin of the known psychological differences. First, let us look briefly at the rival explanations.

Anyone who has had anything to do with children will know that in all sorts of ways children learn that the sexes have different roles. Forty years after the feminist movement of the 1970s, boys are still more likely to get trucks or guns for their birthday presents; girls get dolls or brush-and-comb sets. Girls are put into dresses and told how nice they look; boys are dressed in jeans and praised for their strength and daring. Before the 1970s, children's books almost invariably portrayed fathers going out to work while mothers clean the house and cook the dinner; some still do, although in many countries feminist criticisms of this type of literature – and the fact that more women work – have changed the images presented to children.

Social conditioning exists, certainly, but how well does it explain the existence of differences between the sexes? It is, at best, an incomplete explanation. We still need to know *why* our society – and not just ours, but practically every human society – should shape children in this way. One popular answer is that in earlier, simpler societies, the sexes had different roles because women had to breastfeed their children during the long period before weaning. This meant that the women stayed closer to home while the men went out to hunt. As a result, females evolved a more social and emotional character, while males became tougher and more aggressive. Because physical strength and aggression were the ultimate forms of power in these simple societies, males became dominant. The sex roles that exist today are, on this view, an inheritance from these simpler circumstances, an inheritance that became obsolete once technology made it possible for the weakest person to operate a crane that lifts fifty tons or to fire a missile that kills millions. Nor do women have to be tied to home and children in the way they used to be, because a woman can now combine motherhood and a career.

The alternative view is that although social conditioning plays some role in determining psychological differences between the sexes, biological factors are also at work. This has been supported by a study in which babies just one day old were shown either a live face or a mechanical mobile. Baby girls spent more time looking at the face, and baby boys more time looking at the mobile. In addition, the preferences young females show for playing with dolls, and young males for playing with toy trucks, have even been shown to hold for vervet monkeys! No wonder that parents continue to give their children the toys that they most desire and with which they are most likely to play.

The evidence that the sex difference in aggression has a biological basis is summarized by Eleanor Maccoby and Carol Jacklin in *The Psychology of Sex Differences*:

(1) Males are more aggressive than females in all human societies in which the difference has been studied.

(2) Similar differences are found in humans and in apes and other closely related animals.

(3) The differences are found in very young children, at an age when there is no evidence of any social conditioning in this direction (indeed Maccoby and Jacklin found some evidence that boys are more severely punished for showing aggression than girls).

(4) Aggression has been shown to vary according to the level of sex hormones and females become more aggressive if they receive male hormones.

The evidence for a biological basis of the differences in visual-spatial ability is a little more complicated, but it consists largely of genetic studies that suggest that this ability is influenced by a recessive sex-linked gene. As a result, it is estimated, approximately 50 percent of males have a genetic advantage in situations demanding visual-spatial ability, but only 25 percent of females have this advantage. On the other hand, environmental factors can significantly reduce the male advantage in this area.

Evidence for and against a biological factor in the superior verbal ability of females and the superior mathematical ability of high-achieving males (a result of the greater spread in mathematical ability among males that we mentioned earlier) is, at present, too weak to suggest a conclusion one way or the other.

Adopting the strategy we used before in discussing race and IQ, I shall not go further into the evidence for and against these biological explanations of differences between males and females. Instead, I shall ask what the implications of the biological hypotheses would be.

The differences in the intellectual strengths and weaknesses of the sexes cannot explain more than a small proportion of the difference in positions that males and females hold in our society. For instance, if superior visual-spatial ability is supposed to explain the male dominance of architecture and engineering, why isn't there equality even in areas where the relevant abilities are ones in which women score as well as or better than men? Professions requiring high verbal abilities are an example. It is true that there are more women journalists than engineers, and many women have achieved lasting fame as novelists; yet female journalists and television commentators continue to be outnumbered by males. So even if we accept biological explanations for the patterning of these abilities, we can still argue that women do not have the same opportunities as men to make the most of the abilities they have and reach the top of their field.

On the other hand, the fact that there are more males at both extremes of ability in mathematics, whereas females tend to cluster more around the average level, does support Lawrence Summers' ill-fated remark about the relative scarcity of suitable female candidates for Harvard positions in those areas of science and engineering in which mathematical ability plays a key role. Only those with exceptional ability become professors, and even within that select group, only those among the very best have any prospect of becoming a professor at an elite institution like Harvard. It isn't difficult to see that males are likely to be overrepresented among those at the extreme upper end of the scale of mathematical giftedness.

What of differences in aggression? A first reaction to the suggestion that there is a biological basis to greater male aggression might be that feminists should seize this way of showing the ethical superiority of females, for it means that a woman's greater reluctance to hurt others is part of her nature. But the fact that most violent criminals are male may be only one side of greater male aggression. The other side could be greater male competitiveness, ambition and drive to achieve power. This would have different, and for feminists less welcome, implications. Some years ago an American sociologist, Steven Goldberg, built a provocatively entitled book, *The Inevitability of Patriarchy*, around the thesis that the biological basis of greater male aggression will always make it impossible to bring about a society in which women have as much political power as men. From this claim, it is easy to move to the view that women should accept their inferior position in society and not strive to compete with males or to bring up their daughters to compete with males in these respects. Instead, women should return to their traditional sphere of looking after the home and children. This is just the kind of argument that has aroused the hostility of some feminists towards biological explanations of male dominance.

As in the case of race and IQ, the moral conclusions alleged to follow from the biological theories do not really follow from them at all. Similar arguments apply.

First, whatever the origin of psychological differences between the sexes, social conditioning can emphasize or soften these differences. As Maccoby and Jacklin stress, the biological bias towards, say, male visual-spatial superiority is really a greater natural readiness to learn these skills. Where women are brought up to be independent, their visual-spatial ability is much higher than when they are kept at home and dependent on males. This is no doubt true of other differences as well. Hence, feminists may well be right to attack the way in which we encourage girls and boys to develop in distinct directions, even if this encouragement is not itself responsible for creating psychological differences between the sexes, but only reinforces innate predispositions.

Second, whatever the origin of psychological differences between the sexes, they exist only when averages are taken, and some females are more aggressive and have better visual-spatial ability than some males. We have seen that the genetic hypothesis offered in explanation of male visual-spatial superiority itself suggests that a quarter of all females will have greater natural visual-spatial ability than half of all males. Some females are also among the top one percent of all people in mathematical ability. Our own observations should convince us that there are females who are also more aggressive than some males. So, biological explanations or not, we are never in a position to say: 'You're a woman, so you can't become an engineer or a math professor', or 'Because you are female, you will not have the drive and ambition needed to succeed in politics.' Nor should we assume that no male can possibly have sufficient gentleness and warmth to stay at home with the children while their mother goes out to work. We must assess people as individuals, not merely lump them into 'female' and 'male' if we are to find out what they are really like; and we must keep the roles occupied by females and males flexible if people are to be able to do what they are best suited for.

The third reason is, like the previous two, parallel to the reasons I have given for believing that a biological explanation of racial differences in IQ would not justify racism. The most important human interests are no more affected by differences in aggression than they are by differences in intelligence. Less aggressive people have the same interest in avoiding pain, developing their abilities, having adequate food and shelter, enjoying good personal relationships, and so on, as more aggressive people. There is no reason why more aggressive people ought to be rewarded for their aggression with higher salaries and the ability to provide better for these interests.

Because aggression, unlike intelligence, is not generally regarded as a desirable trait, it is easy to see that greater aggression in itself provides no ethical justification of the greater proportion of men in leading roles in politics, business, the universities and the professions. It may, however, be used to suggest that the present situation is merely the result of competition between males and females under conditions of equal opportunity. Hence, the argument would go, the status quo is not unfair. This suggestion once again raises the further ramifications of biological differences between people that, as I said at the close of our discussion of the race and IQ issue, need to be followed up in more depth.

FROM EQUALITY OF OPPORTUNITY TO EQUALITY OF CONSIDERATION

In our society, large differences in income and social status are commonly thought to be all right, as long as they were brought into being under conditions of equal opportunity. The idea is that there is no injustice in Jill earning $300,000 and Jack earning $30,000, as long as Jack had his chance to be where Jill is today. Suppose that the difference in income is due to the fact that Jill is a doctor whereas Jack is a farm worker. This would be acceptable if Jack had the same opportunity as Jill to be a doctor, and this is taken to mean that Jack was not kept out of medical school because of his race or religion or a disability that was irrelevant to how good a doctor he would be – in effect, if Jack's exam results had been as good as Jill's, or he had satisfied other criteria relevant to being able to practice medicine as well as Jill had, he would have been able to study medicine, become a doctor and earn $300,000 a year. Life, on this view, is a kind of race in which it is fitting that the winners should get the prizes, so long as all get an equal start. The equal start represents equality of opportunity and this, some say, is as far as equality should go.

To say that Jack and Jill had equal opportunities to become a doctor, because Jack would have been accepted into medical school if his results had been as good as Jill's, is to take a superficial view of equal opportunity that will not stand up to further probing. We need to ask *why* Jack's results were not as good as Jill's. Perhaps his education up to that point had been inferior – bigger classes, less qualified teachers, inadequate resources and so on. If so, he was not competing on equal terms with Jill after all. Genuine equality of opportunity requires us to ensure that schools give the same advantages to everyone.

Making schools equal would be difficult enough, but it is the easiest of the tasks that await a thorough-going proponent of equal opportunity. Even if schools are the same, some children will be favoured by the kind of home they come from. A quiet room to study, plenty of books and parents who encourage their child to do well at school could explain why Jill succeeds where Jack, forced to share a room with two younger brothers and take part-time jobs to help support the family, does not. But how does one equalize a home? Or parents? Unless we are prepared to abandon the traditional family setting and bring up our children in communal nurseries, we can't.

This might be enough to show the inadequacy of equal opportunity as an ideal of equality, but the ultimate objection – the one that connects with our previous discussion of equality – is still to come. Even if we did rear our children communally, as on a *kibbutz* in Israel, they would inherit different abilities and character traits, including different levels of aggression and different IQs. Eliminating differences in the child's environment would not affect differences in genetic endowment. True, it would almost certainly reduce the disparity between IQ scores, because it is likely that, at present, social differences accentuate genetic differences; but the genetic differences would remain, and on most estimates they are a significant component of the existing differences in IQ. (Remember that we are now talking of *individuals*. We do not know if race affects IQ, but there is little doubt that differences in IQ between individuals of the same race are, in part, genetically determined.)

So equality of opportunity is not an attractive ideal. It rewards the lucky, who inherit those abilities that allow them to pursue interesting and lucrative careers. It penalizes the unlucky, whose genes make it very hard for them to achieve similar success.

We can now fit our earlier discussion of race and sex differences into a broader picture. Whatever the facts about the social or genetic basis of racial differences in IQ, removing social disadvantages will not suffice to bring about an equal or a just distribution of income – not an equal distribution because those who inherit the abilities associated with high IQ will continue to earn more than those who do not; and not a just distribution because distribution according to the abilities one inherits has nothing to do with what people deserve or need. The same is true of visual-spatial ability, mathematical ability and aggression, if these do lead to higher incomes or status. If, as I have argued, the basis of equality is equal consideration of interests, and the most important human interests have little to do with how high one's IQ is or how aggressive one is, this raises a moral question about a society in which income and social status correlate strongly with these factors.

When we pay people high salaries for programming computers and low salaries for cleaning offices we are, in effect, paying people for having very specific abilities that very probably are to a significant degree inherited, and in any case almost wholly determined before they reach an age at which they are responsible for their actions. From the point of view of justice and utility, there is something wrong here. Both would be better served by a society that adopted the famous Marxist slogan: 'From each according to his ability, to each according to his needs.' If this could be achieved, the differences between the races and sexes would lose their social significance. Only then would we have a society truly based on the principle of equal consideration of interests.

Is it realistic to aspire to a society that rewards people according to their needs rather than their IQ, aggression or other inherited abilities? Don't we have to pay people more to be doctors or lawyers or university professors, or computer programmers, to do the intellectually demanding work essential for our well-being?

There are difficulties in paying people according to their needs rather than their inherited abilities. If one country attempts to introduce such a scheme while others do not, the result is likely to be a brain drain. There are many examples of this already. We can see it, on a small scale, in the number of doctors who have left Canada to work in the United States – not because Canada pays people according to need rather than inherited abilities, but because doctors can earn much more in the United States than in Canada. If any one country were to make a serious attempt to equalize the salaries of doctors and manual workers, there can be no doubt that the number of doctors emigrating would greatly increase. During the communist period in the Soviet Union and its satellite states, emigration had to be severely restricted, for even though there were still steep differentials in income within the communist states, without the restrictions there would have been a crippling outflow of skilled people to the capitalist nations, which rewarded skill more highly. Hence, the East German border guards had orders to shoot to kill people attempting to flee to the West. If bringing about a more just distribution of income in one country requires making the country a giant prison, however, the price of a just distribution may be too high.

To allow these difficulties to lead us to the conclusion that we can do nothing to improve the distribution of income that now exists in capitalist countries would, however, be too pessimistic. There is, in the more affluent Western nations, a good deal of scope for reducing pay differentials before the point is reached at which significant numbers of people begin to think of emigrating. This is, of course, especially true of those countries, like the United States, where pay differentials are presently very great. It is here that pressure for a more equitable distribution can best be applied.

Some might claim that if we did not pay people a lot of money to be doctors or university professors, they would not undertake the studies required to achieve these positions. I do not know what evidence there is in support of this assumption, but it seems to me highly dubious. My own salary is considerably higher than the salaries of the people employed by the university to mow the lawns and keep the grounds clean, but if our salaries were identical I would still not want to swap positions with them – although their jobs are a lot more pleasant than some lowly paid work. Nor do I believe that my doctor would jump at a chance to change places with his receptionist if their salaries did not differ. It is true that my doctor and I have had to study for several years to get where we are, but I at least look back on my student years as among of the most enjoyable of my life.

Although I do not think it is because of the pay that people choose to become doctors rather than receptionists, there is one qualification to be made to the suggestion that payment should be based on need rather than ability. The prospect of earning more money sometimes leads people to make greater efforts to use the abilities they have, and these greater efforts can benefit patients, customers, students or the public as a whole. It might therefore be worth trying to reward *effort*, which would mean paying people more if they worked near the upper limits of their abilities, whatever those abilities might be. This, however, is quite different from paying people for the level of ability they happen to have, which is something they cannot themselves control. As Jeffrey Gray, a British professor of psychology, has written, the evidence for genetic influence on IQ suggests that to pay people differently for 'upper class' and 'lower class' jobs is 'a wasteful use of resources in the guise of "incentives" that either tempt people to do what is beyond their powers or reward them more for what they would do anyway'.

We have, up to now, been thinking of people like university professors, who (at least in some countries) are paid by the government, and doctors, whose incomes are determined either by government bodies, where there is some kind of national health service, or by the government protection given to professional associations like a medical association, which enables the profession to exclude those without certain credentials who might seek to offer similar services at a lower cost. These incomes are therefore already subject to government control and could be altered without drastically changing the powers of government. The business sector is a different matter. Those who are smart and possess entrepreneurial talent will, under any private enterprise system, make more money than their rivals. Taxation can help to redistribute some of this income, but it seems that there are limits to how steeply progressive a tax system can be without leading smart people to spend inordinate amounts of time and energy in finding ingenious new ways to avoid paying tax.

Some would wish to use this argument to argue that justice requires us to abolish private enterprise, worldwide. That may be a nice idea, but it is not going to happen. Private enterprise has a habit of reasserting itself under the most inhospitable conditions. Under communism, as the Russians and East Europeans soon found, black markets emerged, and if you wanted your plumbing fixed swiftly, it was advisable to pay a bit extra on the side. China, though nominally still communist, has become more prosperous only by accepting private enterprise. Only a radical change in human nature – a decline in acquisitive and self-centred desires – could overcome the tendency for people to find a way around any system that suppresses private enterprise. Because no such change in human nature is in sight, we might as well accept that financial rewards will go to those with inherited abilities, rather than those who have the greatest needs.

This doesn't mean that we should forget all about the principle of payment according to needs and effort rather than inherited ability. During the global financial crisis of 2008-09, the huge salaries and bonuses that many senior executives were receiving, even while their companies had their hands out for public funds to ward off insolvency, aroused widespread popular revulsion. At these moments, it is worth remembering that even if their financial judgment had been more astute, these executives would not have deserved those payments. The realistic component of the principle of justice I have been defending is that we should try to create a climate of opinion that will lead to a reduction in excessive payments to senior management and an increase in payments to those whose income barely meets their needs. The problem is how to make this more than a pious wish.

AFFIRMATIVE ACTION

The preceding section suggested that moving to a more egalitarian society in which differences of income are reduced is ethically desirable but likely to prove difficult. Short of bringing about greater equality of income, we might attempt to ensure that members of disadvantaged racial and ethnic groups, and women, should not be on the worse end of major differences in income, status and power to an extent that is disproportionate to their numbers in the community as a whole. Inequalities among members of the same ethnic group may be no more justifiable than those between ethnic groups, or between males and females; but when these inequalities coincide with an obvious difference between people like the differences between African Americans and Americans of European descent, or between males and females, they do more to produce a divided society with a sense of superiority on the one side and a sense of inferiority on the other. Racial and sexual inequality may therefore have a more divisive effect than other forms of inequality. It may also do more to create a feeling of hopelessness among the inferior group, because their sex or their race is not the product of their own actions and there is nothing they can do to change it.

How are racial and sexual equality to be achieved within an inegalitarian society? We have seen that equality of opportunity is practically unrealizable, and if it could be realized might still allow innate differences in aggression or IQ unfairly to determine membership of the upper strata. One way of overcoming these obstacles is to go beyond equality of opportunity and give preferential treatment to members of disadvantaged groups. This is affirmative action (sometimes also called 'reverse discrimination'). It may be the best hope of reducing long-standing inequalities; yet it appears to offend against the principle of equality itself.

Affirmative action is most often used in education and employment. Education is a particularly important area, because it has an important influence on one's prospects of earning a high income, holding a satisfying job and achieving power and status in the community. In the United States, education has been at the centre of the dispute over affirmative action because the Supreme Court has rejected some university admission procedures favouring disadvantaged groups. These cases have arisen because people of European descent were denied admission to courses although their academic records and admission test scores were better than those of some African-American students admitted. The universities did not deny this; they sought to justify it by explaining that they operated admission schemes intended to help disadvantaged students.

For many years, the leading case was *Regents of the University of California v. Bakke*. Alan Bakke applied for admission to the medical school of the University of California at Davis. In an attempt to increase the number of members of minority groups who attended medical school, the university reserved sixteen out of every one hundred places for students belonging to a disadvantaged minority. Because these students would not have won so many places in open competition, fewer students of European descent were admitted than there would have been without this reservation. Some of these students denied places would certainly have been offered them if, scoring as they did on the admission tests, they had been members of a disadvantaged minority. Bakke was among these rejected European American students, and on being rejected he sued the university. Let us take this case as a standard case of affirmative action. Is it defensible?

I shall start by putting aside one argument sometimes used to justify discrimination in favour of members of disadvantaged groups. It is sometimes said that if, say, 20 percent of the population is a racial minority and yet only 2 percent of doctors are from this minority, this is sufficient evidence that, somewhere along the line, there is discrimination on the basis of race. (Similar arguments have been mounted in support of claims of sex discrimination.) Our discussion of the genetics-versus-environment debate indicates why this argument is inconclusive. It *may* be the case that members of the underrepresented group are, *on average,* less gifted for the kind of study one must do to become a doctor. I am not saying that this explanation is true, or even probable, but it is difficult to rule out entirely, just as the disproportionately large number of African-American athletes on the U.S. Olympic athletic team is not in itself proof of discrimination against Americans of European descent. There might, of course, be other evidence suggesting that the small number of doctors from the minority group really is the result of discrimination, but this would need to be shown. In the absence of positive evidence of discrimination, it is not possible to justify affirmative action on the grounds that it merely redresses the balance of discrimination existing in the community.

Another way of defending a decision to accept a minority student in preference to a student from the majority group who scored higher in admission tests would be to argue that standard tests do not give an accurate indication of ability when one student has been severely disadvantaged. This is in line with the point made in the last section about the impossibility of achieving equal opportunity. Education and home background presumably influence test scores. A student with a background of deprivation who scores 55 percent in an admission test may have better prospects of graduating in minimum time than a more privileged student who scores 70 percent. Adjusting test scores on this basis would not mean admitting disadvantaged minority students in preference to better-qualified students. It would reflect a decision that the disadvantaged students really were better qualified than the others. This is not racial discrimination.

The University of California could not attempt this defence, for its medical school at Davis had simply reserved 16 percent of places for minority students. The quota did not vary according to the ability displayed by minority applicants. Nor does the evidence support the view that minority students who benefit from affirmative action are really as well qualified as other students who had better admission scores. The grades of students admitted under affirmative action programs are, on average, lower than those of the class as a whole.

We have seen that the only defensible basis for the claim that all humans are equal is the principle of equal consideration of interests. That principle condemns forms of racial and sexual discrimination which give less weight to the interests of those discriminated against. Could Bakke claim that in rejecting his application the medical school gave less weight to his interests than to those of African-American students?

We have only to ask this question to appreciate that university admission is not normally a result of consideration of the interests of each applicant. It depends rather on matching the applicants against standards that the university draws up with certain policies in mind. Take the most straightforward case: admission rigidly governed by scores on an intelligence test. Suppose those rejected by this procedure complained that their interests had been given less consideration than the interests of applicants of higher intelligence. The university would reply that its procedure did not take the applicants' interests into account at all, and so could hardly give less consideration to the interests of one applicant than it gave to others. We could then ask the university why it used intelligence as the criterion of admission. It might say, first, that to pass the examinations required for graduation takes a high level of intelligence. There is no point in admitting students unable to pass, for they will waste their own time and the university's resources. Secondly, the university may say, the higher the intelligence of our graduates, the more useful they are likely to be to the community. The more intelligent our doctors, the better they will be at preventing and curing disease. Hence, a medical school that selects the most intelligent students is likely to get better value for the community's outlay on medical education.

This particular admission procedure is of course one-sided; a good doctor must have other qualities in addition to a high degree of intelligence. It is only an example, however, and that objection is not relevant to the point I am using the example to make. This point is that no one objects to intelligence as a criterion for selection in the way that they object to race as a criterion; yet those of higher intelligence admitted under an intelligence-based scheme have no more of an intrinsic right to admission than those admitted by reverse discrimination. Higher intelligence, I have argued before, carries with it no right or justifiable claim to more of the good things our society offers. If a university admits students of higher intelligence, it does so not in consideration of their greater interest in being admitted, nor in recognition of their right to be admitted, but because it favours goals that it believes will be advanced by this admission procedure. So if this same university should adopt new goals and use affirmative action to promote them, applicants who would have been admitted under the old procedure cannot claim that the new procedure violates their right to be admitted or treats them with less respect than others. They had no special claim to be admitted in the first place; they were the fortunate beneficiaries of the old university policy. Now that this policy has changed, others benefit, not they. If this seems unfair, it is only because we had become accustomed to the old policy.

So affirmative action cannot justifiably be condemned on the grounds that it violates the rights of university applicants or treats them with less than equal consideration. There is no inherent right to admission, and equal consideration of the interests of applicants is not involved in normal admission tests. If affirmative action is open to objection, it must be because the goals it seeks to advance are bad, because it will not really promote these goals, or because although the goals are good and affirmative action will promote them, there are even more important costs to pursuing an affirmative action program.

The principle of equality might be a ground for condemning the goals of a racially discriminatory admissions procedure. When universities discriminate against already disadvantaged minorities, we suspect that the discrimination really does result from less concern for the interests of the minority. Why else did universities in the American South exclude African Americans until they were compelled to admit them? Then, in contrast to the affirmative action situation, those rejected could justifiably claim that their interests were not being weighed equally with the interests of European Americans who were admitted. Other explanations may have been offered, but they were surely specious.

Opponents of affirmative action have not objected to the goals of social equality and greater minority representation in the professions. They would be hard put to do so. Equal consideration of interests supports moves towards equality because of the principle of diminishing marginal utility, because progress towards equality will reduce the feeling of hopeless inferiority that can exist when members of one race or sex are always worse off than members of another race or the other sex, and because severe inequality between races means a divided community with consequent racial tension.

Within the overall goal of social equality, greater minority representation in professions like law and medicine is desirable for several reasons. Members of minority groups are more likely to work among their own people than those who come from the mainstream ethnic groups, and this may help to overcome the scarcity of doctors and lawyers in poor neighbourhoods where most members of disadvantaged minorities live. They may also have a better understanding of the problems disadvantaged people face than any outsider would have. Minority and female doctors and lawyers can serve as role models to other members of minority groups and to women, breaking down the unconscious mental barriers against aspiring to such positions. Finally, the existence of a diverse student group will help members of the majority ethnic group to learn more about the attitudes of members of the minority group, and thus become better able, as doctors and lawyers, to serve the whole community.

Opponents of affirmative action are on stronger ground when they claim that affirmative action will not promote equality. As Justice Powell said, in the *Bakke* case, 'Preferential programs may only reinforce common stereotypes holding that certain groups are unable to achieve success without special protection.' To achieve real equality, it might be said, members of minority groups and women must win their places on their merits. As long as they get into law school more easily than others, law graduates from disadvantaged minority groups – including those who would have been accepted by their law school under open competition – will be regarded as inferior. More recently, some have claimed that affirmative action produces an academic mismatch that places minority students in classes with students who mostly are more academically gifted than they are. As a result, it is said, they tend to be near the bottom of their class, and are less likely to graduate than if they were in a class that better matched their abilities.

These practical objections raise difficult factual issues. Though they were referred to in the *Bakke* case, they have not been central in the American legal battles over affirmative action. Judges are properly reluctant to decide cases on factual grounds on which they have no special expertise. Alan Bakke won his case because a majority of the judges held that either the U.S. Constitution or the Civil Rights Act of 1964 provides that no person shall, on the grounds of colour, race or national origin, be excluded from any activity receiving Federal financial assistance.

The majority opinion written by Justice Powell added, however, that there would be no objection to a university seeking diversity in its student body, and in the pursuit of that objective, it could include race as one among a number of factors, like athletic or artistic ability, work experience, demonstrated compassion, a history of overcoming disadvantage or leadership potential. The court thus effectively allowed universities to choose their student body in accord with their own goals, so long as they did not use quotas.

That view was upheld by the Supreme Court in *Grutter v. Bollinger*, a 2003 decision involving the University of Michigan Law School. Justice O'Connor, writing the majority opinion, considered that the law school's program passed the test of providing a 'highly individualized, holistic review of each applicant's file, giving serious consideration to all the ways an applicant might contribute to a diverse educational environment'. At the same time, in *Gratz v. Bollinger,* the court rejected the University of Michigan's undergraduate affirmative action program which automatically gave every member of an underrepresented minority group a set amount of extra points towards admission, without conducting the kind of individual and flexible assessment of each applicant provided by the law school.

In the United States, then, managing admissions to achieve diversity is permissible, but racial or ethnic quotas are not. In other countries – and in general, when we look at the issue with an eye to ethics, rather than the law – the distinction between quotas and other ways of giving preference to disadvantaged groups may be less significant. The important point is that affirmative action, whether by quotas or some other method, is not contrary to any sound principle of equality and does not violate any rights of those excluded by it. Properly applied, it is in keeping with equal consideration of interests, in its aspirations at least. The only real doubt is how well it works. On that, the evidence is still being collected and assessed.

A CONCLUDING NOTE: EQUALITY AND DISABILITY

In this chapter, we have been concerned with the interplay of the moral principle of equality and the differences, real or alleged, between groups of people. Perhaps the clearest way of seeing the irrelevance of IQ, or specific abilities, to the moral principle of equality is to consider the situation of people with disabilities, whether physical or intellectual. When we ask how such people ought to be treated, there is no argument about whether their abilities are the same as those of people without disabilities. By definition, they are lacking at least some ability that normal people have. Their disabilities will sometimes mean that they should be treated differently from others. If we are looking for firefighters, we can justifiably exclude someone who is confined to a wheelchair; and if we are seeking a proofreader, a blind person need not apply. The fact that a specific disability may rule a person out of consideration for a particular position does not, however, mean that that person's interests should be given less consideration than those of anyone else. Nor does it justify discrimination against disabled people in any situation in which the particular disability a person has is irrelevant to the employment or service offered.

For centuries, people with disabilities have been subjected to prejudice, in some cases no less severe than those under which racial minorities have suffered. Disabled people have been locked up, out of sight of the public, in appalling conditions. Some were virtual slaves, exploited for cheap labour in households or factories. Under a so-called euthanasia program, the Nazis murdered tens of thousands of intellectually disabled people, many of whom were enjoying their lives but were deemed 'useless mouths' and a blot on the Aryan race. Even today, some businesses will not hire a person in a wheelchair for a job that she could do as well as anyone else. Others seeking a salesperson will not hire someone whose appearance is abnormal, for fear that sales will fall. Similar arguments were used against employing members of racial minorities. We can best overcome such prejudices by becoming more familiar with people who are different from us, which won't happen if they are not employed in positions where they meet members of the public.

We are now just starting to think about the injustices that have been done to people with disabilities and to consider them as a disadvantaged group. That we have been slow in doing so may well be due to the confusion between factual equality and moral equality discussed earlier in this chapter. Because disabled people are different in some significant respects, we have not seen it as discriminatory to treat them differently. We have overlooked the fact that, as in the examples given previously, the person's disability has been irrelevant to the different – and disadvantageous – treatment. There is therefore a need to ensure that legislation that prohibits discrimination on grounds of race, ethnicity or gender also prohibits discrimination on the grounds of disability, unless the disability can be shown to be relevant to the employment or service offered.

Nor is that all. Many of the arguments for affirmative action in the case of those disadvantaged by race or gender apply even more strongly to people with disabilities. Mere equality of opportunity will not be enough in situations in which a disability makes it impossible to become an equal member of the community. Giving disabled people equal opportunity to attend university is not much use if the library is accessible only by a flight of stairs that they cannot use. Many disabled children are capable of benefiting from normal schooling but are prevented from taking part because additional resources are required to cope with their special needs. Because such needs are often very central to the lives of people with disabilities, the principle of equal consideration of interests will give them much greater weight than it will give to the more minor needs of others. For this reason, it will generally be justifiable to spend more on behalf of disabled people than we spend on behalf of others. Just how much more is, of course, a difficult question. Where resources are scarce, there must be some limit. By giving equal consideration to the interests of those with disabilities, and empathetically imagining ourselves in their situation, we can get closer to the right answer.

Some will claim to find a contradiction between this recognition of people with disabilities as a group that has been subjected to unjustifiable discrimination and arguments that appear later in this book defending abortion and euthanasia in the case of a fetus or an infant with a severe disability. For these later arguments presuppose that life is better without a disability than with one; and is this not itself a form of prejudice held by people without disabilities and parallel to the prejudice that it is better to be a member of the European race, or a man, than to be of African descent, or a woman?

The error in this argument is not difficult to detect. It is one thing to argue that people with disabilities who want to live their lives to the full should be given every possible assistance in doing so. It is another, and quite different thing, to argue that if we are in a position to choose, for our next child, whether that child shall begin life with or without a disability, it is mere prejudice or bias that leads us to choose to have a child without a disability. If disabled people who must use wheelchairs to get around were suddenly offered a miracle drug that would, with no side effects, give them full use of their legs, how many of them would refuse to take it on the grounds that life with a disability is in no way inferior to life without a disability? In seeking to raise research funds to overcome and prevent disability, people with disabilities themselves show that the preference for a life without disability is no mere prejudice. Some disabled people might say that they make this choice only because society puts so many obstacles in the way of people with disabilities. They claim that it is social conditions that disable them, not their physical or intellectual condition. This assertion takes the simple truth that social conditions make the lives of the disabled much more difficult than they need be, and twists it into a sweeping falsehood. To be able to walk, to see, to hear, to be relatively free from pain and discomfort, to communicate effectively – all these are, under virtually any social conditions, genuine benefits. To say this is not to deny that people lacking these benefits may triumph over their disabilities and have lives of astonishing richness and diversity. Nevertheless, we show no prejudice against people with disabilities if we prefer, whether for ourselves or for our children, not to be faced with hurdles so great that to surmount them is in itself a triumph.

3

Equality for Animals?

In the previous chapter, I gave reasons for believing that the fundamental principle of equality, on which the idea that humans are equal rests, is the principle of equal consideration of interests. Only a basic moral principle of this kind can allow us to defend a form of equality that embraces almost all human beings, despite the differences that exist between them. (The exceptions are human beings who are not and have never been conscious and therefore have no interests to be considered – a topic to be discussed in Chapters 6 and 7.) Although the principle of equal consideration of interests provides the best possible basis for human equality, its scope is not limited to humans. When we accept the principle of equality for humans, we are also committed to accepting that it extends to some nonhuman animals.

When I wrote the first edition of this book, in 1979, I warned the reader that the suggestion I was making here might seem bizarre. It was then generally accepted that discrimination against members of racial minorities and against women ranked among the most important moral and political issues. Questions about animal welfare, however, were widely regarded as matters of no real significance, except for people who are dotty about dogs and cats. Issues about humans, it was commonly assumed, should always take precedence over issues about animals. Now, thanks to organizations like People for the Ethical Treatment of Animals and vocal animal advocates all over the world, the view that animals are in some sense our equals is less likely to meet with blank stares. It has become more familiar, even if it is still a minority view and often misunderstood.

The belief that issues about humans should always take precedence over issues about animals reflects a popular prejudice against taking the interests of animals seriously – a prejudice no better founded than the prejudice of white slave owners against taking seriously the interests of their African slaves. It is easy for us to criticize the prejudices of our grandfathers, from which our fathers freed themselves. It is more difficult to search for prejudices among the beliefs and values we hold. What is needed now is a willingness to follow the arguments where they lead, without a prior assumption that the issue is not worth our attention.

The argument for extending the principle of equality beyond our own species is simple. It amounts to no more than a clear understanding of the principle of equal consideration of interests. We have seen that this principle implies that our concern for others ought not to depend on what they are like or what abilities they possess (although precisely what this concern requires us to do may vary according to the characteristics of those affected by what we do). It is on this basis that we are able to say that the fact that some people are not members of our race does not entitle us to exploit them, and the fact that some people are less intelligent than others does not mean that their interests may be discounted or disregarded. The principle also implies that the fact that beings are not members of our species does not entitle us to exploit them, and it similarly implies that the fact that other animals are less intelligent than we are does not mean that their interests may be discounted or disregarded.

We saw in the previous chapter that many philosophers have advocated equal consideration of interests, in some form or another, as a basic moral principle. Few recognized that the principle has applications beyond our own species. One of those few was Jeremy Bentham, the founding father of modern utilitarianism. In a forward-looking passage, written at a time when African slaves in the British dominions were still being treated much as we now treat nonhuman animals, Bentham wrote:

The day may come when the rest of the animal creation may acquire those rights which never could have been withholden from them but by the hand of tyranny. The French have already discovered that the blackness of the skin is no reason why a human being should be abandoned without redress to the caprice of a tormentor. It may one day come to be recognised that the number of the legs, the villosity of the skin, or the termination of the *os sacrum*, are reasons equally insufficient for abandoning a sensitive being to the same fate. What else is it that should trace the insuperable line? Is it the faculty of reason, or perhaps the faculty of discourse? But a full-grown horse or dog is beyond comparison a more rational, as well as a more conversable animal, than an infant of a day, or a week, or even a month, old. But suppose they were otherwise, what would it avail? The question is not, Can they *reason?* nor Can they *talk?* but, *Can they suffer?*

In this passage, Bentham points to the capacity for suffering as the vital characteristic that entitles a being to equal consideration. The capacity for suffering – or more strictly, for suffering and/or enjoyment or happiness – is not just another characteristic like the capacity for language or for higher mathematics. Bentham is not saying that those who try to mark 'the insuperable line' that determines whether the interests of a being should be considered happen to have selected the wrong characteristic. The capacity for suffering and enjoying things is a prerequisite for having interests at all, a condition that must be satisfied before we can speak of interests in any meaningful way. It would be nonsense to say that it was not in the interests of a stone to be kicked along the road by a child. A stone does not have interests because it cannot suffer. Nothing that we can do to it could possibly make any difference to its welfare. A mouse, on the other hand, does have an interest in not being tormented, because mice will suffer if they are treated in this way.

If a being suffers, there can be no moral justification for refusing to take that suffering into consideration. No matter what the nature of the being, the principle of equality requires that the suffering be counted equally with the like suffering – in so far as rough comparisons can be made – of any other being. If a being is not capable of suffering, or of experiencing enjoyment or happiness, there is nothing to be taken into account. This is why the limit of sentience (using the term as convenient, if not strictly accurate, shorthand for the capacity to suffer or experience enjoyment or happiness) is the only defensible boundary of concern for the interests of others. To mark this boundary by some characteristic like intelligence or rationality would be to mark it in an arbitrary way. Why not choose some other characteristic, like skin colour?

Racists violate the principle of equality by giving greater weight to the interests of members of their own race when there is a clash between their interests and the interests of those of another race. The white racists who supported slavery typically did not give the suffering of Africans as much weight as they gave to the suffering of Europeans. Similarly, speciesists give greater weight to the interests of members of their own species when there is a clash between their interests and the interests of those of other species. Human speciesists do not accept that pain is as bad when it is felt by pigs or mice as when it is felt by humans.

That, then, is really the whole of the argument for extending the principle of equality to nonhuman animals, but there may be some doubts about what this equality amounts to in practice. In particular, the last sentence of the previous paragraph may prompt some people to reply: 'Surely pain felt by a mouse just is not as bad as pain felt by a human. Humans have much greater awareness of what is happening to them, and this makes their suffering worse. You can't equate the suffering of, say, a person dying slowly from cancer and a laboratory mouse undergoing the same fate.'

I fully accept that in the case described, the human cancer victim normally suffers more than the nonhuman cancer victim. This in no way undermines the extension of equal consideration of interests to nonhumans. It means, rather, that we must take care when we compare the interests of different species. In some situations, a member of one species will suffer more than a member of another species. In this case, we should still apply the principle of equal consideration of interests but the result of so doing is, of course, to give priority to relieving the greater suffering. A simpler case may help to make this clear.

If I give a horse a hard slap across its rump with my open hand, the horse may start, but it presumably feels little pain. Its skin is thick enough to protect it against a mere slap. If I slap a baby in the same way, however, the baby will cry and presumably does feel pain, for the baby's skin is more sensitive. So it is worse to slap a baby than a horse, if both slaps are administered with equal force. But there must be some kind of blow – I don't know exactly what it would be, but perhaps a blow with a heavy stick – that would cause the horse as much pain as we cause a baby by a simple slap. That is what I mean by 'the same amount of pain', and if we consider it wrong to inflict that much pain on a baby for no good reason then we must, unless we are speciesists, consider it equally wrong to inflict the same amount of pain on a horse for no good reason.

There are other differences between humans and animals that cause other complications. Normal adult human beings have mental capacities that will, in certain circumstances, lead them to suffer more than animals would in the same circumstances. If, for instance, we decided to perform extremely painful or lethal scientific experiments on normal adult humans, kidnapped at random from public parks for this purpose, adults who entered parks would become fearful that they would be kidnapped. The resultant terror would be a form of suffering additional to the pain of the experiment. The same experiments performed on non-human animals would cause less suffering because the animals would not have the anticipatory dread of being kidnapped and experimented on. This does not mean, of course, that it would be *right* to perform the experiment on animals, but only that there is a reason, and one that is not speciesist, for preferring to use animals rather than normal adult humans, if the experiment is to be done at all. Note, however, that this same argument gives us a reason for preferring to use human infants – orphans perhaps – or severely intellectually disabled humans for experiments, rather than adults, because infants and severely intellectually disabled humans would also have no idea of what was going to happen to them. So far as this argument is concerned, nonhuman animals and infants and severely intellectually disabled humans are in the same category; and if we use this argument to justify experiments on nonhuman animals, we have to ask ourselves whether we are also prepared to allow experiments on human infants and severely intellectually disabled adults. If we make a distinction between animals and these humans, how can we do it, other than on the basis of a morally indefensible preference for members of our own species?

There are many areas in which the superior mental powers of normal adult humans make a difference: anticipation, more detailed memory, greater knowledge of what is happening and so on. These differences explain why a human dying from cancer is likely to suffer more than a mouse. It is the mental anguish that makes the human's position so much harder to bear. Yet these differences do not all point to greater suffering on the part of the normal human being. Sometimes animals may suffer more because of their more limited understanding. If, for instance, we are taking prisoners in wartime, we can explain to them that although they must submit to capture, search and confinement, they will not otherwise be harmed and will be set free at the conclusion of hostilities. If we capture wild animals, however, we cannot explain that we are not threatening their lives. Animals cannot distinguish attempts to overpower and confine from attempts to kill them; the one causes as much terror as the other.

It may be objected that comparisons of the sufferings of different species are impossible to make, and that for this reason when the interests of animals and humans clash, the principle of equality gives no guidance. It is true that comparisons of suffering between members of different species cannot be made precisely. Nor, for that matter, can comparisons of suffering between different human beings be made precisely. Precision is not essential. As we shall see shortly, even if we were to prevent the infliction of suffering on animals only when the interests of humans will not be affected to anything like the extent that animals are affected, we would be forced to make radical changes in our treatment of animals that would involve the food we eat, the farming methods we use, experimental procedures in many fields of science, our approach to wildlife and to hunting, trapping and the wearing of furs, and areas of entertainment like circuses, rodeos and zoos. As a result, the total quantity of suffering we cause would be hugely reduced.

So far, I have said a lot about the infliction of suffering on animals but nothing about killing them. This omission has been deliberate. The application of the principle of equality to the infliction of suffering is, in theory at least, fairly straightforward. Pain and suffering are bad and should be prevented or minimized, irrespective of the race, sex or species of the being that suffers. How bad a pain is depends on how intense it is and how long it lasts, but pains of the same intensity and duration are equally bad, whether felt by humans or animals. When we come to consider the value of life, we cannot say quite so confidently that a life is a life and equally valuable, whether it is a human life or an animal life. It would not be speciesist to hold that the life of a self-aware being, capable of abstract thought, of planning for the future, of complex acts of communication and so on, is more valuable than the life of a being without these capacities. (I am not saying, at this stage, whether this view is justifiable or not; I am saying only that it cannot simply be rejected as speciesist, because it is not on the basis of species itself that one life is held to be more valuable than another.) The value of life is a notoriously difficult ethical question, and we can only arrive at a reasoned conclusion about the comparative value of human and animal life after we have discussed the value of life in general. This is the topic of the next chapter. Meanwhile, there are important conclusions to be derived from the extension beyond our own species of the principle of equal consideration of interests, irrespective of our conclusions about the value of life.

SPECIESISM IN PRACTICE

Animals as Food

For most people in modern, urbanized societies, the principal form of contact with nonhuman animals is at meal times. The use of animals for food is probably the oldest and the most widespread form of animal use.

There is also a sense in which it is the most basic form of animal use, the foundation stone of an ethic that sees animals as things for us to use to meet our needs and interests.

If animals count in their own right, our use of animals for food becomes questionable. Inuit living a traditional lifestyle in the far north where they must eat animals or starve can reasonably claim that their interest in surviving overrides that of the animals they kill. Most of us cannot defend our diet in this way. People living in industrialized societies can easily obtain an adequate diet without the use of animal flesh. Meat is not necessary for good health or longevity. Indeed, humans can live healthy lives without eating any animal products at all, although a vegan diet requires greater care, especially for young children, and a B12 vitamin supplement should be taken. Nor is animal production in industrialized societies an efficient way of producing food, because most of the animals consumed have been fattened on grains and other foods that we could have eaten directly. When we feed these grains to animals, only about one-quarter – and in some cases, as little as one-tenth – of the nutritional value remains as meat for human consumption. So, with the exception of animals raised entirely on grazing land unsuitable for crops, animals are eaten neither for health nor to increase our food supply. Their flesh is a luxury, consumed because people like its taste. (The livestock industry also contributes more to global warming than the entire transport sector.)

In considering the ethics of the use of animal products for human food in industrialized societies, we are considering a situation in which a relatively minor human interest must be balanced against the lives and welfare of the animals involved. The principle of equal consideration of interests does not allow major interests to be sacrificed for minor interests.

The case against using animals for food is at its strongest when animals are made to lead miserable lives so that their flesh can be made available to humans at the lowest possible cost. Modern forms of intensive farming apply science and technology to the attitude that animals are objects for us to use. Competition in the marketplace forces meat producers to copy rivals who are prepared to cut costs by giving animals more miserable lives. In buying the meat, eggs or milk produced in these ways, we tolerate methods of meat production that confine sentient animals in cramped, unsuitable conditions for the entire duration of their lives. They are treated like machines that convert fodder into flesh, and any innovation that results in a higher 'conversion ratio' is liable to be adopted. As one authority on the subject has said, 'cruelty is acknowledged only when profitability ceases'. To avoid speciesism, we must stop these practices. Our custom is all the support that factory farmers need. The decision to cease giving them that support may be difficult, but it is less difficult than it would have been for a white Southerner to go against the values of his community and free his slaves. If we do not change our dietary habits, how can we censure those slave holders who would not change their own way of living?

These arguments apply to animals reared in factory farms – which means that we should not eat chicken, pork or veal unless we know that the meat we are eating was not produced by factory farm methods. The same is true of beef that has come from cattle kept in crowded feedlots (as most beef does in the United States). Eggs come from hens kept in small wire cages, too small even to allow them to stretch their wings, unless the eggs are specifically sold as 'cage-free' or 'free range'. (At the time of writing, Switzerland has banned the battery cage, and the European Union is in the process of phasing it out. In the United States, California voted in 2008 to ban it, and that ban will come into effect in 2015. A law passed in Michigan in 2009 requires battery cages to be phased out over ten years.) Dairy products also often come from cows confined to a barn, unable to go out to pasture. Moreover, to continue to give milk, dairy cows have to be made pregnant every year, and their calf then taken away from them shortly after birth, so we can have the milk. This causes distress to both the cow and the calf.

Concern about the suffering of animals in factory farms does not take us all the way to a vegan diet, because it is possible to buy animal products from animals allowed to graze outside. (When animal products are labeled 'organic', this should mean that the animals have access to the outdoors, but the interpretation of this rule is sometimes loose.) The lives of free-ranging animals are undoubtedly better than those of animals reared in factory farms. It is still doubtful if using them for food is compatible with equal consideration of interests. One problem is, of course, that using them for food involves killing them (even laying hens and dairy cows are killed when their productivity starts to drop, which is far short of their natural life span), but this is an issue to which, as I have said, we shall return in later chapters. Apart from killing them, there are also many other things done to animals in order to bring them cheaply to our dinner table. Castration, the separation of mother and young, the breaking up of herds, branding, transporting, slaughterhouse handling and finally the moment of slaughter itself – all of these are likely to involve suffering and do not take the animals' interests into account. Perhaps animals can be reared on a small scale without suffering in these ways. Some farmers take pride in producing 'humanely raised' animal products, but the standards of what is regarded as 'humane' vary widely. Any shift towards more humane treatment of animals is welcome, but it seems unlikely that these methods could produce the vast quantity of animal products now consumed by our large urban populations. At the very least, we would have to considerably reduce the amount of meat, eggs and dairy products that we consume. In any case, the important question is not whether animal products *could* be produced without suffering, but whether those we are considering buying *were* produced without suffering. Unless we can be confident that they were, the principle of equal consideration of interests implies that their production wrongly sacrificed important interests of the animals to satisfy less important interests of our own. To buy the results of this process of production is to support it and encourage producers to continue to do it. Because those of us living in developed societies have a wide range of food choices and do not need to eat these products, encouraging the continuation of a cruel system of producing animal products is wrong.

For those of us living in cities where it is difficult to know how the animals we might eat have lived and died, this conclusion brings us very close to a vegan way of life. I shall consider some objections to it in the final section of this chapter.

Experimenting on Animals

Perhaps the area in which speciesism can most clearly be observed is the use of animals in experiments. Here the issue stands out starkly, because experimenters often seek to justify experimenting on animals by claiming that the experiments lead us to discoveries about humans; if this is so, the experimenter must agree that human and nonhuman animals are similar in crucial respects. For instance, if forcing a rat to choose between starving to death and crossing an electrified grid to obtain food tells us anything about the reactions of humans to stress, we must assume that the rat feels stress in this kind of situation.

People sometimes think that all animal experiments serve vital medical purposes and can be justified on the grounds that they relieve more suffering than they cause. This comfortable belief is mistaken. The LD_{50} – a test designed in the 1920s to find the 'Lethal Dose', or level of consumption that will make 50 percent of a sample of animals die – is still used today for some purposes. It is, for example, used to test the popular anti-wrinkle treatment, Botox® Cosmetic. For this purpose, mice are given varying doses. Those given a high enough dose slowly suffocate as their respiratory muscles become paralyzed, undoubtedly after considerable suffering. These tests are not necessary to prevent human suffering: even if there were no alternative to the use of animals to test the safety of the products, it would be better to do without them, and learn to live with wrinkles, as most elderly people always have.

Nor can all university experiments be defended on the grounds that they relieve more suffering than they inflict. In a well-known series of experiments that went on for more than fifteen years, H. F. Harlow of the Primate Research Center, Madison, Wisconsin, reared monkeys under conditions of maternal deprivation and total isolation. He found that in this way he could reduce the monkeys to a state in which, when placed among normal monkeys, they sat huddled in a corner in a condition of persistent depression and fear. Harlow also produced female monkeys so neurotic that when they became mothers they smashed their infant's face into the floor and rubbed it back and forth. Although Harlow himself is no longer alive, some of his former students at other U.S. universities continued to perform variations of his experiments for many years after his death.

In these cases, and many others like them, the benefits to humans are either non-existent or very uncertain; while the losses to members of other species are certain and real. Hence, the experiments indicate a failure to give equal consideration to the interests of all beings, irrespective of species. In the past, argument about animal experimentation has often missed this point because it has been put in absolutist terms: would the opponent of experimentation be prepared to let thousands die from a terrible disease that could be cured only by experimenting on one animal? This is a purely hypothetical question, because no experiment could ever be predicted to have such dramatic results, but so long as its hypothetical nature is clear, I think the question should be answered affirmatively – in other words, if one, or even a dozen animals had to suffer experiments in order to save thousands, I would think it right and in accordance with equal consideration of interests that they should do so.

To the hypothetical question about saving thousands of people through experiments on limited number of animals, opponents of speciesism can reply with a hypothetical question of their own: would experimenters be prepared to perform their experiments on orphaned humans with severe and irreversible brain damage if that were the only way to save thousands? (I say 'orphaned' in order to avoid the complication of the feelings of the human parents.) If experimenters are not prepared to use orphaned humans with severe and irreversible brain damage, their readiness to use nonhuman animals seems to discriminate on the basis of species alone, because apes, monkeys, dogs, cats and even mice and rats are more intelligent, more aware of what is happening to them, more sensitive to pain and so on than many severely brain-damaged humans barely surviving in hospital wards and other institutions. There seems to be no morally relevant characteristic that such humans have that nonhuman animals lack. Experimenters, then, show bias in favour of their own species whenever they carry out experiments on nonhuman animals for purposes that they would not think justified them in using human beings at an equal or lower level of sentience, awareness, sensitivity and so on. If this bias were eliminated, the number of experiments performed on animals would be greatly reduced.

It is possible that a small number of actual experiments on animals could be justified along the lines of the hypothetical justification I accepted previously, that is, without violating the principle of equal consideration of interests. Although the gains from an actual experiment would never be as certain as in the hypothetical example, if the benefit were sufficiently great, the probability of achieving that benefit high enough and the suffering to the animals sufficiently small, a utilitarian could not say that it is wrong to do it. That would also be true if the experiment were to be done on an orphaned, brain-damaged human being. Whether or not the occasional experiment on animals is defensible, current institutional practices of using animals in research are not because, despite some improvements during the past thirty years, these practices still come nowhere near to giving equal consideration to the interests of animals. It would therefore be better to shift funds now going into research on animals to clinical research involving consenting patients and to developing other methods of research that do not make anyone, animal or human, suffer.

Other Forms of Speciesism

I have concentrated on the use of animals as food and in research, because these are examples of large-scale, systematic speciesism. They are not, of course, the only areas in which the principle of equal consideration of interests, extended beyond the human species, has practical implications. There are many other areas that raise similar issues, including the fur trade, hunting in all its different forms, circuses, rodeos, zoos and the pet business. Because the philosophical questions raised by these issues are not very different from those raised by the use of animals as food and in research, I shall leave it to the reader to apply the appropriate ethical principles to them.

SOME OBJECTIONS

When I first put forward the views outlined in this chapter, in 1973, there was no animal liberation or animal rights movement. Now there is, and the hard work of countless animal activists has paid off, not only in greater public awareness of animal abuse, but also in concrete benefits for animals in many different areas. Despite this increasing acceptance of many aspects of the case for equal consideration for the interests of animals and the slow but tangible progress made on behalf of animals in many different areas, a number of objections keep coming up. In this final section of the chapter, I shall attempt to answer the most important of these objections.

How Do We Know That Animals Can Feel Pain?

We can never directly experience the pain of another being, whether that being is human or not. When I see a child fall and scrape her knee, I know that she feels pain because of the way she behaves – she cries, she tells me her knee hurts, she rubs the sore spot and so on. I know that I myself behave in a somewhat similar – if more inhibited – way when I feel pain, and so I accept that the child feels something like what I feel when I scrape my knee.

The basis of my belief that animals can feel pain is similar to the basis of my belief that children can feel pain. Animals in pain behave in much the same way as humans do, and their behaviour is sufficient justification for the belief that they feel pain. It is true that, with the exception of a few animals who have learned to communicate with us in a human language, they cannot actually say that they are feeling pain – but babies and toddlers cannot talk either. They find other ways to make their inner states apparent, however, demonstrating that we can be sure that a being is feeling pain even if the being cannot use language.

To back up our inference from animal behaviour, we can point to the fact that the nervous systems of all vertebrates, and especially of birds and mammals, are fundamentally similar. Those parts of the human nervous system that are concerned with feeling pain are relatively old, in evolutionary terms. Unlike the cerebral cortex, which developed only after our ancestors diverged from other mammals, the basic nervous system evolved in more distant ancestors and so is common to all of the other 'higher' animals, including humans. This anatomical parallel makes it likely that the capacity of vertebrate animals to feel is similar to our own.

The nervous systems of invertebrates are less like our own, and perhaps for that reason we are not justified in having quite the same confidence that they can feel pain. In the case of bivalves like oysters, mussels and clams, a capacity for pain or any other form of consciousness seems unlikely, and if that is so, the principle of equal consideration of interests will not apply to them. On the other hand, scientists studying the responses of crabs and prawns to stimuli like electric shock or a pinch on an antenna have found evidence that does suggest pain. Moreover, the behaviour of some invertebrates – especially the octopus, who can learn to solve novel problems like opening a screw-top glass jar to get at a tasty morsel inside – is difficult to explain without accepting that consciousness has also evolved in at least some invertebrates.

It is significant that none of the grounds we have for believing that animals feel pain hold for plants. We cannot observe behaviour suggesting pain – sensational claims to have detected feelings in plants by attaching lie detectors to them proved impossible to replicate – and plants do not have a centrally organized nervous system like ours.

Animals Eat Each Other, So Why Shouldn't We Eat Them?

This might be called the Benjamin Franklin Objection because Franklin recounts in his *Autobiography* that he was for a time a vegetarian, but his abstinence from animal flesh came to an end when he was watching some friends prepare to fry a fish they had just caught. When the fish was cut open, it was found to have a smaller fish in its stomach. 'Well', Franklin said to himself, 'if you eat one another, I don't see why we may not eat you', and he proceeded to do so.

Franklin was at least honest. In telling this story, he confesses that he convinced himself of the validity of the objection only after the fish was already in the frying pan and smelling 'admirably well'; and he remarks that one of the advantages of being a 'reasonable creature' is that one can find a reason for whatever one wants to do. The replies that can be made to this objection are so obvious that Franklin's acceptance of it does testify more to his hunger on that occasion than to his powers of reason. For a start, most animals who kill for food would not be able to survive if they did not, whereas we have no need to eat animal flesh. Next, it is odd that humans, who normally think of the behaviour of animals as 'beastly' should, when it suits them, use an argument that implies that we ought to look to animals for moral guidance. The most decisive point, however, is that nonhuman animals are not capable of considering the alternatives open to them or of reflecting on the ethics of their diet. Hence, it is impossible to hold the animals responsible for what they do or to judge that because of their killing they 'deserve' to be treated in a similar way. Those who read these lines, on the other hand, must consider the justifiability of their dietary habits. You cannot evade responsibility by imitating beings who are incapable of making this choice.

Sometimes people draw a slightly different conclusion from the fact that animals eat each other. This suggests, they think, not that animals deserve to be eaten, but rather that there is a natural law according to which the stronger prey on the weaker, a kind of Darwinian 'survival of the fittest' in which by eating animals we are merely playing our part.

This interpretation of the objection makes two basic mistakes, one of fact and the other of reasoning. The factual mistake lies in the assumption that our own consumption of animals is part of some natural evolutionary process. This might be true of those who still hunt for food, but it has nothing to do with the mass production of domestic animals in factory farms.

Suppose that we did hunt for our food, though, and this was part of some natural evolutionary process. There would still be an error of reasoning in the assumption that because this process is natural it is right. It is, no doubt, 'natural' for women to produce an infant every year or two from puberty to menopause, but this does not mean that it is wrong to interfere with this process. We need to understand nature and develop the best theories we can to explain why things are as they are, because only in that way can we work out what the consequences our actions are likely to be; but it would be a serious mistake to assume that natural ways of doing things are incapable of improvement.

Ethics and Reciprocity

In the earliest surviving major work of moral philosophy in the Western tradition, Plato's *Republic,* we find the following view of ethics:

They say that to do injustice is, by nature, good; to suffer injustice, evil; but that there is more evil in the latter than good in the former. And so when men have both done and suffered injustice and have had experience of both, any who are not able to avoid the one and obtain the other, think that they had better agree among themselves to have neither; hence they begin to establish laws and mutual covenants; and that which is ordained by law is termed by them lawful and just. This, it is claimed, is the origin and nature of justice – it is a mean or compromise, between the best of all, which is to do injustice and not be punished, and the worst of all, which is to suffer injustice without the power of retaliation.

This was not Plato's own view. He put it into the mouth of Glaucon in order to allow Socrates, the hero of his dialogue, to refute it. It is a view that has never gained general acceptance but has not died away either. Echoes of it can be found in the ethical theories of philosophers like John Rawls and David Gauthier, and it has been used to justify the exclusion of animals from the sphere of ethics, or at least from its core. For if the basis of ethics is that I refrain from doing nasty things to others as long as they don't do nasty things to me, I have no reason to avoid doing nasty things to those who are incapable of appreciating my restraint and controlling their conduct towards me accordingly. Animals, by and large, are in this category. If I am surfing and a shark attacks, my respect for the interests of animals will not help me – I am as likely to be eaten as a surfer who, when not surfing, fishes for sharks from the safety of a boat. Because animals cannot reciprocate, they are, on this view, outside the limits of the ethical contract.

In assessing this conception of ethics, we should distinguish between *explanations* of the origin of ethical judgments and *justifications* of these judgments. The explanation of the origin of ethics in terms of a tacit contract between people for their mutual benefit has some plausibility (though in view of the quasi-ethical social rules that have been observed in the societies of other mammals, it is obviously a historical fantasy). We could accept this account as a historical explanation, however, without thereby committing ourselves to any views about the rightness or wrongness of the ethical system that has resulted. No matter how self-interested the origins of ethics may be, it is possible that once we have started thinking ethically, we are led beyond these mundane premises, for we are capable of reasoning, and reason is not subordinate to self-interest. When we are reasoning about ethics, we are using concepts that, as we saw in the first chapter of this book, take us beyond our own personal interests and even beyond the interests of some sectional group to which we belong. According to the contract view of ethics, this universalizing process should stop at the boundaries of our community; but once the process has begun, we may come to see that it would not be consistent with our other convictions to halt at that point. Just as the first mathematicians, who may have started counting in order to keep track of the number of people in their tribe, had no idea that they were taking the first steps along a path that would lead to the infinitesimal calculus, so the origins of ethics tell us nothing about where ethics should end.

When we turn to the question of justification, we can see that contractual accounts of ethics have many problems. Clearly, such accounts exclude from the ethical sphere a lot more than nonhuman animals. Because profoundly intellectually disabled humans are equally incapable of reciprocating, they must also be excluded. The same goes for infants and very young children. Nor are the problems of the contractual view limited to these special cases. The ultimate reason for entering into the ethical contract is, on this view, self-interest. Unless some additional universal element is brought in, one group of people has no reason to deal ethically with another if it is not in their interest to do so. If we take this seriously, we shall have to revise our ethical judgments very drastically. For instance, the white slave traders who transported African slaves to America had no self-interested reason for treating Africans any better than they did. The Africans had no way of retaliating. If they had only been contractualists, the slave traders could have rebutted the abolitionists by explaining to them that ethics stops at the boundaries of our community and adding that because Africans are not part of our community – as, at the time, they were not – we have no duties to them.

Most striking of all is the impact of the contract model on our attitude to future generations. 'Why should I do anything for posterity? What has posterity ever done for me?' would be the view we ought to take if we have no obligations to those who are unable to reciprocate. How can people who will be alive in the year 2150 do anything to make our lives better or worse? Hence, on the contract view, we need have no worries about problems like the disposal of nuclear waste. True, some nuclear wastes will still be deadly for a quarter of a million years; but as long as we put it in containers that will keep it safe for 100 years, we have done all that ethics demands of us.

These examples should suffice to show that, whatever its origin, the ethics we have now does go beyond a tacit understanding between beings capable of reciprocity. The prospect of returning to such a basis is not appealing. Because no account of the origin of morality compels us to base our morality on reciprocity, and no other arguments in favour of this conclusion have been offered, we should reject this view of ethics.

At this point in the discussion, some contract theorists appeal to a looser view of the contract idea, urging that we include within the moral community all those who have or will have the *capacity* to take part in a reciprocal agreement, irrespective of whether they are in fact able to reciprocate and irrespective of when they will have this capacity. Plainly, this view is no longer based on reciprocity at all, for (unless we care greatly about having our grave kept tidy or our memory preserved forever) later generations cannot enter into reciprocal relationships with us, even though they will one day have the capacity to reciprocate. If contract theorists abandon reciprocity in this manner, however, what is left of the contract account? Why adopt it at all? And why limit morality to those who have the capacity to enter into agreements with us, if in fact there is no possibility of them ever doing so? Rather than cling to the husk of a contract view that has lost its kernel, it would be better to abandon it altogether and consider, on the basis of universalizability, which beings ought to be included within morality.

Differences Between Humans and Animals

That humans and animals are utterly different *kinds* of beings was unquestioned for most of the course of Western civilization. The basis of this assumption was undermined by Darwin's discovery of our origins and the associated decline in the credibility of the story of our divine creation in the image of God. Darwin himself argued that the difference between us and animals is one of degree, rather than of kind – a view that even today, some find difficult to accept. They have searched for ways of drawing a line between humans and animals. To date, these boundaries have been short-lived. For instance, it used to be said that only humans used tools. Then it was observed that the Galapagos woodpecker used a cactus thorn to dig insects out of crevices in trees. Next, it was suggested that even if other animals *used* tools, humans are the only animals who *make* tools. Then Jane Goodall found that chimpanzees in the jungles of Tanzania chewed up leaves to make a sponge for sopping up water and trimmed the leaves from branches to make tools for catching insects. The use of language was another boundary line – but now chimpanzees, bonobos, gorillas and orangutans have learnt to sign in the language used in America by people who are deaf, and parrots have learned to speak – and not merely parrot – English.

Even if these attempts to draw the line between humans and animals had fitted the facts, they would still not carry the moral weight required to justify our treatment of animals. As Bentham pointed out, the fact that an animal does not use language is no reason for ignoring its suffering, and neither is the fact that she does not use tools.

Some philosophers have claimed that there is a more profound difference between humans and animals. They have claimed that animals cannot think or reason, and that accordingly, they have no conception of themselves, no self-awareness. They live from instant to instant and do not see themselves as distinct entities with a past and a future. Nor do they have autonomy, the ability to choose how to live one's life. It has been suggested that autonomous, self-aware beings are in some way much more morally significant than beings who live from moment to moment, without the capacity to see themselves as distinct beings with a past and a future. Accordingly, on this view, the interests of autonomous, self-aware beings ought normally to take priority over the interests of other beings. I shall not now consider whether some nonhuman animals are self-aware and autonomous because in the present context, not much depends on this question. We are now considering only the application of the principle of equal consideration of interests. In the next chapter, when we discuss questions about what makes it wrong to take a life, we shall see that there are reasons for holding that self-awareness makes a difference in debates about whether a being has a right to life; and we shall then investigate the evidence for self-awareness in nonhuman animals. Meanwhile, the more important issue is: does the fact that a being is self-aware entitle that being to some kind of priority of consideration?

The claim that self-aware beings are entitled to more consideration than other beings is compatible with the principle of equal consideration of interests if it amounts to no more than the claim that something that happens to self-aware beings can be contrary to their interests, whereas similar occurrences would not be contrary to the interests of beings who are not self-aware. This might be because the self-aware creature can fit the event into the overall framework of a longer time period, has different desires and so on. This, however, is a point I granted at the start of this chapter, and provided that it is not carried to ludicrous extremes – like insisting that if I am self-aware and a veal calf is not, depriving me of veal causes more suffering than depriving the calf of his freedom to walk, stretch and eat grass – it is not denied by the criticisms I made of animal experimentation and factory farming.

It would be a different matter if it were claimed that, even when a self-aware being did not suffer more than a being that was merely sentient, the suffering of the self-aware being is more important because these are inherently more valuable beings. This introduces non-utilitarian claims of value – claims that do not derive simply from taking a universal standpoint in the manner described in the final section of Chapter 1. Because the argument for utilitarianism developed in that section was admittedly tentative, I cannot use it to rule out all non-utilitarian values. Nevertheless, we are entitled to ask *why* self-aware beings should be considered more valuable and in particular why the alleged greater value of a self-aware being should result in preferring the lesser interests of a self-aware being to the greater interests of a merely sentient being, even where the self-awareness of the former being is not itself at stake. This last point is an important one, for we are not now considering cases in which the lives of self-aware beings are at risk but cases in which self-aware beings will go on living, their faculties intact, whatever we decide. In these cases, if the existence of self-awareness does not mean that the interests of the self-aware being really are greater, and more adversely affected, than the interests of the non-self-aware being, it is not clear why we should bring self-awareness into the discussion at all, any more than we should bring species, race or sex into similar discussions.

There is another possible reply to the claim that self-awareness, or autonomy or some similar characteristic, can serve to distinguish human from nonhuman animals. Recall that there are intellectually disabled humans who have less claim to be regarded as self-aware or autonomous than many nonhuman animals. If we use these characteristics to place a gulf between humans and other animals, we place these less able humans on the other side of the gulf; and if the gulf is taken to mark a difference in moral status, then these humans would have the moral status of animals rather than humans. But none of us would want to use profoundly intellectually disabled humans in painful experiments, or fatten them to satisfy some gourmets' interests in tasting a new kind of meat.

Defending Speciesism

When faced with the objection that their position implies that we would be entitled to treat profoundly intellectually disabled humans as we now treat nonhuman animals, some philosophers fall back on defending speciesism, either because of its instrumental value, or, more boldly, on the grounds that species membership is itself morally significant.

The instrumental defence of speciesism invokes the widely used 'slippery slope' argument. The claim is that a first step in a certain direction will put us on a slippery slope, and we shall not be able to stop sliding into a moral abyss. In the present context, the argument is used to suggest that we need a clear line to divide those beings we can experiment on, or fatten for dinner, from those we cannot. The species boundary makes a nice sharp dividing line, whereas levels of self-awareness, autonomy or sentience do not. Once we allow that any human being, no matter how profoundly intellectually disabled, has no higher moral status than an animal, the argument goes, we have begun to slide down a slope, the next level of which is denying rights to social misfits, and the bottom of which is classifying anyone we do not like as sub-human and eliminating them.

In response to this slippery slope argument, it is important to remember that the aim of my argument is to elevate the status of animals rather than to lower the status of any humans. I do not wish to suggest that intellectually disabled humans should be force-fed with food colourings until they get ill or die – although this would certainly give us a more accurate indication of whether the substance was safe for humans than doing this to rabbits or dogs. I would like our conviction that it would be wrong to treat intellectually disabled humans in this way to be transferred to nonhuman animals at similar levels of self-awareness and with similar capacities for suffering. It is excessively pessimistic to refrain from trying to alter the way we treat animals on the grounds that we might start treating intellectually disabled humans with the same lack of concern we now have for animals, rather than give animals the greater concern that we now have for intellectually disabled humans. If we really are convinced of the dangers of the slippery slope, we can avoid it by insisting that all sentient beings, whether self-aware or not, should have basic rights.

The slippery slope argument may serve as a valuable warning in some contexts, but without some specific reasons for believing that there is a real likelihood that the alleged slide will occur, it cannot bear too much weight. For we could just as well argue that there is a link between the way we treat animals and the way we treat humans that points in the opposite direction. Many studies in psychology and criminology have shown that violent criminals are likely to have a history of animal abuse during their childhood or adolescence. Perhaps if we treated animals better, we would also treat our fellow humans better. Admittedly, this is a speculative claim, but slippery slope arguments also make speculative claims, so the two claims could be taken to cancel each other out. In any case, if the special status we now give to humans allows us to ignore the interests of billions of sentient creatures, we should not be deterred from trying to rectify this situation by the mere possibility that the principles on which we base this attempt will be misused by evil people for their own ends. Instead, we should heighten our vigilance against such misuse.

An argument that comes closer to making species a matter of intrinsic moral significance is that profoundly intellectually disabled humans who do not possess the capacities that mark the normal human off from other animals should nevertheless be treated as if they did possess these capacities, because they belong to a species, members of which normally do possess them. The suggestion is, in other words, that we treat individuals, not in accordance with their actual qualities, but in accordance with the qualities normal for their species.

It is interesting that this suggestion should be made in defence of treating members of our species better than members of another species, when it would be firmly rejected if it were used to justify treating members of our race or sex better than members of another race or sex. In the previous chapter, when discussing the impact of possible differences in IQ between members of different ethnic groups, I made the obvious point that whatever the difference between the *average* scores for different groups, some members of the group with the lower average score will do better than some members of the group with the higher average score, and we ought to treat people as individuals and not according to the average score for their ethnic group, whatever the explanation of that average might be. If we accept this, we cannot consistently accept the suggestion that we should grant profoundly intellectually disabled humans the status or rights normal for their species. For what is the significance of the fact that this time the line is to be drawn around the species rather than around the race or sex? We cannot insist that beings be treated as individuals in the one case and as members of a group in the other.

It has also been argued that although profoundly intellectually disabled humans may not possess higher capacities than other animals, they are nonetheless 'us' and for that reason we have obligations to them that we do not have to those who are not 'us'. This argument begs the question about who we consider ourselves to be. Are we essentially members of the species *Homo sapiens*, or are we essentially self-aware beings or perhaps essentially sentient beings? Personally, I would feel that an intelligent alien with whom I could communicate and share feelings would have more in common with me than a member of my own species who is so profoundly disabled as to be unable to have any conscious experiences at all – even if the latter *looked* much more like me.

It is understandable that human beings who look like us evoke warm feelings that aliens, or some other animals, may not evoke. It would be a mistake, however, to tie morality too closely to our affections. Of course some people may have a closer relationship with the most profoundly intellectually disabled human than they do with any nonhuman animal, and it would be absurd to tell them that they should not feel this way. They simply do, and as such there is nothing good or bad about it. The question is whether our moral obligations to a being should be made to depend on our feelings in this manner. Notoriously, some human beings have a closer relationship with their cat than with their neighbours. Would those who tie morality to affections accept that these people are justified in saving their cats from a fire before they save their neighbours? Even those who are prepared to answer this question affirmatively would, I trust, not want to go along with racists who could argue that if people have more personal relationships with, and greater affection towards, others who have the same skin colour or the same kind of hair, it is all right for them to give preference to the interests of such people. Ethics does not demand that we eliminate personal relationships and partial affections, but it does demand that, when we act, we assess the moral claims of those affected by our actions with some degree of independence from our feelings for them.

Shortly before he died in 2003, the British philosopher Bernard Williams defended speciesism in an article entitled, appropriately enough, "The Human Prejudice." Williams started from the claim that all our values are necessarily 'human values'. In one sense, of course, they are. Because we have yet to encounter any nonhumans who articulate, reflect on and discuss their values, all the values up for discussions are human in the sense that they have been formulated and articulated by human beings. The fact that our values are human in this sense does not exclude the possibility of developing values that would be accepted by any rational being capable of empathy with other beings. Nor – and this is the most important point – does the human nature of our values tell us anything about what our values can or should be and, in particular, whether we should value the pains, pleasures and lives of nonhuman animals less highly than we value our own pains, pleasures and lives. Williams, to his credit, acknowledged that 'it is itself part of a human, or humane, outlook to be concerned with how animals should be treated, and there is nothing in what I have said to suggest that we should not be concerned with that'. What, then, is the significance of the fact that our values are human values? Williams' ultimate defence of 'the human prejudice' is surprisingly crude. He asks us to imagine that our planet has been colonized by benevolent, fair-minded and far-sighted aliens who judge it necessary to remove us. He then says that no matter how fair-minded and well-informed that decision was (we can imagine, perhaps, that our incorrigible aggression was likely, sooner or later, to destroy the planet), we would be right to side with our own species against these aliens. The ultimate question, Williams says, is 'Which side are you on?'

We have heard that question before. In times of war, or racial, ethnic, religious or ideological conflict, 'which side are you on?' is used to evoke group solidarity and suggest that any questioning of the struggle is treason. In the United States in the 1950s, followers of Senator Joseph McCarthy asked it of those who opposed their methods of fighting communism. Senior figures in the administration of President George W. Bush used it to imply that their critics were giving support to terrorists. The question divides the world into 'us' and 'them' and demands that the mere fact of this division transcends the very different question: 'What is the right thing to do?' In these circumstances, the right and courageous thing to do is not to side with the tribal instincts that prompt us to say, 'My tribe (country, race, ethnic group, religion, etc.) right or wrong' but to say, 'I'm on the side that does what is right'. Although it is fantastic to imagine that a fair-minded, well-informed, far-sighted judge could ever decide that there was no alternative to the 'removal' of our species in order to avoid much greater injustice and misery, if this really were the case, we should reject the tribal – or species – instinct and answer Williams' question in the same way.

4

What's Wrong with Killing?

An oversimplified summary of the first three chapters of this book might read like this: the first chapter sets up a conception of ethics from which, in the second chapter, the principle of equal consideration of interests is derived; this principle is then used to illuminate problems about the sense in which humans are equal and, in the third chapter, applied to nonhuman animals.

Thus, the principle of equal consideration of interests has been behind much of our discussion so far; but as I suggested in the previous chapter, the application of this principle when lives are at stake is less straightforward than when we are concerned with interests like avoiding pain and experiencing pleasure. In this chapter, we shall look at some views about the wrongness of taking life, in order to prepare the ground for the following chapters in which we shall turn to some practical issues about when it is wrong to kill someone and when it is wrong to allow someone to die.

HUMAN LIFE

People often say that life is sacred. They almost never mean what they say. They do not mean, as their words seem to imply, that all life is sacred. If they did, killing a pig or pulling up a cabbage would be as abhorrent to them as the murder of a human being. When people say that life is sacred, it is human life they have in mind. But why should human life have special value?

In discussing the doctrine of the sanctity of human life, I shall not take the term 'sanctity' in a specifically religious sense. The doctrine may well have a religious origin, but it is now part of a broadly secular ethic, and it is as part of this secular ethic that it is most influential today. Nor shall I take the doctrine as maintaining that it is *always* wrong to take human life, for this would imply absolute pacifism, and there are many supporters of the sanctity of human life who concede that we may kill in self-defence and some who support capital punishment. We may take the doctrine of the sanctity of human life as simply a way of saying that human life has some very special value, a value quite distinct from the value of the lives of other living things.

The view that human life has unique value is deeply rooted in our society and is enshrined in our law. To see how far it can be taken, consider what happened to Peggy Stinson, a Pennsylvania schoolteacher, who was twenty-four weeks pregnant when she went into premature labor. The baby, whom Peggy and her husband named Andrew, was marginally viable. Despite a firm statement from both parents that they wanted 'no heroics', the doctors in charge of their child used all the technology of modern medicine to keep him alive for nearly six months. Andrew had periodic fits. Towards the end of that period, it was clear that if he survived at all, he would be seriously and permanently impaired. Andrew was also suffering considerably: at one point his doctor told the Stinsons that it must 'hurt like hell' every time Andrew drew a breath. Andrew's treatment cost $104,000, and these events took place in 1977 – today the cost of keeping an infant in intensive care for six months could easily exceed a million dollars.

Andrew Stinson was kept alive, against the wishes of his parents, at a substantial financial cost, notwithstanding evident suffering and despite the fact that after a certain point it was clear that he would never be able to live an independent life or to think and talk in the way that most humans do. Whether it is right to treat an infant human being like this is a question we shall examine in Chapter 7. Here, I want to note the striking contrast between such efforts to preserve a human life and the casual way in which we take the lives of stray dogs, monkeys used in experiments, and the cattle, pigs and chickens we eat. What could justify the difference?

In every society known to us, there has been some prohibition on the taking of life. Presumably no society can survive if it allows its members to kill one another without restriction. Precisely who is protected, however, is a matter on which societies have differed. In many tribal societies, the only serious offence is to kill an innocent member of the tribe itself – members of other tribes may be killed with impunity. In more sophisticated nation-states, protection has generally extended to all within the nation's territorial boundaries, although there have been notorious cases in which a minority was excluded. Nowadays most agree, in theory if not in practice, that, apart from special cases like self-defence, war, possibly capital punishment and one or two other doubtful areas, it is wrong to kill human beings irrespective of their race, religion, class or nationality. The moral inadequacy of narrower principles, limiting respect for life to a tribe, race or nation, is taken for granted; but the argument of the preceding chapter must raise doubts about whether the boundary of our species marks a defensible limit to the protected circle.

At this point, we should pause to ask what we mean by terms like 'human life' or 'human being'. These terms figure prominently in debates about abortion and experimentation on embryos. 'Is the fetus a human being?' is often taken as the crucial question in the abortion debate; but unless we think carefully about these terms, such questions cannot be answered.

It is possible to give 'human being' a precise meaning. We can use it as equivalent to 'member of the species *Homo sapiens*'. Whether a being is a member of a given species is something that can be determined scientifically by an examination of the nature of the chromosomes in the cells of living organisms. In this sense there is no doubt that from the first moments of its existence, an embryo conceived from human sperm and eggs is a human being; and the same is true of the most profoundly and irreparably intellectually disabled human being, even of an anencephalic infant – that is, an infant that, as a result of a defect in the formation of the neural tube, has no brain.

There is another use of the term 'human', one proposed by Joseph Fletcher, a major figure in the development of bioethics. Fletcher compiled a list of what he called 'Indicators of Humanhood' that includes the following: self-awareness, self-control, a sense of the future, a sense of the past, the capacity to relate to others, concern for others, communication and curiosity. This is the sense of the term that we have in mind when we praise someone by saying that she is 'a real human being' or shows 'truly human qualities'. In saying this we are not, of course, referring to the person's membership in the species *Homo sapiens*, which as a matter of biological fact is never in doubt; we are implying that human beings characteristically possess certain qualities, and this person possesses them to a high degree.

These two senses of 'human being' overlap but do not coincide. The embryo, the later fetus, the profoundly intellectually disabled child, even the newborn infant – all are indisputably members of the species *Homo sapiens,* but none are self-aware, have a sense of the future, or the capacity to relate to others. Hence, the choice between the two senses can make an important difference to how we answer such questions as, 'Is the fetus a human being?'

When choosing which words to use in a situation like this, we should choose terms that will enable us to express our meaning clearly, and that do not prejudge the answer to substantive questions. To stipulate that we shall use 'human' in, say, the first of the two senses just described, and that therefore the fetus is a human being and abortion is immoral, would not do. Nor would it be any better to choose the second sense and argue on this basis that the fetus is not a human being so abortion is acceptable. The morality of abortion is a substantive issue, the answer to which cannot depend on a stipulation about how we shall use words. In order to avoid begging any questions, I shall for the moment put aside the tricky term 'human' and substitute two different terms, corresponding to the two different senses of 'human'. For the first sense, the biological sense, I shall simply use the cumbersome but precise expression 'member of the species *Homo sapiens*', and for the second sense, I shall use the term 'person'.

This use of 'person' is itself, unfortunately, liable to mislead, because 'person' is often used as if it meant the same as 'human being'. Yet the terms are not equivalent; there could be a person who is not a member of our species. There could also be members of our species who are not persons. The word 'person' has its origin in the Latin term for a mask worn by an actor in classical drama. By putting on masks, the actors signified that they were acting a role. Subsequently, 'person' came to mean one who plays a role in life, one who is an agent. According to the Oxford Dictionary, one of the current meanings of the term is 'a self-conscious or rational being'. This sense has impeccable philosophical precedents. John Locke defines a person as 'a thinking intelligent being that has reason and reflection and can consider itself as itself, the same thinking thing, in different times and places'.

This definition makes 'person' close to what Fletcher meant by 'human', except that it selects two crucial characteristics – rationality and self-consciousness – as the core of the concept. Quite possibly, Fletcher would have agreed that these two are central and the others more or less follow from them. In any case, I propose to use 'person', in the sense of a rational and self-aware being, to capture those elements of the popular sense of 'human being' that are not covered by 'member of the species *Homo sapiens*'. (I take 'self-conscious' and 'self-aware' to mean the same thing.)

Killing Members of the Species *Homo sapiens*

With the clarification gained by our terminological interlude, and the argument of the preceding chapter to draw on, this section can be very brief. The wrongness of inflicting pain on a being cannot depend on the being's species, and nor can the wrongness of killing it. The biological facts on which the boundary of our species is based do not have moral significance. To give preference to the life of a being simply because that being is a member of our species would put us in a position uncomfortably similar to that of racists who give preference to those who are members of their race.

To those who have read the preceding chapters of this book, this conclusion may seem obvious, for we have worked towards it gradually; but it differs strikingly from the prevailing attitude in our society, which as we have seen treats the lives of all members of our species as uniquely valuable. How is it that our society should have come to accept a view that bears up so poorly under critical scrutiny? A short historical digression may help to explain.

If we go back to the origins of Western civilization, to Greek or Roman times, we find that membership of *Homo sapiens* was not sufficient to guarantee that one's life would be protected. There was no respect for the lives of slaves or other 'barbarians'; and even among the Greeks and Romans themselves, infants had no automatic right to life. Greeks and Romans killed deformed or weak infants by exposing them to the elements on a hilltop. Plato and Aristotle thought that the state should enforce the killing of deformed infants. The celebrated legislative codes said to have been drawn up by Lycurgus and Solon contained similar provisions. In this period, it was thought better to end a life that had begun inauspiciously than to attempt to prolong that life, with all the problems it might bring.

Our present attitudes date from the coming of Christianity. There was a specific theological motivation for the Christian insistence on the importance of species membership: the belief that all born of human parents are immortal and destined for an eternity of bliss or for everlasting torment. With this belief, the killing of *Homo sapiens* took on a fearful significance, because it consigned a being to his or her eternal fate. A second Christian doctrine that led to the same conclusion was the belief that because we are created by God we are his property, and to kill a human being is to usurp God's right to decide when we shall live and when we shall die. As Thomas Aquinas put it, taking a human life is a sin against God in the same way that killing a slave would be a sin against the master to whom the slave belonged. Nonhuman animals, on the other hand, were believed to have been placed by God under man's dominion, as recorded in the Bible (Genesis 1:29 and 9:1–3). Hence, humans could kill nonhuman animals as they pleased, so long as they were not the property of another.

During the centuries of Christian domination of European thought, the ethical attitudes based on these doctrines became part of the unquestioned moral orthodoxy of European civilization. Today, the religious doctrines are no longer universally accepted, but the ethical attitudes to which they gave rise fit in with the deep-seated Western belief in the uniqueness and special privileges of our species; these ethical attitudes have survived. Now that we are reassessing our speciesist view of nature, however, it is also time to reassess our belief in the sanctity of the lives of members of our species.

Killing a Person

We have broken down the doctrine of the sanctity of human life into two separate claims, one that it is especially serious to take the life of a member of our species, and the other that it is especially serious to take the life of a person. We have seen that the former claim cannot be defended. What of the latter? Is there something about the life of a rational and self-conscious being, as distinct from a being that is merely sentient, that makes it much more serious to take the life of the former than the latter?

One line of argument for giving an affirmative answer to this question runs as follows. A self-conscious being is aware of itself as a distinct entity, with a past and a future. (This, remember, was Locke's criterion for being a person.) A being aware of itself in this way will be capable of having desires about its own future. A student may look forward to graduating; a child may want to go to a birthday party; a professor of philosophy may hope to write a book critical of some widely accepted ethical beliefs. To take the lives of any of these people, without their consent, is to thwart their desires for the future. For most mature humans, these forward-looking desires are absolutely central to our lives, so to kill a normal human against his or her wishes is to thwart that person's most significant desires. Killing a snail does not thwart any desires of this kind, because snails are incapable of having such desires. (In this respect, however, human fetuses and even newborn infants are in the same situation as snails. We shall explore the implications of this in a subsequent chapter.)

Admittedly, when a person is killed we are not left with a thwarted desire in the same sense in which I have a thwarted desire when I am hiking through dry country and, pausing to ease my thirst, discover that my water bottle is empty. Then I have a desire that I cannot fulfil, and I feel frustration and discomfort because of the continuing and unsatisfied desire for water. When I am killed, the desires I have for the future do not continue after my death, and I do not suffer from the fact that I cannot satisfy them. Does this mean that preventing the fulfilment of these desires does not matter?

Classical or hedonistic utilitarianism, as we have already noted, judges actions by their tendency to maximize pleasure or happiness and minimize pain or unhappiness. Terms like 'pleasure' and 'happiness' lack precision, but it is clear that they refer to something that is experienced or felt – in other words, to states of consciousness. According to hedonistic utilitarianism, therefore, there is no direct significance in the fact that desires for the future go unfulfilled when people die. If you die instantaneously, whether you have any desires for the future makes no difference to the amount of pleasure or pain you experience. Thus, for the hedonistic utilitarian, the status of 'person' is not *directly* relevant to the wrongness of killing.

Indirectly, however, being a person may be important for the hedonistic utilitarian. Its importance arises in the following manner. If I am a person, I know that I have a future. I also know that my future existence could be cut short. If I think that this is likely to happen at any moment, my present existence will be fraught with anxiety and will presumably be less enjoyable than if I do not think I am likely to die for some time. If I know that people like myself are very rarely killed, I will worry less than if the opposite is the case. Hence, the hedonistic utilitarian can defend a prohibition on killing persons on the indirect ground that it will increase the happiness of people who would otherwise worry that they might be killed. I call this an *indirect* ground because it does not refer to any direct wrong done to the person killed, but rather to a consequence of the killing for others. There is, of course, something odd about objecting to murder, not because of the wrong done to the victim, but because of the effect that the murder will have on others.

One has to be a tough-minded hedonistic utilitarian to be untroubled by this oddness. Remember, though, that we are now only considering what is *especially* wrong about killing a *person*. The hedonistic utilitarian can still regard killing as wrong because it eliminates the happiness that the victim would have experienced had she lived. This direct objection to murder will apply to any being likely to have a happy future, irrespective of whether the being is a person. For present purposes, however, the main point is that the indirect ground does provide a reason why even the hedonistic utilitarian should take the killing of a person, under certain conditions, more seriously than the killing of a being that is not a person. If a being is incapable of conceiving of itself as existing over time, we need not take into account the possibility of it worrying about the prospect of its future existence being cut short. It can't worry about this, for it has no conception of its own future.

I said that the indirect hedonistic utilitarian reason for taking the killing of a person more seriously than the killing of a being that is not a person holds 'under certain conditions'. The most obvious of these conditions is that the killing of the person may become known to other persons, who therefore become fearful of being murdered or gloomy about their prospects of living to a ripe old age. It is of course possible that a person could be killed in complete secrecy, so that no one else knew a murder had been committed. Then, this indirect reason against killing would not apply.

To this last point, however, a qualification must be made. In the circumstances described in the last paragraph, the indirect utilitarian reason against killing would not apply *in so far as we judge this individual case*. There is something to be said, however, against applying utilitarianism – whether classical hedonistic utilitarianism or preference utilitarianism – only or primarily at the level of each individual case. It may be that in the long run, we will achieve better results – greater overall happiness – if we urge people not to judge each individual action by the standard of utility, but instead to think along the lines of some broad principles that will cover all or virtually all of the situations that they are likely to encounter.

Several reasons have been offered in support of this approach. R.M. Hare has suggested a useful distinction between two levels of moral reasoning: the intuitive and the critical. To consider the possible circumstances in which one might maximize utility by secretly killing someone who wants to go on living is to reason at the critical level. Those who are reflective, self-critical or philosophically inclined may find it interesting and helpful to think about such unusual hypothetical cases. In real life, we usually cannot foresee all the complexities of our choices. It is simply not practical to try to calculate the consequences, in advance, of every choice we make. Even if we were to limit ourselves to the more significant choices, there would be a danger that in many cases we would be doing these complex calculations in less than ideal circumstances. We could be hurried or flustered. We might be feeling angry or hurt or competitive. Our thoughts could be coloured by greed or sexual desire or thoughts of vengeance. Our own interests, or the interests of those we love, might be at stake. Or we might just not be very good at thinking about such complicated issues as the likely consequences of a significant choice. For all these reasons, Hare suggests, it will be better if we adopt some broad ethical principles for our everyday ethical life and do not deviate from them. These principles should include those that experience has shown, over the centuries, to be generally conducive to producing the best consequences. In Hare's view, that would include many of the standard moral principles; for example, telling the truth, keeping promises, not harming others and so on. Respecting the lives of people who want to go on living would presumably be among these principles. Even though, at the critical level, we can conceive of circumstances in which better consequences would flow from acting against one or more of these principles, people will do better on the whole if they stick to the principles than if they do not.

On this view, the moral principles we choose to live by should be like a good tennis coach's instructions to a player. The instructions are given with an eye to what will pay off most of the time; they are a guide to playing 'percentage tennis'. Occasionally, a player whose strength is playing from the baseline will rush the net and pull off a winner that has everyone applauding; but if the coach is any good at all, deviations from the instructions laid down will, more often than not, lose. So it is better for a baseline player to put the thought of going to the net out of her mind, except perhaps in carefully defined circumstances. Similarly, if we are guided by a set of well-chosen intuitive principles, we may do better if we do not attempt to calculate the consequences of each significant moral decision we must make, but instead consider what principles apply to our decisions and act accordingly. Perhaps very occasionally we will find ourselves in circumstances in which it is absolutely plain that departing from the principles will produce a much better result than we will obtain by sticking to them, and then we may be justified in making the departure. For most of us most of the time, however, such circumstances will not arise and can be excluded from our thinking. Therefore, even though at the critical level the utilitarian must concede the possibility of cases in which it would be better not to respect a person's desire to continue living – for example, because the person could be killed in complete secrecy, and a great deal of unalleviated misery could thereby be prevented – this kind of thinking has no place at the intuitive level that should guide our everyday actions. So, at least, a utilitarian can argue.

That is, I think, the gist of what the hedonistic utilitarian would say about the distinction between killing a person and killing some other type of being. Preference utilitarianism – the version of utilitarianism that we reach by universalizing our own preferences in the manner described in the opening chapter of this book – gives greater weight to the distinction. According to preference utilitarianism, an action contrary to the preference of any being is wrong, unless this preference is outweighed by contrary preferences. Killing a person who prefers to continue living is therefore wrong, other things being equal. That the victims are not around after the act to lament the fact that their preferences have been disregarded is irrelevant. The wrong is done when the preference is thwarted. (Think about your own preference to go on living. You don't want it to be thwarted, and I doubt very much that you will be persuaded to change your mind about this by the fact that, if you are killed instantly, you will never suffer from the fact that your desire to go on living has been thwarted.)

For preference utilitarians, taking the life of a person will normally be worse than taking the life of some other being, because persons are highly future-oriented in their preferences. To kill a person is therefore, normally, to violate not just one but a wide range of the most central and significant preferences a being can have. Very often, it will make nonsense of everything that the victim has been trying to do in the past days, months or even years. In contrast, beings that cannot see themselves as entities with a future do not have any preferences about their own future existence. This is not to deny that such beings might struggle against a situation in which their lives are in danger, as a fish struggles to get free of the barbed hook in its mouth; but this indicates no more than a preference for the cessation of a state of affairs that causes pain or fear. The behaviour of a fish on a hook suggests a reason for not killing fish by that method but does not in itself suggest a preference utilitarian reason against killing fish by a method that brings about death instantly, without first causing pain or distress. Struggles against danger and pain do not suggest that fish are capable of preferring their own future existence to non-existence. (Again, remember that we are here considering what is especially wrong about killing a person; I am not saying that there are never any preference utilitarian reasons against killing sentient beings that are not persons. We shall return to this question shortly.)

Does a Person Have a Right to Life?

Although preference utilitarianism does provide a direct reason for not killing a person, some may find the reason – even when coupled with the important indirect reasons that any form of utilitarianism will take into account – not sufficiently stringent. For preference utilitarianism, the wrong done to the person killed is serious, but not necessarily decisive. The preference of the victim for continued life could sometimes be outweighed by the strong preferences of others. Many believe that the prohibition on killing people is more absolute than any kind of utilitarian calculation can imply. Our lives, we feel, are things to which we have a *right*, and rights are not to be traded off against the preferences or pleasures of others.

I am not convinced that the notion of a moral right is a helpful or meaningful one, except when it is used as a shorthand way of referring to more fundamental moral considerations, such as the view that – for the reasons offered in the preceding section – for all normal circumstances we should we put the idea of killing people who want to go on living completely out our minds. Nevertheless, because the idea that we have a right to life is a popular one, it is worth asking whether there are grounds for attributing a right to life to a person, as distinct from other living beings.

Michael Tooley, a contemporary American philosopher, has argued that the only beings who have a right to life are those who can conceive of themselves as distinct entities existing over time – in other words, persons, as we have used the term. His argument is based on the claim that there is a conceptual connection between the desires a being is capable of having and the rights that the being can be said to have. As Tooley puts it:

The basic intuition is that a right is something that can be violated and that, in general, to violate an individual's right to something is to frustrate the corresponding desire. Suppose, for example, that you own a car. Then I am under a prima facie obligation not to take it from you. However, the obligation is not unconditional: it depends in part upon the existence of a corresponding desire in you. If you do not care whether I take your car, then I generally do not violate your right by doing so.

Tooley admits that it is difficult to formulate the connections between rights and desires precisely because there are problem cases, like people who are asleep or temporarily unconscious. He does not want to say that such people have no rights because they have, at that moment, no desires. Nevertheless, Tooley holds, the possession of a right must in some way be linked with the capacity to have the relevant desires, if not with having the actual desires themselves.

The next step is to apply this view about rights to the case of the right to life. To put the matter as simply as possible – more simply than Tooley himself does and no doubt *too* simply – if the right to life is the right to continue existing as a distinct entity, then the desire relevant to possessing a right to life is the desire to continue existing as a distinct entity. But only a being who is capable of conceiving herself as a distinct entity existing over time – that is, only a person – could have this desire. Therefore, only a person could have a right to life.

This is how Tooley first formulated his position, in a striking article entitled "Abortion and Infanticide", published in 1972. The problem of how precisely to formulate the connections between rights and desires, however, led Tooley to alter his position in a subsequent book with the same title, *Abortion and Infanticide*. He there argues that an individual cannot at a given time – say, now – have a right to continued exist-ence unless the individual is of a kind such that it can now be in its interests that it continues to exist. One might think that this makes a dramatic difference to the outcome of Tooley's position, for although a newborn infant would not seem to be capable of conceiving itself as a distinct entity existing over time, we commonly think that it can be in the interests of an infant to be saved from death, even if the death would have been entirely without pain or suffering. We certainly do this in retrospect. If my mother told me that when I was a baby, my pram rolled into the path of a speeding train, and it was only the quick action of a stranger that saved me, I might say that that stranger is my greatest benefactor, for without her swift thinking I would never have had the happy and fulfilling life that I am now living. Tooley argues, however, that the retrospective attribution of an interest in living to the infant is a mistake. I am not the infant from whom I developed. The infant could not look forward to developing into the kind of being I am, or even into any intermediate being, between the being I now am and the infant. I cannot even recall being the infant; there are no mental links between us. Continued existence cannot be in the interests of a being who *never* has had the concept of a continuing self – that is, never has been able to conceive of itself as existing over time. If the train had instantly killed the infant, the death would not have been contrary to the interests of the infant, because the infant would never have had the concept of existing over time. It is true that I would then not be alive, but I can say that it is in my interests to be alive only because I do have the concept of a continuing self. I can with equal truth say that it is in my interests that my parents met, because if they had never met, they could not have created the embryo from which I developed, and so I would not be alive. This does not mean that the creation of this embryo was in the interests of any potential being who was lurking around, waiting to be brought into existence. There was no such being, and had I not been brought into existence, there would not have been anyone who missed out on the life I have enjoyed living. Similarly, we make a mistake if we now construct an interest in future life in the newborn infant who in the first days following birth can have no concept of continued existence and with whom I have no mental links.

Hence, in his book Tooley reaches, though by a more circuitous route, a conclusion that is practically equivalent to the conclusion he reached in his article. To have a right to life, one must have, or at least at one time have had, the concept of having a continuing existence. Note that this formulation avoids any problems in dealing with sleeping or unconscious people; it is enough that they, at one time, have had the concept of continued existence for us to be able to say that continued life may be in their interests. This makes sense: my desire to continue living – or to complete the book I am writing, or to travel to Nepal next year – does not cease whenever I am not consciously thinking about these things. We often desire things without the desire being at the forefront of our minds. The fact that we have the desire is apparent if we are reminded of it, or suddenly confronted with a situation in which we must choose between two courses of action, one of which makes the fulfilment of the desire less likely. In a similar way, when we go to sleep our desires for the future do not cease to exist. They will still be there when we wake. As the desires are still part of us, so too our interest in continued life remains part of us while we are asleep or unconscious.

Respect for Autonomy

To this point, our discussion of the wrongness of killing people has focused on their capacity to envisage their future and have desires related to it. Another implication of being a person may also be relevant to the wrongness of killing. There is a strand of ethical thought, associated with Kant but including many modern writers who are not Kantians, according to which respect for autonomy is a basic moral principle. 'Autonomy' here refers to the capacity to choose and to act on one's own decisions. Rational and self-aware beings presumably have this capacity, whereas beings who cannot consider the alternatives open to them are not capable of choosing in the required sense and, hence, cannot be autonomous. In particular, only a being who can grasp the difference between dying and continuing to live can autonomously choose to live. Hence, killing a person who does not choose to die fails to respect that person's autonomy; and as the choice of living or dying is about the most fundamental choice anyone can make, the choice on which all other choices depend, killing a person who does not choose to die is the gravest possible violation of that person's autonomy.

Not everyone agrees that respect for autonomy is a basic moral principle or a valid moral principle at all. Utilitarians do not respect autonomy for its own sake; although as we have seen, they might give great weight to a person's desire to go on living, either directly as a preference utilitarian would or as evidence that the person's life was on the whole a happy one, as a hedonistic utilitarian would. But a utilitarian cannot place the same stress on autonomy as those who take respect for autonomy as an independent moral principle. The hedonistic utilitarian might have to accept that in some cases it would be right to kill a person who does not choose to die on the grounds that the person will otherwise lead a miserable life, and the preference utilitarian may have to reach a similar conclusion if a person's desire to go on living is outweighed by the equally strong desires of others. This is true, however, only on the critical level of moral reasoning. As we saw earlier, utilitarians may encourage people to adopt, in their daily lives, principles that will in almost all cases lead to better consequences when followed than any alternative action. The principle of respect for autonomy would be a prime example of such a principle. We shall discuss actual cases that raise this issue in the chapter on euthanasia.

It may be helpful here to draw together our conclusions about the wrongness of taking a person's life. We have seen that there are four possible reasons for holding that it is especially serious to take a person's life: the hedonistic utilitarian concern with the effects of the killing on others; the preference utilitarian concern with the frustration of the victim's desires and plans for the future; the argument that the capacity to conceive of oneself as existing over time is a necessary condition of a right to life; and respect for autonomy. Although at the level of critical reasoning a hedonistic utilitarian would accept only the first, indirect, reason and a preference utilitarian only the first two reasons, at the intuitive level utilitarians of both kinds would probably advocate the idea of a right to life as well as respect for autonomy. The distinction between critical and intuitive levels thus leads to a greater degree of convergence, at the level of everyday moral decision making, between utilitarians and non-utilitarians than we would find if we took into account only the critical level of reasoning. In any case, none of the four reasons for giving special protection to the lives of persons can be rejected out of hand. We shall therefore bear all four in mind when we turn to practical issues involving killing.

Before we do turn to practical questions about killing, however, we have still to consider whether killing is wrong when the being that is killed is neither a member of our species nor a person.

CONSCIOUS LIFE

Many beings are sentient and capable of experiencing pleasure and pain, but they are not rational and self-conscious and, therefore, are not persons. I shall refer to these as 'merely conscious' beings. Many nonhuman animals fall into this category; so must newborn infants and some intellectually disabled humans. Exactly which of these lack self-awareness is something we shall consider in the next chapters. If Tooley is right, beings that lack self-awareness cannot be said to have a right to life, in the full sense, though it might be wrong to kill them for other reasons. In the present section, we shall ask if it is wrong to take the life of a merely conscious being and, if so, why.

Killing a Merely Conscious Being

The most obvious reason for thinking that it is wrong to kill a being capable of experiencing pleasure or pain is the one that a hedonistic utilitarian would give: because of the pleasure it can experience. If we value our own pleasures – like the pleasures of eating, of sex, of the warmth of the sun on our skin, or of swimming on a hot day – then the universal aspect of ethical judgments requires us to extend our positive evaluation of our own experience of these pleasures to the similar experiences of all who can experience them. But death is the end of all pleasurable experiences. Thus, the fact that beings will experience pleasure in the future is a reason for saying that it would be wrong to kill them. Of course, a similar argument about pain points in the opposite direction, and this argument counts against killing only when we believe that the pleasure that beings are likely to experience outweighs the pain they are likely to suffer. So what this amounts to is that we should not cut short a pleasant life.

This seems simple enough: we value pleasure, and killing those who lead pleasant lives eliminates the pleasure they would otherwise experience, therefore such killing is wrong. Note that this claim goes beyond the simple argument for preference utilitarianism based on universalizing our own preferences that I outlined in Chapter 1. The merely conscious being does not have a preference for continued life. Perhaps while having a pleasurable experience it has a preference for that experience to continue, or while having a painful experience it has a preference for that experience to end, but it will not have any preferences for the long-term future, and the desires it has do not survive periods of sleep or temporary unconsciousness, because unlike a self-aware being, it has no conception of its own future existence after a period of sleep. Thus if we are concerned only about the thwarting of preferences, for a merely conscious being, painless killing and administering an anesthetic seem to be equivalent. Killing does not thwart any more desires than putting the being to sleep. The being will be able to continue to satisfy its preferences after it awakes, but from the being's subjective perspective it is as if a new being, with new preferences, came into existence. Tooley's claim about newborn infants applies here to all merely conscious beings: in the subject experience of the being itself, there is no sense of continuity between its mental life before it falls asleep and after it wakes. That is why the claim, in the first sentence of this paragraph, that 'we value pleasure' needs to be understood in terms that go beyond the preference utilitarian starting point for ethics. It asserts that pleasure is a value – and thus, that there are things of value, independently of a being preferring them.

This particular value is easy to accept. Isn't it obvious that pleasure is of positive value and pain is of negative value? Jeremy Bentham, the founder of the utilitarian school, even went so far as to say that the words 'benefit, advantage, pleasure, good, or happiness' all come to the same thing, and 'a thing is said to promote the interest, or to be *for* the interest, of an individual, when it tends to add to the sum total of his pleasures: or, what comes to the same thing, to diminish the sum total of his pains'. Some philosophers think Bentham was wrong about this: they think that something can be in my interest if it is what I most want, whether or not it will give me the most pleasure or the least pain. To defend Bentham's view, we would have to regard pleasure and pain as objective values (in the case of pain, an objective negative value or disvalue), not based merely on the universalizing of our preferences. To defend that claim, we would need to explain the nature of such objective values and how we come to know of them. These would be philosophically controversial claims, but not necessarily indefensible ones.

Suppose, then, that we did accept the idea that pleasure is objectively good and pain is objectively bad, and that we agreed with Bentham that to say that something promotes the interest of an individual is to say that it tends to add to the sum total of his, or her, pleasures, after subtracting pains. We now face another difficult issue. Stating the argument in terms of the interests of an individual conceals the fact that there are two ways of reducing the amount of pleasure in the world: one is to eliminate pleasures from the lives of those leading pleasant lives; the other is to eliminate those leading pleasant lives. The former leaves behind beings who experience less pleasure than they otherwise would have. The latter does not. This means that we cannot move automatically from valuing a pleasant life rather than an unpleasant one, to valuing a pleasant life rather than no life at all. For, it might be objected, being killed does not make us worse off; it makes us cease to exist. Once we have ceased to exist, we shall not miss the pleasure we would have experienced.

You may think that this is sophistical – an instance of the ability of academic philosophers to find distinctions where there are no significant differences. Why not, you may ask, regard killing a being as just the same as reducing the pleasures of an existing being to zero? One reason for thinking that there might be a morally significant difference between the two ways of reducing the amount of pleasure in the world is that we do think there is a morally significant difference between the two parallel ways of increasing the amount of pleasure in the world, one of which is to increase the pleasure of those who now exist, and the other is to increase the number of those who will lead pleasant lives. If killing those leading pleasant lives is bad because of the loss of pleasure, then it would seem to be good to increase the number of those leading pleasant lives. We could do this by having more children, provided we could reasonably expect their lives to be pleasant, or by rearing large numbers of animals under conditions that would ensure that their lives would be pleasant. Would it really be good to create more pleasure by creating more pleased beings?

There seem to be two possible approaches to these perplexing issues. The first approach is simply to accept that it is good to increase the amount of pleasure in the world by increasing the number of pleasant lives and bad to reduce the amount of pleasure in the world by reducing the number of pleasant lives. This approach has the advantage of being straightforward and clearly consistent, but it requires us to hold that if we could increase the number of beings leading pleasant lives without making others worse off, it would be good to do so. To see whether you are troubled by this conclusion, it may be helpful to consider a specific case. Imagine that a couple are trying to decide whether to have children. Suppose that so far as their own happiness is concerned, the advantages and disadvantages balance out. Children will interfere with their careers at a crucial stage of their professional lives, and they will have to give up their favourite recreation, backcountry hiking, for a few years at least. On the other hand, they know that, like most parents, they will get joy and fulfilment from having children and watching them develop. Suppose that if others will be affected, here too the good and bad effects will cancel each other out. Finally, suppose that because the couple could provide their children with a good start in life, and the children would be citizens of a developed nation with a high living standard, it is probable that their children will lead enjoyable lives. Should the couple count the likely future pleasure of their children as a significant reason for having children? I doubt that many couples would, but if we accept this first approach, they should.

I shall call this approach the 'total' view because on this view we should aim to increase the total amount of pleasure (strictly, the net total amount of pleasure after deducting the total amount of pain) and we should be indifferent to whether this is done by increasing the pleasure of existing beings or increasing the number of beings who exist.

The second approach is to be concerned only about beings who exist and those who will exist independently of what we do – as we noted in discussing the social contract view of ethics, it would be wrong to disregard the interests of future generations merely because they do not exist now. We can call this the 'prior existence' view because it is concerned with beings who exist, or whose existence is already determined, prior to the decision we are making. The prior existence view denies that there is value in increasing pleasure by creating additional beings. It is more in harmony with the intuitive judgment most people have (I think) that couples are under no moral obligation to have children simply because the children are likely to lead enjoyable lives and no one else is adversely affected. But how do we square the prior existence view with our intuitions about the reverse case, when a couple are considering having a child who, perhaps because it will inherit a genetic defect, would lead a thoroughly miserable life and die before its second birthday? We would think it wrong for a couple knowingly to conceive such a child; but if the pleasure a possible child will experience is not a reason *for* bringing it into the world, why is the pain a possible child will experience a reason *against* bringing it into the world? The prior existence view must either hold that there is nothing wrong with bringing a miserable being into the world or explain the asymmetry between cases of possible children who are likely to have enjoyable lives and possible children who are likely to have miserable lives.

Denying that it is bad knowingly to bring a miserable child into the world is hardly likely to appeal to those who adopted the prior existence view in the first place because it seemed more in harmony with their intuitive judgments than the total view; but a convincing explanation of the asymmetry is not easy to find. Perhaps the best one can say – and it is not very good – is that there is nothing directly wrong in conceiving a child who will be miserable, but once such a child exists, because its life can contain nothing but misery, we should reduce the amount of pain in the world by an act of euthanasia. This is, at best, paradoxical, for it implies that there is nothing wrong with conceiving a child even though one knows that, once the child exists, it will be morally obligatory to kill it. In addition if, as in most societies today, euthanasia is a crime that renders one liable to a long term of imprisonment, one might have overriding reasons for *not* killing the miserable child once it exists. In that case, on this view, one has no reason against conceiving a child who will have a miserable life even when there is an overriding reason not to end that life once the child exists. The parents can foresee that the child they bring into existence is likely to exist in misery for several decades, and yet they will, on the prior existence view, have done nothing wrong.

This leaves us with counterintuitive consequences for both the total and the prior existence view. Where has this taken us with regard to our original question, whether it is wrong to cut short a pleasant life? On either the total view or the prior existence view, we can hold that it is wrong, but our answers commit us to different things in each case. We can only take the prior existence approach if we accept that it is not wrong to bring a miserable being into existence – or else offer an explanation for why this should be wrong and yet it would not be wrong to fail to bring into existence a being whose life will be pleasant. Alternatively, we can take the total approach, but then we must accept that it is also good to create more beings whose lives will be pleasant – and this has some odd practical implications. The importance of the choice between the two views will become more apparent in the chapters that follow.

Comparing the Value of Different Lives

If we can give an affirmative – albeit somewhat shaky – answer to the question whether the life of a merely conscious being has some value, can we also compare the value of different lives at different levels of consciousness or self-awareness? We are not, of course, going to attempt to assign numerical values to the lives of different beings, or even to produce an ordered list. The best that we could hope for is some idea of the principles that, when supplemented with the appropriate detailed information about the lives of different beings, might serve as the basis for such a list. The most fundamental issue, however, is whether we can accept the idea of ordering the value of different lives at all.

Some say that it is anthropocentric, even speciesist, to order the value of different lives in a hierarchical manner. If we do so, we shall, they say, inevitably put ourselves at the top and other beings closer to us in proportion to the resemblance between them and ourselves. Instead, we should accord equal value to every life. Those who take this view recognize, of course, that a person's life may include the study of philosophy whereas a mouse's life cannot; but they say that the pleasures of a mouse's life are all that the mouse has, and are as important to the mouse as the pleasures of studying philosophy are to the most enthusiastic student of the subject.

Is it speciesist to judge that the life of a normal adult member of our species is more valuable than the life of a normal adult mouse? It is possible to defend such judgments only if we can find some neutral ground, some impartial standpoint from which we can make the comparison.

The difficulty of finding neutral ground is a very real practical difficulty, but I am not convinced that it presents an insoluble theoretical problem. I would frame the question we need to ask in the following manner. Imagine that I have the peculiar property of being able to turn myself into an animal, so that like Puck in *A Midsummer Night's Dream* 'sometimes a horse I'll be, sometimes a hound'. Suppose that when I am a horse, I really am a horse, with all and only the mental experiences of a horse, and when I am a human being, I have all and only the mental experiences of a human being. Now let us make the additional supposition that I can enter a third state in which I remember exactly what it was like to be a horse and exactly what it was like to be a human being. What would this third state be like? In some respects – the degree of self-awareness and rationality involved, for instance – it might be more like a human existence than an equine one, but it would not be a human existence in every respect. In this third state, then, I could compare horse existence with human existence. Suppose that I were offered the opportunity of another life, and given the choice of life as a horse or as a human being, the lives being in each case about as good as horse or human lives can reasonably be expected to be. I would then be deciding, in effect, between the value of the life of a horse (to the horse) and the value of the life of a human (to the human).

Undoubtedly, this scenario requires us to suppose a lot of things that could never happen and some things that strain our imagination. The coherence of an existence in which one is neither a horse nor a human, but remembers what it is like to be both, might be questioned. Nevertheless, I think I can make some sense of the idea of choosing from this position; and I am fairly confident that from this position, some forms of life would be seen as preferable to others.

If it is true that we can make sense of the choice between existence as a horse and existence as a human, then – whichever way the choice would go – we can make sense of the idea that the life of one kind of animal possesses greater value than the life of another; and if this is so, then the claim that the life of every being has equal value is on very weak ground. We cannot defend this claim by saying that every being's life is all-important for it, because we have now accepted a comparison that takes a more objective – or at least intersubjective – stance and thus goes beyond the value of the life of a being considered solely from the point of view of that being.

So it would not necessarily be speciesist to rank the value of different lives in some hierarchical ordering. *How* we should go about doing this is another question, and I have nothing better to offer than the imaginative reconstruction of what it would be like to be a different kind of being. Some comparisons may be too difficult. We may have to say that we have not the slightest idea whether it would be better to be a fish or a snake; but then, we do not very often find ourselves forced to choose between killing a fish or a snake. Other comparisons might not be so difficult.

In general, it does seem that the more highly developed the mental life of the being, the greater the degree of self-awareness and rationality and the broader the range of possible experiences, the more one would prefer that kind of life, if one were choosing between it and a being at a lower level of awareness. Can utilitarians defend such a preference? In a famous passage, John Stuart Mill attempted to do so:

Few human creatures would consent to be changed into any of the lower animals, for a promise of the fullest allowance of a beast's pleasures; no intelligent human being would consent to be a fool, no instructed person would be an ignoramus, no person of feeling and conscience would be selfish and base, even though they should be persuaded that the fool, the dunce, or the rascal is better satisfied with his lot than they are with theirs . . . It is better to be a human being dissatisfied than a pig satisfied; better to be Socrates dissatisfied than a fool satisfied. And if the fool, or the pig, are of a different opinion, it is because they only know their own side of the question. The other party to the comparison knows both sides.

As many critics have pointed out, this argument is open to challenge. Does Socrates really know what it is like to be a fool? Can he truly experience the joys of idle pleasure in simple things, untroubled by the desire to understand and improve the world? We may doubt it. But another significant aspect of this passage is less often noticed. Mill's argument for preferring the life of a human being to that of an animal (with which most modern readers would be quite comfortable) is exactly paralleled by his argument for preferring the life of an intelligent human being to that of a fool. Given the context and the way in which the term 'fool' was commonly used in his day, it seems likely that by this he means what we would now refer to as a person with an intellectual disability. With this further conclusion, some modern readers will be distinctly uncomfortable; but as Mill's argument suggests, it is not easy to embrace the preference for the life of a human over that of a nonhuman animal without at the same time endorsing a preference for the life of a normal human being over that of another human at a similar intellectual level to that of the nonhuman in the first comparison.

Mill's argument is difficult to reconcile with hedonistic utilitarianism, because it just does not seem true that the more intelligent being necessarily has a greater capacity for happiness; and even if we were to accept that the capacity is greater, the fact that, as Mill acknowledges, this capacity is less often filled (the fool is satisfied, Socrates is not) would have to be taken into consideration. Would a preference utilitarian have a better prospect of defending the judgments Mill makes? That would depend on how we compare different preferences, held with differing degrees of awareness and self-consciousness. It does not seem impossible that we should find ways of ranking such different preferences, but at this stage the question remains open.

This chapter has focused on the killing of beings that are self-aware, or at least conscious. It is intended to serve as a basis for the discussions to follow on the killing of nonhuman animals, embryos and fetuses; those who wish to die; and infants who suffer such severe damage that their parents consider it would be better if the child were to die. We will consider whether there is anything wrong about taking non-conscious life – the lives of trees or plants, for instance – in Chapter 10.

5

Taking Life

Animals

In the preceding chapter, we examined some general principles about the value of life. In this and the following two chapters, we shall draw from that discussion some conclusions about three cases of killing that have been the subject of heated debate: abortion, euthanasia and killing animals. Of these three, the question of killing animals has aroused the least controversy. Nevertheless, for reasons that will become clear later, it is impossible to defend a position on abortion and euthanasia without taking some view about the killing of nonhuman animals. So we shall look at that question first.

CAN A NONHUMAN ANIMAL BE A PERSON?

We have seen that there are reasons for holding that the killing of a person is more seriously wrong than the killing of a being who is not a person. This is true whether we accept preference utilitarianism, Tooley's argument about the right to life or the principle of respect for autonomy. Even a hedonistic utilitarian would say that there may be indirect reasons why it is worse to kill a person. So in discussing the wrongness of killing nonhuman animals, it is important to ask if any of them are persons.

It sounds odd to call an animal a person, but this may be no more than a symptom of our habit of keeping our own species sharply separated from others. In any case, we can avoid the linguistic oddness by rephrasing the question in accordance with our definition of 'person'. What we are really asking is whether any nonhuman animals are rational and self-conscious beings, aware of themselves as distinct entities with a past and a future.

In ancient myths and in contemporary stories and movies, we imagine being able to talk to animals. That dream was at least partially realized in 1967 when two scientists at the University of Nevada, Allen and Beatrice Gardner, guessed that the failure of previous attempts to teach chimpanzees to talk was due to the chimpanzees' lacking, not the intelligence required for using language, but the vocal equipment needed to reproduce the sounds of human language. The Gardners therefore decided to treat a young chimpanzee as if she were a human baby without vocal chords. They communicated with her, and with one another when in her presence, by using American Sign Language, a language widely used by deaf people.

The technique worked. The chimpanzee, whom they called 'Washoe,' learnt to understand about 350 different signs and to use about 250 of them correctly. She put signs together to form simple sentences and, in doing so, provided strong evidence of a sense of self. When shown her own image in a mirror and asked 'Who is that?' she replied: 'Me, Washoe.' Later Washoe moved to Ellensburg, Washington, where she lived with other chimpanzees under the care of Roger and Deborah Fouts. Here, she adopted an infant chimpanzee and soon began not only signing to him but even deliberately teaching him signs, for example, by moulding his hands into the sign for 'food' in an appropriate context. Washoe died in 2007 at the age of forty two.

Gorillas, bonobos and orangutans have also been able to learn sign language, although the extent of their ability is controversial. For more than thirty years, Francine Patterson has been signing and speaking English with Koko, a lowland gorilla. She claims that Koko now has a working vocabulary of more than 500 signs and understands an even larger number of spoken English words. In front of a mirror, Koko will make faces or examine her teeth. Chantek, an orangutan, has been taught sign language by Lyn Miles. When shown a photograph of a gorilla pointing to her nose, Chantek was able to imitate the gorilla by pointing to his own nose. Apes also use signs to refer to past or future events, thus showing a sense of time. The Fouts hold regular festivities for the chimpanzees at Ellensburg. Each year, after Thanksgiving, Roger and Deborah Fouts set up a Christmas tree covered with edible ornaments. The chimpanzees use the sign combination 'candy tree' to refer to the Christmas tree. In 1989, when snow began to fall just after Thanksgiving but the tree had not yet appeared, a chimpanzee named Tatu asked: 'Candy tree?' The Fouts interpreted this as showing, not only that Tatu remembered the tree, but also that she knew that this was the season for it. Later, Tatu also remembered that the birthday of one of the chimpanzees, Dar, followed closely on that of Deborah Fouts. The chimpanzees got ice cream for their birthdays; and after the festivities for Deborah's birthday were over, Tatu asked: 'Dar ice cream?'

Suppose that on the basis of such evidence, we accept that the signing apes are self-conscious. Are they exceptional among all the nonhuman animals in this respect precisely because they can use language? Or is it merely that language enables these animals to demonstrate to us a characteristic that they, and other animals, possessed all along?

Some philosophers have argued that thinking requires language: one cannot think without formulating one's thoughts in words. The Oxford philosopher Stuart Hampshire, for example, has written:

The difference here between a human being and an animal lies in the possibility of the human being expressing his intention and putting into words his intention to do so-and-so, for his own benefit or for the benefit of others. The difference is not merely that an animal in fact has no means of communicating, or of recording for itself, its intention, with the effect that no one can ever know what the intention was. It is a stronger difference, which is more correctly expressed as the senselessness of attributing intentions to an animal which has not the means to reflect upon, and to announce to itself or to others, its own future behaviour... It would be senseless to attribute to an animal a memory that distinguished the order of events in the past, and it would be senseless to attribute to it an expectation of an order of events in the future. It does not have the concepts of order, or any concepts at all.

Obviously, Hampshire was wrong to distinguish so crudely between humans and animals; for as we have just seen, the signing apes have shown that they do have 'an expectation of an order of events in the future' Hampshire wrote before apes had learned to use sign language, so this lapse may be excusable. Suppose that his argument were to be rephrased so that it referred to animals who have not learned to use a language, rather than all animals. Would it then be sound? If so, no being without language can be a person. This applies, presumably, to young humans as well as to non-signing animals. It might be argued that many species of animals do use language, just not our language. Certainly most social animals have some means of communicating with one another, whether it be the melodious songs of the humpback whales, the buzzes and whistles of dolphins, the alarm calls of vervet monkeys, which vary according to the kind of predator sighted, the howls and barks of dogs,

the songs of birds and even the dance performed by honey bees returning to the hive, from which other bees learn the distance and direction
of the food source from which the bee has come. Whether these forms of
communication amount to language, in the required sense, is doubtful.
Because pursuing this issue would take us too far from our topic, I shall
assume that they do not, and consider what can be learned from the
non-linguistic behaviour of animals.

Hampshire's argument is an example of a pitfall to which philosophers
of previous generations were especially prone: reaching conclusions from
the armchair on a topic that demands investigation in the real world.
There is nothing altogether inconceivable about a being possessing the
capacity for conceptual thought without having a language, and there
are instances of animal behaviour that are extraordinarily difficult, if
not downright impossible, to explain except under the assumption that
the animals are thinking conceptually. In one experiment, for example,
German researchers presented a chimpanzee named Julia with two series
of five closed and transparent containers. At the end of one series was
a box with a banana; the box at the end of the other series was empty.
The box containing the banana could only be opened with a distinctively
shaped key; this was apparent from looking at the box. This key could
be seen inside another locked box; and to open that box, Julia needed
another distinctive key, which had to be taken out of a third box which
could only be opened with its own key, which was inside a fourth locked
box. Finally, in front of Julia, were two initial boxes, open and each
containing a distinctive key. Julia was able to choose the correct initial key
with which she could open the next box in the series that led, eventually,
to the box with the banana. To do this, she must have been able to reason
backwards from her desire to open the box with the banana to her need
to have the key that would open it, to her need for the key that would
open that box, and so on. Because Julia had not been taught any form of
language, her behaviour proves that beings without language can think
in quite complex ways.

Nor is it only in laboratory experiments that the behaviour of animals
points to the conclusion that they possess both memory of the past and
expectations about the future, that they are self-aware and that they
form intentions and act on them. For several years, Frans de Waal and
his colleagues watched chimpanzees living in semi-natural conditions
in two acres of forest at Arnhem Zoo in the Netherlands. They often
observed co-operating activity that requires planning. For example, the

chimpanzees liked to climb the trees and break off branches so that they could eat the leaves. To prevent the rapid destruction of the small forest, the zookeepers placed electric fencing around the trunk of the trees. The chimpanzees overcame this by breaking large branches from dead trees (which had no fences around them) and dragging them to the base of a live tree. One chimpanzee then held the dead branch while another climbed up it, over the fence and into the tree. The chimpanzee who got into the tree in this way shared the leaves thus obtained with the one holding the branch.

De Waal also observed deliberately deceptive behaviour that clearly shows both self-awareness and an awareness of the intentions of another. Chimpanzees live in groups in which one male will be dominant and will attack other males who mate with receptive females. Despite this, a good deal of sexual activity goes on when the dominant male is not watching. Male chimpanzees often seek to interest females in sexual activity by sitting with their legs apart, displaying their erect penis. (Human males who expose themselves in a similar way may be continuing a form of primate behaviour that has become socially inappropriate.) On one occasion, a junior male was enticing a female in this manner when the dominant male walked over. The junior male covered his erection with his hands so that the dominant male could not see it.

Not only philosophers like Hampshire, but also some scientists have argued that 'mental time travel' – the ability to imagine a future event – is unique to humans. As so often happens with attempts to draw lines between humans and animals, this one had to be stated in a very precise form in order to be at all plausible. Everyone who has a dog as a companion knows that the dog can anticipate going for a walk. The ability unique to humans is therefore said to be that of anticipating the future beyond one's current set of motivations. So this claim is not refuted by a dog who brings her lead and puts it at the feet of her human companion. The dog, it is said, is simply in the grip of her desire to go for a walk and is acting on that desire. Humans, in contrast, can plan on satisfying motivations that they do not presently feel – as when we go shopping to make sure there will be something to eat for dinner, even though we are not hungry now. Many animals will hide food for future use, as squirrels do, but can it be shown that this involves conscious forethought, rather than purely instinctive behaviour?

Jane Goodall has described an incident showing forward planning by Figan, a young wild chimpanzee in the Gombe region of Tanzania. In order to bring the animals closer to her observation post, Goodall had hidden some bananas in a tree:

One day, sometime after the group had been fed, Figan spotted a banana that had been overlooked – but Goliath [an adult male ranking above Figan in the group's hierarchy] was resting directly underneath it. After no more than a quick glance from the fruit to Goliath, Figan moved away and sat on the other side of the tent so that he could no longer see the fruit. Fifteen minutes later, when Goliath got up and left, Figan without a moment's hesitation went over and collected the banana. Quite obviously he had sized up the whole situation: if he had climbed for the fruit earlier, Goliath would almost certainly have snatched it away. If he had remained close to the banana, he would probably have looked at it from time to time. Chimps are very quick to notice and interpret the eye movements of their fellows, and Goliath would possibly, therefore, have seen the fruit himself. And so Figan had not only refrained from instantly gratifying his desire but had also gone away so that he could not 'give the game away' by looking at the banana.

For many years, Goodall's observation was dismissed as a mere anecdote. Now, however, similar behaviour has been observed in pigs, both in natural circumstances and in controlled experiments. A pig who knows where to find food will not go there if she is being followed by a heavier pig who does not know where the food is. It seems that she is aware that the heavier pig would push her aside and take the food. Instead, she learns to behave in ways that minimize the chances that the other pig will be able to take her food – for example, she goes to the food only when the heavier pig is out of sight or much further away from the food than she is.

Another example of behaviour that shows an ability to look forward in time comes from Mathias Osvath's sustained observation of Santino, a chimpanzee in a Swedish zoo. Over a decade, Santino has regularly collected and cached stones. He does this in the morning, before visitors are admitted to the zoo. Several hours later, he goes to his stones, which he has placed on the side of his enclosure where visitors appear, and throws them at the visitors. He has even discovered how to detect, by knocking, places where the concrete in his enclosure is thin enough for him to break it into pieces of a suitable size for throwing. He then breaks it in these weak spots and adds the pieces to his cache of natural stones. In winter, when the zoo is closed to visitors, he does not collect stones. Throwing rocks isn't instinctive in chimpanzees, and nor, of course, is breaking up concrete. Santino does these things calmly, when there are no visitors present, so he cannot be gripped by the same motivation he has when he gets excited by their presence.

A still more rigorous demonstration of an animal's ability to anticipate its own future desires comes, remarkably enough, from experiments, not with apes or other primates, but with scrub jays. Scientists have used two characteristics of these birds to design an ingenious experiment. Like us, scrub jays store food for later consumption. Also like us, after gorging on one kind of food, they become satiated with it and prefer something different. Experimenters gave one group of birds pine nuts and then allowed them to store either pine nuts or kibble. Before they had access to their cache, they again got pine nuts. After becoming familiar with this routine, the jays preferred to store kibble. If they were fed kibble on both occasions, however, they preferred to store pine nuts. This could be explained by the fact that at the time of storing the food, the birds were satiated with what they had been eating, and just preferred to store the other kind of food. With another group of jays, however, the experimenters varied the routine. This time they gave the birds one food and allowed them to store it – but before these birds got access to their cache, they were fed the *other* kind of food from the one that they had been fed before they were able to store food. These birds preferred to store the food that they had just eaten, even though they were satiated with it. It is difficult to see any explanation for the different behaviour of these birds other than their ability to anticipate that, before they could get at their cached food, they would be satiated, not with the food they had just eaten, but with the other kind of food, and so would prefer the one that they did not want now but would want then. If that is the case, scrub jays not only have exactly what Hampshire said creatures without language could not have, 'an expectation of an order of events in the future', but more remarkably still, they also have desires based on their awareness that their future desires will be different from their present ones.

KILLING NONHUMAN PERSONS

I think we should conclude, on the basis of the evidence just summarized, that some nonhuman animals are persons, as we have defined the term. To judge the significance of this, we must set it in the context of our earlier discussion in which I argued that the only defensible version of the doctrine of the sanctity of human life was what we might call the 'doctrine of the special significance of taking personal life'. I suggested that if most human beings have lives of special significance, or have a special claim for their lives to be protected, this must be tied up with the fact that most human beings are persons. So if some nonhuman animals are persons too, they also have a special claim for their lives to be protected. Whether we base these special moral features of the lives of human persons on preference utilitarianism, on a right to life deriving from their capacity to see themselves as continuing selves, or on respect for autonomy, these arguments must apply to nonhuman persons as well. Only the indirect utilitarian reason for not killing persons – the fear that such acts are likely to arouse in other persons – applies less readily to nonhuman persons, because nonhumans are less likely than humans to learn about killings that take place at a distance from them. This reason does not apply to all killings of human persons either, however, because sometimes it is possible to kill in such a way that no one learns that a person has been killed.

Hence, we should reject the doctrine that killing a member of our species is always more significant than killing a member of another species. Some members of other species are persons; some members of our own species are not. No objective assessment can support the view that it is always worse to kill members of our species who are not persons than it is to kill members of other species who are. On the contrary, as we have seen, there are strong arguments for thinking that to take the lives of persons is, in itself, more serious than taking the lives of those who are not persons. So it seems that killing a chimpanzee is, other things being equal, worse than the killing of a human being who, because of a profound intellectual disability, is not and never can be a person. (Often, of course, other things are not equal: for instance, the attitudes of parents of humans with profound intellectual disability are relevant.)

The great apes may be the clearest cases of nonhuman persons, but as we have seen, there is evidence of future-directed thinking in several other species. Self-awareness is sometimes linked to knowing that when you look in a mirror, you are seeing yourself rather than another being. This has been tested by putting a coloured dye on a part of the animal where it will be seen in the mirror but cannot be seen otherwise – for example, on an ape, the forehead. (The dye is put on when the animal is asleep so that she does not notice.) Then the animal is given a mirror, with which she has previously become familiar. If she looks in the mirror and then touches the dyed spot, this indicates that she knows that the image in the mirror is herself. All the great apes can pass the mirror test, but so too can elephants, dolphins and even magpies. Magpies belong to the crow family, as do scrub jays, which as we have already seen are capable of taking their future desires into account. Alex, an African gray parrot, who was taught a vocabulary of between fifty and one hundred words by Irene Pepperberg, understood concepts like 'colour' and 'shape' as well as 'same' and 'different'. He did not take the mirror test, but Pepperberg's meticulously recorded account of his abilities and behaviour leaves little doubt that he too was self-aware to some extent. Human children less than one year old typically fail the mirror test, but by the time they are eighteen months old, most can pass it.

Passing the mirror test may show self-awareness, but failing it does not prove that an animal is not self-aware. In contrast to apes, monkeys do not show signs of self-recognition, although some can learn to use mirrors to locate food that they cannot otherwise see. Dogs have not passed the mirror test, but that may be because they rely more on their sense of smell than on sight. Many people who live with dogs and cats are convinced that their animal companions are self-conscious and have a sense of the future. If dogs and cats qualify as persons, the mammals we use for food cannot be far behind. We think of dogs as being more 'human' than pigs, but we have already seen that pigs can plan ahead and grasp whether another pig does or does not know the location of food. Are we turning persons into bacon? Additionally, because at least some birds appear to be persons, we should be cautious about excluding chickens, too. In flocks of up to ninety birds, chickens appear to recognize one another as individuals, always knowing whether another bird is above or below them in the pecking order. They also have the capacity for self-control and to envisage at least the near future. In one experiment, chickens were taught that pecking one key would, after two seconds, bring them access to food for three seconds; whereas pecking a different key would, after six seconds, bring them access to food for twenty-two seconds. The hens preferred to wait for the opportunity to feed longer. At a more anecdotal level, many people who keep free range hens and lock them up at night describe them as eager to get outside in the mornings – an attitude that suggests anticipating the future.

Of the animals that regularly appear on our plates, fish may seem the least likely to be persons, but the category is an extremely broad one: there are approximately 28,000 species of fish, more than all the other vertebrates combined. They vary widely in their abilities. In 2003, the journal *Fish and Fisheries* published a special issue on learning in fish, the introduction of which described fish as 'steeped in social intelligence, pursuing Machiavellian strategies of manipulation, punishment and reconciliation . . . and cooperating to inspect predators and catch food.' Whether any of this involves conscious planning is unclear, but we do know that the popular myth that fish can remember things for only three seconds is quite wrong – experiments have shown that they can remember the location of a hole in a net even if they have not been near the net for eleven months. As for invertebrates, the veined octopus has been observed to pick up coconut half shells discarded by tourists and carry them a considerable distance – which makes movement quite awkward for this small octopus – in order to assemble them later as a kind of protective shelter. Given what we know of the learning abilities of octopuses, it is not too far-fetched to interpret this behaviour as indicating that the octopus is aware of its own future need for shelter and is planning ahead.

It is difficult to establish when another being has a sense of its own self, or of the past and the future. If it is wrong to kill a person when we can avoid doing so, and there is real doubt about whether a being we are thinking of killing is a person, the best thing to do is to give that being the benefit of the doubt. The rule here is the same as that among deer hunters: if you see something moving in the bushes and are not sure if it is a deer or a hunter, don't shoot! (We may think that the hunters shouldn't shoot in either case, but the rule is a sound one within the ethical framework that hunters use.) On these grounds, much killing of nonhuman animals is open to objection. It may be justifiable of course, for overriding reasons, but it is in need of justification.

On the other hand, even for those nonhuman animals who are self-aware, and hence meet our definition of "person" it is still true that they are not likely to be nearly as much focused on the future as normal human beings are. Gary Varner, in his *Personhood and Animals in the Two-Level Utilitarianism of R.M. Hare*, argues for a more demanding definition of a person than the one I have used. To be a person, in his view, one must have a biographical sense of self. Humans, he points out, typically tell stories about their lives, weaving narratives that bring together where they have come from, where they are now and what they hope for in the future. Only beings with a sophisticated language, Varner suggests, have this kind of biographical sense of their lives, which means that only humans will have it – and not all humans, either, because not all humans are capable of language. Varner believes that this biographical sense of one's life gives a life a special significance that is lacking in the lives of other beings. Some nonhuman animals, in his view, are 'near-persons' in that they have some self-awareness but not a biographical sense of self.

Roger Scruton, a British philosopher, has said that the untimely death of a human being is a tragedy because there are likely to be things that she hoped to accomplish but now will not be able to achieve. The premature death of a cow is not a tragedy in this sense, because whether cows live one year or ten, there is nothing that they hope to achieve. Even those great apes who can use sign language do not talk to us about their plans for the distant future. Scrub jays hide food for the next day, but as far as we know, they do not embark on long-term projects that will pay off in the years ahead. (If it could be shown that squirrels and other animals who hide food for the winter are doing this with conscious foresight of their future needs, that would be an impressive counter-example, but this behaviour may be instinctive.)

Accepting these differences between normal mature humans and non-human animals, we could see the wrongness of killing, not as a black and white matter, dependent on whether the being killed is or is not a person, but as a matter of degree, dependent on, among other things, whether the being killed was fully a person or was a near-person or had no self-awareness at all, the extent to which, by our best estimate, the being had future-directed desires, and how central those desires were to the being's life. The criminal law can reasonably take a different view on the grounds that public policy is better served by laws that draw sharp boundaries, but the relevant moral considerations suggest a continuum.

KILLING OTHER ANIMALS

Arguments against killing based on the capacity to see oneself as an individual existing over time apply to some nonhuman animals, but presumably there are others who, though conscious, are not persons. Let's assume that there are some animals about whom we can be confident that they are not persons, or even near-persons. The rightness or wrongness of killing these animals then seems to rest on utilitarian considerations, for they are not autonomous and – at least if Tooley's analysis of rights is correct – do not qualify for a right to life.

Before we discuss the utilitarian approach to killing in itself, we should remind ourselves that a wide variety of indirect reasons will figure in the utilitarian's calculations. Many modes of killing used on animals do not inflict an instantaneous death, so there is pain in the process of dying. There is also the effect of the death of one animal on his or her mate or other members of the animal's social group. There are many species of birds, and a few mammals, in which the bond between male and female lasts for a lifetime. The death of one member of this pair presumably causes distress and a sense of loss and sorrow for the survivor. The mother-child relationship in mammals can be a source of intense suffering if either is killed or taken away. (Dairy farmers routinely remove calves from their mothers at an early age so that the milk will be available for humans; anyone who has lived on a dairy farm will know that, for days after the calves have gone, their mothers keep calling for them.) In some species, the death of one animal may be felt by a larger group – as the behaviour of wolves and elephants suggests. All these factors would lead the utilitarian to oppose some killing of animals, whether or not the animals are persons. These factors would not, however, be reasons for opposing killing in itself, apart from the pain and distress it may cause.

Deciding on the correct utilitarian verdict on killing that is painless and causes no loss to others is complicated, because it depends both on how we choose between the two versions of utilitarianism outlined in the previous chapter, that is, the total or the prior existence view, and also on whether we are hedonistic or preference utilitarians. I will begin by supposing that we are hedonistic utilitarians, because this makes the discussion of the differences between the total and the prior existence views more straightforward, and only subsequently will I consider what impact a switch to preference utilitarianism makes.

On the prior existence view, it is wrong to kill any being whose life is likely to contain, or can be brought to contain, more pleasure than pain. This view implies that it is normally wrong to kill animals for food, because usually we could argue that these animals would have had a few pleasant months or even years before they died – and the pleasure we get from eating them would not outweigh this. In contrast, the total view can lead to a different outcome. In *Social Rights and Duties,* a collection of essays and lectures published in 1896, Leslie Stephen, a British essayist – and the father of the novelist Virginia Woolf – writes:

Of all the arguments for Vegetarianism none is so weak as the argument from humanity. The pig has a stronger interest than anyone in the demand for bacon. If all the world were Jewish, there would be no pigs at all.

Stephen's point is that although meat eaters are responsible for the death of the animal they eat and for the loss of pleasure experienced by that animal, they are also responsible for the creation of more animals, because if no one ate meat there would be no more animals bred for fattening. The loss meat eaters inflict on one animal is thus compensated for by the benefit they confer on the next. The argument is periodically revived by those who seek to defend meat eating – in the twenty-first century, for example, by Michael Pollan in his best-seller *The Omnivore's Dilemma*, and also by the British chef and food writer Hugh Fearnley-Whittingstall. We may call it 'the replaceability argument', for it assumes that if we kill one animal, we can replace it with another as long as that other will lead a life as pleasant as the one killed would have led, if it had been allowed to go on living. Hedonistic utilitarians who accept the total view must agree with this, for that version of utilitarianism regards sentient beings as valuable only insofar as they make possible the existence of intrinsically valuable experiences like pleasure. It is as if sentient beings are receptacles of something valuable, and it does not matter if a receptacle gets broken so long as there is another receptacle to which the contents can be transferred without any getting spilt. (This metaphor should not be taken too seriously, however; unlike precious liquids, pleasure and other experiences cannot exist independently from a conscious being, and so even on the total view, sentient beings cannot properly be thought of merely as receptacles.)

The first point to note about the replaceability argument is that even if it is valid when the animals in question have pleasant lives, it would not justify eating the flesh of animals reared in modern factory farms, where the animals are so crowded together and restricted in their movements that their lives seem to be more of a burden than a benefit to them. Pollan and Fearnley-Whittingstall are aware of this. They unequivocally condemn factory farming and recommend that we avoid its products.

A second point is that if it is good to create happy life, then presumably it is good for there to be as many happy beings on our planet as it can possibly hold. Defenders of meat eating had better hope that they can find a reason why it is better for there to be happy people rather than just the maximum possible number of happy beings, because otherwise the argument implies that we should eliminate almost all human beings in order to make way for the much larger numbers of smaller happy animals that could sustainably replace them. If, however, the defenders of meat eating do come up with a reason for preferring the creation of happy people to, say, happy mice, then their argument will not support meat eating at all. For with the exception of some areas suitable only for pasture, the surface of our globe can support more people if we grow plant foods than if we raise animals.

A third point is that if replaceability holds for animals, it must hold for humans at a similar mental level. Suppose that whenever a child is born, the parents are offered the option of creating a clone of their child to serve as an organ donor for the child later in life. The clones are gestated in artificial wombs and then reared separately from other human beings in order to prevent the parents becoming so attached to them that they will be reluctant to remove the clone's organs. While in embryonic form, the clones are genetically modified so that their mental abilities never develop beyond those of a human infant. Intellectually incapable of understanding their fate, they will lead lives similar to those of happy, well-cared-for infants until the time comes for them to be killed – humanely, of course. Their hearts and other organs are then used to prolong the lives of the children – now usually adults – from whom they were cloned. Those who receive the organs pay for them, and the revenue from these sales makes it possible to rear new clones from the next generation of babies. Suppose that there is one religious group, let's say Buddhism, that objects to this practice, refuses to use clones, and urges us to accept the idea of living a natural lifespan, which Buddhists see as ethically better than using organs from clones to prolong our lives. To this a modern Leslie Stephen might reply: 'Of all the arguments for a natural lifespan, none is so weak as the argument from humanity. The clone has a stronger interest than anyone in the demand for organs. If all the world were Buddhist, there would be no clones at all.' Given our earlier rejection of speciesism, it isn't easy to see how we can use the replaceability argument to defend meat eating without also accepting it as a defence of this form of organ banking.

These three points undoubtedly reduce the appeal of the replaceability argument as a defence of meat eating, but they do not go to the heart of the matter. Are some sentient beings really replaceable? The total view and the replaceability argument have been widely criticised, but none of the critics have offered satisfactory solutions to the underlying problems to which these positions offer a consistent, if uncongenial, answer.

Henry Salt, a nineteenth-century English vegetarian and author of a book called *Animals' Rights*, thought that the argument rested on a simple philosophical error:

The fallacy lies in the confusion of thought that attempts to compare existence with non-existence. A person who is already in existence may feel that he would rather have lived than not, but he must first have the *terra firma* of existence to argue from: the moment he begins to argue as if from the abyss of the non-existent, he talks nonsense, by predicating good or evil, happiness or unhappiness, of that of which we can predicate nothing.

Salt claims that the Roman philosopher Lucretius, who lived in the first century before the Christian era, refuted Stephen's 'vulgar sophism' in the following passage of *De Rerum Natura:*

> What loss were ours, if we had known not birth?
> Let living men to longer life aspire,
> While fond affection binds their hearts to earth:
> But who never hath tasted life's desire,
> Unborn, impersonal, can feel no dearth.

When I wrote the first edition of *Animal Liberation*, I accepted Salt's view. I thought that it was absurd to talk as if one conferred a favour on a being by bringing it into existence, because at the time one confers this favour, there is no being at all. But I have since changed my mind on this point. As we saw in the preceding chapter, we do seem to do something bad if we knowingly bring a miserable being into existence, and if this is so, it is difficult to explain why we do not do something good when we knowingly bring a happy being into existence.

Derek Parfit has offered a thought experiment that amounts to an even stronger case for the replaceability view. He asks us to imagine that two women are each planning to have a child. The first woman is already three months pregnant when her doctor gives her both bad and good news. The bad news is that the fetus she is carrying has a defect that will significantly diminish the future child's quality of life – although not so adversely as to make the child's life utterly miserable, or not worth living at all. The good news is that this defect is easily treatable. All the woman has to do is take a pill that will have no side effects, and the future child will not have the defect. In this situation, Parfit very plausibly suggests, we would all agree that the woman should take the pill and that she does wrong if she refuses to take it.

The second woman sees her doctor before she is pregnant, when she is about to stop using contraception. She also receives bad and good news. The bad news is that she has a medical condition, the effect of which is that if she conceives a child within the next three months, the child will have the same defect that the first woman's child will have if she does not take the pill. This defect is not treatable, but the good news is that the woman's condition is a temporary one, and if she waits three months before becoming pregnant, her child will not have the defect. Here too, Parfit suggests, we would all agree that the woman should wait before becoming pregnant and that she does wrong if she does not wait.

Suppose that the first woman does not take the pill, and the second woman does not wait before becoming pregnant, and that as a result each has a child with a significant disability. It would seem that they have each done something wrong. Is their wrongdoing of equal magnitude? If we assume that it would have been no more difficult for the second woman to wait three months before becoming pregnant than it would have been for the first woman to take the pill, it would seem that the answer is yes, what they have done is equally wrong. But now consider what this answer implies. The first woman has harmed her child. That child can say to her mother: 'You should have taken the pill. If you had done so, I would not now have this disability, and my life would be significantly better.' If the child of the second woman tries to make the same claim, however, her mother can respond: 'If I had waited three months before becoming pregnant, you would never have existed. I would have produced another child, from a different egg and different sperm. Your life, even with your disability, is worth living. You never had a chance of existing without the disability. So I have not harmed you at all.' This reply seems a complete defence to the charge of having harmed the child now in existence. If, despite this, we persist in our belief that it was wrong of the woman not to postpone her pregnancy, in what does the wrongness consist? It cannot lie in bringing into existence the child to whom she gave birth, for that child has an adequate quality of life. Could it lie in *not* bringing a possible being into existence – to be precise, in not bringing into existence the child she would have had if she had waited three months? If we explain the wrongness of the second woman's decision in this way, we are rejecting the prior existence view in favour of the total view, or something closer to it. We are also a step closer to accepting replaceability, for our explanation implies that we should give weight to the interests of beings who would come into existence, if we chose to bring them into existence.

Because some people are unsure what to say about the case of the two women – in particular, whether what they do is equally wrong – I will add one more example, adapting a case that Parfit calls 'Depletion' so that it becomes very like the choice that developed nations are facing now on what to do about climate change. We could continue to use the cheapest energy available to give ourselves, our children and perhaps our grandchildren a high standard of living. In discussions of climate policy, this is often referred to as 'Business As Usual'. If we do this, however, the warming of the planet will mean that sometime in the next century, things will get much worse for future generations and will remain much worse for several centuries – although we shall assume, for the purposes of this discussion, that they will not get *so* bad that people in these future centuries will not have a life that is not worth living. Alternatively, we could follow a policy we will call 'Sustainability': this involves a quick end to the use of fossil fuels, with significantly changed lifestyles, different industries, less travel, less meat and many other changes. We and our children and perhaps our grandchildren would be slightly worse off under Sustainability than under Business As Usual, but more distant future generations would, for many centuries, be much better off. Overall, if we consider the welfare of every generation, including ours, as far as we can foresee, Sustainability has much better consequences than Business As Usual. But imagine that we are selfish, and don't care much about future generations, beyond our own grandchildren, and so we decide to opt for Business As Usual.

Have we done something wrong? Surely we have; but who have we wronged? It may seem that we have wronged the people who will live in later centuries, because they will have less good lives than they would have had if we had opted for Sustainability. But this response overlooks the fact that our choice of policies will have such widespread effects that it will also change who meets whom, and who has children with whom. For example, people will travel less and so will meet different people. New industries will develop in different parts of the country, and people will move there to find employment. Who we are depends on who our parents are – if my parents had never met, I would not exist. Probably my mother and my father would have had other children, with other partners, and none of those children would have been me. So if we choose Business as Usual, we can pre-empt any complaints from twenty-third-century people by leaving them a document explaining that if we had chosen Sustainability, they would not have been better off, but rather they would not have been at all. Moreover, if their lives are not so bad as not to be worth living, they are better off existing than not existing.

What is wrong with this justification of Business as Usual? On the prior existence view, it is difficult to see what could be wrong with it. The prior existence view tells us to do what is best for those who exist, or will exist anyway, and following Business As Usual does that. The people who are made worse off by our continuation of Business As Usual are people who would not have existed if we had chosen Sustainability. The example shows that to focus only on those who exist or will exist anyway leaves out something vital to the ethics of this decision. We can, and should, compare the lives of those who will exist with the lives of those who might have existed, if we had acted differently. Contrary to Salt, we can and should 'argue as if from the abyss of the non-existent'. We can condemn the decision to continue with Business As Usual only by taking into account the fact that, if we switch to Sustainability, the lives of those who will exist would be much better than the lives of those who will exist under Business As Usual. Granted, the people for whose sake we should switch to Sustainability will remain, in Lucretius's words, 'unborn, impersonal' if we do not make that switch. Never having tasted 'life's desire', they will 'feel no dearth' of life. Yet the quality of the lives they would have led is inescapably relevant to our decision.

If then we should, in making ethical decisions, at least sometimes take account of the impact we could have on the lives of people the existence of whom is, at the time we are making the decision, uncertain, we need to ask: at what stage in the development from people we might bring into existence to people actually in existence does replaceability cease to apply? What characteristic makes the difference?

Here, there is a difference between preference utilitarianism and hedonistic utilitarianism. Preference utilitarians can draw a distinction between self-aware individuals, leading their own lives and wanting to go on living, and those with no future-directed preferences. They would agree with Lucretius that there is a difference between killing living beings who 'to longer life aspire' and failing to create a being who, unborn and impersonal, can feel no loss of life. But what of beings who, though alive, cannot aspire to longer life because they lack the conception of themselves as living beings with a future? These being are also, in a sense, 'impersonal'. We might say that we do them no personal wrong, which a preference utilitarian might understand as meaning that because they have no future-directed preferences, we are not acting contrary to any of their preferences if we kill them instantly and painlessly. So perhaps the capacity to see oneself as existing over time, and thus to aspire to longer life (as well as to have other non-momentary, future-directed interests), is the characteristic that marks out those beings who cannot be considered replaceable.

This conclusion is in harmony with Tooley's views about what it takes to have a right to life. For a preference utilitarian, concerned with the satisfaction of preferences rather than experiences of suffering or happiness, there is a similar fit with the distinction already drawn between killing those who are rational and self-conscious and killing those who are not. Rational, self-conscious beings are individuals, leading lives of their own, and cannot in any sense be regarded merely as receptacles for containing a certain quantity of happiness. Beings that are conscious, but not self-conscious, on the other hand, more nearly approximate the image of receptacles for experiences of pleasure and pain, because their preferences will be of a more immediate sort. Given the evidence we have just reviewed, it is not easy to say with confidence which animals might be conscious but not self-conscious, but it is reasonable to suppose that there are some in this category. They will not have desires that project their images of their own existence into the future. Their conscious states are not internally linked over time. If they become unconscious, for example by falling asleep, then before the loss of consciousness they would have no expectations or desires for anything that might happen subsequently; and if they regain consciousness, they have no awareness of having previously existed. Therefore, if they were killed while unconscious and replaced by a similar number of other members of their species who will be created only if the first group are killed, there would, from the perspective of their awareness, be no difference between that and the same animals losing and regaining consciousness.

For a merely conscious being, death is the cessation of experiences, in much the same way that birth is the beginning of experiences. Death cannot be contrary to an interest in continued life any more than birth could be in accordance with an interest in commencing life. To this extent, with merely conscious beings, birth and death cancel each other out; whereas with self-aware beings, the fact that one may desire to continue living means that death inflicts a loss for which the birth of another is insufficient compensation.

The test of universalizability supports this view. If I imagine myself in turn as a self-conscious being and a merely conscious being, it is only in the former case that I could have forward-looking desires that extend beyond periods of sleep or temporary unconsciousness, for example a desire to complete my studies, a desire to have children, or simply a desire to go on living, in addition to desires for immediate satisfaction or pleasure, or to get out of painful or distressing situations. Hence, it is only in the former case that my death involves a greater loss than just a temporary loss of consciousness, and my death is not adequately compensated for by the creation of a being with similar prospects of pleasurable experiences.

In reviewing the first edition of this book, the late H. L. A. Hart, a major figure in twentieth-century philosophy of law, suggested that for a utilitarian, self-conscious beings must be replaceable in just the same way as non-self-conscious beings are. The type of utilitarianism one holds will, in Hart's view, make no difference here, because:

Preference Utilitarianism is after all a form of maximizing utilitarianism: it requires that the overall satisfaction of different persons' preferences be maximized just as Classical Utilitarianism requires overall experienced happiness to be maximized . . . If preferences, even the desire to live, may be outweighed by the preferences of others, why cannot they be outweighed by new preferences created to take their place?

It is of course true that preference utilitarianism is a form of maximizing utilitarianism in the sense that it directs us to maximize the satisfaction of preferences, but that does not mean that we should regard the thwarting of existing preferences as something that can be outweighed by creating new preferences – whether in existing beings or in beings we bring into existence – that we will then satisfy. For whereas the satisfaction of an existing preference is a good thing, how we should evaluate the package deal that involves creating and then satisfying a preference is a very different question. If I put myself in the place of another with an unsatisfied preference and ask myself if I would, other things being equal, want that preference satisfied, the answer is self-evidently yes, because that is just what it is to have an unsatisfied preference. If, on the other hand, I ask myself whether I wish to have a new preference created that can then be satisfied, I may say that it all depends on what the preference is. If I think of a case in which the satisfaction of the preference will be highly pleasurable, I may say yes. If we know that we are going to eat well in the evening, we may take a walk beforehand to be sure that we have a good appetite; and people take all kinds of supposed aphrodisiacs in order to stimulate sexual desire when they know that the circumstances for satisfying that desire are propitious. In these cases, the creation of the new desire leads to more pleasure, and most people prefer more pleasure; so the creation of the new desire is a means of achieving something that I desire anyway. If, on the other hand, I think of the creation of a preference that is more like a privation, I will say no, I don't want it, even if I will be able to satisfy it. We don't deliberately make ourselves thirsty because we know that there will be plenty of water on hand to quench our thirst. This suggests that the creation and satisfaction of a preference is in itself neither good nor bad: our response to the idea of the creation and satisfaction of a preference varies according to whether the experience as a whole will be desirable in terms of other longstanding preferences we may have. If not, there is no value in creating a new desire just so that we can then satisfy it.

Consistently with this conclusion, we might think of the creation of an unsatisfied preference as putting a debit in a kind of moral ledger of debits and credits. The satisfaction of the preference merely cancels out the debit. This 'debit model' of the ethical significance of preferences has the advantage of explaining the puzzling asymmetry in our obligations regarding bringing children into existence, which is mentioned in the previous chapter. We consider it wrong to bring into existence a child who, because of a genetic defect, will lead a thoroughly miserable existence for a year or two and then die; yet we do not consider it good or obligatory to bring into existence a child who, in all probability, will lead a happy life. The debit view of preferences explains why this should be so: to bring into existence a child, most of whose preferences we will be unable to satisfy, is to create a debit that we cannot cancel and is therefore wrong. To create a child whose preferences will be satisfied is to create a debit that will be erased when the desires are satisfied. On the debit view, this is ethically neutral. The model can also explain why, in Parfit's example, what the two women do is equally wrong – for although neither thwarts any existing preferences, both quite unnecessarily bring into existence a child who is likely to have a larger negative balance in the moral ledger than a child they could have brought into existence. Similarly, it explains why continuing with Business As Usual is wrong – it too leaves larger negative balances in the moral ledger than would be the case if we switched to Sustainability.

There is, however, one serious objection to this account of preferences: if the creation of each preference is a debit that is cancelled only when the desire is satisfied, it would follow that it is wrong, other things being equal, to bring into existence a child who will on the whole be very happy and will be able to satisfy nearly all, but not quite all, of her preferences. Because everyone has some unsatisfied desires, even the best life anyone can realistically hope to lead is going to leave a small debit in the ledger. The conclusion to be drawn is that it would have been better if none of us had been born!

Is that too absurd to take seriously? It is reminiscent of the philosophy of pessimism defended by the nineteenth-century German philosopher Arthur Schopenhauer, and also of some strands of Buddhist thinking. For Schopenhauer and perhaps for Buddha, we are always striving for something, and when we attain it, instead of achieving lasting satisfaction, new desires emerge that need to be satisfied. Because the only satisfaction we can achieve is transient relief from a negative state, life is not worth living, and the best we can hope for is to escape from the cycle of birth and death. David Benatar, a South Africa philosopher, has recently defended something like Schopenhauer's pessimism in his book *Better Never to Have Been: The Harm of Coming into Existence.* Benatar argues that bringing someone into existence harms them in a way that is not compensated for by the positive experiences they may have. One of Benatar's arguments for this claim is grounded on something like the debit view of preferences: to have an unfulfilled desire is, he holds, to be in a state of dissatisfaction, and that is a bad thing. Moreover, we spend most of our lives with unfulfilled desires, and the occasional satisfactions that are all most of us can achieve are insufficient to outweigh these prolonged negative states.

Let us revisit the climate change scenario and add a third option to which this kind of pessimism points. We can call it the Party & Go option. Advocates of this option want us to become even more profligate with our energy usage than in the Business As Usual scenario; but to ensure that our actions are not going to leave any kind of larger negative balance in the overall moral ledger of our planet, they urge that we all get sterilized. The people who now exist will be the last generation on Earth. Suppose, implausibly, that everyone agrees to this, no one minds being the last generation, and our actions will not make nonhuman animals worse off (or perhaps we will sterilize all of them, too). If the pessimists are correct, this would be the right thing to do, and we might think that those who hold the debit view of preferences must accept that it would be right or, at least, not wrong. For if to bring someone into existence will inevitably leave a negative balance in the moral ledger, why should we do it? We should do it only, presumably, if otherwise there will be a bigger negative balance in the moral ledgers of those who already exist – that is, if they want to have children or want there to be generations that come after them. If the assumptions on which Party & Go is based can be granted, however, that is not the case. Those who already exist will lead better lives if there are no future generations.

Does the debit view of preferences leave us with any basis on which to reject Party & Go? To refresh your memory on what is at stake here: remember that the debit view of preferences was a response to Hart's argument that a preference utilitarian should regard *all* beings as replaceable, whether they desire to go on living or not. If the debit view of preferences requires us to accept Party & Go, many would consider that an objection to the debit view, and hence an objection to my attempt to argue that persons are not replaceable. I think, however, that we can reject Party & Go while retaining the debit view of preferences, but to do so requires an appeal to a notion of value that goes beyond the minimalist basis for preference utilitarianism outlined in Chapter 1 of this book.

Consider two different universes. In the Nonsentient Universe, there is never any sentient life at all. In the Peopled Universe, there are several billion self-aware beings. They lead rich and full lives, experiencing the joys of love and friendship, of fulfilling and meaningful work, and of bringing up children. They seek knowledge, successfully adding to their understanding of themselves and the universe they inhabit. They respond to the beauties of nature, cherish the forests and animals that pre-date their own existence, and create literature and music that is on a par with the works of Shakespeare and Mozart. They manage to prevent or relieve many forms of suffering, but they are mortal and are not able to satisfy all their desires. Is it better that the Peopled Universe exist rather than the Nonsentient Universe?

Can we answer this question by universalizing our own preferences? We might say that we would prefer to live the kind of life that is lived in the Peopled Universe than not to live at all. R. M. Hare once suggested that we could take this approach to abortion. Because I enjoy my life, I am pleased that my parents did not abort the fetus from which I developed. Therefore, other things being equal, he argued, we should not abort fetuses if we have reason to believe that the fetus will develop into a person who will enjoy being alive; and if, should the fetus be aborted, there will be fewer such persons (that is, the aborted fetus will not subsequently be replaced by another that would not otherwise have existed). But there is a significant difference between putting yourself in the place of other existing beings who will be affected by your act and putting yourself in the place of beings who might not exist at all. In one case, we are satisfying existing preferences, and in the other, bringing preferences into existence. To draw on the example to which I have already referred, if people are thirsty, that is a reason for giving them water, but it doesn't follow that we have a reason for making people thirsty and then offering them water. Similarly, no obligation to bring more beings into existence follows from the fact that, if we do, they will be able to satisfy most of their preferences. Hence, to take into account the interests of merely possible future beings – as we can scarcely avoid doing in some scenarios – goes beyond the original minimalist idea of preference utilitarianism based on universalizing our own preferences. It may be based on a judgment that there is value in certain kinds of lives. We could try to distinguish two kinds of value: preference-dependent value, which depends on the existence of beings with preferences and is tied to the preferences of those specific beings, and value that is independent of preferences. When we say that the Peopled Universe is better than the Nonsentient Universe, we are referring to value that is independent of preferences. Henry Sidgwick, the nineteenth-century utilitarian, said that if we reflect carefully, we will see that the only thing that is intrinsically or ultimately good – good for its own sake – is a form of consciousness, or state of mind, that we regard as desirable. He thought that this desirable consciousness is pleasure, and, like other hedonistic utilitarians, would have thought that the Peopled Universe is better because it contains a surplus of pleasure over pain and the Nonsentient Universe does not. To say that pleasure is good and pain is bad is to assert not only that there are preference-independent values, but to say that pleasure and pain are such values. If there are preference-independent values, there are many other possible views about what is of value, in this sense. My account of the Peopled Universe was designed to capture a variety of possible views about what kinds of consciousness are desirable. We could hold a pluralist view of value and consider that love, friendship, knowledge and the appreciation of beauty, as well as pleasure or happiness, are all of value. My point here is not to determine the nature of preference-independent value but to show that some notion of it provides a basis for objecting to the Party & Go option, as well as the Business as Usual option, in our climate change example.

Hedonistic utilitarians must face a different objection. Because they would prefer any universe that contains a surplus of pleasure over pain to a universe with neither pleasure nor pain, they must prefer, not only the Peopled Universe to the Nonsentient Universe, but also the Happy Sheep Universe, where the only sentient beings are sheep who have plenty of grass on which to graze. Lambs gambol happily in the fields, grow up, reproduce, and when their offspring are mature, die swiftly and without suffering. Whether hedonistic utilitarians would prefer the Happy Sheep Universe over the Peopled Universe would depend on which has the greater surplus of pleasure over pain and, as we saw at the end of the previous chapter, whether we agree with Mill's assessment of the pleasures and pains of animals and normal human beings.

It seems obvious to me that both the Peopled Universe and the Happy Sheep Universe are better than the Nonsentient Universe, but at this point we are dealing with such basic values that it is difficult to find an argument that would persuade someone who denies this. Remember that the Peopled Universe is not our actual universe. It may be that there is more suffering and misery than happiness in our actual universe, especially if we consider the extremes of suffering that exist in it. So I am not here committed to an optimistic view of our actual universe, but only to the view that if life were really good for everyone, without terrible suffering, that would be a better universe than the Nonsentient one. Still, I admit that it would be possible for a preference utilitarian to bite the bullet here and say that the Nonsentient Universe is as good as the Peopled Universe – and explain our reluctance to embrace this conclusion by saying that it is the outcome of our evolved instinct to reproduce and care for our offspring.

In discussing this choice of universes, I have been met with the objection that the Nonsentient Universe cannot be compared, ethically, with any other universe. It is neither worse nor better than any other universe. It doesn't have zero value on a scale that gives a positive value to the Peopled Universe, it is just outside the scope of ethics and no scale of value applies to it. That might seem plausible until we imagine a Hellish Universe peopled exclusively by small children who suffer agonizing pain for several years, with no redeeming aspects of their lives, and then die. The same people who deny that we can compare the Peopled Universe with the Nonsentient Universe are prepared to agree that this is worse than the Nonsentient Universe. That implies that we can compare the Nonsentient Universe with universes containing sentient beings. Moreover, we can imagine a whole series of universes, with progressively less sentience in them, stretching from the Peopled Universe to the Nonsentient Universe. The one closest to the Nonsentient Universe might have no sentient life, ever, except for one shrimp, which lives, has a brief flash of consciousness and then dies. It seems very odd to claim that we can rank that universe on the same scale as the Peopled Universe, but as soon as the universe does not have even that momentary consciousness, it becomes incomparable with all the others.

In the thirty years since the first edition of this book was published, many philosophers have put forward ingenious solutions to the problem of how we should think about decisions that affect who will exist. A view that most philosophers find even tolerably satisfactory is still to be found, and any new suggestion is bound to give rise to some difficulties or counter-intuitive results. That is not in itself a reason for rejecting the view, because the difficulties may still be less serious than the difficulties afflicting all other views. It is, therefore, a consideration in favour of the kind of value I have been suggesting that, in combination with the debit view of preferences, it helps us to formulate answers to these baffling questions. It enables us to move beyond the prior existence view, which is clearly not adequate for dealing with some of these questions, without forcing us to accept that all sentient beings, even those who are self-aware, are replaceable. Moreover, if provides a basis for rejecting Party & Go as a strategy for dealing with climate change. Nevertheless, this combination of preference utilitarianism and an idea of intrinsic value that is not dependent on preferences sacrifices one of the great advantages of any form of utilitarianism that is based on just one value, which is that there is no need to explain how different values are to be traded off against one another. Instead, because this view suggests that there are two kinds of values, one personal and based on preferences and the other impersonal, it isn't easy to see how we are to proceed when the two kinds of values clash.

Before we leave the topic of killing animals, I should emphasize that to hold that merely conscious beings are replaceable is not to say that their interests do not count. I hope that the third chapter of this book makes it clear that their interests do count. As long as sentient beings are conscious, they have an interest in satisfying their desires, or in experiencing as much pleasure and as little pain as possible. Sentience suffices to place a being within the sphere of equal consideration of interests, but it does not mean that the being has a personal interest in continuing to live.

CONCLUSIONS

If the arguments in this chapter are correct, there is no single answer to the question: 'Is it normally wrong to kill an animal?' The term 'animal' – even in the restricted sense of 'nonhuman animal' – covers too diverse a range of lives for one principle to apply to all of them.

Some nonhuman animals appear to conceive of themselves as distinct beings with a past and a future, and this provides a direct reason against killing them, the strength of which will vary with the degree to which the animal is capable of having desires for the future. Our increasing knowledge of the intellectual capacities of nonhuman animals has extended the number of species to which this reason against killing can reasonably be applied. Twenty years ago, we could confidently attribute self-awareness only to great apes. Now, we can include not only elephants and dolphins but also some birds. It is hard to know what further research may show. We should therefore try to give the benefit of the doubt to monkeys, dogs, cats, pigs, seals, bears, cattle, sheep and so on, perhaps even to birds and fish – much depends how far we are prepared to go in extending the benefit of the doubt, where a doubt exists. Our discussion has raised a question mark over the justifiability of a great deal of killing of animals carried out by humans, even when this killing takes place painlessly and without causing suffering to other members of the animal community. (Most of this killing, of course, does not take place under such ideal conditions.)

When we come to animals that, as far as we can tell, lack self-awareness, the best direct reason against killing points to the loss of a pleasant or enjoyable life. Where the life taken would not, on balance, have been pleasant or enjoyable, no direct wrong is done. Even when the animal killed would have lived pleasantly, it is at least arguable that no wrong is done if the animal killed will, as a result of the killing, be replaced by another animal living an equally pleasant life. Taking this view involves holding that a wrong done to an existing being can be made up for by a benefit conferred on an as yet non-existent being. Thus, it is possible to regard merely conscious animals as interchangeable with one another in a way that beings with a sense of their own future are not. This means that in some circumstances – when animals lead pleasant lives, are killed painlessly, their deaths do not cause suffering to other animals and the killing of one animal makes possible its replacement by another that would not otherwise have lived – the killing of animals without self-awareness is not wrong.

Is it possible, along these lines, to justify raising any animals for their meat, not in factory farm conditions but roaming freely around a farm-yard? Suppose that we could be confident that chickens, for example, are not aware of themselves as existing over time (and as we have seen, this assumption is questionable). Assume also that the birds can be killed painlessly, and the survivors do not appear to be affected by the death of one of their numbers. Assume, finally, that for economic reasons we could not rear the birds if we did not eat them. Then the replaceability argument appears to justify killing the birds, because depriving them of the pleasures of their existence can be offset against the pleasures of chickens who do not yet exist and will exist only if existing chickens are killed.

As a piece of critical moral reasoning, this argument may be sound, but its application is limited. It cannot justify factory farming, where animals do not have pleasant lives. Nor does it normally justify the killing of wild animals. A duck shot by a hunter (assuming for the sake of the argument that ducks are not self-aware and that the shooter can be relied on to kill the duck instantly) was probably leading a pleasant life, but the shooting of a duck does not lead to its replacement by another. Unless the duck population is at the maximum that can be sustained by the available food supply, the killing of a duck ends a pleasant life without starting another and is, for that reason, wrong on straightforward utilitarian grounds.

Even in the case of animals with some self-awareness, killing for food will not always be wrong. Many people who think nothing of buying factory-farmed ham or chicken from a supermarket are quick to condemn hunting; yet hunting is more defensible than factory farming. Consider deer hunting in those parts of the United States where there are no longer any predators, other than human beings, to keep the deer population in check. Deer then reproduce to the point where they no longer have enough to eat, and they begin to degrade the environment. Eventually many of them will starve. Hunters argue that a quick death from a bullet is better for the deer than slow starvation, and environmentalists point out that the high density of deer may cause other species, both plants and animals, to become endangered. That death from a well-aimed bullet is preferable to starvation is undeniable, and this holds even if deer are self-aware. In practice, because not all hunters aim well and some will injure the animals rather than kill them, some form of fertility control would be better than permitting hunting. (It is an indication of our lack of concern about killing animals that there has been so little research into developing practical methods of contraception or sterilization for wild animals.) Let's assume, however, that there is no feasible method of fertility control; that the hunter is a good enough shot to kill the deer without inflicting suffering; and that if the deer are not shot they will die slowly and painfully in the coming winter. When that is the situation, it seems that a consequentialist cannot object to the deer being killed. To do so would require holding that we are responsible for the deaths we inflict but not for the deaths that 'nature' will bring about if we do nothing. That argument is similar to one sometimes used to distinguish active euthanasia from 'allowing nature to take its course', and as we shall see when we discuss it in Chapter 7, it is not defensible. Hunting under these circumstances, however, covers only a few of the billions of premature deaths humans inflict on animals each year.

It is sometimes argued that even vegans cannot avoid responsibility for killing, because a tractor plowing a field to plant crops may crush field mice, and moles can be killed when their burrows are destroyed by the plow. Harvesting crops removes the ground cover in which small animals shelter, making it possible for predators to kill them. Steven

Davis, an animal scientist at Oregon State University, has claimed that the number of animals killed by growing crops is greater than the number killed by rearing beef cattle on pasture, even including the deaths of the cattle. His findings have been used by other defenders of meat-eating, including Michael Pollan. Davis has, however, failed to take into account the fact that an area of land used for crops will feed about ten times as many people as the same area of land used for grass-fed beef. When that difference is fed into the calculations, Davis's argument is turned on its head and proves that vegans are responsible for killing only about a fifth as many animals as those who eat grass-fed beef.

None of this discussion is intended to suggest that people who need to kill animals in order to survive – people living in poverty who are struggling to get enough to feed themselves and their families, or those living a traditional hunting and gathering existence – should not do so. If cows, pigs, chickens and the other animals we usually eat are self-aware, they are still not self-aware to anything like the extent that humans normally are. I agree with Varner and Scruton that the more one thinks of one's life as a story that has chapters still to be written, and the more one hopes for achievements yet to come, the more one has to lose by being killed. For this reason, when there is an irreconcilable conflict between the basic survival needs of animals and of normal humans, it is not speciesist to give priority to the lives of those with a biographical sense of their life and a stronger orientation towards the future.

6

Taking Life

The Embryo and Fetus

THE PROBLEM

Few ethical issues have been as bitterly fought over during the past forty years as abortion, and neither side has had much success in altering the opinions of its opponents. Until 1967, abortion was illegal in almost all the Western democracies except Sweden and Denmark. Then Britain changed its law to allow abortion on broad social grounds, and in the 1973 case of *Roe v. Wade*, the United States Supreme Court held that women have a constitutional right to an abortion in the first six months of pregnancy. Conservative presidents have changed the composition of the Supreme Court, but to date it has continued to uphold the core of the *Roe v. Wade* decision while allowing states to restrict access to abortion in various minor ways. In recent decades, European nations, including Roman Catholic countries like Italy, Spain and France, have liberalised their abortion laws. Even Ireland and Poland now permit abortion in some circumstances. Worldwide, only a handful of countries, mostly in Latin America, prohibit abortion entirely.

In 1978, the birth of Louise Brown – the first human to have been born from an embryo that had been fertilised outside a human body – raised a new issue about the status of early human life. The achievement of Robert Edwards and Patrick Steptoe in demonstrating the possibility of in vitro fertilization, or IVF, was the result of several years of experimentation on early human embryos – none of which had survived – and since then more embryos have been used in experiments aimed at improving the success rate of this means of enabling otherwise infertile couples to have children. IVF is now a routine procedure for certain types of infertility, and millions of people owe their existence to it. IVF can also be used by couples who have a high risk of having a child with a genetic abnormality. Their embryos can be screened in the laboratory for genetic abnormalities, and only those embryos that do not carry the abnormality are implanted. This avoids the need for prenatal diagnosis and abortion, but still destroys human embryos.

Because the IVF procedure often produces more embryos than can safely be transferred to the uterus of the woman from whom the egg came, embryo freezing has been developed so that surplus embryos can be frozen and stored until they are needed. Normal children can develop from these embryos, but if the original transfer of a 'fresh' embryo results in the desired child, the frozen embryos may not be wanted. As a result, there are now large numbers of embryos preserved in special freezers around the world. (In the United States alone, there are more than 400,000 frozen embryos.) A few of these unwanted frozen embryos may be given to other infertile couples who cannot produce their own eggs or sperm, but the fate of the others is uncertain. In many cases, contact with the couple from whom the egg and sperm came has been lost. Scientists have become interested in using some of these surplus or abandoned embryos in order to obtain stem cells, which they believe may offer the potential for finding cures for Parkinson's disease, juvenile diabetes, Alzheimer's, spinal cord injuries, heart disease and other medical conditions. Because the process of obtaining the stem cells destroys the embryo, however, it has become embroiled in the same ethical and political controversy as abortion over the question of when it is wrong to destroy early human life. In 2001, President George W. Bush prohibited the use of federal funds for research using stem cell lines derived from embryos after the date of his announcement. This decision was promptly reversed by President Barack Obama after he took office in 2009, but his executive order permitting the use of federal funds was itself overturned by a federal judge in 2010, who ruled that it is contrary to a law preventing the use of federal funds for research that destroys embryos.

In this chapter we shall consider the moral status of the early embryo and of the fetus. I shall mostly use the term 'fetus', but it should be understood to include the embryo, unless the context makes it clear that this is not the case.

The issue of when it is wrong to destroy early human life needs careful thought because the development of the human being is a gradual process. Immediately after conception, the fertilized egg is just a single cell, and its death has little emotional resonance for most of us – in fact, in normal conception, the woman in whose body fertilization takes place will not even know that the egg was fertilized or, should there be an early miscarriage, that the conception was lost. After several days, it is still only a tiny cluster of cells without a single anatomical feature of the human being it will later become. The cells that will eventually become the embryo proper are at this stage indistinguishable from the cells that will become the placenta and amniotic sac. Up to about fourteen days after fertilization, we cannot even tell if the embryo is going to be one or two individuals, because splitting can take place, leading to the formation of identical twins. At fourteen days, the first anatomical feature, the so-called primitive streak, appears in the position in which the backbone will later develop. At this point, the embryo could not possibly be conscious or feel pain. Yet this embryo will, in the normal process of development, gradually develop into an adult human being. To kill a human adult is murder, and, except in special circumstances, some of which will be discussed in the next chapter, is unhesitatingly and universally condemned. The absence of any obvious sharp line that divides the fertilized egg from the adult creates the problem.

I shall begin by stating the position of those opposed to abortion, which I shall refer to as the conservative position. I shall then examine some of the standard liberal responses and show why they are inadequate. Finally, I shall use our earlier discussion of the value of life to approach the issue from a broader perspective. In contrast to the common opinion that the moral question about abortion is a dilemma with no solution, I shall show that, at least within the bounds of non-religious ethics, there is a clear-cut answer and those who take a different view are mistaken.

THE CONSERVATIVE POSITION

The central argument against abortion, put as a formal argument, would go something like this:

First premise: It is wrong to kill an innocent human being.
Second premise: A human fetus is an innocent human being.
Conclusion: Therefore, it is wrong to kill a human fetus.

The usual liberal response is to deny the second premise of this argument. So it is on whether the fetus is a human being that the issue is joined, and the dispute about abortion is often taken to be a dispute about when a human life begins.

On this issue the conservative position is difficult to shake. The conservative points to the continuum between the fertilized egg and child and challenges the liberal to point to any stage in this gradual process that marks a morally significant dividing line. Unless there is such a line, the conservative says, we must either upgrade the status of the earliest embryo to that of the child, or downgrade the status of the child to that of the embryo; but no one wants to allow children to be dispatched on the request of their parents, and so the only tenable position is to grant the fetus the protection we now grant the child.

Is it true that there is no morally significant dividing line between fertilized egg and child? Those commonly suggested are: birth, viability, quickening and the onset of consciousness. Let us consider these in turn.

Birth

Birth is the most visible possible dividing line and the one that would suit liberals best. It coincides to some extent with our sympathies – we are less disturbed by the destruction of a fetus we have never seen than at the death of a being we can all see, hear and cuddle. Is this enough to make birth the line that decides whether a being may or may not be killed? The conservative can plausibly reply that the fetus/baby is the same entity, whether inside or outside the womb, with the same human features (whether we can see them or not) and the same degree of awareness and capacity for feeling pain. A prematurely born infant may well be *less* developed in these respects than a fetus nearing the end of its normal term. It seems peculiar to hold that we may not kill the premature infant but may kill the more developed fetus. The location of a being – inside or outside the womb – should not make that much difference to the wrongness of killing it.

Viability

If birth does not mark a crucial moral distinction, should we push the line back to the time at which the fetus could survive outside the womb? This overcomes one objection to taking birth as the decisive point, for it treats the viable fetus on a par with the infant, born prematurely, at the same stage of development. Viability is where the United States Supreme Court drew the line in *Roe v. Wade*. The Court held that the state has a legitimate interest in protecting potential life, and this interest becomes 'compelling' at viability 'because the fetus then presumably has the capability of meaningful life outside the mother's womb'. Therefore, statutes prohibiting abortion after viability would not, the Court said, be unconstitutional. The judges who wrote the majority decision gave no indication why the mere capacity to exist outside the womb should make such a difference to the state's interest in protecting potential life. After all, if we talk, as the Court did, of *potential* human life, then the fetus before the time of viability is as much a potential adult human as the fetus after that time. (I shall return to this issue of potentiality shortly; but it is a different issue from the conservative argument we are now discussing, which claims that the fetus is already a human being and not just a potential human being.)

There is another important objection to making viability the cut-off point. The point at which the fetus can survive outside the mother's body varies according to the state of medical technology. Until the development of modern methods of intensive care, it was generally accepted that a baby born more than two months premature could not survive. Now a six-month-old fetus – three months premature – can often be pulled through, thanks to sophisticated medical techniques, and fetuses born after as little as five and a half months of gestation have survived.

In the light of these medical developments, do we say that a six-month-old fetus should not be aborted now but could have been aborted without wrongdoing fifty years ago, when it would have been unlikely to survive? The same comparison can also be made, not between the present and the past, but between different places. A six-month-old fetus might have a fair chance of survival if born in a city where the latest medical techniques are used, but no chance at all if born in a remote New Guinea village. Suppose that for some reason a woman, six months pregnant, was to fly from New York to a New Guinea village and that, once she had arrived in the village, there was no way she could return quickly to a city with modern medical facilities. Are we to say that it would have been wrong for her to have an abortion before she left New York, but now that she is in the village she may go ahead? The trip does not change the nature of the fetus, so why should it remove its claim to life?

The liberal might reply that the fact that the fetus is totally dependent on the mother for its survival means that it has no right to life independent of her wishes. In other cases, however, we do not hold that total dependence on another person means that that person may decide whether one lives or dies. A newborn baby is totally dependent on its mother if it happens to be born in an isolated area in which there is no other lactating woman or the means for bottle feeding. An elderly woman may be totally dependent on her son looking after her, and a hiker who breaks her leg five days' walk from the nearest road may die if her companion does not bring help. We do not think that in these situations the mother may take the life of her baby, the son the life of his aged mother, or a hiker the life of her injured companion. So it is not plausible to suggest that the dependence of the nonviable fetus on its mother gives her the right to kill it; and if dependence does not justify making viability the dividing line, it is hard to see what does.

Quickening

If neither birth nor viability marks a morally significant distinction, there is less still to be said for a third candidate, quickening. Quickening is the time when the mother first feels the fetus move, and in traditional Catholic theology, this was thought to be the moment at which the fetus gained its soul. If we accepted that view, we might think quickening important, because the soul is, on the Christian view, what marks humans off from animals. The idea that the soul enters the fetus at quickening is, however, an outmoded piece of superstition, discarded now even by Catholic theologians. Putting aside these religious doctrines makes quickening insignificant. It is no more than the time when the fetus is first felt to move of its own accord; the fetus is alive before this moment, and ultrasound studies have shown that fetuses do in fact start moving as early as six weeks after fertilization, long before they can be felt to move. In any case, the capacity for physical motion – or the lack of it – has nothing to do with the seriousness of one's claim for continued life. We do not see the lack of such a capacity as negating the claims of paralysed people to go on living.

Consciousness

Movement might be thought to be indirectly of moral significance, insofar as it is an indication of some form of awareness – and as we have already seen, consciousness and the capacity to feel pleasure or pain are of real moral significance. Despite this, neither side in the abortion debate has made much mention of the development of consciousness in the fetus. Those opposed to abortion may show films about the 'silent scream' of the fetus when aborted, but the intention behind such films is merely to stir the emotions of the uncommitted. Opponents of abortion really want to uphold the right to life of the human being from conception, irrespective of whether it is conscious or not. For those in favour of abortion, to appeal to the absence of a capacity for consciousness has seemed a risky strategy. On the basis of the studies showing that movement takes place as early as six weeks after fertilization, coupled with other studies that have found some brain activity as early as the seventh week, it has been suggested that the fetus could be capable of feeling pain at this early stage of pregnancy. That possibility has made liberals very wary of appealing to the onset of consciousness as a point at which the fetus has a right to life. We shall return to the issue of consciousness later in this chapter.

Our discussion has shown that the liberal search for a morally crucial dividing line between the newborn baby and the fetus has failed to yield any event or stage of development that can bear the weight of separating those with a right to life from those who lack such a right in a way that clearly shows that, when most abortions take place, the fetus lacks a right to life. The conservative is on solid ground in insisting that the development from the embryo to the infant is a gradual process, not marked by any obvious point at which there is a change in moral status sufficient to justify the difference between regarding the killing of an infant as murder and the killing of a fetus as something that a pregnant woman should be free to choose as she wishes.

SOME LIBERAL ARGUMENTS

Some liberals do not challenge the conservative claim that the fetus is an innocent human being, but they nevertheless argue that abortion is permissible. I shall consider three arguments for this view.

The Consequences of Restrictive Laws

The first argument is that laws prohibiting abortion do not stop abortions but merely drive them underground. Women who want to have abortions are often desperate. They will go to backyard abortionists or try folk remedies. Abortion performed by a qualified medical practitioner is as safe as any medical operation, but attempts to procure abortions by unqualified people often result in serious medical complications and sometimes death. Thus, the effect of prohibiting abortion is not so much to reduce the number of abortions performed as to increase the difficulties and dangers for women with unwanted pregnancies. Moreover, when abortion was illegal, some abortion providers bribed the police to turn a blind eye to what they were doing, thus contributing to police corruption.

This argument has been influential in gaining support for more liberal abortion laws. It was accepted by the Canadian Royal Commission on the Status of Women, which concluded that: 'A law that has more bad effects than good ones is a bad law... As long as it exists in its present form thousands of women will break it.' In those Latin American countries that prohibit abortion or allow it only in very limited circumstances, illegal abortions are widespread and a major cause of death and injury in young women.

The main point to note about this argument is that it is not an argument against the view that abortion is morally wrong, but rather an argument against prohibiting abortion. This is an important distinction, often overlooked in the abortion debate. The present argument well illustrates the distinction, because one could accept it and quite consistently advocate that the law should allow abortion on request, while at the same time deciding oneself – if one were pregnant or counselling another who was pregnant – that it would be wrong to have an abortion. It is a mistake to assume that the law should always enforce morality. Attempts to enforce right conduct may lead to consequences no one wants and no decrease in wrongdoing. If that is the case, they are better abandoned.

So this first argument is an argument about abortion law, not about the ethics of abortion. Even within those limits, however, it is open to challenge, for it fails to meet the conservative claim that abortion is the deliberate killing of an innocent human being and in the same ethical category as murder. Those who take this view of abortion will not rest content with the assertion that restrictive abortion laws do no more than drive women to backyard abortionists. They will insist that this situation can be changed and the law properly enforced. They may also suggest measures to make pregnancy easier to accept for those women who become pregnant against their wishes. Conservatives may also say that there will be some deterrent effect of the law even if it isn't properly enforced and that the lives of the unborn saved by this deterrent effect outweigh the harm done to women by backyard abortionists.

If the initial conservative argument against abortion is not contested, then these are reasonable responses, and for this reason the first argument does not succeed in avoiding the central ethical issue of whether it is wrong to kill a fetus.

Not the Law's Business?

The second argument is again an argument about abortion laws rather than the ethics of abortion. In the 1950s, the British government set up a committee under Sir John Wolfenden to inquire into whether homosexual acts and prostitution should remain crimes. Wolfenden's report did not contest the immorality of such acts but recommended that the law should be changed because 'there must remain a realm of private morality and immorality that is, in brief and crude terms, not the law's business'. This view is widely accepted among liberal thinkers and can be traced back to John Stuart Mill's *On Liberty*. The 'one very simple principle' of this work is, in Mill's words

that the only purpose for which power can be rightfully exercised over any member of a civilised community, against his will, is to prevent harm to others ... He cannot rightfully be compelled to do or forbear because it will be better for him to do so, because it will make him happier, because in the opinions of others, to do so would be wise or even right.

Mill's view is often and properly quoted in support of the repeal of laws that create 'victimless crimes' – laws prohibiting homosexual relations between consenting adults, the use of marijuana and other drugs, prostitution, gambling and so on. Abortion is often included in this list. Those who consider abortion a victimless crime say that, although everyone is entitled to hold and act on his or her own view about the morality of abortion, no section of the community should try to force others to adhere to its own particular view. In a pluralist society, we should tolerate others with different moral views and leave the decision to have an abortion up to the woman concerned.

The fallacy involved in numbering abortion among the victimless crimes should be obvious. The dispute about abortion is, largely, a dispute about whether or not abortion does have a 'victim'. Opponents of abortion maintain that the victim of abortion is the fetus. Those not opposed to abortion may deny that the fetus counts as a victim. They might, for instance, say that a being cannot be a victim unless it has interests that are violated, and the fetus has no interests. This dispute could be resolved in different ways, but whichever way it may go, one cannot simply ignore it on the grounds that people should not attempt to force others to follow their own moral views. My view that what Hitler did to the Jews is wrong is a moral view, and if there were any prospect of a revival of Nazism I would certainly do my best to force others to act in accordance with this view. Mill's principle is defensible only if it is restricted, as Mill restricted it, to acts that do not harm others. To use the principle as a means of avoiding the difficulties of resolving the ethical dispute over abortion is to take it for granted that abortion does not harm an 'other' – which is precisely the point that needs to be proven before we can legitimately apply the principle to the case of abortion.

A Feminist Argument

The last of the three arguments that seek to justify abortion without denying that the fetus is an innocent human being is that a woman has a right to choose what happens to her own body. This argument became prominent with the rise of the women's movement in the 1970s and has been elaborated by American philosophers sympathetic to feminism. An influential version of it by Judith Jarvis Thomson makes use of an ingenious analogy. Imagine, she says, that you wake up one morning and find yourself in a hospital bed, somehow connected to an unconscious man in an adjacent bed. You are told that this man is a famous violinist with kidney disease. The only way he can survive is for his circulatory system to be plugged into the system of someone else with the same blood type, and you are the only person whose blood is suitable. So a society of music lovers kidnapped you, had the connecting operation performed, and there you are. Because you are now in a reputable hospital you could, if you choose, order a doctor to disconnect you from the violinist; but the violinist will then certainly die. On the other hand, if you remain connected for only (only?) nine months, the violinist will have recovered and you can be unplugged without endangering him.

Thomson believes that if you found yourself in this unexpected predicament, you would not be morally required to allow the violinist to use your kidneys for nine months. It might be generous or kind of you to do so, but to say this is, Thomson claims, quite different from saying that you would be doing wrong if you did not do it.

Note that Thomson's conclusion does not depend on denying that the violinist is an innocent human being, with the same right to life as any other innocent human being. On the contrary, Thomson affirms that the violinist does have a right to life – but to have a right to life does not, she says, entail a right to the use of another's body, even if without that use one will die.

The parallel with pregnancy, especially pregnancy due to rape, should be obvious. A woman pregnant through rape finds herself, through no choice of her own, linked to a fetus in much the same way as the person is linked to the violinist. True, a pregnant woman does not normally have to spend nine months in bed, but even if she had a medical condition that made it necessary for her to stay in bed for the entire pregnancy, opponents of abortion would not regard this as a sufficient justification for abortion. Giving up a newborn baby for adoption might be more difficult, psychologically, than parting from the violinist at the end of his illness; but this too does not seem a sufficient reason for killing the fetus. Accepting for the sake of the argument that the fetus does count as a fully fledged human being with corresponding morally significant interests, having an abortion when the fetus is not viable has the same moral significance as unplugging oneself from the violinist. So if we agree with Thomson that it would not be wrong to unplug oneself from the violinist, we must also accept that, whatever the status of the fetus, abortion is not wrong – at least not when the pregnancy results from rape.

Can Thomson's argument be extended beyond cases of rape? Suppose that you found yourself connected to the violinist, not because you were kidnapped by music lovers, but because you had intended to enter the hospital to visit a sick friend; and when you got into the elevator, you carelessly pressed the wrong button and ended up in a section of the hospital normally visited only by those who have volunteered to be connected to patients who would not otherwise survive. A team of doctors, waiting for the next volunteer, assumed you were it, jabbed you with an anesthetic and connected you. If Thomson's argument was sound in the kidnap case, it is probably sound here too, because nine months unwillingly supporting another is a high price to pay for ignorance or carelessness. If so, the argument might apply beyond rape cases to the much larger number of women who become pregnant through ignorance, carelessness or contraceptive failure.

Is the argument sound? The short answer is: it is sound if the particular theory of rights that lies behind it is sound; and it is unsound if that theory of rights is unsound.

The theory of rights in question can be illustrated by another of Thomson's fanciful examples: suppose I am desperately ill, and the only thing that can save my life is the touch of my favourite film star's cool hand on my fevered brow. Well, Thomson says, even though I have a right to life, this does not mean that I have a right to force the film star to come to me or that he is under any moral obligation to fly over and save me – although it would be frightfully nice of him to do so. Thus, Thomson does not accept that we are always obliged to take the best course of action, all things considered, or to do what has the best consequences. She accepts, instead, a system of rights and obligations that allows us to justify our actions independently of their consequences.

I shall say more about this conception of rights in Chapter 8. At this stage, it is enough to notice that a utilitarian would reject this theory of rights and would reject Thomson's judgment in the case of the violinist. The utilitarian would hold that, however outraged I may be at having been kidnapped, if the consequences of disconnecting myself from the violinist are, on balance and taking into account the interests of everyone affected, worse than the consequences of remaining connected, I ought to remain connected. This does not mean that utilitarians would regard a woman who disconnected herself as wicked or deserving of blame. They might recognize that she has been placed in an extraordinarily difficult situation, one in which to do what is right involves a considerable sacrifice. They might even grant that most people in this situation would follow self-interest rather than do the right thing. Nevertheless, they would hold that to disconnect oneself is wrong.

In rejecting Thomson's theory of rights, and with it her judgment in the case of the violinist, the utilitarian would also be rejecting her argument for abortion. Thomson claimed that her argument justified abortion even if we allowed the life of the fetus to count as heavily as the life of a normal person. The utilitarian would say that it would be wrong to refuse to sustain a person's life for nine months if that was the only way the person could survive. Therefore, if the life of the fetus is given the same weight as the life of a normal person, the utilitarian would say that it would be wrong to refuse to carry the fetus until it can survive outside the womb.

This concludes our discussion of the usual liberal replies to the conservative argument against abortion. We have seen that liberals have failed to establish a morally significant dividing line between the newborn baby and the fetus, and their arguments – with the possible exception of Thomson's argument if her theory of rights can be defended – also fail to justify abortion in ways that do not challenge the conservative claim that the fetus is an innocent human being. Nevertheless, it would be premature for conservatives to assume that their case against abortion is sound. It is now time to bring into this debate some more general considerations about the value of life.

THE VALUE OF FETAL LIFE

Let us go back to the beginning. The central argument against abortion from which we started was:

First premise: It is wrong to kill an innocent human being.
Second premise: A human fetus is an innocent human being.
Conclusion: Therefore, it is wrong to kill a human fetus.

The first set of replies we considered accepted the first premise of this argument but objected to the second. The second set of replies rejected neither premise but objected to drawing the conclusion from these premises (or objected to the further conclusion that abortion should be prohibited by law). None of the replies questioned the first premise of the argument. Given the widespread acceptance of the doctrine of the sanctity of human life, this is not surprising; but the discussion of this doctrine in the earlier chapters of this book shows that this premise is less secure than many people think.

The weakness of the first premise of the conservative argument is that it relies on our acceptance of the special status of *human* life. We have seen that 'human' is a term that straddles two distinct notions: being a member of the species *Homo sapiens* and being a person. Once the term is dissected in this way, the weakness of the conservative's first premise becomes apparent. If 'human' is taken as equivalent to 'person', the second premise of the argument, which asserts that the fetus is a human being, is clearly false; for one cannot plausibly argue that a fetus is either rational or self-conscious. If, on the other hand, 'human' is taken to mean no more than 'member of the species *Homo sapiens*', then the conservative defence of the life of the fetus is based on a characteristic lacking moral significance, and so the first premise is false. The point should by now be familiar: whether a being is or is not a member of our species is, in itself, no more relevant to the wrongness of killing it than whether it is or is not a member of our race. The belief that mere membership of our species, irrespective of other characteristics, makes a great difference to the wrongness of killing a being is a legacy of religious doctrines that even those opposed to abortion hesitate to bring into the debate.

Recognizing this simple point transforms the abortion issue. The key question is no longer 'when does a human life begin?' because we can now see that granting that the fetus is a living human being does not resolve the question of whether it is wrong to kill it. We can look at the fetus for what it is – the actual characteristics it possesses – and can value its life on the same scale as the lives of beings with similar characteristics which are not members of our species. This change of perspective makes it apparent that the 'Pro Life' or 'Right to Life' movement is misnamed. Those who protest against abortion but dine regularly on the bodies of chickens, pigs and calves can hardly claim to have concern for 'life' as such. Their concern about embryos and fetuses suggests only a biased concern for the lives of members of our own species. On any fair comparison of morally relevant characteristics, like rationality, self-consciousness, awareness, autonomy, pleasure and pain and so on, the calf, the pig and the much derided chicken come out well ahead of the fetus at any stage of pregnancy – whereas if we make the comparison with an embryo, or a fetus of less than three months, a fish shows much more awareness.

My suggestion, then, is that we accord the fetus no higher moral status than we give to a nonhuman animal at a similar level of rationality, self-consciousness, awareness, capacity to feel and so on. Because no fetus is a person, no fetus has the same claim to life as a person. Until a fetus has some capacity for conscious experience, an abortion terminates an existence that is – considered as it is and not in terms of its potential – more like that of a plant than of a sentient animal like a dog or a cow. (The issue of the difference the potential of the fetus should make is still to be discussed.)

THE FETUS AS A SENTIENT BEING

Once the fetus is sufficiently developed to be conscious, though not self-conscious, abortion should not be taken lightly (if a woman ever does take abortion lightly). So we need to ask when the fetus becomes conscious. It is not surprising that those on different sides of the abortion debate tend to give different answers to this question. By asserting that the fetus is conscious early in pregnancy, and describing the pain that they believe the fetus experiences during the abortion process, those opposed to abortion add an emotionally powerful argument to their case against abortion. Those who take a liberal view on abortion typically prefer not to think about the possibility that the fetus can feel pain during an abortion.

To resolve the issue, we need both scientific knowledge of the development of the brain and nervous system of the fetus and – because scientists cannot directly observe pain but only what we believe to be its physiological correlates – a view about what level of development is required for the existence of consciousness and a capacity to experience pain. As we have seen in considering pain in animals very different from ourselves, like invertebrates, it is difficult to know if there can be pain, or consciousness of any kind, without a functioning cerebral cortex. In humans, prior to about eighteen weeks of gestation, the cerebral cortex is not sufficiently developed for synaptic connections to take place within it – in other words, the signals that give rise to pain in an adult are not being received. Between eighteen and twenty-five weeks, the brain of the fetus reaches a stage at which there is some nerve transmission in those parts associated with consciousness. Even then, however, the fetus appears to be in a persistent state of sleep and, therefore, may not be able to perceive pain. The fetus begins to 'wake up' at a gestational age of around thirty weeks. This is, of course, well beyond the stage of viability, and a 'fetus' that was alive and outside the womb at this stage would be a premature baby and not a fetus at all.

In order to give the fetus the benefit of the doubt, it would be reasonable to use the earliest point at which it can plausibly be claimed that the fetus is able to feel anything as the boundary after which the fetus should be protected. Thus, we should disregard the uncertain evidence about wakefulness and take instead the point at which the brain is physically capable of receiving signals necessary for awareness. This suggests eighteen weeks of gestation as the earliest time at which the fetus can feel pain. Prior to that stage, to believe that the fetus is conscious we would have to hold that the fetus has some way of feeling pain that does not require synaptic connections in the cerebral cortex. This is possible, but we have no evidence of it. Fortunately, the overwhelming majority of abortions are performed much earlier than eighteen weeks – in the United States, over 85 percent of abortions are done in the first trimester, that is, when the fetus is less than thirteen weeks old. Therefore, most abortions are unlikely to involve any experience of pain for the fetus.

After eighteen weeks of gestation, the interests of the fetus in not suffering should be taken into account in the same way that we should take into account the interests of sentient, but not self-conscious, nonhuman animals. As we have seen, killing a sentient creature can be justified, but it is important that the killing be done as painlessly as possible. In the case of nonhuman animals, the importance of humane killing is widely accepted (even if laws requiring humane killing are often inadequately enforced). Oddly, in the case of abortion, relatively little attention is paid to the possible suffering of the fetus. This is not because abortion is known to kill the fetus swiftly and humanely. Not long ago, late abortions – which are the ones in which the fetus may be able to suffer – were performed by injecting a salt solution into the amniotic sac that surrounds the fetus. This causes the fetus to have convulsions and die between one and three hours later. This method is rarely used today, but it has been abandoned primarily because of risks it poses for the pregnant woman rather than from any concern to avoid causing the fetus to suffer. Today, late abortions are likely to be carried out by the use of prostaglandin, a synthetic hormone that causes contractions similar to labour but may also cause convulsions and can result in live births. To prevent the risk of live births, digoxin can be injected into the heart of the fetus, which kills it rapidly. This method should be used, not only

because it prevents live births, but because it avoids unnecessary fetal
suffering.

THE FETUS AS POTENTIAL LIFE

Up to this point, we have taken into account only the actual characteristics of the fetus and not its potential characteristics. On the basis
of its actual characteristics, some opponents of abortion will admit, the
fetus compares unfavourably with many nonhuman animals; it is when
we consider its potential to become a mature human being, they will say,
that membership of the species *Homo sapiens* becomes important, and
the importance of the life of the fetus far surpasses that of any chicken,
pig or calf. Now is the time to look at this other argument. We can state
it as follows:

First premise: It is wrong to kill a potential human being.
Second premise: A human fetus is a potential human being.
Conclusion: Therefore, it is wrong to kill a human fetus.

The second premise of this argument is stronger than the second premise
of the preceding argument. Whereas it is problematic whether a fetus
actually *is* a human being – it depends on what we mean by the term –
it cannot be denied that the fetus is a potential human being, whether
by 'human being' we mean 'member of the species *Homo sapiens*' or a
rational and self-conscious being, a person. The strong second premise
of the new argument is, however, purchased at the cost of a weaker first
premise, for the wrongness of killing a potential human being – even
a potential person – is more open to challenge than the wrongness of
killing an actual person.

It is of course true that the potential rationality, self-consciousness and
so on of a fetal *Homo sapiens* surpasses that of a cow or pig; but it does
not follow that the fetus has a stronger claim to life. There is no rule that
says that a potential X has the same value as an X or has all the rights of
an X. There are many examples that show just the contrary. To pull out
a sprouting acorn is not the same as cutting down a venerable oak. To
drop a fertile egg into a pot of boiling water is very different from doing
the same to a live chicken. Prince Charles is (at the time of writing) a
potential King of England, but he does not now have the rights of a king.

In the absence of any general inference from 'A is a potential X' to
'A has the rights of an X', we should not accept that a potential person
should have the rights of a person, unless we can be given some specific
reason why this should hold in this particular case. What could that

reason be? This question becomes especially pertinent if we recall the grounds on which, in the previous chapter, it was suggested that the life of a person merits greater protection than the life of a being which is not a person. These reasons – the indirect classical utilitarian concern with not arousing in others the fear that they may be the next killed, the weight given by the preference utilitarian to a person's desires, Tooley's link between a right to life and the capacity to see oneself as a continuing mental subject, and the principle of respect for autonomy – are all based on the fact that persons see themselves as distinct entities with a past and future. None of the reasons apply to those who are not now and never have been capable of seeing themselves in this way. If these are the grounds for not killing persons, the mere potential for becoming a person does not count against killing.

It might be said that this reply misunderstands the relevance of the potential of the human fetus and that this potential is important, not because it creates in the fetus a right or claim to life, but because anyone who kills a human fetus deprives the world of a future rational and self-conscious being. If rational and self-conscious beings are intrinsically valuable in a way that other conscious beings are not, to kill a human fetus is to deprive the world of something with special intrinsic value, and therefore wrong. Yet the claim that rational and self-conscious beings are of especially high intrinsic value cannot serve as a reason for objecting to all abortions, or even to abortions carried out merely because the pregnancy is inconveniently timed. Suppose a woman has been looking forward to joining a Himalayan mountain-climbing expedition in June – climbing being one of her passions and this expedition being a rare opportunity to climb in a region new to her – but in January she learns that she is two months pregnant. She and her partner have often discussed the kind of family they want to have, and they both want to have two children sometime within the next five years. This pregnancy is unwanted only because the timing is so bad. Opponents of abortion would presumably think an abortion in these circumstances particularly outrageous, for neither the life nor the health of the mother is at stake – only the enjoyment she gets from climbing mountains. Yet if abortion is wrong only because it deprives the world of a future person, this abortion is not wrong. It does not prevent the entry of a person into the world, it merely delays it.

On the other hand, to argue against abortion on the grounds that it prevents beings of high intrinsic value coming into the world is implicitly to condemn practices that reduce the future human population: contraception, whether by 'artificial' means or by 'natural' means such as abstinence on days when the woman is likely to be fertile, and also celibacy. This argument does not provide any reason for thinking abortion worse than any other means of population control. If the world is already overpopulated, the argument provides no reason at all against abortion.

Is there any other significance in the fact that the fetus is a potential person? Paul Ramsey, a former Professor of Religion at Princeton University, wrote that modern genetics, by teaching us that the first fusion of sperm and ovum creates a 'never-to-be-repeated' informational speck, leads us to the conclusion that 'all destruction of fetal life should be classified as murder'. President George W. Bush said something similar in 2001 when, in defending his restrictions on federal funding for stem cell research, he claimed that every embryo is unique, 'like a snowflake'. But the fact that something is unique is not in itself a reason for preserving it – we don't try to preserve snowflakes. A canine fetus is also, no doubt, genetically unique. Does this mean that it is as wrong to abort a dog as a human? When identical twins are conceived, the genetic information is repeated. Would Ramsey or Bush therefore have thought it permissible to abort one of a pair of identical twins?

Developments in reproductive technology have put the argument from uniqueness under more pressure, especially when it is used – as President Bush used it – as an argument against the destruction of embryos to obtain stem cells. It is now a relatively simple matter to allow an embryo to develop to the stage at which it consists of two or four cells and then divide it in half. This procedure creates two genetically identical embryos, each of which can, if implanted into a woman's uterus, develop normally. (The procedure is similar to what happens naturally when an embryo splits and becomes identical twins.) If the reason why it is wrong to destroy an embryo is that each embryo is unique, then we could divide embryos in this way and destroy only one of them, thus preserving uniqueness. I doubt that this would be acceptable to many of those who think it wrong to destroy human embryos.

This kind of embryo splitting is a form of cloning, but not, of course, the much more heavily publicized form that resulted in the birth of the cloned sheep Dolly. Dolly was cloned from an adult cell. The scientists took the nucleus of a cell from a sheep's mammary gland and placed it inside an egg from which the nucleus had been removed. The resulting embryo was then transferred to the uterus of a second sheep. Dolly was genetically identical to the sheep from which the mammary gland cell had been taken. This form of cloning has now been done with many species, including cats, dogs, horses and monkeys, and there is no scientific reason to think that it could not be done with humans. Thus, our genetic uniqueness is on the threshold of becoming a matter of choice – if we wish to clone ourselves, we probably could. But pro-life advocates are no more likely to accept that we can destroy a cloned embryo, because it is not genetically unique, than they are to agree to the destruction of one of a pair of identical twins.

The possibility of cloning poses a different problem for arguments against destroying embryos based on their potential. We now know that a variety of cells, both from adults and from embryos, can develop into new human beings. Stem cells are a good example, because it has been shown that, when transferred to an enucleated egg, they readily develop into new beings. A plausible way of construing the argument from potential is to see it as the claim that if an entity can develop into a new human being, we should grant that entity a moral status similar to that of a human being. If we accept that claim, however, we seem to be committed to granting this moral status, not only to embryos, but also to all of these other cells that can develop into human beings. Thus, the attempt to defuse the controversy over obtaining stem cells from embryos by using adult stem cells instead of embryonic ones would misfire, because the stem cells themselves, whatever their origin, have the potential to develop into new human beings. Once we realize that so many cells have the potential to become new human individuals, however, we can also see the absurdity of the claim that we should protect all potential human beings.

TWO MORE ARGUMENTS AGAINST ABORTION

Two further arguments against abortion are worth mentioning separately, because they both accept that it is not satisfactory merely to assert that the fetus is a member of the species *Homo sapiens*, and therefore that it is wrong to kill it.

The first of these arguments was put forward by Don Marquis in a widely reprinted article called "Why Abortion is Immoral". Marquis begins by asking why killing one of us – say you, the reader – would be wrong. His answer to this is that to kill you would be wrong because it deprives you of your future, and that is something of value to you. If this is so, then it is, other things being equal, wrong to kill a being who can be expected to have a future like yours in the relevant respects and, hence, of value to them. The fetus can be expected to have such a future. So killing a fetus is wrong, because it deprives it of 'a future like ours'.

This objection to abortion does not apply if the fetus cannot be expected to have a future like ours. Suppose, for instance, that prenatal diagnosis shows that the fetus has the gene for Tay-Sachs disease, an incurable condition that causes paralysis and eventually death, usually by the age of four. Marquis accepts that his argument does not provide any reason against killing such a fetus. This leads many advocates of the pro-life position to reject his view, but this flexibility should rather be seen as a strength of the position (and an indication that it is not simply the traditional defence of the sanctity of human life in new guise).

Marquis thus avoids the objection that his view is a form of speciesism, but it is more difficult for him to avoid the objection that applies to arguments based on the potential of the fetus. If what is wrong with killing the fetus is that we deprive it of a valuable future, isn't that also wrong when we decide not to have a child at all? Or when we decide to have only two children rather than three? In that respect, abortion, reliable contraception and abstinence are all equally effective in preventing the existence of a being with a valuable future.

Marquis acknowledges that what he calls 'the contraceptive objection' is the strongest counter to his argument, but he believes he has a cogent reply: 'The wrong of killing is primarily a wrong to the individual who is killed; at the time of contraception there is no individual to be wronged.' In other words, on Marquis's ethic, you can only do wrong if you wrong an existing individual. That's a widely shared view. It seems obvious that it is worse to kill a person who is looking forward to that valuable future than it is to fail to bring into existence a person who would, if conceived, have a valuable future – indeed, that is the basis of the preference utilitarian reason against killing, as discussed in Chapters 4 and 5. This difference dwindles, however, when we have in mind, not a person who is looking forward to his or her future, but a fetus that is not conscious and never has been conscious. The fetus itself, if killed before awareness commences, experiences nothing different than it would have experienced if it had not been conceived – for in both cases there are no experiences at all. The only difference is that in the abortion case we can say, 'there existed a fetus that experienced nothing and then ceased to exist'; whereas in the contraception situation we can only say that no fetus came into existence. This is too slender a difference on which to rest the distinction between an immoral act and a morally innocuous one.

The problem gets even worse if we consider what we might call 'the totipotent cell objection'. Marquis is not committed to the view that an individual exists from the moment that the sperm penetrates the egg. Considering when the individual who will have the future of value first comes into existence, he writes:

The fact that the cells produced up to the sixteen cell stage are totipotent, and therefore can split into one or more individuals suggests a difficulty with the view that a human individual (a later stage of which is an adult) begins to exist at conception. Indeed, perhaps at the sixteen cell stage there are sixteen human individuals.

If Marquis is right about this, it only makes things more difficult for his position. As we saw earlier, we can divide the two-cell or four-cell embryo, thus creating identical twins or quadruplets. (Leaving the division to the sixteen-cell stage reduces the chances of success, as by this time the totipotency of the cells is waning.) If we divide, say, the four-cell embryo into quadruplets and transfer them to a woman's uterus, or perhaps better, the uteruses of four women, each one can be expected to have a future of value. Is it therefore immoral not to do this – to allow the embryo to continue to grow, thus reducing the number of lives with futures of value from four to one? This seems absurd, yet Marquis cannot say here that there is no existing individual to take into account, because he has acknowledged that – perhaps – each totipotent cell is a human individual. Of course, we could deny that each totipotent cell is an individual, but for Marquis to defend his position in this way reveals how crucially the application of his argument – and the decision that an act is immoral – depends on making fine distinctions about the status of various entities rather than on whether the act has better or worse consequences than something else one could have done.

Patrick Lee and Robert George, two noted American opponents of abortion and the destruction of embryos, have recently revived a view that has roots deep in the Catholic moral tradition but does not seek support from religious premises. In a manner somewhat similar to Marquis, Lee and George reject any explicit appeal to the mere fact that the embryo or fetus is a member of the species *Homo sapiens* and disavow any use of the argument from potential, agreeing that 'the right to life must be based on what is true of the entity now, not just what is true of its future'. They go on to say: 'it is true of the human embryo now that he or she is a distinct individual with a rational nature, even though it will take him or her several years fully to actualise his or her basic, natural capacities so they are immediately exercisable'. Given that we all agree that the human embryo cannot reason, has never been able to reason, and will not be able to reason for a long time, is it more accurate to say that the human embryo is 'a distinct individual with a rational nature' or to say that the human embryo 'is a distinct individual with the potential to become a rational being'? If we have to choose between these two ways of putting it, it is the latter that gives a more accurate description of the embryo. It does not have 'a rational nature'. What it has is the genetic coding that will, under favourable circumstances, lead it to develop into a being with a rational nature. While disavowing any argument from potential, in the end what Lee and George appear to rely upon is the embryo's potential to reason. For if they were to insist that the right to life is based on the human embryo's existing property of having a rational nature, what could they mean? Only, it seems, that it is an organism that, unlike some other organisms, for example an adult dog, has a genetic coding that will lead to the human individual having, in some years time, a rational nature. If this is the argument, Lee and George still owe us an account of why *that* property is sufficient to make it worse to kill a being than it is to kill an adult dog who lacks that property but has a greater present capacity to be aware of, and have preferences about, its life. Why should we decide which beings it is most seriously wrong to kill by reference to a genetic coding that will, in some years' time, lead to a capacity to reason? It is hard to see how, without slipping back into either a religious argument or an argument from potential, this claim could be defended.

THE STATUS OF THE EMBRYO IN THE LABORATORY

The preceding discussion of abortion also enables us to resolve the newer debate about the moral status of early human embryos outside the human body. This emergence of this issue shows that we cannot bypass the issue of the moral status of the embryo and fetus by asserting that, even if the embryo counts as much as an adult human being, a woman still has the right to control her own body and therefore may choose to end her pregnancy. When the embryo is not in a woman's body, that argument does not apply. One might therefore think that the case against embryo experimentation is stronger than the case for abortion. For one argument in favour of abortion does not apply, and the major arguments against abortion – either that the embryo is entitled to protection because it is a human being or that the embryo is entitled to protection because it is a potential human being – do. In fact, however, the two arguments against abortion do not apply as straightforwardly to the embryo in the laboratory as one might imagine.

First, is the embryo already a human being? We have already seen that even if we acknowledge that a human life begins at conception, that does not justify the conclusion that it is wrong to destroy an embryo or fetus, because claims for a right to life should not be based on species membership. Also if, as I have argued, the fetus is not a person, it is even more apparent that the embryo cannot be one. There is a further interesting point to be made against the claim that the early embryo is a human being: human beings are individuals, and whether the early embryo is an individual human being is contentious. As we have just noted, human embryos occasionally split into two or more genetically identical twins. This can happen at any time up to about fourteen days after fertilization. When we have an embryo prior to this point, we cannot be sure if what we are looking at will give rise to one or more human adults.

This poses a problem for those who stress the continuity of our exist-ence from conception to adulthood. Suppose we have an embryo in a dish on a laboratory bench. If we think of this embryo as the first stage of an individual human being, we might call it Mary. Now suppose the embryo divides into two. Is one of them still Mary and the other Jane? If so, which one is Mary? There is nothing to distinguish the two, no way of saying that the one we call Jane split off from the one we call Mary, rather than vice versa. So should we say that Mary is no longer with us, and instead we have Jane and Helen? What happened to Mary? Did she die? Should we mourn her? David Oderberg, who seeks to defend the view that the human adult is one and the same individual as the zygote or early embryo from which he or she developed, has suggested that we could properly mourn the loss of Mary, although because we know so little about her, we would not, of course, mourn her in the way we would mourn someone we knew well. An attitude of mourning implies that there is something to be sad about, and it is hard to see *anything* about the formation of twins that one should be sad about – unless, of course, one does not want to cope with the burden of having two babies at once. Unless we have some reason to want the cluster of cells we called Mary to realize its potential in the form of Mary rather than in the form of Jane and Helen, what reason is there to mourn even a tiny bit? Indeed, we can now see that naming this cluster of cells 'Mary' is already to assume that it is a particular individual, and perhaps it is that which makes it possible to think that there is the loss of an individual one could mourn. If we think of it as a cluster of cells, with the number of individuals who will develop from it still unknown, then there is no temptation to imagine that a life has been lost. It would make just as much sense to mourn the loss of Jane and Helen, if the embryo does develop into just one child. (We don't yet know what causes an embryo to divide. Does it make a difference if the division is predetermined by the inherent nature of the embryo – and we simply don't *know* if this is going to happen – rather than if splitting depends on factors independent of the embryo itself, perhaps in the body of the pregnant woman? If the former is the case, there may be a better argument for saying that in some sense whatever child or children result from the embryo existed from the moment that the sperm penetrates the egg; whereas if division depends on something external to the embryo, that view is more difficult to defend. Of course, if splitting is the result of human intervention – if we decide to divide the embryo at the two-cell stage – it would be impossible to say that both twins existed before that operation was performed.)

So there is a case for denying that the early embryo is an individual human being, but it is by no means a conclusive one. It provides some basis for the laws and guidelines in Britain and various other countries that allow experimentation on the embryo up to fourteen days after fertilization. I will not take the discussion further, however, because I have already given reasons why, even if the embryo before fourteen days is an individual human being, it does not follow that it is wrong to destroy it. Hence, laws limiting destructive experimentation on embryos to the first fourteen days of their existence are unnecessarily restrictive.

Arguments for protecting embryos in the laboratory based on their potential also face more difficulties when applied to early embryos than when applied to the fetus in the womb. In the normal process of human sexual reproduction inside the body, the embryo remains unattached for the first seven to fourteen days and then implants in the wall of the uterus. As long as unattached embryos existed only inside the woman's body, there was no way of observing them during that period. The very existence of the embryo could not be definitively established until after implantation. Under these circumstances, once the existence of an embryo was known, that embryo had a good chance of becoming a person, unless its development was deliberately interrupted. The probability of such an embryo becoming a person was therefore very much greater than the probability of an egg in a fertile woman uniting with sperm from that woman's partner and leading to a child. There is also, in human sexual reproduction, a further important distinction between the embryo and the egg and sperm. Whereas the embryo inside the female body has some definite chance (we shall shortly consider how great a chance) of developing into a child *unless* a deliberate human act interrupts its growth, the egg and sperm can only develop into a child if there *is* a human act – the sexual act. So in the one case, all that is needed for the embryo to have a prospect of realizing its potential is for those involved to refrain from stopping it; in the other case, they have to carry out a positive act. The development of the embryo inside the female body can therefore be seen as a mere unfolding of a potential that is inherent in it. (Admittedly, this is an oversimplification, for it ignores the positive acts involved in childbirth and in caring for the newborn child, but it is close enough.) The development of the separated egg and sperm is more difficult to regard in this way, because no further development will take place unless the couple have sexual intercourse or use artificial insemination.

Now consider what has happened as a result of the successful development of IVF. The procedure involves removing one or more eggs from a woman's ovary, placing them in the appropriate fluid in a glass dish, and then adding sperm to the dish. In competent laboratories, this leads to fertilization in about 80 percent of the eggs thus treated. The embryo can then be kept in the dish for a few days while it grows and its cells divide. If it appears to be growing normally, it will either be transferred to a woman's uterus or frozen for later use, in case the woman does not become pregnant from the embryo or embryos transferred. Although the transfer itself is a simple procedure, it is after the transfer that things are most likely to go wrong, for reasons that are not fully understood; with even the most successful IVF teams, the probability of a given embryo that has been transferred to the uterus actually implanting there and leading to a live birth is generally less than 20 percent, and in women older than thirty-seven, generally less than 10 percent (IVF clinics frequently cite much higher 'success rates', but their figures are based on live births 'per treatment cycle' and a cycle typically involves the transfer of two or three embryos.) In summary, then, before the advent of IVF, in every instance in which we knew of the existence of a normal human embryo, it would have been true to say of that embryo that, unless it was deliberately interfered with, it would most likely develop into a person. The process of IVF, however, leads to the creation of embryos that cannot develop into a person unless there is some deliberate human act (the transfer to the uterus) and that even then, in the best of circumstances, will most likely not develop into a person.

The upshot of all this is that IVF has reduced the difference between what can be said about the embryo and what can be said about the egg and sperm, when still separate but considered as a pair. Before IVF, any normal human embryo known to us had a far greater chance of becoming a child than any egg plus sperm prior to fertilization taking place. With IVF, there is a much more modest difference in the probability of a child resulting from a two-cell embryo in a glass dish, and the probability of a child resulting from an egg and some sperm in a glass dish. To be specific, if we assume that a laboratory succeeds in fertilizing 80 percent of the eggs it collects from its patients and its rate of pregnancy per embryo transferred is 20 percent, then when the laboratory has received the egg, the chance of that egg developing into a child is 16 percent; whereas once it has an embryo, the probability of a child resulting from that embryo is 20 percent. So if the embryo is a potential person, why are not the egg-and-sperm, considered jointly, also a potential person? Yet no member of the pro-life movement wants to rescue eggs and sperm in order to save the lives of the people that they have the potential to become.

Consider the following, not *too* improbable scenario. In the IVF laboratory, a woman's egg has been obtained. It sits in one dish on the bench. The sperm from her partner sits in an adjacent dish, ready to be mixed into the solution containing the egg. Then some bad news arrives: the obstetrician has discovered that the woman has a health condition that prevents her uterus being able to receive an embryo for at least a month, and the laboratory does not have the ability to freeze embryos. There is therefore no point in going ahead with the procedure. A laboratory assistant is told to dispose of the egg and sperm. She does so by tipping them down the sink. So far, so good; but a few hours later, when the assistant returns to prepare the laboratory for the next procedure, she notices that the sink is blocked. The egg and its fluid are still there, in the bottom of the sink. She is about to clear the blockage, when she realizes that the sperm has been tipped into the sink too. Quite possibly, the egg has been fertilised! Now what is she to do? Those who draw a sharp distinction between the egg-and-sperm and the embryo must hold that, whereas the assistant could quite innocently pour the egg and sperm down the sink, it would be wrong to clear the blockage now. This is difficult to accept. Potentiality seems not to be such an all-or-nothing concept; the difference between the egg-and-sperm and the embryo is one of degree, related to the probability of development into a person.

Traditional defenders of the right to life of the embryo have been reluctant to introduce degrees of potential into the debate, because once the notion is accepted, it seems undeniable that the early embryo is less of a potential person than the later embryo or the fetus. This could easily be understood as leading to the conclusion that the prohibition against destroying the early embryo is less stringent than the prohibition against destroying the later embryo or fetus. Nevertheless, some defenders of the argument from potential have invoked probability. Among these has been the Roman Catholic theologian John Noonan:

As life itself is a matter of probabilities, as most moral reasoning is an estimate of probabilities, so it seems in accord with the structure of reality and the nature of moral thought to found a moral judgment on the change in probabilities at conception... Would the argument be different if only one out of ten children conceived came to term? Of course this argument would be different. This argument is an appeal to probabilities that actually exist, not to any and all states of affairs which may be imagined... If a spermatozoon is destroyed, one destroys a being which had a chance of far less than 1 in 200 million of developing into a reasoning being, possessed of the genetic code, a heart and other organs, and capable of pain. If a fetus is destroyed, one destroys a being already possessed of the genetic code, organs and sensitivity to pain, and one which had an 80 per cent chance of developing further into a baby outside the womb who, in time, would reason.

The article from which this quotation is taken was once influential in the abortion debate, often quoted and reprinted by those opposed to abortion, but the development of our understanding of the reproductive process has made Noonan's position untenable. The initial difficulty is that Noonan's figures for embryo survival even in the uterus are no longer regarded as accurate. At the time Noonan wrote, the estimate of pregnancy loss was based on clinical recognition of pregnancies at six to eight weeks after fertilization. At this stage, the chance of losing the pregnancy through spontaneous abortion is about 15 percent. Recent technical advances allowing earlier recognition of pregnancy, however, provide startlingly different figures. If pregnancy is diagnosed before implantation (within fourteen days of fertilization), the probability of a birth resulting falls to 25 to 30 percent. After implantation, this increases initially to 46 to 60 percent, and it is not until six weeks gestation that the chance of birth occurring increases to 85 to 90 percent.

Noonan claimed that his argument is '... an appeal to probabilities that actually exist, not to any and all states of affairs which may be imagined'. Once we substitute the real probabilities of embryos, at various stages of their existence, becoming persons, however, Noonan's argument no longer supports the moment of fertilization as the time at which the embryo gains a significantly different moral status. Indeed, if we were to require an 80 percent probability of further development into a baby – the figure Noonan himself mentions – we would have to wait until nearly six weeks after fertilization before the embryo would have the significance Noonan wants to claim for it.

At one point in his argument Noonan refers to the number of sperm involved in a male ejaculation, and he says that there is only one chance in 200 million of a sperm becoming part of a living being. This focus on the sperm rather than the egg is curious (perhaps an instance of male bias?), but even if we let that pass, new technology provides still one more difficulty for the argument. There is now a means of overcoming male infertility caused by a low sperm count. The egg is removed as in the normal in vitro procedure; but instead of adding a drop of seminal fluid to the dish with the egg, a single sperm is picked up with a fine needle and micro-injected under the outer layer of the egg. So if we compare the probability of the embryo becoming a person with the probability of the egg – together with the single sperm that has been picked up by the needle and is about to be micro-injected into the egg – becoming a person, we will be unable to find any sharp distinction between the two. Does that mean that it would be wrong to stop the procedure once the sperm has been picked up? Noonan's argument from probabilities would seem to commit him either to this implausible claim, or to accepting that we may destroy human embryos. This procedure also undermines Ramsey's claim about the importance of the unique genetic blueprint – that 'never-to-be-repeated' informational speck having been determined in the case of the embryo but not in the case of the egg and sperm. For that, too, is here determined before fertilization.

In this section, I have tried to show how the special circumstances of the embryo in the laboratory affect the application of the arguments discussed elsewhere in this chapter about the status of the embryo or fetus. I have not attempted to cover all aspects of the ethics of in vitro fertilization and embryo experimentation. To do that, it would be necessary to investigate several other issues, including the appropriateness of allocating scarce medical resources to this area at a time when the world has a serious problem of overpopulation. Further uses of IVF, such as donating or selling embryos to others, employing a surrogate to bear the child, using IVF to enable older women to have children (in 2008, a 70-year-old Indian woman used the technique to become the oldest woman reliably recorded as having had a child), or selecting from among a number of embryos for the one that meets some criteria of genetic desirability, raise separate ethical issues. They are important, but to cover them would take us too far from the main themes of this book.

ABORTION AND INFANTICIDE

There remains one major objection to the argument I have advanced in favour of abortion. We have already seen that the strength of the conservative position lies in the difficulty liberals have in pointing to a morally significant line of demarcation between an embryo and a newborn baby. The standard liberal position needs to be able to point to some such line, because liberals usually hold that it is permissible to kill an embryo or fetus but not a baby. I have argued that the life of a fetus (and even more plainly, of an embryo) is of no greater value than the life of a nonhuman animal at a similar level of rationality, self-awareness, capacity to feel and so on, and that because no fetus is a person, no fetus has the same claim to life as a person. Now we have to face the fact that these arguments apply to the newborn baby as much as to the fetus. A week-old baby is not a rational and self-aware being, and there are many nonhuman animals whose rationality, self-awareness, capacity to feel and so on, exceed that of a human baby a week or a month old. If, for the reasons I have given, the fetus does not have the same claim to life as a person, it appears that the newborn baby does not either. Thus, although my position on the status of fetal life may be acceptable to many, the implications of this position for the status of newborn life are at odds with the virtually unchallenged assumption that the life of a newborn baby is as sacrosanct as that of an adult. Indeed, some people seem to think that the life of a baby is more precious than that of an adult. Lurid tales of German soldiers bayoneting Belgian babies figured prominently in the wave of anti-German propaganda that accompanied Britain's entry into the First World War, and it seemed to be tacitly assumed that this was a greater atrocity than the murder of adults.

I do not regard the conflict between the position I have taken and widely accepted views about the sanctity of infant life as a ground for abandoning my position. In thinking about ethics, we should not hesitate to question ethical views that are almost universally accepted if we have reasons for thinking that they may not be as securely grounded as they appear to be. It is true that infants appeal to us because they are small and helpless, and there are no doubt very good evolutionary reasons why we should instinctively feel protective towards them. It is also true that infants cannot be combatants, and killing infants in wartime is the clearest possible case of killing civilians, which is prohibited by international convention. In general, because infants are harmless and morally incapable of committing a crime, those who kill them lack the excuses often offered for the killing of adults. None of this shows, however, that the death of an infant is as bad as the death of an (innocent) adult.

In attempting to reach a considered ethical judgment about this matter, we should put aside feelings based on the small, helpless and – sometimes – cute appearance of human infants. To think that the lives of infants are of special value because infants are small and cute is on a par with thinking that a baby seal, with its soft white fur coat and large round eyes deserves greater protection than a gorilla, who lacks these attributes. Nor can the helplessness or the innocence of the infant *Homo sapiens* be a ground for preferring it to the equally helpless and innocent fetal *Homo sapiens*, or, for that matter, to laboratory rats who are 'innocent' in exactly the same sense as the human infant, and, in view of the experimenters' power over them, almost as helpless.

If we can put aside these emotionally moving but strictly irrelevant aspects of the killing of a baby, we can see that the grounds for not killing persons do not apply to newborn infants. The indirect, classical utilitarian reason does not apply, because no one capable of understanding what is happening when a newborn baby is killed could feel threatened by a policy that gave less protection to the newborn than to adults. In this respect, Bentham was right to describe infanticide as 'of a nature not to give the slightest inquietude to the most timid imagination'. Once we are old enough to comprehend the policy, we are too old to be threatened by it.

Similarly, the preference utilitarian reason for respecting the life of a person cannot apply to a newborn baby. Newborn babies cannot see themselves as beings that might or might not have a future, and so they cannot have a desire to continue living. For the same reason, if a right to life must be based on the capacity to want to go on living, or on the ability to see oneself as a continuing mental subject, a newborn baby cannot have a right to life. Finally, a newborn baby is not an autonomous being, capable of making choices, and so to kill a newborn baby cannot violate the principle of respect for autonomy. In all this, the newborn baby is on the same footing as the fetus, and hence fewer reasons exist against killing both babies and fetuses than exist against killing those who are capable of seeing themselves as distinct entities, existing over time.

It would, of course, be difficult to say at what age children begin to see themselves as distinct entities existing over time. But a difficulty in drawing the line is not a reason for drawing it in a place that is obviously wrong, any more than the notorious difficulty in saying how much hair a man has to have lost before we can call him 'bald' is a reason for saying that someone whose pate is as smooth as a billiard ball is not bald. Granted, where rights are at risk, we should err on the side of safety. There is some plausibility in the view that, for legal purposes, because birth provides the only sharp, clear and easily understood line, the law of homicide should continue to apply from the moment of birth. Because this is an argument at the level of public policy and the law, it is quite compatible with the view that, on purely ethical grounds, the killing of a newborn infant is not comparable with the killing of an older child or adult. Alternatively, recalling Hare's distinction between the critical and intuitive levels of moral reasoning, one could hold that the ethical judgment we have reached applies only at the level of critical morality; for everyday decision making, we should act as if an infant has a right to life from the moment of birth. In the next chapter, however, we shall consider another possibility: that there should be at least some circumstances in which a full legal right to life comes into force, not at birth, but only a short time after birth – perhaps a month. This would provide the ample safety margin mentioned previously.

If these conclusions seem too shocking to take seriously, it may be worth remembering that our present absolute protection of the lives of infants is a distinctively Christian attitude rather than a universal ethical value. Infanticide has been practised in societies ranging geographically from Tahiti to Greenland and varying in culture from nomadic Australian aborigines to the sophisticated urban communities of ancient Greece or mandarin China or Japan before the late nineteenth century. In some of these societies, infanticide was not merely permitted but, in certain circumstances, deemed morally obligatory. Not to kill a deformed or sickly infant was often regarded as wrong, and infanticide was probably the first, and in several societies the only, form of population control.

We might think that we are more 'civilized' than these 'primitive' peoples, but it is not easy to feel confident that we are more civilized than the best Greek and Roman moralists, nor than the highly sophisticated civilizations of China and Japan. In ancient Greece, it was not just the Spartans who exposed their infants on hillsides: both Plato and Aristotle recommended the killing of deformed infants. Romans like Seneca, whose compassionate moral sense strikes the modern reader (or me, anyway) as superior to that of the early and mediaeval Christian writers, also thought infanticide the natural and humane solution to the problem posed by sick and deformed babies. The change in Western attitudes to infanticide since Roman times is, like the doctrine of the sanctity of human life of which it is a part, a product of Christianity. Perhaps it is now possible to think about these issues without assuming the Christian moral framework that has, for so long, prevented any fundamental reassessment.

None of this is meant to suggest that someone who goes around randomly killing babies is morally on a par with a woman who has an abortion. We should put very strict conditions on permissible infanticide; but these restrictions should owe more to the effects of infanticide on others than to the intrinsic wrongness of killing an infant. Obviously, in most cases, to kill an infant is to inflict a terrible loss on those who love and cherish the child. My comparison of abortion and infanticide was prompted by the objection that the position I have taken on abortion also justifies infanticide. I have admitted this charge to the extent that the *intrinsic* wrongness of killing the late fetus and the *intrinsic* wrongness of killing the newborn infant are not markedly different. In cases of abortion, however, we assume that the people most affected – the parents-to-be or at least the mother-to-be – want to have the abortion. Thus, infanticide can only be equated with abortion when those closest to the child do not want it to live. As an infant can be adopted by others in a way that a pre-viable fetus cannot be, such cases will be rare. (Some of them are discussed in the following chapter.) Killing an infant whose parents do not want it dead is, of course, an utterly different matter, just as forcing a woman to have an abortion she does not want to have is utterly different from allowing a woman to choose to have an abortion.

7

Taking Life

Humans

At the end of the last chapter, we looked beyond abortion to the issue of infanticide, thus confirming the suspicions of supporters of the sanctity of human life that once abortion is accepted, euthanasia lurks around the corner. For them, that is an added reason for opposing abortion. Euthanasia has, they point out, been rejected by doctors since the fifth century BC, when physicians first took the Oath of Hippocrates and swore 'to give no deadly medicine to anyone if asked, nor suggest any such counsel'. Moreover, they argue, the Nazi extermination programme is a terrible modern example of what can happen once we give the state the power to kill innocent human beings.

It is true that if one accepts abortion on the grounds provided in the preceding chapter, the case for killing other human beings, in certain circumstances, is strong. As I shall try to show in this chapter, however, this is not something to be regarded with horror, and the use of the Nazi analogy is utterly misleading. On the contrary, once we abandon those doctrines about the sanctity of human life that – as we saw in Chapter 4 – collapse as soon as they are questioned, it is the refusal to accept killing that, in some cases, is horrific.

When the first edition of this book appeared in 1979, no country had legalized euthanasia, although in Switzerland a physician could prescribe lethal drugs to patients seeking aid in dying. Thirty years on, voluntary euthanasia and/or physician-assisted suicide is legal in the Netherlands, Switzerland, Belgium, Luxembourg, and the American states of Oregon, Washington and Montana. Before we consider the justifiability of these practices, some terminological clarification will be helpful.

FORMS OF AID IN DYING

Like abortion, providing aid in dying is highly controversial, and the politics of the issue has affected the terms used. In the United States, the discussion has focused on whether, if a patient asks a doctor for help in dying, the doctor ought to be allowed to prescribe something that will, if the patient takes it, end the patient's life swiftly and humanely. This has been legalized in the states of Oregon and Washington following citizen-initiated referenda that were passed by a majority of voters, and the Montana Supreme Court declared in 2009 that it is not contrary to law. It is usually called 'physician-assisted suicide' but in the United States, at least, 'suicide' has such negative associations that organizations seeking to legalize it prefer to call it 'death with dignity' or 'aid in dying.' These terms are too vague for philosophical discussions. 'Death with dignity' can mean almost anything, depending on what one considers a dignified way to die. 'Aid in dying' is barely more specific. It could refer to acts that make a dying person more comfortable, without shortening life, like giving modest amounts of pain relief, or it could refer to giving a patient, on request, a lethal injection. In addition, neither of these expressions says anything about *who* assists the patient to die. The term 'physician-assisted dying' gets closer to what happens, but it still does not emphasize that it is the patient who takes the step of ending her own life. Although it is certainly true that patients who are terminally ill and choose to end their own life to avoid further suffering are making a very different decision from people who kill themselves because they are emotionally disturbed, that does not change the basic fact that all these people are ending their own lives rather than continuing to live for as long as they can. Hence, we should not shy away from the term 'physician-assisted suicide,' because that offers the most precise description of what happens when a physician, acting on a request from the patient, provides a prescription for a drug which the patient then takes to end her life. In using this term, we should try to dismiss any negative associations that the term 'suicide' may have. Many cultures have considered suicide, in certain circumstances, to be a rational, honourable, and even sometimes a noble act. The Stoic philosopher Seneca wrote that a wise person 'lives as long as he ought, not as long as he can'. Cato the Younger, a Roman politician renowned for his integrity and refusal to take bribes, committed suicide when he was unable to stop Julius Caesar's overthrow of the Roman republic. According to Plutarch's account, Caesar said 'Cato, I grudge your death' – acknowledging that in ending his life,

Cato had done something truly noble. So let's use that term, without prejudicing our discussion of whether, in the circumstances we shall be discussing, physician-assisted suicide is justifiable or should be legal.

Physician-assisted suicide can be considered as one form of euthanasia, but the latter term has a wider meaning. According to the dictionary, 'euthanasia' refers to 'a gentle and easy death', but it is now used to refer to the killing of those who are incurably ill and in great pain or distress, in order to spare them further suffering or distress. Hence, it differs from physician-assisted suicide in that the physician or other person providing euthanasia may do the killing, for example, by giving the patient a lethal injection. Within the usual definition of euthanasia there are three different types, each of which raises distinctive ethical issues. It will help our discussion if we begin by setting out the three forms of euthanasia and place them within the broader framework. We can then assess the justifiability of each form.

Voluntary Euthanasia

Voluntary euthanasia is euthanasia carried out at the voluntary request of the person killed, who must be, when making the request, mentally competent and adequately informed. Euthanasia can be voluntary even if a person is not mentally competent right up to the moment of death because a person may, while in good health, make a written request for euthanasia specifying the conditions under which, if she should cease to be mentally competent, she would wish to die. In killing a person who has made such a request, has re-affirmed it from time to time, and is now in one of the states described, one could truly claim to be acting with her consent; and this would therefore be voluntary euthanasia.

In the Netherlands, a series of court cases during the 1980s upheld a doctor's right to assist a patient to die. The courts did not distinguish between providing a patient with a prescription for a lethal dose of a drug and giving the patient a lethal injection – in fact, in the Netherlands most doctors think it better that the physician be present when the patient dies to make sure that nothing goes wrong. Moreover, some patients are unable to swallow, or keep down, a large dose of a drug, and so injections are generally preferred.

In 2002, the Dutch parliament legalized voluntary euthanasia, as long as doctors comply with certain guidelines (which will be described later in this chapter). Belgium did the same later in the year. In 2008, Luxembourg became the third country to legalize voluntary euthanasia.

Involuntary Euthanasia

I shall regard euthanasia as involuntary when the person killed is capable of consenting to her own death but does not do so, either because she is not asked or because she is asked and chooses to go on living. Admittedly, this definition lumps two different cases under one heading. There is a significant difference between killing someone who chooses to go on living and killing someone who has not consented to being killed, but if asked would have consented. In practice, though, it is hard to imagine cases in which a person is capable of consenting, and would have consented if asked, but was not asked. Why not ask? Only in the most bizarre situations could one conceive of a reason for not obtaining the consent of a person both able and willing to consent.

Killing someone who has not consented to being killed can properly be regarded as euthanasia only when the motive for killing is the desire to prevent unbearable suffering on the part of the person killed. It is, of course, odd that anyone acting from this motive should disregard the wishes of the person for whose sake the action is done. Genuine cases of involuntary euthanasia appear to be very rare.

Nonvoluntary Euthanasia

These two definitions leave room for a third kind of euthanasia. If a human being is not capable of understanding the choice between life and death, euthanasia would be neither voluntary nor involuntary, but nonvoluntary. Those unable to give consent would include incurably ill or severely disabled infants and people who through accident, illness or old age have permanently lost the capacity to understand the issue involved, without having previously requested or rejected euthanasia in these circumstances.

In 1988 Samuel Linares, an infant, swallowed a small object that stuck in his windpipe, causing a loss of oxygen to the brain. Had such a case occurred fifty years earlier, Samuel would undoubtedly have died soon afterwards, and no decision would have had to be made. Instead, given the availability of modern medical technology, he was admitted to a Chicago hospital in a coma and placed on a respirator. Eight months later he was still comatose, still on the respirator, and the hospital was planning to move Samuel to a long-term care unit. Shortly before the move, Samuel's parents visited him in the hospital. His mother left the room, while his father produced a pistol and told the nurse to keep away.

He then disconnected Samuel from the respirator and cradled the baby in his arms until he died. When he was sure Samuel was dead, he gave up his pistol and surrendered to police. He was charged with murder, but the grand jury refused to issue a homicide indictment, and he subsequently received a suspended sentence on a minor charge arising from the use of the pistol.

In Canada in 1993, Robert Latimer killed his twelve-year-old disabled daughter Tracey by placing her in the cabin of the family truck and piping exhaust fumes into it. Evidence suggested that Tracey, who had a severe form of cerebral palsy, could not walk, talk, or feed herself and had suffered considerable pain. Latimer said that his priority was 'to put her out of her pain'. He was convicted of murder and sentenced to life imprisonment with a minimum of ten years before parole. Many Canadians felt the sentence was unreasonably harsh, but several appeals failed to free Latimer. He was granted parole in 2008.

Obviously, such cases raise different issues from those raised by voluntary euthanasia. There is no desire to die on the part of the person killed. The question can be raised whether, in such cases, the death is carried out for the sake of the infant or for the sake of the family as a whole. Caring for Samuel Linares would have been a great and no doubt futile burden for the family and a drain on the state's limited medical resources; but if he was comatose, he could not have been suffering, and death could not be said to be in (or contrary to) his interests. It is therefore not euthanasia, strictly speaking, as I have defined the term. It might nevertheless be a justifiable ending of a human life.

Because cases of infanticide and nonvoluntary euthanasia are the kind of cases most nearly akin to our previous discussions of the status of animals and the human fetus, we shall consider them first.

JUSTIFYING INFANTICIDE AND NONVOLUNTARY EUTHANASIA

As we have seen, euthanasia is nonvoluntary when the subject has never had the capacity to choose to live or die. This is the situation of the severely disabled infant or the older human being who has been profoundly intellectually disabled since birth. Euthanasia or other forms of killing are also nonvoluntary when the subject is not now but once was capable of making the crucial choice and did not then express any preference relevant to her present condition.

The case of someone who has never been capable of choosing to live or die is a little more straightforward than that of a person who had, but has now lost, the capacity to make such a decision. We shall, once again, separate the two cases and take the more straightforward one first. For simplicity, I shall concentrate on infants, although everything I say about them would apply to older children or adults whose mental age is and has always been that of an infant.

Life and Death Decisions for Disabled Infants

If we were to approach the issue of life or death for a seriously disabled human infant without any prior discussion of the ethics of killing in general, we might be unable to resolve the conflict between the widely accepted obligation to protect the sanctity of human life and the goal of reducing suffering. Some say that such clashes of fundamental values can only be resolved by a 'subjective' decision, or that life and death questions must be left to God and Nature. Our previous discussions have, however, prepared the ground, and the principles established and applied in the preceding three chapters make the issue much less baffling than most take it to be.

In Chapter 4, we saw that the fact that a being is a human being, in the sense of a member of the species *Homo sapiens*, is not relevant to the wrongness of killing it; instead, characteristics like rationality, autonomy and self-awareness make a difference. Infants lack these characteristics. Killing them, therefore, cannot be equated with killing normal human beings or any other self-aware beings. The principles that govern the wrongness of killing nonhuman animals that are sentient but not rational or self-aware must apply here too. As we saw, the most plausible arguments for attributing a right to life to a being apply only if there is some aware-ness of oneself as a being existing over time or as a continuing mental self. Nor can respect for autonomy apply where there is no capacity for autonomy. The remaining principles identified in Chapter 4 are utilit-arian. Hence, the quality of life that the infant can be expected to have is important.

This conclusion is not limited to infants who, because of irreversible intellectual disabilities, will never be rational, self-aware beings. We saw in our discussion of abortion that the potential of a fetus to become a rational, self-aware being cannot count against killing it at a stage when it lacks these characteristics – not, that is, unless we are also prepared to count the value of rational self-aware life as a reason against contraception and celibacy. No infant – disabled or not – has as strong an intrinsic claim to life as beings capable of seeing themselves as distinct entities existing over time.

The difference between killing disabled and normal infants lies, not in any supposed right to life that the latter has and the former lacks, but in other considerations about killing. Most obviously, there is the difference that often exists in the attitudes of the parents. The birth of a child is usually a happy event for the parents. They are likely to have planned for the child. The mother has carried it for nine months. From birth, a natural affection begins to bind the parents to it. So one important reason why it is normally a terrible thing to kill an infant is the effect the killing will have on its parents.

It is different when the infant is born with a serious disability. Birth abnormalities vary, of course. Some are trivial and have little effect on the child or its parents, but others turn the normally joyful event of birth into a threat to the happiness of the parents and of any other children they may have.

Parents may, with good reason, regret that a disabled child was ever born. In those circumstances, the effect that the death of the child will have on its parents can be a reason for, rather than against, killing it. Of course, this is not always the case. Some parents want even the most gravely disabled infant to live as long as possible, and their desire is then a reason against killing the infant. But what if this is not the case? In the discussion that follows, I shall assume that the parents do not want the disabled child to live. I shall also assume that the disability is so serious that – again in contrast to the situation of an unwanted but normal child today – there are no other couples keen to adopt the infant. This is a realistic assumption even in a society in which there is a long waiting list of couples wishing to adopt normal babies. It is true that from time to time, when a case of an infant who is severely disabled and is being allowed to die has been publicised, couples have come forward offering to adopt the child. Unfortunately, such offers are the product of the highly publicised dramatic life-and-death situation and do not extend to the less publicised but far more common situations in which parents feel themselves unable to look after a severely disabled child, and the child then languishes in an institution.

Consider, for instance, Tay-Sachs disease, a genetic condition that within the first year of life causes the child's muscles to atrophy. The child becomes blind, deaf, unable to swallow and eventually paralysed. The child also suffers mental deterioration and has seizures. Even with the best medical care, children with Tay-Sachs disease usually die before their fifth birthday. This seems to be a life that can reasonably be judged not to be worth living. When the life of an infant will be so miserable as not to be worth living, from the internal perspective of the being who will lead that life, both the 'prior existence' and the 'total' version of utilitarianism entail that if there are no 'extrinsic' reasons for keeping the infant alive – like the feelings of the parents – it is better that the child should be helped to die without further suffering.

A more difficult problem arises – and the convergence between the two views ends – when we consider disabilities that make the child's life prospects significantly less promising than those of a normal child, but not so bleak as to make the life one not worth living. Haemophilia may serve as an example. The haemophiliac lacks the element in normal blood that makes it clot and thus risks prolonged bleeding, especially internal bleeding, from the slightest injury. If allowed to continue, this bleeding leads to permanent crippling and eventually death. The bleeding is painful, and although improved treatments have eliminated the need for constant blood transfusions, haemophiliacs still have to spend a lot of time in hospital. They are unable to play most sports and live constantly on the edge of crisis. Nevertheless, haemophiliacs do not appear to spend their time wondering whether to end it all; most find life definitely worth living, despite the difficulties they face.

Given these facts, suppose that a newborn baby is diagnosed as a haemophiliac. The parents, daunted by the prospect of bringing up a child with this condition, are not anxious for him to live. Could euthanasia be defended here? Our first reaction may well be a firm 'no', for the infant can be expected to have a life that is well worth living, even if not quite as good as that of a normal child. The 'prior existence' version of utilitarianism supports this judgment. The infant exists. His life can be expected to contain a positive balance of happiness over misery. To kill him would deprive him of this positive balance of happiness. Therefore, it would be wrong.

On the 'total' version of utilitarianism, on the other hand, we cannot reach a decision on the basis of this information alone. The total view makes it necessary to ask whether the death of the haemophiliac infant would lead to the creation of another being who would not otherwise have existed. In other words, if the haemophiliac child is killed, will his parents have another child whom they would not have if the haemophiliac child lives? If they would, is the second child likely to have a better life than the one killed?

Often it will be possible to answer both these questions affirmatively. Like the mountaineer we considered in the previous chapter, a woman may plan to have two children. If one dies while she is of child-bearing age, she may conceive another in its place. Suppose a woman planning to have two children has one normal child, and then gives birth to a haemophiliac child. The burden of caring for that child may make it impossible for her to cope with a third child; but if the disabled child were to die, she would have another. It is also plausible to suppose that the prospects of a happy life are better for a normal child than for a haemophiliac.

If we favour the total view rather than the prior existence view, then we have to take account of the probability that when the death of a disabled infant will lead to the birth of another infant with better prospects of a happy life, the total amount of happiness will be greater if the disabled infant is killed. The loss of happy life for the first infant is outweighed by the gain of a happier life for the second. Therefore, if killing the haemophiliac infant has no adverse effect on others, it would, according to the total view, be right to kill him.

The total view treats infants as replaceable, in much the same way as it treats animals that are not self-aware as replaceable (as we saw in Chapter 5). Many will think that the replaceability argument cannot be applied to human infants. The direct killing of even the most hopelessly disabled infant is still officially regarded as murder. How then could the killing of infants with far less serious problems, like haemophilia, be accepted? Yet on further reflection, the implications of the replaceability argument do not seem quite so bizarre. For there are disabled members of our species whom we now deal with exactly as the argument suggests we should. These cases closely resemble the ones we have been discussing. There is only one difference, and that is a difference of timing – the timing of the discovery of the problem and the consequent killing of the disabled being.

Prenatal diagnosis is now routine for pregnant women. There are various medical techniques for obtaining information about the fetus during the early months of pregnancy. At one stage in the development of these techniques, it was possible to discover the sex of the fetus but not whether the fetus would suffer from haemophilia. Haemophilia is a sex-linked genetic defect from which only males suffer – females can carry the gene and pass it on to their male offspring without themselves being affected. So a woman who knew that she carried the gene for haemophilia could, at that stage, avoid giving birth to a haemophiliac child only by finding out the sex of the fetus and aborting all males fetuses. Statistically, only half of these male children of women who carried the defective gene would have suffered from haemophilia, and so half of the fetuses being killed were normal. This practice was widespread in many countries and yet did not cause any great outcry. Now that we have techniques for identifying haemophilia before birth, we can be more selective, but the principle is the same: women are offered, and usually accept, abortions in order to avoid giving birth to children with haemophilia.

The same can be said about several other conditions that can be detected before birth. Down syndrome is one of these. Children with this condition have intellectual disabilities, and most will never be able to live independently, but their lives, like those of children, can be joyful. The risk of having a Down syndrome child increases sharply with the age of the mother, and for this reason in many countries prenatal diagnosis is offered to all pregnant women over thirty-five. The overwhelming majority of pregnant women who are told that their child will have Down syndrome end their pregnancy, and many start another pregnancy, which in most cases leads to the birth of a child without this condition.

Prenatal diagnosis, followed by abortion in selected cases, is common practice in countries with liberal abortion laws and advanced medical techniques. I think this is as it should be. As the arguments of the last chapter indicate, I believe that abortion can be justified. Note, however, that neither haemophilia nor Down syndrome is so crippling as to make life not worth living from the inner perspective of the person with the condition. To abort a fetus with one of these disabilities, intending to have another child who will not be disabled, is to treat fetuses as replaceable. If the mother has previously decided to have a certain number of children, then what she is doing, in effect, is rejecting one potential child in favour of another. She could, in defence of her actions, say: the loss of life of the aborted fetus is outweighed by the gain of a better life for the normal child that will be conceived only if the disabled one dies.

When death occurs before birth, replaceability does not conflict with generally accepted moral convictions. That a fetus is known to be disabled is widely accepted as grounds for abortion. Yet, in discussing abortion, we saw that birth does not mark a morally significant dividing line. It is not easy to defend the view that fetuses may be 'replaced' before birth but newborn infants may not be. Nor is there any other point, such as viability, that does a better job of dividing the fetus from the infant. Self-awareness, which could provide a basis for holding that it is wrong to kill one being and replace it with another, is not to be found in either the fetus or the newborn infant. Neither the fetus nor the newborn infant is an individual capable of regarding itself as a distinct entity with a life of its own to lead, and it is only for newborn infants, or for still earlier stages of human life, that replaceability should be considered to be an ethically acceptable option.

Some disability advocates object strongly to this conclusion. They say that to replace either a fetus or a newborn infant because of a disability is wrong, for it suggests to disabled people living today that their lives are less worth living than the lives of people who are not disabled. Yet that belief is the only way to make sense of actions that we all take for granted. Recall thalidomide: this drug, when taken by pregnant women, caused many children to be born without arms or legs. Once the cause of the abnormal births was discovered, the drug was taken off the market, and the company responsible had to pay compensation. If we *really* believed that there is no reason to think the life of a disabled person is likely to be any worse than that of a normal person, we would not have regarded the use of thalidomide by pregnant women as a tragedy. No compensation would have been sought by parents or awarded by the courts. The children would merely have been 'different'. We could even have left the drug on the market, so that women who found it a useful sleeping pill during pregnancy could continue to take it. If this sounds grotesque, that is only because we are all in no doubt at all that it is better to be born with limbs than without them. To believe this involves no disrespect at all for those who are lacking limbs; it simply recognizes the reality of the difficulties they face.

In any case, the position taken here does not imply that it would be *better* that no people born with severe disabilities should survive; it implies only that the parents of such infants should be able to make this decision. Nor does this imply lack of respect or equal consideration for people with disabilities who are now living their own lives in accordance with their own wishes. As we saw at the end of Chapter 2, the principle of equal consideration of interests rejects any discounting of the interests of people on grounds of disability.

Even those who reject abortion and the idea that the fetus is replaceable are likely to regard *possible* people as replaceable. Recall the second woman in Parfit's case of the two women, described in Chapter 5. She was told by her doctor that if she went ahead with her plan to become pregnant immediately, her child would have a disability (it could have been haemophilia); but if she waited three months, her child would not have the disability. If we think she would do wrong not to wait, it can only be because we are comparing the two possible lives and judging one to have better prospects than the other. Of course, at this stage no life has begun; but the question is, when does a life, in the morally significant sense, really begin? In Chapters 4 and 5, we saw several reasons for saying that life only gains its full moral significance when there is awareness of one's existence over time.

Regarding newborn infants as replaceable, as we now regard fetuses, would have considerable advantages over prenatal diagnosis followed by abortion. Prenatal diagnosis still cannot detect all major disabilities. Some disabilities, in fact, are not present before birth; they may be the result of extremely premature birth or of something going wrong in the birth process itself. At present, parents can choose whether to keep their disabled offspring only if the disability happens to be detected during pregnancy. There is no logical basis for restricting parents' choice to these particular disabilities. If newborn infants were not regarded as having a right to life until some time after birth, it would allow parents, in consultation with their doctors, to choose on the basis of far greater knowledge of the infant's condition than is possible before birth.

All these remarks have been concerned with the wrongness of ending the life of the infant considered in itself rather than for its effects on others. When we take effects on others into account, the picture may alter. Obviously, to go through the whole of pregnancy and labour only to give birth to a child who one decides should not live would be a difficult, perhaps heartbreaking, experience. For this reason, many women would prefer prenatal diagnosis and abortion rather than live birth with the possibility of infanticide; but if the latter is not morally worse than the former, this would seem to be a choice that the woman herself should be allowed to make.

Another factor to take into account is the possibility of adoption. When there are more couples wishing to adopt than normal children available for adoption, a childless couple may be prepared to adopt a haemophiliac. This would relieve the mother of the burden of bringing up a haemophiliac child and enable her to have another child, if she wished. Then the replaceability argument could not justify infanticide, for bringing the other child into existence would not be dependent on the death of the haemophiliac. The death of the haemophiliac would be a straightforward loss of a life of positive quality not outweighed by the creation of another being with a better life.

The issue of ending life for disabled newborn infants is not without complications, both factual and philosophical. Philosophically, the most difficult issue is whether to accept the prior existence or the total version of utilitarianism (or some other view altogether), because in the case of infants with disabilities whose lives are nevertheless worth living, the justifiability of a decision to end the infant's life will depend on which view we choose. Nevertheless, the main point remains clear, even after the various objections and complications have been considered: killing a disabled infant is not morally equivalent to killing a person. Very often it is not wrong at all.

Other Nonvoluntary Life and Death Decisions

In the preceding section, we discussed justifiable killing of beings who have never been capable of choosing to live or die. Ending a life without consent may also be considered in the case of those who were once persons capable of choosing to live or die but now, through accident or old age, have permanently lost this capacity and did not, prior to losing it, express any views about whether they wished to go on living in such circumstances. These cases are not rare. Many hospitals care for motor accident victims whose brains have been damaged beyond all possible recovery. They may survive, in a coma or perhaps barely conscious, for many years. Rita Greene, a nurse, was twenty-four when she became ill and went into a persistent vegetative state. She died at the age of sixty-three without ever having recovered consciousness. Estimates of the number of people in a persistent vegetative state in the United States at any given time range from 10,000 to 40,000. In other developed countries, where life-prolonging technology is not used so aggressively, there are far fewer long-term patients in this condition.

Decisions about the treatment of people in a persistent vegetative state sometimes come before the courts and receive extensive publicity. None has received more attention than the case of Terri Schiavo, who died in a Florida hospice in 2005 after spending fifteen years in what her doctors said was a persistent vegetative state. Michael Schiavo, Terri's husband, wanted her feeding tube removed so that she would die. He claimed that this was in accordance with her wishes, as previously expressed to him. Robert and Mary Schindler, her parents, denied this and also claimed that she showed signs of awareness and so was not in a persistent vegetative state. Court decisions favoured Michael Schiavo, and the feeding tube that was keeping Terri Schiavo alive was withdrawn. The case was soon taken up as a cause by those opposed to abortion and euthanasia. They succeeded in persuading the Florida legislature to pass a new law to keep

Terri's case before the Florida courts, and when the courts again failed to order that Terri be kept alive, Congress was recalled from a break to pass a special law allowing the Schindlers to take their case to a federal court. President George W. Bush flew from his Texas ranch to Washington to sign the law, but the federal court also held that Michael Schiavo had the right to make the decision to withdraw his wife's feeding tube. The U.S. Supreme Court refused to hear an appeal from that decision, and Terri died. An autopsy showed that Terri Schiavo's brain was severely atrophied, and that no treatment could have reversed the loss of brain matter.

It is possible that a small percentage of patients diagnosed as being in a persistent vegetative state do have some awareness. Improved imaging techniques enable us to see, however, that for many patients in a persistent vegetative state, there is no blood flow to the parts of the brain responsible for consciousness. Without blood flow, the brain rapidly decays; and so in those patients, the existence of consciousness, or the recovery of it, can definitely be excluded. Once it is clear that a patient in a persistent vegetative state has no awareness, and never again can have any awareness, her life has no intrinsic value. These patients are alive biologically but not biographically. If this verdict seems harsh, ask yourself whether there is anything to choose between the following options: (a) instant death; or (b) instant coma, followed by death without recovery in ten years. I can see no advantage in survival in a comatose state if death without recovery is certain.

There is, however, one important respect in which these patients differ from disabled infants. In discussing infanticide in the final section of Chapter 6, I cited Bentham's comment that infanticide need not 'give the slightest inquietude to the most timid imagination'. This is because those old enough to be aware of the killing of disabled infants are necessarily outside the scope of the policy. This cannot be said of decisions about how to treat those who once were rational and self-aware. So a possible objection to ending the life of such a patient would be that it will lead to insecurity and fear among those who are not now, but might come to be, within its scope. For instance, elderly people, knowing that nonvoluntary euthanasia is sometimes applied to senile elderly patients who lack the capacity to accept or reject death, might fear that every injection or tablet will be lethal. This fear might be quite irrational, but it would be difficult to convince people of this, particularly if old age really had affected their memory or powers of reasoning. This objection could be met by a procedure allowing those who do not wish to be subjected to nonvoluntary euthanasia under any circumstances to register their refusal. If this became routine, it would have the additional benefit of preventing lengthy and costly legal cases like that of Terri Schiavo.

JUSTIFYING VOLUNTARY EUTHANASIA

Where euthanasia and physician-assisted suicide are illegal, doctors who help their terminally ill patients to die are risking serious criminal charges. Although juries are extremely reluctant to convict in cases of this kind, the law is clear that neither a request to be killed, nor the degree of suffering, nor the incurable condition of the person killed are defences to a charge of murder. Advocates of voluntary euthanasia propose that this law be changed so that a doctor may lawfully respond to a patient's desire to die without further suffering. The case for voluntary euthanasia has some common ground with the case for nonvoluntary euthanasia, in that death is a benefit for the one killed – or at least, in the case of people who are irreversibly unconscious, not a harm. The two kinds of euthanasia differ, however, in that voluntary euthanasia involves the killing of a person, a rational and self-aware being. (People who are rational and self-aware at the time they make a request may no longer be rational and self-aware at the time when the request is acted on, but for simplicity I shall disregard this complication.)

We have seen that it is possible to justify ending the life of a human being who lacks the capacity to consent. We must now ask in what way the ethical issues are different when the being is capable of consenting and does in fact consent.

Let us return to the general principles about killing proposed in Chapter 4. I argued there that killing a being with a sense of his or her own future is a more serious matter than killing a merely conscious being. I gave four distinct grounds on which this could be argued:

1. The classical utilitarian claim that because self-aware beings are capable of fearing their own death, killing them has worse effects on others.
2. The preference utilitarian calculation that counts the thwarting of the victim's desire to go on living as an important reason against killing.
3. A theory of rights according to which to have a right one must have the ability to desire that to which one has a right, so that to

have a right to life one must be able to desire one's own continued existence.

4. Respect for the autonomous decisions of rational agents.

Now suppose we have a situation in which a person suffering from a painful and incurable disease wishes to die. Do any of the four grounds for holding that it is normally worse to kill a person provide reasons against killing when the individual is a person who wants to die?

The classical utilitarian objection does not apply to killing that takes place only with the genuine consent of the person killed. That people are killed under these conditions would have no tendency to spread fear or insecurity, because if we do not wish to be killed, we simply do not consent. In fact, the argument from fear points in favour of voluntary euthanasia, for if voluntary euthanasia is not permitted we may, with good cause, be fearful that our deaths will be unnecessarily drawn out and distressing. In the Netherlands, a nationwide government-commissioned study found that 'many patients want an assurance that their doctor will assist them to die should suffering become unbearable'. Often, having received this assurance, no request for euthanasia eventuated. The availability of euthanasia brought comfort without euthanasia having to be provided.

Preference utilitarianism also points in favour of, not against, voluntary euthanasia. Just as preference utilitarianism must count a desire to go on living as a reason against killing, so it must count a desire to die as a reason for killing.

Next, according to the theory of rights we have considered, it is an essential feature of a right that one can waive one's rights if one so chooses. I may have a right to privacy; but I can, if I wish, install webcams in every room of my house and leave them on 24/7. No one who looks at the resulting images on my Web site violates my right to privacy, because I have waived the right. Similarly, to say that I have a right to life is not to say that it would be wrong for my doctor to end my life, if I choose to waive my right to life.

Lastly, the principle of respect for autonomy tells us to allow rational agents to live their own lives according to their own autonomous decisions, free from coercion or interference; but if rational agents should autonomously choose to die, then respect for autonomy will lead us to assist them to do as they choose.

So, although there are reasons for thinking that killing a self-aware being is normally worse than killing any other kind of being, in the special case of voluntary euthanasia most of these reasons count for euthanasia rather than against it. Surprising as this result might at first seem, it really does no more than reflect the fact that what is special about self-aware beings is that they can know that they exist over time and will, unless they die, continue to exist. Normally this continued existence is fervently desired, but when the foreseeable continued existence is dreaded rather than desired, the wish to die may take the place of the normal wish to live, reversing the reasons against killing. Thus, the case for voluntary euthanasia is arguably much stronger than the case for nonvoluntary euthanasia.

Some opponents of the legalization of voluntary euthanasia might concede that all this follows, if we have a genuinely free and rational decision to die; but, they add, we can never be sure that a request to be killed is the result of a free and rational decision. Will not the sick and elderly be pressured by their relatives to end their lives quickly? Will it not be possible to commit outright murder by pretending that a person has requested euthanasia? Even if there is no pressure or falsification, can anyone who is ill, suffering pain, and very probably in a drugged and confused state of mind make a rational decision about whether to live or die?

We now have a growing body of experience with the legalization of voluntary euthanasia and physician-assisted suicide, and that provides a basis for responding to these concerns. Although the Dutch parliament did not legalize euthanasia until 2002, this followed almost two decades during which Dutch physicians could be sure that they would not be prosecuted for carrying out euthanasia, as long as they followed guidelines developed by the courts in a series of cases in which physicians had been charged with euthanasia and acquitted. When euthanasia was legalized, similar conditions became part of the law. In the Netherlands, euthanasia is lawful only if:

- it is carried out by a physician;
- the patient has explicitly requested euthanasia in a manner that leaves no doubt that the patient's desire to die is voluntary, well-informed and well-considered;
- the patient has a condition causing protracted physical or mental suffering which the patient finds unbearable;
- there is no reasonable alternative (reasonable from the patient's point of view) to alleviate the patient's suffering; and

- the doctor has consulted another independent professional who
  agrees with his or her judgment.

These guidelines make murder in the guise of euthanasia very difficult
to carry out, and there has been no suggestion that this is occurring in
the Netherlands. Since the law was passed, governments of different
political complexions have held power, with the Christian Democrats
taking the leading role in successive coalition governments. Nevertheless,
there has been no move to repeal the legalization of euthanasia. It is not
a coincidence that the next nations to legalize euthanasia, Belgium and
Luxembourg, are neighbours of the Netherlands and that their laws are
similar to the Dutch law. The majority of Belgians, in particular, are
well-placed to observe the practice of euthanasia in the Netherlands,
because they speak Dutch. It is implausible that these countries would
have legalized euthanasia if there were clear evidence of serious abuses
in the Netherlands.

Similarly, Oregon legalized physician-assisted suicide in 1997, so there
is now considerable experience of that practice in one part of the United
States. There has been no evidence of any abuse of the law. Once again,
a neighbour has observed and then followed. At the elections held in
2008, the voters of Washington passed a law very similar to Oregon's.

Another common objection to euthanasia is that doctors can be mistaken. In rare instances, patients diagnosed by two competent doctors as
suffering from an incurable condition have survived and enjoyed years of
good health. Possibly the legalization of voluntary euthanasia would, over
the years, mean the deaths of one or two people who would otherwise
have recovered from their immediate illness and lived for some extra
years. This is not, however, the knockdown argument against euthanasia
that some imagine it to be. Against a very small number of unnecessary
deaths that might occur if euthanasia is legalized we must place the very
large amount of pain and distress that will be suffered quite pointlessly,
by patients who really are terminally ill, if euthanasia is not legalized.
Longer life is not such a supreme good that it outweighs all other considerations. (If it were, there would be many more effective ways of saving
life – such as a ban on smoking or a reduction of speed limits to ten
kilometres per hour, not to mention the issue of foreign aid that is the
topic of the next chapter.) The possibility that two doctors may make a
mistake means that the person who opts for euthanasia is deciding on
the balance of probabilities and giving up an extremely small chance of
survival in order to avoid suffering that is overwhelmingly likely to end

in death. This may be a perfectly rational choice. Probability is the guide of life, and of death too.

Against this, some will reply that improved care for the terminally ill has eliminated pain and made voluntary euthanasia unnecessary. But it is not only physical pain that makes people wish to die: they may suffer from bones so fragile they fracture at sudden movements, uncontrollable nausea and vomiting, slow starvation due to a cancerous growth, inability to control one's bowels or bladder, difficulty in breathing and so on. These symptoms often cannot be eliminated, at least not without keeping the patient unconscious all the time.

Dr. Timothy Quill from Rochester, New York, has described how he prescribed barbiturate sleeping pills for 'Diane', a patient with a severe form of leukaemia, knowing that she wanted the tablets in order to be able to end her life. Dr. Quill had known Diane for many years and admired her courage in dealing with previous serious illnesses. In an article in the *New England Journal of Medicine,* Dr. Quill wrote:

It was extraordinarily important to Diane to maintain control of herself and her own dignity during the time remaining to her. When this was no longer possible, she clearly wanted to die. As a former director of a hospice program, I know how to use pain medicines to keep patients comfortable and lessen suffering. I explained the philosophy of comfort care, which I strongly believe in. Although Diane understood and appreciated this, she had known of people lingering in what was called relative comfort, and she wanted no part of it. When the time came, she wanted to take her life in the least painful way possible. Knowing of her desire for independence and her decision to stay in control, I thought this request made perfect sense ... In our discussion it became clear that preoccupation with her fear of a lingering death would interfere with Diane's getting the most out of the time she had left until she found a safe way to ensure her death.

Not all dying patients who wish to die are fortunate enough to have a doctor like Timothy Quill. Betty Rollin has described, in her moving book *Last Wish,* how her mother developed ovarian cancer that spread to other parts of her body. One morning her mother said to her:

I've had a wonderful life, but now it's over, or it should be. I'm not afraid to die, but I am afraid of this illness, what it's doing to me ... There's never any relief from it now. Nothing but nausea and this pain ... There won't be any more chemotherapy. There's no treatment anymore. So what happens to me now? I know what happens. I'll die slowly ... I don't want that ... Who does it benefit if I die slowly? If it benefits my children I'd be willing. But it's not going to do you any good. ... There's no point in a slow death, none. I've never liked doing things with no point. I've got to end this.

Betty Rollin found it very difficult to help her mother to carry out her desire: 'Physician after physician turned down our pleas for help (How many pills? What kind?).' After her book about her mother's death was published, she received hundreds of letters, many from people, or close relatives of people, who had tried to die, failed, and suffered even more. Many of these people were denied help from doctors, because although suicide is legal in most jurisdictions, assisted suicide is not.

Dr. Jack Kevorkian, a Michigan pathologist, sought to help people who want to die but cannot get assistance from their own doctor. Initially, he helped people to die with a 'suicide machine' consisting of a metal pole with three different bottles attached to a tube of the kind used to provide an intravenous drip. He would insert the tube in the patient's vein, but with the switch set so that only a harmless saline solution can pass through it. The patient could then flip a switch allowing a coma-inducing drug to come through the tube; this was automatically followed by a lethal drug contained in the third bottle. Dr. Kevorkian announced that he was prepared to make the machine available to any terminally ill patient who wished to use it. In June 1990, Janet Adkins, who was suffering from Alzheimer's disease but still competent to make the decision to end her life, contacted Dr. Kevorkian and told him of her wish to die rather than go through the slow and progressive deterioration that the disease involves. Dr. Kevorkian was in attendance while she made use of his machine. He then reported Janet Adkins' death to the police. He was subsequently charged with murder, but the judge refused to allow the charge to proceed to trial, on the grounds that Janet Adkins had caused her own death. During the next eight years, Dr. Kevorkian assisted many other people to die. He was repeatedly charged with assisting suicide, but no jury convicted him of that offence. When his licence to practise medicine was withdrawn, and he was no longer able to obtain the lethal drug he had been using, he altered the 'suicide machine' so that it released carbon monoxide, through a gas mask, to the patient. Finally in 1998, Kevorkian decided to help Thomas Youk, who was dying from ALS, also known as Lou Gehrig's disease, and had asked Kevorkian to end his life. Those suffering from ALS lose control of their muscles, and so as the inevitable end approaches, they are unable to flip switches or take drugs. Kevorkian crossed the line from assisted suicide to voluntary euthanasia by giving Youk a lethal injection. Moreover, in a clear challenge to the legal authorities, he released a video taken while he was giving the injection. This time, a jury convicted him of second-degree homicide, and he served eight years in prison before being released on parole.

Philip Nitschke prefers to work at the edge of the law rather than to challenge it directly. Nitschke was practicing medicine in Australia's Northern Territory when that region legalized voluntary euthanasia. Nitschke helped four terminally ill people end their lives before the law was overturned by the Federal government in 1997. Convinced that people have a right to end their own lives if they choose to do so, he founded Exit International, an organization that runs workshops in Australia, New Zealand, the United Kingdom and the United States advising people on how to end their lives reliably and safely. He has co-authored *The Peaceful Pill Handbook* to provide the same knowledge to those who cannot attend the workshops. The hard copy version of the book has been banned in Australia, but is available in the United States, and Nitschke has made an electronic version available online (although it is an offense to download it in Australia). Whatever one thinks about the ethics of voluntary euthanasia and physician-assisted suicide, whether such information should be publicly available is itself an ethical question, given the possibility of misuse by those who are not terminally or incurably ill. Many advocates of the legalization of voluntary euthanasia and physician-assisted suicide are themselves against publishing 'do it yourself' guides to dying, arguing that laws restricting aid in dying to doctors provide important safeguards. Nitschke might agree that this would be desirable, but consider that because there are still few countries in which either voluntary euthanasia or physician-assisted suicide is legal, the importance of helping those who have good reason to end their lives outweighs the small risk of misuse.

Does the idea of giving everyone access to a 'peaceful pill' perhaps give too much weight to individual freedom and autonomy? After all, we do not allow people free choices on matters like, for instance, the taking of heroin. This is a restriction of freedom but, in the view of many, one that can be justified on paternalistic grounds. If preventing people becoming heroin addicts is justifiable paternalism, why isn't preventing people having themselves killed?

The question is a reasonable one, because respect for individual freedom can be carried too far. John Stuart Mill thought that the state should never interfere with the individual except to prevent harm to others. The individual's own good, Mill thought, is not a proper reason for state intervention. But Mill may have had too high an opinion of the rationality of most human beings. It may occasionally be right to prevent people making choices that are obviously not rationally based and which we can be sure they will later regret. The prohibition of voluntary euthanasia cannot be justified on paternalistic grounds, however, for voluntary euthanasia is an act for which good reasons exist. Voluntary euthanasia occurs only when, to the best of medical knowledge, a person is suffering from an incurable and painful or extremely distressing condition. In these circumstances one cannot say that to choose to die quickly is obviously irrational. The strength of the case for voluntary euthanasia lies in this combination of respect for the preferences, or autonomy, of those who decide for euthanasia; and the clear rational basis of the decision itself. When information about ending one's life is made easily available, people may decide to end their lives without such a clear rational basis. Legal, regulated voluntary euthanasia and physician-assisted suicide have far less potential for abuse, and when they are available, there is no need to make it easy for people to find out how to kill themselves.

NOT JUSTIFYING INVOLUNTARY EUTHANASIA

Involuntary euthanasia resembles voluntary euthanasia in that it involves the killing of those capable of consenting to their own death. It differs in that they do not consent. This difference is crucial, as the argument of the preceding section shows. All the four reasons against killing self-aware beings apply when the person killed does not choose to die.

Something very like involuntary euthanasia appears to have taken place in a hospital in New Orleans during the floods caused by Hurricane Katrina in 2005. Memorial Medical Center, a community hospital that was holding more than 200 patients at the time, was cut off by the rising water. Three days after the hurricane hit, the hospital had no electricity, the water supply had failed, and toilets could no longer be flushed. Some patients who were dependent on ventilators died. In stifling heat, doctors and nurses were hard-pressed to care for surviving patients lying on soiled beds. Adding to the anxiety were fears that law and order had broken down in the city, and the hospital itself might be a target for armed bandits.

Helicopters were called in to evacuate patients. Priority was given to those who were in better health, and could walk. State police arrived and told staff that because of the civil unrest, everybody had to be out of the hospital by 5 P.M.

On the eighth floor, Jannie Burgess, a 79-year-old woman with advanced cancer, was on a morphine drip and close to death. To evacuate her, she would have to be carried down six flights of stairs and would require the attention of nurses who were needed elsewhere. If she were left unattended, however, she might come out of her sedation and be in pain. One of the physicians present instructed the nurse to increase the morphine 'giving her enough until she goes'. Another physician told nursing staff that several patients on the seventh floor were also too ill to survive. She injected them with morphine and another drug that slowed their breathing until they died.

At least one of the patients injected with this lethal combination of drugs appears to have otherwise been in little danger of imminent death. Emmett Everett was a 61-year-old man who had been paralysed in an accident several years earlier and was in the hospital for surgery to relieve a bowel obstruction. When others from his ward were evacuated, he asked not to be left behind; but he weighed 380 lbs (172 kg), and it would have been extremely difficult to carry him down the stairs and then up again to where the helicopters were landing. He was told the injection he was being given would help with the dizziness from which he suffered.

Whether any of these killings can be justified in these circumstances is debatable, but the killing of Emmett Everett, in my view, cannot be. Significantly, the physicians' actions were not the result of a slippery slope from the acceptance of voluntary euthanasia or physician-assisted suicide, for those practices have always been illegal in Louisiana. Rather, from what the physicians told Sheri Fink, on whose *The New York Times* report the previous account is based, the physicians saw what they were doing as an application of the doctrine of double effect, on which physicians commonly draw when giving morphine to relieve pain in a terminally ill patient, though they know it will shorten life. We shall discuss that doctrine shortly.

Would it ever be possible to justify involuntary euthanasia on paternalistic grounds, to save someone extreme agony? We can imagine a case in which the agony is so great, and so certain, that it overrides all four reasons against killing self-aware beings. Yet to make this decision one would have to be confident that one can judge when a person's life is so bad as to be not worth living – and that one is in a better position to make that judgment than the person herself. But the fact that the other person wishes to go on living is good evidence that her life is worth living. What better evidence could there be?

The only kind of case in which the paternalistic argument is at all plausible is one in which the person to be killed does not realize what agony she will suffer in the future, and if she is not killed now she will have to live through to the very end. On these grounds, one might kill a person who has – though she does not yet realize it – fallen into the hands of homicidal sadists who will torture her to death. These cases are, fortunately, more commonly encountered in fiction than reality.

Here, the distinction between critical and intuitive levels of moral reasoning (see pp. 78–80, Chapter 4) is again relevant. If in real life we are unlikely ever to encounter a case of justifiable involuntary euthanasia, then it may be best to dismiss from our minds the fanciful cases in which one might imagine defending it and treat the rule against involuntary euthanasia as, for all practical purposes, absolute. At the intuitive level, the level of moral reasoning we apply in our daily lives, we can simply say that euthanasia is only justifiable if those killed either:

a. lack the ability to consent to death, because they lack the capacity to understand the choice between their own continued existence or non-existence; or
b. have the capacity to choose between their own continued life and death and have made an informed, voluntary and settled decision to die.

ACTIVE AND PASSIVE EUTHANASIA

The conclusions we have reached in this chapter violate one of the most fundamental tenets of Western ethics – that killing an innocent human being is always wrong. I have already shown that my conclusions are, at least in the area of disabled infants, a less radical departure from existing practice than one might suppose because of the widespread support for prenatal diagnosis and abortion of a pregnancy that will lead to a disabled child. In this section, I shall argue that there is another area of accepted medical practice that is not intrinsically different from the practices that I advocate. Against this background, the conclusions we have reached may seem less shocking than they otherwise would.

'Baby Doe' – a legal pseudonym – was born in Bloomington, Indiana, in 1982, with Down syndrome and some additional problems, including an improperly formed oesophagus – the passage from the mouth to the stomach. This meant that Baby Doe could not receive nourishment by mouth. Surgery to fix the problem was offered, but the parents, after discussing the situation with their obstetrician, refused. Without surgery, Baby Doe would soon die. Baby Doe's father later said that as a school-teacher he had worked closely with Down syndrome children, and that he and his wife had decided that it was in the best interests of Baby Doe, and of their family as a whole (they had two other children), to refuse consent for the operation. The hospital authorities, uncertain of their legal position, took the matter to court. Both the local county court and the Indiana State Supreme Court upheld the parents' right to refuse consent to surgery. The case attracted national media attention, and an attempt was made to take it to the United States Supreme Court; but before this could happen, Baby Doe died.

One result of the Baby Doe case was that the United States government, headed at the time by President Ronald Reagan, issued regulations directing that all infants are to be given necessary life-saving treatment, irrespective of disability. But the new regulations were strongly resisted by the American Medical Association and the American Academy of Pediatrics. In court hearings on the regulations, even Dr. C. Everett Koop, Reagan's surgeon general and the driving force behind the attempt to ensure that all infants should be treated, had to admit that there were some cases in which he would not provide life-sustaining treatment. Dr. Koop mentioned three conditions in which, he said, life-sustaining treatment was not appropriate: anencephalic infants (infants born without a brain); infants who had, usually as a result of extreme prematurity, suffered such severe bleeding in the brain that they would never be able to breathe without a respirator and would never be able even to recognize another person; and infants lacking a major part of their digestive tract, who could only be kept alive by means of a drip providing nourishment directly into the bloodstream.

The regulations were eventually accepted only in a watered-down form, allowing some flexibility to doctors. Even so, a subsequent survey of American paediatricians specialising in the care of newborn infants showed that 76 percent thought that the regulations were not necessary, 66 percent considered the regulations interfered with parents' rights to determine what course of action was in the best interests of their children, and 60 percent believed that the regulations did not allow adequate consideration of infants' suffering.

In a series of British cases, the courts have accepted the view that the quality of a child's life is a relevant consideration in deciding whether life-sustaining treatment should be provided. In a case called *In re B*, concerning a baby like Baby Doe, with Down syndrome and an intestinal obstruction, the court said that surgery should be carried out, because the infant's life would not be 'demonstrably awful'. In another case, *Re C*, where the baby had a poorly formed brain combined with severe physical handicaps, the court authorised the paediatric team to refrain from giving life-prolonging treatment. This was also the course taken in the case of *Re Baby J*, this infant was born extremely prematurely and was blind, deaf and would probably never have been able to speak.

A survey of European physicians working in neonatal intensive care units in France, Germany, Italy, Luxembourg, the Netherlands, Spain, Sweden and the United Kingdom showed that in all these countries, a majority had set limits to the intensive care given to an infant because it had an incurable condition. They had, for example, withheld resuscitation after a baby's heart had stopped or not put the baby on a respirator. Thus, though many would disagree with Baby Doe's parents' decision (because people with Down syndrome can live enjoyable lives and are often warm and loving individuals), virtually everyone recognizes that in more severe conditions, allowing an infant to die is the only humane and ethically acceptable course to take. The question is: if it is right to allow infants to die, why is it wrong to kill them?

This question has not escaped the notice of the doctors involved. Frequently, they answer it by invoking a verse by the nineteenth-century poet, Arthur Clough:

> Thou shalt not kill; but need'st not strive
> Officiously to keep alive.

Unfortunately for those who appeal to Clough's immortal lines as an authoritative ethical pronouncement, they come from a biting satire – 'The Latest Decalogue' – the intent of which is to mock the attitudes described. The opening lines, for example, are:

> Thou shalt have one god only; who
> Would be at the expense of two.
> No graven images may be
> Worshipped except the currency.

So Clough cannot be numbered on the side of those who think it wrong to kill, but right not to try too hard to keep alive. Is there, nonetheless, something to be said for this idea? The view that there is something to be said for it is often termed 'the acts and omissions doctrine'. It holds that there is an important moral distinction between performing an act that has certain consequences – say, the death of a disabled child – and omitting to do something that has the same consequences. If this doctrine is correct, the doctor who gives the child a lethal injection does wrong; the doctor who omits to give the child antibiotics, knowing full well that without antibiotics the child will die, does not.

What grounds are there for accepting the acts and omissions doctrine? Few champion the doctrine for its own sake as an important ethical first principle. It is, rather, an implication of one view of ethics, of a view that holds that so long as we do not violate specified moral rules that place determinate moral obligations on us, we do all that morality demands of us. These rules are of the kind made familiar by the Ten Commandments and similar moral codes: 'Do not kill', 'Do not lie', 'Do not steal' and so on. Characteristically they are formulated in the negative, so that to obey them it is necessary only to abstain from the actions they prohibit. Hence, obedience can be demanded of every member of the community.

An ethic consisting of specific duties, prescribed by moral rules that everyone can be expected to obey, must make a sharp moral distinction between acts and omissions. Take, for example, the rule: 'Do not kill.' If this rule is interpreted, as it has been in the Western tradition, as prohibiting only the taking of innocent human life, it is not too difficult to avoid overt acts in violation of it. Few of us are murderers. It is not so easy to avoid letting innocent humans die. Many people die because of insufficient food or poor medical facilities. If we could assist some of them but do not do so, we are letting them die. Taking the rule against killing to apply to omissions would make living in accordance with it a mark of saintliness or moral heroism rather than a minimum required of every morally decent person.

An ethic that judges acts according to whether they do or do not violate specific moral rules must, therefore, place moral weight on the distinction between acts and omissions. An ethic that judges acts by their consequences will not do so, for the consequences of an act and an omission will often be, in all significant respects, indistinguishable. For instance, deciding not to put a premature infant who cannot breathe unaided on a respirator has consequences just as fatal as giving the child a lethal injection.

The acts and omissions issue poses the choice between these two basic approaches in an unusually clear and direct way. What we need to do is imagine two parallel situations differing only in that in one a person performs an act resulting in the death of another human being, whereas in the other she omits to do something, with the same result. Here is a description of a relatively common situation, taken from an essay by Sir Gustav Nossal, an eminent Australian medical researcher:

An old lady of 83 has been admitted [to a nursing home for the aged] because her increasing degree of mental confusion has made it impossible for her to stay in her own home, and there is no one willing and able to look after her. Over three years, her condition deteriorates. She loses the ability to speak, requires to be fed, and becomes incontinent. Finally, she cannot sit in an armchair any longer, and is confined permanently to bed. One day, she contracts pneumonia.

In a patient who was enjoying a reasonable quality of life, pneumonia would be routinely treated with antibiotics. Should this patient be given antibiotics? Nossal continues:

The relatives are contacted, and the matron of the nursing home tells them that she and the doctor she uses most frequently have worked out a loose arrangement for cases of this type. With advanced senile dementia, they treat the first three infections with antibiotics, and after that, mindful of the adage that 'pneumonia is the old person's friend', they let nature take its course. The matron emphasises that if the relatives desire, *all* infections can be vigorously treated. The relatives agree with the rule of thumb. The patient dies of a urinary tract infection six months later.

This patient died when she did as a result of a deliberate omission. Many people would think that this omission was well-justified. They might question whether it would not have been better to omit treatment even for the initial occurrence of pneumonia. There is, after all, no moral magic about the number three. Would it also have been justifiable, at the time when a decision not to give an antibiotic was taken, to give an injection that would bring about the patient's death in a peaceful way?

Comparing these two possible ways of bringing about a patient's death at a particular time, is it reasonable to hold that the doctor who gives the injection is a murderer who deserves to go to jail, whereas the doctor who decides not to administer antibiotics is practising good and compassionate medicine? That may be what courts of law would say, but surely it is an untenable distinction. In both cases, the outcome is the death of the patient. In both cases, the doctor knows that this will be the result and decides what she will do on the basis of this knowledge, because she judges this result to be better than the alternative. In both cases, the doctor must take responsibility for her decision – it would not be correct for the doctor who decided not to provide antibiotics to say that she was not responsible for the patient's death because she did nothing. Doing nothing in this situation is itself a deliberate choice, and one cannot escape responsibility for its consequences.

One might say, of course, that the doctor who withholds antibiotics does not kill the patient, she merely allows the patient to die; but one must then answer the further question why killing is always wrong and letting die is sometimes right. The answer that most advocates of the distinction give is simply that there is a moral rule against killing innocent human beings and none against allowing them to die. This answer treats a conventionally accepted moral rule as if it were beyond questioning; it does not go on to ask whether we should have a moral rule against killing (but not against allowing to die). We have already seen that the conventionally accepted principle of the sanctity of human life is untenable. The moral rules that prohibit killing but accept 'letting die' cannot be taken for granted either.

Reflecting on these cases leads us to the conclusion that there is no *intrinsic* moral difference between killing and allowing to die. That is, there is no difference which depends solely on the distinction between an act and an omission. (This does not mean that all cases of allowing to die are morally equivalent to killing. Other factors – extrinsic factors – will sometimes be relevant. This will be discussed further in the next chapter.) Allowing to die – sometimes called 'passive euthanasia' – is already accepted as a humane and proper course of action in certain cases. If there is no intrinsic moral difference between killing and allowing to die, active euthanasia should also be accepted as humane and proper in certain circumstances.

Others have suggested that the difference between withholding treatment necessary to prolong life and giving a lethal injection lies in the intention with which the two are done. Those who take this view resort to the 'doctrine of double effect', a doctrine widely held among Roman Catholic moral theologians and moral philosophers, to argue that one action (for example, refraining from life-sustaining treatment) may have two effects (in this case, not causing additional suffering to the patient and shortening the patient's life). They then argue that as long as the *directly intended* effect is the beneficial one that does not violate an absolute moral rule, the action is permissible. Though we foresee that our action (or omission) will result in the death of the patient, this is merely an unwanted side effect. But the distinction between directly intended effect and side effect is a contrived one, and the doctrine can easily be misused, as we have seen in the case of Memorial Medical Center in New Orleans after Hurricane Katrina. We cannot avoid responsibility simply by directing our intention to one effect rather than another. If we foresee both effects, we must take responsibility for the foreseen effects of what we do. We often want to do something but cannot do it because of its other, unwanted consequences. For example, a chemical company might want to get rid of toxic waste in the most economical manner, by dumping it in the nearest river. Would we allow the executives of the company to say that all they directly intended was to improve the efficiency of the factory, thus promoting employment and keeping down the cost of living? Would we regard the pollution as excusable because it is merely an unwanted side effect of furthering these worthy objectives? Obviously, the defenders of the doctrine of double effect would not accept such an excuse. In rejecting it, however, they would have to rely on a judgment that the cost – the polluted river – is disproportionate to the gains. Here, a consequentialist judgment lurks behind the doctrine of double effect. The same is true when the doctrine is used in medical care. Normally, saving life takes precedence over relieving pain. If in the case of a particular patient it does not, this can only be because we have judged that the patient's prospects for a future life of acceptable quality are so poor that in this case relieving suffering can take precedence. This is, in other words, not a decision based on acceptance of the sanctity of human life, but a decision based on a disguised quality of life judgment.

Equally unsatisfactory is the common appeal to a distinction between 'ordinary' and 'extraordinary' means of treatment, coupled with the belief that it is not obligatory to provide extraordinary means. Together with my colleague, Helga Kuhse, I carried out a survey of paediatricians and obstetricians in Australia and found that they had remarkable ideas about what constituted 'ordinary' and 'extraordinary' means. Some even thought that the use of antibiotics – the cheapest, simplest and most common medical procedure – could be extraordinary. The reason for this range of views is easy to find. When one looks at the justifications given by moral theologians and philosophers for the distinction, it turns out that what is 'ordinary' in one situation can become 'extraordinary' in another. For example, in the landmark case of Karen Ann Quinlan, a young New Jersey woman who was in a coma, breathing with the aid of a respirator and considered to have no prospect of recovery, a Roman Catholic bishop testified that the use of a respirator was 'extraordinary' and hence optional because Quinlan had no hope of recovery from the coma. Obviously, if doctors had thought that Quinlan was likely to recover, the use of the respirator would not have been optional and would have been declared 'ordinary'. On the other hand, when the respirator was removed and Quinlan, to most people's surprise, continued to breathe on her own, her parents, who were Roman Catholics, did not seek the removal of her feeding tube. Quinlan survived for another nine years but never recovered from her coma.

In 2004, during the controversy over Terri Schiavo, Pope John Paul II stated firmly that a feeding tube must not be withdrawn from people in a vegetative state, saying that 'the administration of water and food, even when provided by artificial means, always represents a natural means of preserving life, not a medical act'. It is hard to see how the use of a feeding tube is not a medical act – inserting one is not something that people without health care training can do. Is there really a significant moral difference between withdrawing a respirator and withdrawing a feeding tube? The patient's prospects of at least a minimal quality of life (and, where resources are limited and could be used more effectively to save lives elsewhere, the cost of the treatment) should determine whether a given form of treatment is to be provided or not.

Indeed, because of extrinsic differences – especially differences in the time it takes for death to occur – active euthanasia may be the more humane course. In the 1970s, Dr. John Lorber, a British physician, recommended that infants born with the most severe form of spina bifida – then a relatively common birth defect in which the baby has a wound on the back exposing the nerves – should be allowed to die, because he considered that their prospects of a worthwhile life were poor. Lorber openly acknowledged that the object of not treating these infants is that they should die soon and painlessly. Yet when he charted the fate of twenty-five infants born with spina bifida on whom it had been decided not to operate, he found that fourteen were still alive after one month and seven after three months. An Australian clinic following Lorber's approach to spina bifida found that of seventy-nine untreated infants, five survived for more than two years. For both the infants, and their families, this must have been a long, drawn-out ordeal. It is also (although in a society with a reasonable level of affluence this should not be the primary consideration) a considerable burden on the hospital staff and the community's medical resources. (Today, far fewer babies are born with spina bifida, partly because of the discovery that taking folic acid early in pregnancy reduces the incidence of the condition and partly because spina bifida can now be detected during pregnancy and most fetuses with the condition are aborted.)

Consider, to take another example, infants born with Down syndrome and a blockage in the digestive system which, if not removed, will make it impossible for the baby to eat. Like 'Baby Doe', these infants may be allowed to die. Yet the blockage can be removed and has nothing to do with the degree of intellectual disability the child will have. Moreover, the death resulting from the failure to operate in these circumstances is, though sure, neither swift nor painless. The infant dies from dehydration or hunger. Baby Doe took about five days to die, and in other recorded instances of this practice, it has taken up to two weeks for death to come.

It is interesting, in this context, to think again of our earlier argument that membership of the species *Homo sapiens* does not entitle a being to better treatment than a being at a similar mental level who is a member of a different species. We could also have said – except that it seemed too obvious to need saying – that membership of the species *Homo sapiens* is not a reason for giving a being *worse* treatment than a member of a different species. Yet in respect of euthanasia, this needs to be said. If your dog is ill and in pain with no chance of recovery, the humane thing to do is take her to the vet, who will end her suffering swiftly with a lethal injection. To 'allow nature to take its course', withholding treatment while your dog dies slowly and in distress over days, weeks or months, would obviously be wrong. It is only our misplaced respect for the doctrine of the sanctity of human life that prevents us from seeing that what it is obviously wrong to do to a dog, it is equally wrong to do to a human being who has never been able to express a view about such matters.

To summarize: passive ways of ending life result in a drawn-out death. They introduce irrelevant factors (a blockage in the intestine or the presence of an easily curable infection) into the selection of those who shall die. If we are able to admit that our objective is a swift and painless death, we should not leave it up to chance to determine whether this objective is achieved. Having chosen death, we should ensure that it comes in the best possible way.

THE SLIPPERY SLOPE: FROM EUTHANASIA TO GENOCIDE?

Before we leave this topic, we must consider an objection that looms so large in the anti-euthanasia literature that it merits a section to itself. It is, for instance, the reason why Dr. John Lorber rejected active euthanasia. He wrote:

I wholly disagree with euthanasia. Though it is fully logical, and in expert and conscientious hands it could be the most humane way of dealing with such a situation, legalizing euthanasia would be a most dangerous weapon in the hands of the State or ignorant or unscrupulous individuals. One does not have to go far back in history to know what crimes can be committed if euthanasia were legalized.

Would euthanasia be the first step down a slippery slope? In the absence of prominent moral footholds to check our descent, would we slide all the way down into the abyss of state terror and mass murder? The experience of Nazism, to which Lorber no doubt is referring, has often been invoked as a spectre to warn us against euthanasia. Here is a more specific example, from an article by another doctor, Leo Alexander:

Whatever proportions [Nazi] crimes finally assumed, it became evident to all who investigated them that they had started from small beginnings. The beginnings at first were merely a subtle shift in emphasis in the basic attitude of the physicians. It started with the acceptance of the attitude, basic in the euthanasia movement, that there is such a thing as life not worthy to be lived. This attitude in its early stages concerned itself merely with the severely and chronically sick. Gradually the sphere of those to be included in the category was enlarged to encompass the socially unproductive, the ideologically unwanted, the racially unwanted and finally all non-Germans. But it is important to realize that the infinitely small wedged-in lever from which this entire trend of mind received its impetus was the attitude toward the nonrehabilitable sick.

Alexander singles out the Nazis' so-called euthanasia program as the root of all the horrendous crimes the Nazis later committed, because that program implied 'that there is such a thing as life not worthy to be lived'. Lorber could hardly agree with Alexander on this, because his recommended procedure of not treating infants with the worst form of spina bifida is based on exactly this judgment. Although people sometimes talk as if we should never judge a human life to be not worth living, there are times when such a judgment is obviously correct. A life of physical suffering, unredeemed by any form of pleasure or by a minimal level of self-awareness, is not worth living. As we have already noted, life with Tay-Sachs disease is a plausible example of a life not worth living. Surveys undertaken by health care economists in which people are asked how much they value being alive in certain states of health, regularly find that people give some states a negative value – that is, they indicate that they would prefer to be dead than to survive in that condition. Apparently, the life of the elderly woman described by Sir Gustav Nossal was, in the opinion of the matron of the nursing home, the doctor, and the relatives, not worth living. If we can set criteria for deciding who is to be allowed to die and who is to be given treatment, then why should it be wrong to set criteria, perhaps the same criteria, for deciding who should be killed?

So it is not the attitude that some lives are not worth living that marks out the Nazis from normal people who do not commit mass murder. What then is it? Is it that they went beyond passive euthanasia and practised active euthanasia? Many, like Lorber, worry about the power that a program of active euthanasia could place in the hands of an unscrupulous government. This worry is not negligible but should not be exaggerated. Unscrupulous governments already have within their power more plausible means of getting rid of their opponents than euthanasia administered by doctors on medical grounds. 'Suicides' can be arranged. 'Accidents' can occur. If necessary, assassins can be hired, and their crimes blamed on others. Our best defence against such possibilities is to do everything possible to keep our government democratic, open, and in the hands of people who would not seriously wish to kill their opponents. Once the wish is serious enough, governments will find a way, whether euthanasia is legal or not.

In fact, the Nazis did not have a euthanasia program, in the proper sense of the word. Their so-called euthanasia program was not motivated by concern for the suffering of those killed. If it had been, they would not have kept their operations secret, deceived relatives about the cause of death of those killed, or exempted from the program certain privileged classes, such as veterans of the armed services or relatives of the euthanasia staff. Nazi 'euthanasia' was never voluntary and often was involuntary rather than nonvoluntary. 'Doing away with useless mouths' – a phrase used by those in charge – gives a better idea of the objectives of the program than 'mercy-killing'. Both racial origin and ability to work were among the factors considered in the selection of patients to be killed. It was the Nazi belief in the importance of maintaining a pure Aryan *Volk* – a quasi-mystical racist concept that was thought of as more important than mere individuals' lives – that made both the so-called euthanasia program and later the entire holocaust possible. Proposals for the legalization of euthanasia, on the other hand, are based on respect for autonomy and the goal of avoiding pointless suffering.

Hence, there is little prospect that legalizing euthanasia will lead us to slide into the abyss of Nazi-style atrocities. It could still be argued that no matter how arbitrary the distinctions between human and nonhuman, fetus and infant, and killing and allowing to die, may be, the rule that it is always wrong to kill an innocent human being at least marks a workable line. The distinction between an infant whose life may be worth living and one whose life definitely is not is much more difficult to draw. Perhaps people who see that some kinds of human beings may be killed in certain circumstances are more likely to conclude that it is not wrong to kill others not very different from the first kind. So will the boundary of acceptable killing be pushed gradually back? In the absence of any logical stopping place, will the outcome be the loss of all respect for human life?

If our laws were altered so that anyone could carry out an act of euthanasia, the absence of a clear line between those who might justifiably be killed and those who might not would pose a real danger; but that is not what advocates of euthanasia propose. If acts of euthanasia can only be carried out by a member of the medical profession, with the concurrence of a second doctor, it is not likely that the propensity to kill would spread unchecked throughout the community. Doctors already have a good deal of power over life and death through their ability to withhold treatment. There has been no suggestion that doctors who begin by allowing severely disabled infants to die from pneumonia will move on to withhold antibiotics from political extremists or patients who belong to a racial minority. In fact, legalizing euthanasia might well act as a check on the power of doctors because it would bring what some doctors do now, on their own initiative and in secret, into the open and under the scrutiny of another doctor.

There is, anyway, little historical evidence to suggest that a permissive attitude towards the killing of one category of human beings leads to a breakdown of restrictions against killing other humans. Ancient Greeks regularly killed or exposed infants but appear to have been at least as scrupulous about taking the lives of their fellow citizens as medieval Christians or modern Americans. In traditional Eskimo societies, it was the custom for a man to kill his elderly parents, but the murder of a normal healthy adult was almost unheard of. I mention these practices, not to suggest that they should be imitated, but only to indicate that lines can be drawn at places other than where we now draw them. If these societies could separate human beings into different categories without transferring their attitudes from one group to another, we with our more sophisticated legal systems and greater medical knowledge should be able to do the same.

All of this is not to deny that departing from the traditional sanctity of life ethic carries with it a small but nevertheless finite risk of unwanted consequences. Against this risk we must balance the tangible harm to which the traditional ethic gives rise – harm to those whose misery is needlessly prolonged. We must also ask if the widespread acceptance of abortion and passive euthanasia has not already revealed flaws in the traditional ethic that make it a weak defence against those who lack respect for individual lives. A sounder, if less clear-cut, ethic may in the long run provide a firmer ground for resisting unjustifiable killing.

8

Rich and Poor

SOME FACTS ABOUT POVERTY

At the end of the twentieth century, the World Bank sent out a team of researchers to record the views of 60,000 women and men living in extreme poverty. Visiting seventy-three countries, the research team heard, over and over, that poverty meant these things:

- You are short of food for all or part of the year, often eating only one meal per day, sometimes having to choose between stilling your child's hunger or your own, and sometimes being able to do neither.
- You can't save money. If a family member falls ill and you need money to see a doctor, or if the crop fails and you have nothing to eat, you have to borrow from a local moneylender; he will charge you so much interest that the debt continues to mount, and you may never be free of it.
- You can't afford to send your children to school; or if they do start school, you have to take them out again if the harvest is poor.
- You live in an unstable house, made with mud or thatch that you need to rebuild every two or three years, or after severe weather.
- You have no close source of safe drinking water. You have to carry it a long way, and even then, it can make you ill unless you boil it.

Along with these material deprivations goes, very often, a humiliating state of powerlessness, vulnerability and a deep sense of shame or failure.

Extreme poverty, as defined by the World Bank, means not having enough income to meet the most basic human needs for adequate food, water, shelter, clothing, sanitation, health care or education. In 2008, the

Bank calculated that this requires a daily income that is the purchasing power equivalent of about US$1.25 per day in the United States. This is not the foreign exchange equivalent of US$1.25, which might not be so bad, because as everyone who travels from a rich country to a poor one knows, the currencies of rich countries often have much greater purchasing power in poor countries. The World Bank's definition takes that difference into account: the poor earn only as much as will buy, in their currency, the quantity of necessities that $1.25 will buy in the United States. The bank estimates that 1.4 billion people have less income than this.

In industrialized countries, people are poor by comparison to others in their society. Their poverty is relative – they have enough to meet their basic needs and usually access to free health care as well. The 1.4 billion people living in extreme poverty in developing countries are poor by an absolute standard: they have difficulty meeting their basic needs. Absolute poverty kills. According to UNICEF, the United Nations International Children's Emergency Fund, 8.8 million children under five years old died from avoidable, poverty-related causes in 2008. That comes to 24,000 – think of it as a football stadium full of children – dying unnecessarily every day. (The number of children dying has been falling steadily since the 1960s but still remains far too high.) Millions of adults also die because of absolute poverty. Life expectancy in the rich nations is now seventy-eight years; in developing countries, it is around fifty. When absolute poverty does not cause death, it still causes misery of a kind not often seen in the affluent nations. Malnutrition in young children stunts both physical and mental development. Millions of people on poor diets suffer from deficiency diseases, like goiter, or blindness caused by a lack of vitamin A. The food value of what the poor eat is further reduced by parasites such as hookworm and ringworm, which are endemic in conditions of poor sanitation and health education.

Death and disease apart, absolute poverty remains a miserable condition of life, with inadequate food, shelter, clothing, sanitation, health services and education. This is the 'normal' situation of our world. At least ten times as many people died from preventable, poverty-related diseases on September 11, 2001, as died in the terrorist attacks on the World Trade Center and the Pentagon on that black day. The terrorist attacks led to trillions of dollars being spent on the 'war on terrorism' and on security measures that have inconvenienced every air traveller since then. The deaths caused by poverty were ignored. So whereas very few people have died from terrorism since September 11, 2001, approximately 30,000 people died from poverty-related causes on September 12, 2001, and on every day between then and now, and will die tomorrow. Even when we consider larger events, like the Asian tsunami of 2004, which killed approximately 230,000 people, or the 2010 earthquake in Haiti that killed up to 200,000, we are still talking about numbers that represent just one week's toll for preventable, poverty-related deaths – and that happens fifty-two weeks in every year.

SOME FACTS ABOUT AFFLUENCE

We can juxtapose a picture of 'absolute affluence' against this picture of absolute poverty. Those who are absolutely affluent are not necessarily affluent by comparison with their neighbours, but they have more income than they need to provide themselves adequately with all the basic necessities of life. After buying (either directly or through their taxes) food, shelter, clothing, basic health services and education, the absolutely affluent still have money to spend on luxuries. The absolutely affluent choose their food for the pleasures of the palate, not to stop hunger; they buy new clothes to look good, not to keep warm; they move house to be in a better neighbourhood or have more space for the children to play, not to keep out the rain; and after all this, there is still money to spend on home entertainment centres and exotic holidays.

At this stage, I am making no ethical judgments about absolute affluence; I am merely pointing out that it exists. Its defining characteristic is a significant amount of income above the level necessary to provide for the basic human needs of oneself and one's dependents. By this standard, the majority of citizens of Europe, North America, Japan, Australia, New Zealand and the oil-rich Middle Eastern states are all absolutely affluent. There are also hundreds of millions of affluent people in countries like China, India and Brazil, although there is also extreme poverty in those countries. These affluent people have wealth that they could, without threatening their own basic welfare, transfer to the extremely poor.

At present, very little is being transferred. In 1970, the United Nations General Assembly set a modest target for the amount of foreign aid that the rich nations should give: 0.7 percent of Gross National Income, or 70 cents for every hundred dollars a nation earns. Forty years later, only Denmark, Luxembourg, The Netherlands, Norway and Sweden have reached that level. In 2008, the United States and Japan, the two largest economies among the affluent nations, gave only 0.19 percent, or 19 cents in every $100 they earned. Australia and Canada did only slightly better, at 0.32 percent, whereas France, Germany and Britain were around the average for affluent nations, giving between 0.38 and 0.43 percent. In comparison to their income, what the rich nations are giving is relatively trivial.

THE MORAL EQUIVALENT OF MURDER?

These facts suggest that, by giving far less than they could, rich people are allowing more than a billion people to continue to live in conditions of deprivation and to die prematurely. This conclusion applies not only to governments but to each affluent individual, for each of us has the opportunity to do something about the situation; for instance, to give our time or money to voluntary organizations that are helping to provide health care, safe drinking water, education and better agricultural techniques for the poor. If, then, allowing someone to die is not intrinsically different from killing someone, it would seem that we are all murderers.

Is this verdict too harsh? Many will reject it as self-evidently absurd. They would sooner take it as showing that allowing to die cannot be equivalent to killing than as showing that living in an affluent style without contributing to an aid agency is ethically equivalent to going over to Ethiopia and shooting a few peasants. They point to several significant differences between spending money on luxuries, when we could use it to save lives, and deliberately shooting people. Let us look at some of these differences and then consider which of them really are morally significant.

First, the motivation will normally be different. Those who deliberately shoot others go out of their way to kill. Motivated by malice, sadism or some equally unpleasant motives, they want their victims dead. A person who buys an iPod presumably wants to enhance her enjoyment of music – not in itself a terrible thing. At worst, spending money on luxuries instead of giving it away indicates selfishness and indifference to the sufferings of others, characteristics that may be undesirable but are not comparable to actual malice or similar motives.

Second, it is not difficult for most of us to act in accordance with a rule against killing people: it is, on the other hand, very difficult to obey a rule that commands us to save all the lives we can. To live a comfortable or even luxurious life, it is not necessary to kill anyone, but we do have to allow to die some whom we might have saved, for the money that we need to live comfortably could have been given away. Thus, the duty to avoid killing is much easier to discharge completely than the duty to save. Saving every life we possibly could save would mean cutting our standard of living down to the bare essentials needed to keep us alive.* To discharge this duty completely would require a degree of moral heroism utterly different from that required by mere avoidance of killing.

A third difference is the greater certainty of the outcome of shooting when compared with not giving aid. If I point a loaded gun at someone at close range and pull the trigger, it is virtually certain that the person will be killed; whereas the money that I could give might be spent on a project that turns out to be unsuccessful and helps no one.

Fourth, when people are shot, there are identifiable individuals who have been harmed. We can point to them and to their grieving families. When I buy my iPod, I cannot know who my money would have saved if I had given it away.

Fifth, it might be said that the plight of the hungry is not my doing, and so I cannot be held responsible for it. The starving would have been starving if I had never existed. If I kill, however, I am responsible for my victims' deaths, for those people would not have died if I had not killed them.

These differences need not shake our previous conclusion that there is no intrinsic difference between killing and allowing to die. They are extrinsic differences, that is, differences normally but not necessarily associated with the distinction between killing and allowing to die. We can imagine cases in which someone allows another to die for malicious or sadistic reasons. We can imagine a world in which there are so few people needing assistance and they are so easy to assist, that our duty not to allow people to die is as easily discharged as our duty not to kill. We can imagine situations in which the outcome of not helping is as sure as shooting. We can imagine cases in which we can identify the person we allow to die. We can even imagine a case of allowing to die in which, if I had not existed, the person would not have died – for instance, a case in which if I had not been in a position to help (though I didn't help), someone else would have been in my position and would have helped. These imaginary situations aside, however, it is true that the extrinsic differences that *normally* mark off killing and allowing to die help to explain why we *normally* regard killing as much worse than allowing to die. To explain our conventional ethical attitudes, however, is not to justify

* Strictly, we would need to cut down to the minimum level compatible with earning the income which, after providing for our needs, left us most to give away. Thus, if my present position pays me $100,000 a year but requires me to spend $30,000 a year on living in a more expensive location than I otherwise might, I cannot save more people by moving to an inexpensive rural area if that will mean taking a job that pays only $60,000.

them. Do the five differences not only explain, but also justify, our attitudes? Let us consider them one by one.

(1) Take the lack of an identifiable victim first. Research has shown that people offered an opportunity to give to a poor child are more likely to give if they are shown a photograph of the child and told her name and age than if they are not given any identifying details. But this may show no more than that, during the millions of years in which our ancestors lived in small face-to-face groups, we developed an instinctive response to help individuals. In contrast, we did not develop any response to giving more anonymous forms of aid, for which there was no opportunity anyway. Should this make any difference to our ethical obligations? Suppose that I am a travelling salesperson, selling tinned food, and I learn that a batch of tins contains a contaminant, the known effect of which, when consumed, is to double the risk that the consumer will die from stomach cancer. Suppose I continue to sell the tins. My decision may have no identifiable victims. Some of those who eat the food will die from stomach cancer. The proportion of consumers dying in this way will be twice that of the community at large, but who among the consumers died because they ate what I sold, and who would have contracted the disease anyway? It is impossible to tell; but surely this impossibility makes my decision no less reprehensible than it would have been had the contaminant had more readily detectable, though equally fatal, effects. Moreover, if this is true for killing an unidentifiable individual, why should it be any different for failing to save one?

(2) The lack of certainty that by giving money I could save a life does reduce the wrongness of not giving, by comparison with deliberate killing; but it is insufficient to show that not giving is acceptable conduct. The motorist who speeds through pedestrian crossings, heedless of anyone who might be on them, is not a murderer. She may never actually hit a pedestrian; yet if she knowingly risks killing an innocent person, what she does is very wrong indeed.

(3) The idea that we are responsible for our acts but not for our omissions is more puzzling. On the one hand, we feel ourselves to be under a greater obligation to help those whose misfortunes we have caused. (It is for this reason that advocates of increased foreign aid often argue that the rich nations have created the poverty of the poor nations, through forms of economic exploitation that go back to the colonial system.) On the other hand, any consequentialist would insist that we are responsible for all the consequences of our actions; and if a consequence of my spending money on an iPod is that someone dies, I am responsible

for that death. It is true that the person would have died even if I had never existed, but what is the relevance of that? The fact is that I do exist, and the consequentialist will say that our responsibilities derive from the world as it is, not as it might have been.

One way of making sense of the non-consequentialist view of responsibility is to base it on a theory of rights of the kind proposed by John Locke and more recently defended by libertarians like Robert Nozick and Jan Narveson. If everyone has a right to life, and this right is a right *against* others who might threaten my life but not a right *to* assistance from others when my life is in danger, then we can understand the feeling that we are responsible for killing but not for omitting to save. The former violates the rights of others, the latter does not.

Should we accept such a theory of rights? If we build up our theory of rights by imagining, as Locke and Nozick do, individuals living independently from one another in a 'state of nature', it may seem natural to adopt a conception of rights in which as long as each leaves the other alone, no rights are violated. I might, on this view, quite properly have maintained my independent existence if I had wished to do so. So if I do not make you any worse off than you would have been if I had had nothing at all to do with you, how can I have violated your rights? The factual basis of this theory is doubtful. Thomas Pogge challenges it in *World Poverty and Human Rights*, arguing that several features of the world economic order show that we contribute to the impoverishment of some people to our own benefit. To take just one example, we rely on oil and minerals bought from countries ruled by dictators who use the money to enrich themselves or to strengthen their armies and entrench themselves in power. These dictators have no moral right to the wealth that lies beneath the soil of the countries in which they have seized power. The proceeds should go to the people of the country as a whole. The dictators are robbers and murderers, and we are receivers of stolen goods. Our willingness to hand over billions of dollars to dictators in return for oil and mineral rights also creates a huge incentive for anyone who fancies their chances of overthrowing an existing government, and thus increases instability in these countries, which in turn contributes to poverty. (Climate change creates another problem for the view that we are not harming the poor – but that is the topic of the next chapter.)

Even if we put aside such problems with the factual basis of the libertarian argument, we need to ask why we should start from the unhistorical, abstract and ultimately inexplicable idea of a human being living independently. Our ancestors were – like other primates – social beings long before they were human beings, and they could not have developed the abilities and capacities of human beings if they had not been social beings first. We are not, now, isolated individuals, and we never have been. So why should we assume that rights must be restricted to rights against interference? We might, instead, adopt the view that taking rights to life seriously is incompatible with standing by and watching people die when one could easily save them.

(4) What of the difference in motivation? That a person does not positively wish for the death of another lessens the severity of the blame she deserves, but not by as much as is suggested by our present attitudes to giving aid. The behaviour of the speeding motorist is again comparable, for such motorists usually have no desire at all to kill anyone. They merely want to get somewhere sooner, or they enjoy speeding and are indifferent to the consequences. Despite their lack of malice, those who kill with cars deserve not only blame but also severe punishment.

(5) The difference I have left for last is the most significant. The fact that to avoid killing people is normally not difficult whereas to save all one possibly could save is heroic must make an important difference to our attitude to failure to do what the respective principles demand. Not to kill is a minimum standard of acceptable conduct we can require of everyone. In contrast, to save all one possibly could is not something that can realistically be required, especially not in societies accustomed to giving as little as ours do. Given the generally accepted standards, people who give, say, 10 percent of what they earn to help the poor are more aptly praised for their above-average generosity than blamed for giving less than they might. The appropriateness of praise and blame is, however, a separate issue from the rightness or wrongness of actions. The former evaluates the agent; the latter evaluates the action. Perhaps many people who give 10 percent really ought to give 50 percent, but to blame them for not giving more could be counterproductive. It might make them feel that what is required is too demanding, and if one is going to be blamed anyway, one might as well not give anything at all. That an ethic that puts saving all one possibly can on the same footing as not killing would be an ethic for saints or heroes should not lead us to assume that the alternative must be an ethic that makes it obligatory not to kill but puts us under no obligation to save anyone. There are positions in between these extremes, as we shall see.

Let's summarize the five differences that normally exist between killing and allowing to die in the context of extreme poverty and overseas aid. The lack of an identifiable victim is of no moral significance, though it may play an important role in explaining our attitudes. The idea that we are directly responsible for those we kill, but not for those we do not help, depends on a questionable notion of responsibility and may need to be based on a dubious theory of rights. Differences in certainty and motivation are ethically significant and show that not aiding the poor is not to be condemned as murdering them; it could, however, be on a par with killing someone as a result of reckless driving, which is serious enough. Finally, the difficulty of completely discharging the duty of saving all one possibly can makes it inappropriate to blame those who fall short of this target in the same way that we blame those who kill; but this does not show that the act itself is less serious. Nor does it excuse those who make no effort to save anyone.

In any case, whereas failing to save a life may not always be ethically on par with deliberate killing, it is clear that how we respond to the existence of both absolute poverty and absolute affluence is one of the great moral issues of our time. So let us consider afresh whether we have an obligation to assist those whose lives are in danger and, if so, how this obligation applies to the present world situation.

THE OBLIGATION TO ASSIST

The Argument for an Obligation to Assist

On my way to give a lecture, I pass a shallow ornamental pond and notice that a small child has fallen in and is in danger of drowning. I look around to see where the parents, or babysitter, are, but to my surprise, I see that there is no one else around. It seems that it is up to me to make sure that the child doesn't drown. Would anyone deny that I ought to wade in and pull the child out? This will mean getting my clothes muddy, ruining my shoes and either cancelling my lecture or delaying it until I can find something dry to change into; but compared with the avoidable death of a child none of these things are significant.

A plausible principle that would support the judgment that I ought to pull the child out is this: if it is in our power to prevent something very bad happening, without thereby sacrificing anything of comparable moral significance, we ought to do it. This principle seems uncontroversial. It will obviously win the assent of consequentialists; but non-consequentialists should accept it too, because the injunction to prevent what is bad applies only when nothing comparably significant is at stake. Thus, the principle cannot lead to the kinds of actions of which non-consequentialists strongly disapprove – serious violations of individual rights, injustice, broken promises and so on. If non-consequentialists regard any of these as comparable in moral significance to the bad thing that is to be prevented, they will automatically regard the principle as not applying in those cases in which the bad thing can only be prevented by violating rights, doing injustice, breaking promises or whatever else is at stake. Most non-consequentialists hold that we ought to prevent what is bad and promote what is good. Their dispute with consequentialists lies in their insistence that this is not the sole ultimate ethical principle: that it is *an* ethical principle is not denied by any plausible ethical theory.

Nevertheless, the uncontroversial appearance of the principle that we ought to prevent what is bad when we can do so without sacrificing anything of comparable moral significance is deceptive. If it were taken seriously and acted on, our lives and our world would be fundamentally changed. For the principle applies, not just to rare situations in which one can save a child from a pond, but to the everyday situation in which we can assist those living in absolute poverty. In saying this, I assume that absolute poverty, with its hunger and malnutrition, lack of shelter, illiteracy, disease, high infant mortality and low life expectancy, is a bad thing. Additionally, I assume that it is within the power of the affluent to reduce absolute poverty, without sacrificing anything of comparable moral significance. If these two assumptions and the principle we have been discussing are correct, we have an obligation to help those in absolute poverty that is no less strong than our obligation to rescue a drowning child from a pond. Not to help would be wrong, whether or not it is intrinsically equivalent to killing. Helping is not, as conventionally thought, a charitable act that is praiseworthy to do but not wrong to omit. It is something that everyone ought to do.

Set out more formally, this argument would look like this.

First premise: If we can prevent something bad without sacrificing anything of comparable significance, we ought to do it.

Second premise: Extreme poverty is bad.

Third premise: There is some extreme poverty we can prevent without sacrificing anything of comparable moral significance.

Conclusion: We ought to prevent some extreme poverty.

The first premise is the substantive moral premise on which the argument rests, and I have tried to show that it can be accepted by people who hold a variety of ethical positions.

The second premise is unlikely to be challenged. It would be hard to find a plausible ethical view that did not regard extreme poverty, with the suffering and deaths of both adults and children that it causes, not to mention the lack of education, sense of hopelessness, powerlessness and humiliation that are also its effects, as a bad thing.

The third premise is more controversial, even though it is cautiously framed. It claims only that some extreme poverty can be prevented without the sacrifice of anything of comparable moral significance. It thus avoids the objection that any aid I can give is just 'drops in the ocean', for the point is not whether my personal contribution will make any noticeable impression on world poverty as a whole (of course it won't) but whether it will prevent some poverty. This is all the argument needs to sustain its conclusion, because the second premise says that any extreme poverty is bad and not merely the total amount of extreme poverty. If without sacrificing anything of comparable moral significance we can provide just one family with the means to raise itself out of extreme poverty, the third premise is vindicated.

Nevertheless, some will argue that I can't have any confidence that my donation to an aid organization will save a life or will help people to lift themselves out of extreme poverty. Often these arguments are based on demonstrably false beliefs, such as the idea that aid organizations use most of the money given to them for administrative costs, so that only a small fraction gets through to the people who need it, or that corrupt governments in developing nations will take the money. In fact, the major aid organizations use no more than 20 percent of the funds they raise for administrative purposes, leaving at least 80 percent for the programs that directly help the poor; and they do not donate to governments but work directly with the poor, or with grassroots organizations in developing countries that have a good record of helping the poor.

Measuring the effectiveness of an aid organization by the extent to which it can reduce its administrative costs is, however, a common mistake. Administrative costs include the salaries of experienced people who can ensure that your donation will fund projects that really help the poor in a sustainable, long-term way. An organization that does not employ such people may have lower administrative costs than one that does, but it will still achieve less with your donation.

GiveWell.org is not an aid organization but an organization that seeks hard evidence about which organizations are most effective. It has, for example, compared the cost per life saved of various organizations that work to combat the diseases that kill many of those 8.8 million children who die each year from poverty-related causes. According to GiveWell, there are several organizations that can save a life for somewhere in the range of $600 to $1200, and on the GiveWell.org Web site, you can see which it ranks most highly. Because you can give to one of the top-ranked organizations, it seems clear that the third premise of the argument is true for people who spend at least a few hundred dollars a year on things they do not really need. They can save a life, or prevent some extreme poverty, without sacrificing anything of comparable moral significance.

I have left the notion of moral significance unexamined in order to show that the argument does not depend on any specific values or ethical principles. On any defensible view of what is morally significant, the third premise will be true for most people living in industrialized nations. Our affluence means that we have income we can dispose of without giving up the basic necessities of life, and we can use this income to reduce extreme poverty. Just how much we will think ourselves obliged to give up will depend on what we consider to be of comparable moral significance to the poverty we could prevent: stylish clothes, expensive dinners, a sophisticated stereo system, exotic holidays, a luxury car, a larger house, private schools for our children and so on. For a utilitarian, none of these is likely to be of comparable significance to the reduction of extreme poverty; and those who are not utilitarians surely must, if they subscribe to the principle of universalizability, accept that at least *some* of these things are of far less moral significance than the extreme poverty that could be prevented by the money they cost. So the third premise seems to be true on any plausible ethical view – although the precise amount of extreme poverty that can be prevented before anything of comparable moral significance is sacrificed will vary according to the ethical view one accepts.

Objections to the Argument

Taking Care of Our Own

Anyone who has worked to increase foreign aid will have come across the argument that we should look after those near us, our families and then the poor in our own country before we think about poverty in distant places.

No doubt we instinctively prefer to help those who are close to us. Few could stand by and watch a child drown; many can ignore the avoidable deaths of children in Africa or India. The question, however, is not what we usually do, but what we ought to do, and it is difficult to see any sound moral justification for the view that distance, or community membership, makes a crucial difference to our obligations.

Consider, for instance, racial affinities. Should people of European origin help poor Europeans before helping poor Africans? Most of us would reject such a suggestion, and our discussion of the principle of equal consideration of interests in Chapter 2 has shown why we should reject it: people's need for food has nothing to do with their race, and if Africans are in greater need than Europeans, it would be a violation of the principle of equal consideration to give preference to Europeans.

The same point applies to citizenship or nationhood. Every affluent nation has some relatively poor citizens, but absolute poverty is limited largely to the developing nations. In the United States, a family of four is officially classified as poor if they have an annual income of less than $22,000. It can be very difficult to support a family on that income in the United States, but clearly it will take several thousand dollars to make a significant improvement in the lives of people in that situation. In developing countries, on the other hand, it costs less than $1,000 to save the life of a child who would otherwise die from a poverty-related disease, and to double the income of ten families living in extreme poverty would take less than $5,000. (The figure is merely for comparison – I am not suggesting that the best way to reduce poverty is to give money directly to the poor.) Because everyone's resources are limited, it makes sense to use them where they can have the most beneficial impact. Under these circumstances, it would be wrong to decide that only those fortunate enough to be citizens of our own affluent community will share our abundance.

We feel obligations of kinship more strongly than those of citizenship. What kind of parents could give away their last bowl of rice if their own children were starving? To do so would seem unnatural. Indeed, it would be contrary to our nature as biologically evolved mammals with offspring who are dependent on us for many years – but that alone would not show that it was wrong to do so. In any case, we are not faced with that situation but with one in which our own children are well fed, well clothed, well educated and would now like new bikes or more sophisticated computer games. In these circumstances, any special obligations we might have to our children have been fulfilled, and the needs of strangers make a stronger claim on us.

The element of truth in the view that we should first take care of our own lies in the advantage of a recognized system of responsibilities. When families and local communities look after their own poorer members, ties of affection and personal relationships achieve ends that would otherwise require a large, impersonal bureaucracy. Hence, it would be absurd to propose that from now on we all regard ourselves as equally responsible for the welfare of everyone in the world; but the argument for an obligation to assist does not propose that. It applies only when some are in extreme poverty, and others can help without sacrificing anything of comparable moral significance. To allow one's own kin to sink into extreme poverty would be to sacrifice something of comparable significance; and well before that point had been reached, the breakdown of the system of family and community responsibility would be a factor to weigh the balance in favour of a modest preference for family and community. This modest degree of preference is, however, decisively outweighed by existing discrepancies in wealth and property.

Property Rights

Do people have a right to private property, a right that contradicts the view that they are under an obligation to give some of their wealth away to those in absolute poverty? According to some theories of rights, people who have acquired their property without the use of unjust means like force and fraud may be entitled to great wealth and every conceivable luxury while others starve. This individualistic conception of rights is in contrast to other views, like the Christian doctrine that holds that property exists for the satisfaction of human needs; and so, as Thomas Aquinas wrote, 'whatever a man has in superabundance is owed, of natural right, to the poor for their sustenance'. A socialist would also, of course, see wealth as belonging to the community rather than the individual; whereas utilitarians, whether socialist or not, would be prepared to override property rights to prevent great evils.

Does the argument for an obligation to assist others therefore presuppose one of these other theories of property rights and reject the idea of a strong individual right to property? Not necessarily. A theory of property rights can insist on our *right* to retain wealth without pronouncing on whether the rich *ought* to give to the poor. Robert Nozick, for example, rejected the use of compulsory means like taxation to redistribute income, but he suggested that we can achieve the ends we deem morally desirable by voluntary means. So Nozick would have rejected the claim that rich people have an 'obligation' to give to the poor, insofar as this implies that the poor have a right to our aid, but could have agreed that giving is something we ought to do and failing to give – though within one's rights – is wrong, for there is more to an ethical life than respecting the rights of others.

The argument for an obligation to assist can survive, with only minor modifications, even if we accept an individualistic theory of property rights. In any case, however, I do not think we should accept such a theory. It leaves too much to chance to be an acceptable ethical view. For instance, many of those whose forefathers happened to inhabit some sandy wastes around the Persian Gulf are now fabulously wealthy, because oil lay under those sands; whereas many of those whose forefathers settled on better land south of the Sahara live in extreme poverty, because of drought and bad harvests. Can this distribution be acceptable from an impartial point of view? If we imagine ourselves about to begin life as a citizen of either Kuwait or Chad – but we do not know which – would we accept the principle that citizens of Kuwait are under no obligation to assist people living in Chad?

Population and the Ethics of Triage

Perhaps the most serious objection to the argument that we have an obligation to assist is that because the major cause of extreme poverty is overpopulation, helping those currently in poverty will only ensure that yet more people are born to live in poverty in the future.

In its most extreme form, this objection is taken to show that we should adopt a policy of 'triage'. The term comes from medical policies adopted in wartime. With too few doctors to cope with all the casualties, the wounded were divided into three categories: those who would probably survive without medical assistance, those who might survive if they received assistance but otherwise probably would not, and those who even with medical assistance probably would not survive. Only those in the middle category were treated. The idea, of course, was to use limited medical resources as effectively as possible. For those in the first category, medical treatment was not strictly necessary; for those in the third category, it was likely to be useless. In the 1970s, some suggested that we should apply the same policies to countries, according to their prospects of becoming self-sustaining. If we were to accept that view, we would not aid countries that, even without our help, will soon be able to feed their populations. We would not aid countries that, even with our help, will not be able to limit their population to a level they can feed. We would aid those countries where our help might make the difference between success and failure in bringing food and population into balance.

In support of this view, Garrett Hardin offered a metaphor: we in the rich nations are like the occupants of a crowded lifeboat adrift in a sea full of drowning people. If we try to save the drowning by bringing them aboard, our boat will be overloaded and we shall all drown. Because it is better that some survive than none, we should leave the others to drown. In the world today, according to Hardin, 'lifeboat ethics' apply. The rich should leave the poor to starve, for otherwise the poor will drag the rich down with them. He cited India and Bangladesh as examples of countries in which the population was increasing beyond the carrying capacity of the land they occupied. So, he suggested they should be left alone until famine, disease and natural disasters had reduced their population to the level at which they can support it.

Against this view, some writers have argued that overpopulation is a myth. The world produces ample food to feed its population and could, according to some estimates, feed several times as many. People are hungry not because there are too many people but because of inequitable land distribution and because the international political and economic system exploits the poor nations for the benefit of the rich.

The world does produce enough to feed its inhabitants – in fact we waste vast quantities of grain and soybeans by feeding them to animals, getting back from the animals only a small fraction of the nutritional value of the plant foods we put into them. We also waste further significant quantities of grain by turning it into biofuel so we can drive more. In fact, the amount of grain we feed to animals would be enough to give *all* of the 1.4 billion people now living in extreme poverty more than twice the calories they need.

Since Hardin wrote about 'lifeboat ethics,' the populations of India and Bangladesh have continued to grow, but the capacities of those countries to feed their populations have proved much greater than Hardin thought possible. These countries now have a smaller proportion of their people going hungry than they had when Hardin advocated shutting off aid to them. Nevertheless, it is hard not to be alarmed by the population growth rates of some African nations. By 2050, the population of Nigeria, for example, is expected to almost double from its present size of 144 million. By then, Ethiopia, now with 77 million people, is predicted to have 146 million, and the Democratic Republic of Congo will have 187 million, almost three times its current population of 63 million. The question is: how should we respond to these rapid rates of population growth in countries that already have a large proportion of their population living in extreme poverty? Advocates of triage propose that we allow the population growth of such countries to be checked by a rise in death rates – that would mean, in practice, by famines, malnutrition, increased infant mortality or epidemics of infectious diseases.

These consequences are so horrible that we are inclined to reject, without further thought, triage on this scale. How could we sit by our televisions watching millions starve while we do nothing? Would not that be the end of all notions of human equality and respect for human life? Anyone whose initial reaction to triage was not one of repugnance would be an unpleasant sort of person. Yet initial reactions based on strong feelings are not always reliable guides. Advocates of triage are rightly concerned with the long-term consequences of our actions. They say that helping people who are extremely poor now merely ensures that there will be more extremely poor and starving people in the future. When we tire of helping, or our capacity to help is finally unable to cope, the suffering will be greater than it would be if we stopped helping now. If this were correct, there would be nothing we could do to prevent extreme poverty, in the long run, and so we would have no obligation to assist. Nor does it seem reasonable to hold that under these circumstances people have a right to our assistance. If we do accept such a right irrespective of the consequences, we are saying that, in Hardin's metaphor, we should continue to haul the drowning into our lifeboat until the boat sinks and we all drown.

If triage is to be rejected, it must be tackled on its own ground, within the framework of consequentialist ethics. Here it is vulnerable. Any consequentialist ethics must take probability of outcome into account. A course of action that will certainly produce some benefit is to be preferred to an alternative course that may lead to a slightly larger benefit but is equally likely to result in no benefit at all. Only if the greater magnitude of the uncertain benefit outweighs its uncertainty should we choose it. Better one certain unit of benefit than a 10 percent chance of five units; but better a 50 percent chance of three units than a single certain unit. The same principle applies when we are trying to avoid evils.

Advocates of shutting off aid to the poorest countries predict that this will result in a very great evil: population control by famine and disease. Tens of millions would die slowly. Hundreds of millions would continue to live in extreme poverty, at the very margin of existence. Against this prospect, those who support this policy place a possible evil that is greater still: the same process of famine and disease taking place in, say, fifty years' time when the world's population will be at least 50 percent greater than its present level and the number who will die from famine or struggle on in extreme poverty will be that much greater. The question is: how probable is this forecast that continued assistance now will lead to greater disasters in the future?

Forecasts of population growth are notoriously fallible, and theories about the factors that affect it remain speculative. The most widely accepted model of population changes postulates that countries pass through a 'demographic transition' as their standard of living rises. When people are very poor and have no access to modern medicine, their fertility is high, but population is kept in check by high death rates, especially infant mortality. The introduction of sanitation, modern medical techniques and other improvements reduces child mortality, and initially population grows rapidly. Some poor countries, especially in sub-Saharan Africa, are now in this phase. As child mortality falls, however, couples begin to realize that to have the same number of children surviving to maturity as in the past, they do not need to give birth to as many children as their parents did. The need for children to provide economic support in old age may also diminish. Improved education and the emancipation and employment of women reduce the birth rate, and so population growth begins to level off. Most rich nations have reached this stage, and their populations are – aside from immigration – growing only very slowly, if at all.

If this model is right, there is an alternative to the disasters accepted as inevitable by those who think that aid only promotes population growth. We can assist poor countries to raise the living standards of the poorest members of their population. We can encourage the governments of these countries to enact land reform measures, improve education, educate women and provide them with alternatives to a purely child-bearing role. We can also help other countries to make contraception and sterilization widely available. There is a fair chance that these measures will hasten the onset of the demographic transition and bring population growth down to a manageable level. According to United Nations estimates, the total fertility rate in developing countries fell from six births per woman in the late 1960s to less than three births at the beginning of the twenty-first century. Notable successes in encouraging the use of contraception during this period have occurred in Thailand, Indonesia, Mexico, Colombia, Brazil and Bangladesh. These achievements reflected a relatively low expenditure in developing countries – considering the size and significance of the problem – with only a small part of the money coming from developed nations. So expenditure in this area seems likely to be highly cost-effective. Admittedly, there are signs that the decline in fertility is slowing, and even stalling, in some countries, so there is a real need to remain focused on the dangers of continued population growth. Nevertheless, the evidence concerning the impact on population growth of improvements in economic security and education, and in making contraceptives more widely available, is sufficient to render shutting off aid ethically unacceptable. We cannot allow millions to die from starvation and disease when there is a reasonable probability that population growth can be brought under control without such horrors.

Population growth is not a reason against giving aid but a reason for reconsidering the kind of aid to give. This may mean putting more resources into education, especially the education of women, or into the provision of contraceptive services. Whatever kind of aid proves most effective in specific circumstances, the obligation to assist is not reduced.

One awkward question remains. What should we do about a poor and already overpopulated country that, for religious or nationalistic reasons, restricts the use of contraceptives and refuses to slow its population growth? Should we nevertheless offer development assistance? Or should we make our offer conditional on effective steps being taken to reduce the birth rate? To the latter course, some would object that putting conditions on aid is an attempt to impose our own ideas on independent sovereign nations. So it is – but is this imposition unjustifiable? If the argument for an obligation to assist is sound, we have an obligation to reduce extreme poverty; but we have no obligation to make sacrifices that, to the best of our knowledge, have no prospect of reducing extreme poverty in the long run – and could even increase it. Hence, we have no obligation to assist countries whose governments have policies that will undermine the effectiveness of our aid. This could be very harsh on poor citizens of these countries – for they may have no say in their government's policies – but we will help more people in the long run by using our resources where they are most effective. (The same principles may apply, incidentally, to countries that refuse to take other steps that could make assistance effective – like refusing to allow women to be educated.)

Leaving it to the Government

We often hear that foreign aid should be a government responsibility and not left to private charity. Giving privately, it is said, allows the government to escape its responsibilities. If we give, the government won't see the need to do so.

Because increasing government aid is the surest way of significantly increasing the total amount of aid given, I would agree that the governments of affluent nations should give more aid than they give now – as long as it is given for projects that effectively help those in extreme poverty. Less than 25 cents in every $100 dollars of gross national income is a scandalously small amount for a nation as wealthy as the United States to give to relieve extreme poverty in the world's poorest countries – and that figure includes both government aid and non-government charitable donations. Even the official UN target of 0.7 percent seems much less than affluent nations can and should give – though it is a target few have reached. But is this a reason against each of us giving as much as we can through voluntary agencies? To believe that it is seems to assume that the more people there are who give through voluntary agencies, the less likely it is that the government will do its part. Is this plausible? The opposite view – that if no one gives voluntarily, the government will assume that its citizens are not in favour of overseas aid and will cut its programme accordingly – is more reasonable. In any case, unless there is a definite probability that by refusing to give we would be helping to bring about an increase in government assistance, refusing to give privately is wrong for the same reason that shutting off aid because of the risks of overpopulation is wrong: it is a refusal to prevent a definite evil for the sake of a very uncertain gain. The onus of showing how a refusal to give privately will make the government give more is on those who refuse to give.

This is not to say that giving privately is enough. As active concerned citizens, we should campaign for entirely new standards for both public and private aid. We should also work for fairer trading arrangements between rich and poor countries, including an end to rich nations paying subsidies to their agricultural producers that make it impossible for poor countries to compete in global markets. Perhaps it is more important to be politically active in the interests of the poor than to give to them oneself – but why not do both? Unfortunately, many use the view that aid is the government's responsibility as a reason against giving but not as a reason for being politically active.

Too High a Standard?

The final objection to the argument I have given for an obligation to assist is that it is too demanding; it sets a standard so high that only a saint could attain it. This objection comes in at least three versions. The first maintains that, human nature being what it is, we cannot achieve so high a standard; and because it is absurd to say that we ought to do what we cannot do, we must reject the claim that we ought to give so much. The second version asserts that even if we could achieve so high a standard, to do so would be undesirable. The third version of the objection is that to set so high a standard is undesirable because it will be perceived as too difficult to reach and will discourage many from even attempting to do so.

Those who put forward the first version of the objection often make observations about human nature. They point out that we all are much more concerned about our own interests, and those of our immediate family, than we are about the interests of strangers. That is, they may add, because we have evolved from a natural process in which those with a high degree of concern for their own interests, or the interests of their offspring and kin, tended to leave more descendants in future generations than those who were not so concerned with their own interests or those of their kin. Thus, the biologist Garrett Hardin has argued, in support of his 'lifeboat ethics', that altruism can only exist 'on a small scale, over the short term, and within small, intimate groups'; and Richard Dawkins has written, in his provocative book *The Selfish Gene*: 'Much as we might wish to believe otherwise, universal love and the welfare of the species as a whole are concepts which simply do not make evolutionary sense.'

I have already noted, in discussing the objection that we should first take care of our own, the very strong tendency for partiality in human beings. Our preference for our own interests, and those of our close kin, over the interests of strangers is no doubt a natural outcome of the evolutionary process. What this means is that we would be foolish to expect widespread conformity to a standard that demands impartial concern, and for that reason it would scarcely be appropriate or feasible to condemn all those who fail to reach such a standard. Yet to act impartially, though it might be very difficult, is not impossible. The commonly quoted maxim '*ought* implies *can*' does not apply here. That maxim is a reason for rejecting such moral judgments as, 'You ought to have saved all the people from the sinking ship', when in fact if you had taken one more person into the lifeboat, it would have sunk and you would not have saved any. In that situation, it is absurd to say that you ought to have done what you could not possibly do. When we have money to spend on luxuries and others are starving, however, it is clear that we *can* all give much more than we do give, and we can therefore all come closer to the impartial standard proposed in this chapter. Nor is there, as we approach closer to this standard, any barrier beyond which we cannot go.

A remarkable illustration of what is possible for a family to do began in Atlanta, Georgia, in 2006 when the car in which Kevin Salwen was driving his fourteen-year-old daughter Hannah was halted by a stoplight. On one side Hannah saw a gleaming Mercedes coupe, and on the other she saw a homeless man. 'You know, Dad,' she said, pointing, 'if *that* man had a less nice car, that man *there* could have a meal.' That started a conversation that continued at home. Instead of scoffing at the idea, Hannah's mother challenged her: 'What do you want to do: sell our house, move into one half the size, give up your room?' Over a series of family discussions, the Salwens, a well-off family of four, decided to do just that: sell their home, give half the money they received for it to the poor and, with the other half, buy a smaller home. Friends thought they were crazy, but they were confident that they were doing the right thing. As a result, they were able to give more than $800,000 to help rural villagers in Ghana lift themselves out of poverty. Many people would consider moving to a smaller home a sacrifice, but Kevin Salwen says that even in terms of self-interest, it made sense: 'Giving away half of something we had too much of (our house) brought us a togetherness, trust and joy we never had.'

Admittedly, the Salwens' decision still left them comfortably off. They could have given more without sacrificing anything comparable in significance to the lives that they could, by giving even more, have saved. So this example does not demonstrate that this standard is achievable, but it does show how a family can break through barriers that most of us take for granted. Zell Kravinsky pushed those barriers even further. After making more than $40 million though canny real estate investments, he gave away almost all of it, living with his family in a modest suburban home. Then, on learning that people die from kidney disease while waiting for a transplant to become available, and studying research showing that the chances of anyone needing both kidneys are as low as 1 in 4000, he went to a city hospital that served mostly African Americans and donated one of his kidneys to a stranger. With examples like these, we cannot say that the impartial standard is mistaken because it is impossible for us – for anyone one of us, individually – to achieve it. We don't really know how far in the direction of impartiality it is possible to go. Unlike the Salwens or Zell Kravinsky, most people never try.

The second version of the objection has been put by several philosophers during the past decade, among them Susan Wolf in a forceful article entitled "Moral Saints". Wolf argues that if we all took the kind of moral stance defended in this chapter, we would have to do without a great deal that makes life interesting: opera, gourmet cooking, elegant clothes and professional sport, for a start. The kind of life we come to see as ethically required of us would be a single-minded pursuit of the overall good, lacking that broad diversity of interests and activities that, on a less demanding view, can be part of our ideal of a good life for a human being. To this, however, one can respond that although the rich and varied life that Wolf upholds as an ideal may be the most desirable form of life for a human being in a world of plenty, it is wrong to assume that it remains a good life in a world in which buying luxuries for oneself means accepting the continued avoidable suffering of others. A doctor faced with hundreds of injured victims of a train crash can scarcely think it defensible to treat fifty of them and then go to the opera, on the grounds that going to the opera is part of a well-rounded human life. The life-or-death needs of others must take priority. Looking at the world as a whole, and our ability to make a difference, we are like the doctor in that we live in a time when we all have an opportunity to help to mitigate a disaster.

Associated with this second version of the objection is the claim that an impartial ethic of the kind advocated here makes it impossible to have serious personal relationships based on love and friendship. These relationships are, of their nature, partial. We put the interests of our loved ones, our family and our friends ahead of those of strangers. If we did not do so, would these relationships survive? I have already indicated, in the response I gave when considering the objection that we should first take care of our own, that there is a place within an impartially grounded moral framework for recognising some degree of partiality for kin, and the same can be said for other close personal relationships. Clearly, for most people personal relationships are among the necessities of a flourishing life, and to give them up would be to sacrifice something of great moral significance. Moreover, for most people, to give up such relationships would diminish, not only their happiness and their mental health, but also their effectiveness as an agent of change. Hence, no such sacrifice is required by the principle for which I am here arguing.

The third version of the objection asks: might it not be counterproductive to demand that people give up so much? Might not people say, 'As I can't do what is morally required anyway, I won't bother to give at all'? If, however, we were to set a more realistic standard, people might make a genuine effort to reach it. Thus, setting a lower standard might actually result in more aid being given.

It is important to get the status of this third version of the objection clear. Its accuracy as a prediction of human behaviour is quite compatible with the argument that we are obliged to give to the point at which by giving more we sacrifice something of comparable moral significance to what we achieve by our donation. What would follow from the objection is that public advocacy of this standard of giving is undesirable. It would mean that, in order to do the maximum to reduce extreme poverty, we should advocate a standard lower than the amount we think people really ought to give. Of course we ourselves – those of us who accept the original argument, with its higher standard – would know that we ought to do more than we publicly propose people ought to do, and we might actually give more than we urge others to give. There is no inconsistency here, because in both our private and our public behaviour we are trying to do what will most reduce extreme poverty.

For a consequentialist, this apparent conflict between public and private morality is always a possibility and not in itself an indication that the underlying principle is wrong. The consequences of a principle are one thing, the consequences of publicly advocating it another. A variant of this idea is already acknowledged by the distinction between the intuitive and critical levels of morality, of which I have made use in previous chapters. If we think of principles that are suitable for the intuitive level of morality as those that should be generally advocated, these are the principles that, when advocated, will give rise to the best consequences. Where aid is concerned, they will be the principles that lead to the largest amount being given by the affluent to the poor – as long as the money is given to an organization that will use it with maximum effectiveness.

Is it true that the standard set by our argument is so high as to be counterproductive? There is not much evidence to go by, but discussions of the argument with students and others have led me to think it might be. On the other hand, the conventionally accepted standard – a few coins in a collection tin when one is waved under your nose – is obviously far too low. What level should we advocate? In my book *The Life You Can Save* – and on the corresponding website, www.thelifeyoucansave.com – I have suggested a progressive scale, like a tax scale. It begins at just 1 percent of income; and for 90 percent of taxpayers, it does not require giving more than 5 percent. This is therefore an entirely realistic amount, and one that people could easily give with no sacrifice – and indeed, often with a personal gain, because there are many psychological studies showing that those who give are, as the Salwen family found, happier than those who do not. I do not really know if the scale I propose is the one that will, if widely advocated, achieve the greatest total amount donated, but I calculated that if everyone in the affluent world gave according to that scale, it would raise $1.5 trillion each year – which is eight times what the United Nations task force headed by the economist Jeffrey

Sachs calculated would be needed to meet the Millennium Development Goals set by the leaders of all the world's nations when they met at the UN Millennium Development Summit in 2000. Those goals included reducing by half the proportion of the world's people living in extreme poverty and the proportion of people who suffer from hunger, as well as reducing by two-thirds the death toll among children under five years old – thus saving six million lives every year – and enabling children everywhere to have a full course of primary schooling.

This surprising outcome – that if everyone with abundance were to contribute to the effort to reduce extreme poverty and all that goes with it, the amount each of us would need to give would be quite modest – shows that the argument with which this chapter began is demanding only because so few of those with the ability to help the poor are doing anything significant to help them. We do not need to transfer half or a quarter or even a tenth of the wealth of the rich to the poor. If few are helping, those few have to cut very deep before they get to the point at which giving more would involve sacrificing something of comparable moral significance to the life saved by their gift. If we all, or even most of us, gave according to the much more modest scale I have suggested, none of us would have to give up much. That is why this is a suitable standard for public advocacy. What we need to do is to change our public ethics so that for anyone who can afford to buy luxuries – and even a bottle of water is a luxury if there is safe drinking water available free – giving something significant to those in extreme poverty becomes an elementary part of what it is to live an ethical life.

9

Climate Change

In the previous chapter, we briefly considered the argument that the only obligation we have to strangers is not to harm them. For most of human existence, that view would have been easy to live by. Our ancestors lived in groups of no more than a few hundred people, and those on the other side of a river or mountain range might as well have been living in a separate world. We developed ethical principles to help us to deal with problems within our community, not to help those outside it. The harms that it was considered wrong to cause were generally clear and well defined. We developed inhibitions against, and emotional responses to, such actions, and these instinctive or emotional reactions still form the basis for much of our moral thinking.

Today, we are connected to people all over the world in ways our ancestors could not have imagined. The discovery that human activities are changing the climate of our planet has brought with it knowledge of new ways in which we can harm one another. When you drive your car, you burn fossil fuel that releases carbon dioxide into the atmosphere. You are changing the chemical composition of the atmosphere and, hence, the climate. What does this do to others?

In some parts of the world, what you are doing is already apparent. According to the World Health Organization, the warming of the planet caused an additional 140,000 deaths in 2004, as compared with the number of deaths there would have been had average global temperatures remained as they were during the period 1961 to 1990. This means that climate change is already causing, every week, as many deaths as occurred in the terrorist attacks on September 11, 2001. The immediate causes of the additional death are mostly climate-sensitive diseases such as malaria, dengue, and diarrhoea, which is more common when there is a lack of safe water. Malnutrition resulting from crops that fail because of high temperatures or low rainfall is also responsible for many extra deaths.

Changes are also already apparent in the fertile, densely settled delta regions in Egypt, Bangladesh, India and Vietnam, which are at risk from rising sea levels. The Sunderbans, islands in the Ganges delta that are home to four million Indians, are disappearing – two islands have vanished entirely; in total, an area of land measuring thirty-one square miles has disappeared over the last thirty years. Hundreds of families have had to move to camps for displaced people. Some small Pacific nations like the Maldives, Kiribati and Tuvalu, which consist of low-lying coral atolls, are in similar danger; within a few decades, these nations may be submerged beneath the waves.

These are only the first signs of much greater change to come. In 2007, the Fourth Assessment Report of the Intergovernmental Panel on Climate Change, the scientific body established by the United Nations Environment Program and the World Meteorological Association, found that a temperature rise, by 2080, in the range of 2.0°C to 2.4°C would put stress on water resources used by 1.2 billion people. Rising sea levels would expose, each year, an additional 16 million people to coastal flooding. If temperatures rise as much as 3.3°C over the same period, the stress on water resources would affect 2.5 to 3.2 billion people, and each year would expose an additional 29 million to coastal flooding.

What we are doing to strangers in other communities right now is, therefore, far more serious and far more widespread than the harm we would do if we were in the habit of occasionally sending out a group of warriors to rape and pillage a village or two. Yet causing imperceptible harm at a distance by the release of waste gases is a completely new form of harm, and so we lack any kind of instinctive inhibitions or emotional response against causing it. We have trouble seeing it as harm at all.

The polar bear perched on a melting chunk of ice has become an icon of the campaign against global warming, making the point that it is not only humans who will suffer from climate change. Millions of animals will die in droughts and floods. Some will be able to move as their environments change, but for others there will be nowhere to go. In some regions, for instance, alpine species will be able to move higher up mountains as temperatures increase, but in others – Australia is one example – alpine plants and animals are already clinging to the most elevated regions of the country, and there is nowhere higher to go. Global warming will cause extinctions on a vast scale.

In the previous chapter, I argued against the view that the only obligation we have to strangers is to avoid harming them; but even if we were
to take that view, the facts of climate change would demonstrate clearly
that we *are* harming hundreds of millions, perhaps billions, of the world's
poor. It would seem, therefore, that on *any* plausible view, we have an
obligation to stop harming them and to compensate them for the harm
we have already caused them – harm that will continue to unfold for the
next century at least, even if we cut all greenhouse gas emissions to zero
today. We need international arrangements to deal with climate change,
and we need a global ethic on which to base these arrangements. This
chapter will discuss what this global ethic might look like and what the
responsibilities of both nations and individuals are in respect of climate
change.

'ENOUGH AND AS GOOD'

Imagine that we live in a village in which everyone puts their waste down
a giant drain. No one quite knows what happens to the waste after it goes
down the drain, but because it disappears and doesn't seem to bother
anyone, no one worries about it. No matter how much we pour down
the drain, others can do the same. For as long as anyone can remember,
the capacity of the drain to dispose of our waste has seemed limitless. We
believe that we can take what we want and still leave, in the words of the
seventeenth-century English philosopher John Locke, 'enough and as
good left in common for others'. This, on Locke's view, is a key factor in
our being able to acquire property from natural resources. Now imagine
that we start producing more waste, and suddenly we find that the drain's
capacity is not limitless after all; on the contrary, it is being used to the
full. At this point, when we continue to throw our wastes down the drain
we are no longer leaving 'enough and as good for others', and hence our
right to unchecked waste disposal becomes questionable.

Think of our atmosphere as that giant drain and our wastes as carbon
dioxide, methane and other greenhouse gases. We have just discovered
that the atmosphere's capacity to absorb our gases without harmful consequences is limited. The evidence shows that we are already using it
beyond its capacity. Before the industrial revolution, carbon dioxide in
our atmosphere amounted to only 270 parts per million (ppm). Then
humans began to burn coal in large quantities, and later oil and gas.
In 2010, carbon dioxide in the atmosphere reached 390 ppm. This
is a higher level than at any time in recorded history, and it is still

increasing at 2 ppm each year. There is general agreement that if we cause average temperatures to increase by 2°C, dangerous, large-scale consequences, much more severe than anything we have seen so far, are probable. Until about 2008, most scientists agreed on 450 ppm as the level of carbon dioxide in our atmosphere that should not be exceeded if we are to prevent a greater increase than 2°C. On current trends, we will reach 450 ppm of carbon dioxide in the atmosphere by 2040.

Allowing levels of carbon dioxide in the atmosphere to reach 450 ppm is already taking a grave risk. In the first decade of the twenty-first century, global warming repeatedly exceeded the predictions made by earlier reports of the Intergovernmental Panel on Climate Change, and we developed a better understanding of the dangers of feedback loops in planetary warming. The melting of arctic ice is one visible example of something happening more rapidly than scientists had predicted. It also illustrates the dangers of a feedback loop. Four hundred years ago, explorers sought the legendary 'Northeast Passage' that would enable them to sail across the north of Europe and Russia to China. They found the arctic ice impenetrable and gave up their quest. In 2009, commercial vessels successfully navigated the Northeast Passage. The large area of the Arctic Ocean that is now ice-free in summer is a symptom of global warming. In addition, it is itself a cause of further warming. Ice and snow reflect the sun's rays back upwards. An ice-free ocean surface absorbs more warmth from the sun. Our greenhouse gas emissions have, by causing enough warming to melt arctic ice, created a feedback loop that will generate more warming, even if we were to stop emitting all greenhouse gases tomorrow. Other feedback loops pose even greater danger. In Siberia, vast quantities of methane, an extremely potent greenhouse gas, are locked up in what used to be called 'permafrost' – regions in which the ground was permanently frozen. Areas that used to be frozen are now thawing, and as they thaw they release the methane, contributing to further warming and to the thawing of further regions, releasing more methane.

Evidence of this kind led James Hansen, of the U.S. National Aeronautics and Space Administration, and his colleagues to conclude, in an article published in *Science* in 2008, that if we wish 'to preserve a planet similar to that on which civilization developed and to which life on Earth is adapted,' we need to reduce carbon dioxide to 'at most 350 ppm'. That is, of course, a level that we passed some years ago. So if we think of the atmosphere as a giant drain, then the drain is already overused. We

need to cut back on our usage. How can we decide who should cut back
the most?

WHAT IS AN EQUITABLE DISTRIBUTION?

Historical Responsibility

In addressing the question of justice in distribution in his book *Anarchy,
State and Utopia*, the philosopher Robert Nozick made a useful distinction
between 'historical' principles and 'time-slice' principles. An historical
principle is one that says: to understand whether a given distribution of
goods is just or unjust, we must ask how the distribution came about; we
must know its history. Are the parties entitled, by an originally justifiable
acquisition and a chain of legitimate transfers, to what they now have? If
so, the present distribution is just. If not, rectification or compensation
will be needed to produce a just distribution. In contrast, a time-slice
principle just looks at the existing distribution, at this moment of time,
and asks on that basis if it is just.

One historical principle, often applied in the case of pollution, is 'You
broke it, you fix it' – also known as 'The polluter pays'. If a chemical
factory pollutes a river, then the owner of the factory is responsible for
cleaning up the river. If we apply this principle to climate change, then
it would assign responsibility for fixing the problem to each country in
proportion to the amount that the country has contributed to causing
the problem. Historical emissions of carbon dioxide are relevant, because
most of the carbon dioxide emitted a century ago is still in the atmosphere
today.

In discussions at the United Nations on climate change in 1997, the
Brazilian government proposed that emission reduction targets should
be set according to the impact of a nation's historic emissions on temperature rise. A scientific group was set up to evaluate the proposal and
indicate whether the data existed to allow conclusions to be reached on
what contributions different nations or regions had made to the increase
in global temperatures. This group eventually reported, in 2008, that the
data was adequate for this, especially for fossil fuel emissions, although
contributions due to changes in forestry and agriculture were more difficult to quantify. The group took as its period for measuring contributions from 1890 to 2000, noting that different dates would give slightly
different results. It concluded that the United States is responsible for
20 percent of the temperature rise and the European nations that are

members of the Organization for Economic Cooperation and Development (OECD) are responsible for 14 percent. Somewhat surprisingly – and perhaps disconcertingly for the Brazilians – Latin America also comes out as contributing 14 percent of the temperature rise, although the study notes that this figure falls as low as 8 percent if different data for forestry and land use changes are used. On the other hand, all of East Asia, including China, has contributed only 10 percent, and South Asia, including India, only 7 percent. On the 'You broke it, you fix it' view, therefore, it is the United States and the long-industrialized European nations, perhaps together with Latin America, that ought to bear the largest share of the burden of solving the problem.

China has offered support for the Brazilian proposal, but with the explicit proviso that historic contributions to climate change should be considered on a per capita basis. *Carbon Equity,* a report prepared by five Chinese academic and policy-oriented think tanks for the 2009 conference on climate change in Copenhagen, argues that the fact that China has a much larger population than the United States has to be taken into account in apportioning responsibility for the greenhouse problem. The assumption here, which seems reasonable, is that each person is entitled to an equal share of the atmosphere, and we should be looking at the extent to which people in some nations have, in past centuries, used more than their share. The report calculates that over the period from 1850 to 2004, the average American has been responsible for putting twenty-one times as much carbon dioxide into the atmosphere as the average Chinese and fifty-three times as much as the average Indian. On average, Britons and Canadians are responsible for sixteen times as much carbon being in the atmosphere as Chinese and forty times as much as Indians. The principle of historical responsibility thus indicates that almost all of the sacrifices required to stop global warming should be made by the older industrialized nations.

One sometimes hears the objection that the industrial revolution has benefited the entire world, not only the industrialized nations, and hence that the emissions required for industrialization should not be regarded as only the responsibility of the industrialized nations. It's true that the industrial revolution made possible the development of science and technology, and this has benefited and is continuing to benefit billions of people all over the world. But it also enabled the industrialized nations to colonize much of the world and, even after the era of colonization, to dominate the global trading system. This has greatly benefited those living in the industrialized nations, whereas its impact on the colonized nations was, at best, much more mixed. So even if industrialization has been, on balance, a benefit rather than a harm for the world as a whole, it is a benefit that has accrued disproportionately to those in the industrialized nations themselves, and the emissions can fairly be seen as their responsibility.

Another objection to holding the industrialized nations responsible for all their emissions since the industrial revolution is that for most of this period they did not know that these emissions would be harmful. That's true, though as early as 1896, the distinguished scientist Svante Arrhenius predicted that burning fossil fuels would lead to a build-up of carbon dioxide in the atmosphere that would heat the planet. (He thought, however, that this would be a good thing, making the earth's climate 'more equable' and stimulating food production. Perhaps that benign view of global warming had something to do with his location in Sweden.) Human-induced global warming was not seriously studied until the 1970s, however, and climate change only became an issue of international concern in the 1980s. At U.S. congressional hearings in 1987 – at the time the hottest year on record, but now already not even one of the ten hottest years – James Hansen warned of the dangers of global warming. Other scientists supported him. The following year, the Intergovernmental Panel on Climate Change was set up, and two years later that body reported that the threat of climate change was real, and a global treaty was needed to deal with it. The United Nations Framework Convention on Climate Change was agreed to at the "Earth Summit" held in Rio de Janeiro in 1992. This convention, accepted by 181 governments, including all the major industrialized nations, calls for greenhouse gases to be stabilized 'at a low enough level to prevent dangerous anthropogenic interference with the climate system'. The nations of the world have not done what they said they would do. Instead, their greenhouse gas emissions continued to grow. (The Kyoto Protocol, agreed to by most industrialized nations in 1997, was an attempt to get action from the industrialized nations that would fulfil the pledges made at the Rio Earth Summit five years earlier. The United States, then the world's largest emitter of greenhouse gases, and one with a particularly high per capita level of emissions, did not ratify it.)

Though not legally binding, the Rio de Janeiro commitment demonstrates that in 1992 the developed nations were aware of the need for action. The study of the Brazilian proposal to consider historical contributions, referred to previously, also examined what the outcome would be if the starting date for historical responsibility were not 1890 but

1990 – a date by which there could be no claim of ignorance about the fact that greenhouse gas emissions posed a risk of bringing about dangerous climate change. Although this much more recent starting date did of course reduce the contributions of the older industrialized nations, the difference was smaller than might be expected. The contribution of the United States declined from 20 percent to 16 percent, and that of the European OECD nations fell from 14 percent to 11 percent. China's contribution increased to around 13 percent, but India's remained near 5 percent; Africa's contributions remain extremely small whatever dateline is used. The per capita contributions of the industrialized nations remain lopsidedly greater, because of course the population of the United States is only about one quarter that of China. Thus, even if we accept the argument that the 'You broke it, you fix it' rule applies only from the time when the biggest emitters knew that their emissions were risking dangerous anthropogenic climate change, it would still be the case that the United States and the industrialized nations of Europe ought to be doing much more than any other nations to solve the problem.

Equal Shares

At a 2009 United Nations Summit meeting on climate change, the president of Rwanda, Paul Kagame, pointed out that climate change will probably have a more severe impact on Africa than on any other part of the world – and yet Africa has fewer resources to draw on to meet this challenge. Many models of the changes that global warming is likely to bring show that precipitation will decrease nearer the equator and increase nearer the poles. The rainfall on which hundreds of millions rely to grow their food will become less reliable. Moreover, the poor nations depend on agriculture far more than the rich. In the United States, agriculture represents only 4 percent of the economy; in Malawi it is 40 percent, and 90 percent of Malawians are subsistence farmers, virtually all of them dependent on rainfall. Similar patterns of dependence on farming and rainfall are common across Africa.

It is also obviously true that the poorer nations lack the resources to adapt. In southern Australia, when several states were faced with a long-term trend of declining rainfall, governments built costly desalination plants to ensure that major cities will not run out of water. In the Netherlands, the government has raised dykes to keep out rising sea levels and is designing amphibious houses that can rise and float, while remaining securely moored, if rivers flood. Other countries cannot afford such expensive ways of providing water and controlling flooding from rising sea levels.

President Kagame went on to point out that climate change is only 'very marginally, if at all, a problem of Africa's making'. We have seen that he was right about this too. Nevertheless, he offered to wipe the slate clean and forget about the responsibility of the industrialized nations for causing the problem. Because we are all facing a struggle for survival, he said, he did not want 'a new round of blame game' which would not only be in poor taste but also counterproductive. Instead, he proposed that every human being is entitled to an equal share of the atmosphere. At the same United Nations meeting, Sri Lanka made a similar proposal.

'Equal shares' has the great merit of simplicity. It is a time-slice principle – it takes no account of the past and gives everyone an equal share of the atmosphere from now on. Like other developing nations, Rwanda and Sri Lanka are using far less than their equal per capita share, and so even if they give up their right to make a claim against the industrialized nations on the basis of historical responsibility, they will still do well on an equal shares basis.

What would equal shares mean in practice? Suppose that we aim to stabilize greenhouse gas emissions at a level that will prevent us exceeding 450 ppm carbon dioxide. It is controversial how much carbon we could emit per person while remaining below that level, but one plausible figure is two tons of carbon dioxide per person per year. (Emissions are sometimes expressed in terms of carbon rather than carbon dioxide. One ton of carbon is equivalent to 3.7 tons of carbon dioxide, so two tons of carbon dioxide is not much more than half a ton of carbon. We should also remember that the figure for 'carbon dioxide' really means 'carbon dioxide equivalent' for it includes other greenhouse gases such as methane, converted at a rate that takes into account their potency to heat up the planet.) Now compare actual per capita emissions for some key nations with this estimate of two tons of carbon dioxide per person that could be emitted each year. In 2010, the United States, Canada and Australia all produced about twenty tons of carbon dioxide per person per year, while Germany produced eleven tons, China about four, India not much more than one ton, and Sri Lanka only about two-thirds of a ton. This means that Sri Lanka could triple its emissions and India could almost double its emissions while still remaining within their per capita shares. China would need to halve its current emissions, Germany would have to reduce them by more than 80 percent, and most dramatically of all, the United States, Canada and Australia would have to reduce their emissions to only one-tenth of present levels.

It is, of course, not possible for industrialized nations like Germany and the United States to make such dramatic reductions in the short term, or at least not without devastating economic consequences that would be likely, in a democracy, to lead to a change of government and a reversal of the policy. Before we conclude that this makes the principle of equal per capita shares an unrealistic idea, however, there are two mitigating factors to consider. The first is that making greenhouse gas emission quotas tradeable would ease the transition to a low-emissions economy. Emissions trading works on the simple economic principle that if you can buy something more cheaply than you can produce it yourself, you are better off buying it than producing it. In this case, what you buy will be a transferable quota to produce greenhouse gases, allocated on the basis of an equal per capita share. International carbon trading means that cuts in carbon emissions will be made at the lowest possible cost, thus doing the least possible damage to the global economy. Moreover, a carbon trading scheme gives countries with few greenhouse gas emissions – generally, poor countries – an incentive to keep their emissions low, so that they have more emissions quota to sell to rich countries that are over their quota. Thus, an international emissions trading scheme could contribute towards solving the problem of poverty discussed in the previous chapter. It would involve the transfer of resources from rich nations to poor ones – not as altruism, but as payment for a valuable commodity.

There are, however, some serious objections to an international carbon trading scheme. One is whether such a scheme would be verifiable – that is, whether the emissions of each nation could be properly checked against the nation's quota – and what would happen if it were not. Without a reliable means of verifying emissions cuts, nothing will be achieved. Secondly, payments from rich nations to poor nations will only reduce poverty if the governments to which they are paid use them for that purpose. In the case of governments that refused to do so – which, as we saw in the previous chapter, often happens when dictatorial or corrupt governments earn royalties from the sale of oil and minerals – it would be better for the payments to be held in trust until a government emerges that can demonstrate that it will use the funds for the benefit of its people as a whole.

The third objection to an international emissions trading scheme is one that James Hansen has made to any 'cap and trade' system – that is, any system that sets an overall cap on emissions, divides them up into emission permits for nations or corporations or individuals, and then allows these permits to be traded. Hansen points out that such schemes have a perverse effect on altruistic actions. If I decide to cut my greenhouse gas emissions by buying a fuel-efficient hybrid car, this does not reduce the emissions total for my country. The cap determines the total, and if some people reduce their emissions, this will make the price of emission permits fall. Thus, fossil fuels will be cheaper than they would have been if some people had not altruistically decided to reduce their emissions, and others who are not altruistic will no doubt decide to buy a bigger car, or use more energy, because of the price fall. Hansen therefore prefers a tax on the carbon content of fossil fuels, with the proceeds divided equally between all of a country's legal residents – he calls it a 'fee and dividend' scheme. This would reward those who reduce their carbon footprint, and doing so would reduce the overall emissions total. In response, the economist Paul Krugman acknowledges that a cap and trade system does reduce the opportunities for climate altruism, but he denies that altruism is going to enable us to cut emissions to the extent we need. He also points out that allowing permits to be traded uses the mechanism of the market to ensure that emissions are reduced at the lowest possible cost – why reduce emissions at a high cost if someone else can reduce them for much less and still profit by selling their permits to you? Thus, in Krugman's view and in the view of most economists, a carbon fee or tax is less efficient than a cap and trade system.

This discussion of the advantages and disadvantages of a carbon trading scheme is, however, a digression from our discussion of whether it is possible for developed nations to reduce their emissions to the extent needed to avoid catastrophe. A carbon trading scheme was one factor that may make this task a little more possible than it at first seems. A second factor is that the cuts do not need to be made all at once. The German Advisory Council on Global Change, a scientific body that advises the German government, has suggested that the total amount of permissible emissions of carbon dioxide should not be calculated for a single year, but rather should be set for the entire period between now and 2050 and designed to make it likely that global temperatures do not rise more than 2°C. For this purpose, the council suggested a maximum of 750 billion tons of carbon dioxide to be emitted between 2010 and 2050 (although even with this amount, the council warned that there would be no more than a two-thirds probability that the temperature rise could be kept below 2°C). This total, the council proposed, should be divided between countries on the basis of equal per capita shares. Countries could then produce their own 'road maps' showing how they would reduce their carbon dioxide emissions so as not to exceed their carbon budgets before 2050.

Although the German proposal gives industrialized countries time to make changes, for those countries with the highest current per capita emissions outputs, the time is very short. About sixty countries, mostly industrialized nations, will, at current rates, use up their budget in less than twenty years. Germany, for example, if it continued to emit at the same rate as it did in 2008, would use up its emissions budget in just ten years, requiring it to have zero emissions for the next thirty years. (It is therefore commendable that Angela Merkel, the German chancellor, has accepted the equal shares principle, saying: ' . . . our long-term measure can only be that per capita CO_2 emissions in the world must be equalized.') The United States, Australia and Canada are currently on track to use up their budgets in just six years. Another group of thirty countries, which includes China, Mexico and Thailand, will, at current rates, use up their budgets in twenty to forty years. The remaining ninety-five countries do not need to reduce their emissions, as at current rates their budgets will last at least forty years. Brazil is in this group. So too is India, which would take eighty-eight years to exhaust its budget at current levels. Some of the poorest nations emit so little carbon that at current rates it would take them several centuries to use up their budget. At the extreme end of this spectrum, the small African nation of Burkina Faso would take 2,892 years to use up its budget – which means that under an international cap and trade scheme, it would be able to sell a large amount of its quota to those nations that will have the most difficulty in meeting their targets.

Apart from the question of whether the rich nations could realistically comply with the equal per capita share approach, another objection to this approach is that if a country's population grows, then that country gets a larger allocation; while everyone else's allocation diminishes because the total permissible emissions level must remain constant. Thus, a country with a rapidly growing population is imposing a burden on other countries, forcing them to reduce their emissions still further. It would be better to have a system that gives countries an incentive to slow population growth. We could do this by setting national allocations that are tied to today's population rather than letting them rise with an increase in population. Because different countries have different proportions of young people about to reach reproductive age, however, this provision would produce greater hardship in countries with younger populations than in those with older populations. That problem could be avoided if national allocations were based on an estimate of a country's population at some future date. The Population Division of the United Nations Department of Economic and Social Affairs publishes predictions of the population that each nation will reach in 2050. Using this figure as the basis for the per capita allocation would encourage countries to aim to remain below their projected population, for any country that could achieve this would have a larger per person allocation than that to which its actual population would entitle it. Conversely, a country would have a reduced emission quota per actual resident if its population growth exceeded the UN population forecast.

Luxury versus Subsistence

In *A Theory of Justice*, perhaps the most influential work on justice published in the twentieth century, John Rawls argued that if devoting more resources to those who are worse off will improve their situation, then that is what justice requires us to do. In the 1992 United Nations Framework Convention on Climate Change, the importance of favouring those who are worse off was recognized by a provision stating that the countries signing the convention 'have a right to, and should, promote sustainable development'. This accepts the importance of development for poor countries, but the right to development is constrained by the need for development to be sustainable. The countries of the world therefore have, in the wording of the convention, 'common but differentiated responsibilities'.

In 1993, the philosopher Henry Shue argued that a just allocation of quotas to emit greenhouse gases would distinguish between 'subsistence emissions' and 'luxury emissions' so that methane from rice paddies in poor countries would not rank equally with emissions from large vehicles used for recreational driving in the rich nations. At a United Nations General Assembly debate on climate change in 2007, a diplomat representing China used the same language, saying that 'emissions of subsistence' and 'development emissions' of poor countries should be accommodated by any future agreements, whereas the 'luxury emissions' of rich countries should be restricted. Whether one chooses an egalitarian, Rawlsian, or utilitarian principle of justice, that is difficult to deny.

Drawing a distinction between subsistence and luxury emissions shows convincingly that Burkina Faso is under no obligation to restrict emissions that are helpful for its development – but then, as we have seen, that is also apparent from an application of the principle of equal per capita shares. The distinction between subsistence emissions and luxury emissions is of only limited use to China, however, because there are already more Chinese living an affluent lifestyle, and therefore responsible for a high level of emissions, than there are, say, Germans. Admittedly, almost all Germans are responsible for a high level of emissions, whereas only a small proportion of Chinese are, but if China is calling on rich countries to restrict their 'luxury emissions', it can scarcely ignore the luxury emissions coming from its own elite.

A FORM OF AGGRESSION?

All of the three principles we have discussed have something to be said for them, and the choice between them is difficult. We could try to combine them, modifying the basic idea of equal per capita shares by giving some weight to historical contributions and some to a country's need to develop and provide the means for all its citizens to reach a minimum standard of living. Without going into the complexities of such possible combinations, it is clear that on any of these principles, or on any combination of them, the rich nations cannot justify their continued high output of greenhouse gases. It is impossible to think of a plausible ethical principle by which they could justify it. We can therefore conclude that they are doing something wrong.

What exactly is the nature of the wrongdoing? At an African Union summit in 2007, President Yoweri Museveni of Uganda told the nations of Europe and North America: 'You are causing aggression to us by causing global warming ... Alaska will probably become good for agriculture, Siberia will probably become good for agriculture, but where does that leave Africa?' We have already seen that the facts to which Museveni refers are basically accurate. Nevertheless, his use of the term 'aggression' shocks us. Can he be right?

When we think of 'aggression', we imagine troops moving across a border, or planes bombing enemy positions. In emitting high levels of greenhouse gases, the rich nations are not deliberately attacking another country, but their actions may be even more devastating than conventional forms of aggressive war. Because of what the rich nations are doing, lands that now grow crops will become barren, glaciers that for millennia have fed rivers will dwindle, the sea will take over fertile fields, tropical diseases will spread, and people will starve or become refugees. For at least the past twenty years, the rich countries have known that their actions risk causing these effects; and from some time in the first decade

of the twenty-first century, they have known that their actions very probably will have these effects. The fact that these harms are an unwanted
but unavoidable side effect of pursuing otherwise innocuous goals, like
giving people the kind of lifestyle they desire, is no justification for causing such harms. According to the doctrine of double effect, knowingly
causing harm can be justified if the harm is not intended, the goal is sufficiently important to outweigh the harm caused, and there is no other
way of achieving the goal without causing at least as great a harm. In the
case of global warming, however, the reverse is the case: the harm caused
far outweighs the good obtained. President George W. Bush admitted
as much early in his presidency when, asked if he would do something
about global warming, he said: 'We will not do anything that harms our
economy, because first things first are the people who live in America.'
Shortly afterwards Ari Fleischer, his spokesperson, was asked at a press
briefing whether the president would call on drivers to sharply reduce
their fuel consumption, Fleischer replied: 'That's a big no. The President
believes that it's an American way of life, and that it should be the goal of
policymakers to protect the American way of life.' Such remarks suggest
that the United States was bringing life-threatening harm to hundreds of
millions of people because its leader put a higher priority on preserving
its citizens' economic interests, and their rights to burn as much fuel
as they wish, than on the survival of people outside the United States.
Though George W. Bush is no longer in power, unless the United States
drastically changes course on emissions, that will remain true. One could
say the same about other developed nations, even if their leaders are
more guarded in their comments.

What we are doing to the people most at risk from global warming,
therefore, is similar in its impact to waging aggressive war on them.
It differs in its motivation, but that will be little consolation to them.
Moreover, because we know what we are doing and yet do not stop doing
it, we cannot shirk responsibility for it. We are culpable for the harm we
are doing to them.

WHAT OUGHT INDIVIDUALS TO DO?

The next question to ask is: what obligation does this place on us as
individual citizens of the culpable nations? When we looked at our individual responsibilities as affluent individuals in a world with a billion
people living in extreme poverty, the answer was clear. We may well try
to change the behaviour of our government, urging it to increase its aid

to the world's poor and to make that aid as effective as possible, but we also can and should act on our own, even if – or especially if – the government does not live up to its obligations. As long as we can, by giving to aid agencies, stop something very bad from happening without sacrificing anything of comparable moral significance ourselves, then giving to those agencies is what we ought to do. That does seem to be the situation: a given donation can have a significant, discernible impact – not on the problem of poverty as a whole, but on a child and the child's family. Can we say the same about climate change?

At first glance it seems that we can. Suppose that, like the average American, I am personally responsible for emitting the equivalent of twenty tons of carbon dioxide every year. I use air-conditioning to keep my house cool in summer, with the electricity coming largely from coal-fired power stations, and I use oil to heat it in winter. My diet is heavy in beef and dairy products, I drive a car, and I fly to Florida for my winter vacation. Then I become concerned about climate change, so I switch to eating mostly plant-based foods, improve my home insulation, install solar hot water, heating and electricity generation, ride my bike or the train instead of driving, and take vacations closer to home. Amazingly, I manage to cut my greenhouse gas emissions to two tons a year. Will the change in my lifestyle have a significant, discernible impact on anyone? It surely won't have an impact that anyone can detect. Even if we assume that the result of my actions is that eighteen fewer tons of carbon dioxide go into the atmosphere each year, that is too small a quantity to have any discernible effect on anyone. That's not to say that it won't have any effect at all, but rather that we cannot know what effect – if any – it has.

We often find ourselves faced with actions that seem to be wrong, even though it isn't obvious that they will have bad consequences. A favourite example of philosophers is taking a short cut across a beautiful lawn. Assume that all of us would save a few seconds by taking the short cut, but none of us want to see the lawn damaged. Still, what difference will it make if *I* take the short cut, just this once? The grass will not show any perceptible damage from one person walking on it. To this the usual reply is: 'What if everyone did that?' If everyone did it, of course, an unsightly muddy path would form, and none of us want to see that. The suggestion is that, because it would be bad if everyone were to do it, it must be wrong for me to do it.

'What if everyone did that?' isn't always a good objection to an action. 'What if everyone became a philosopher? We would all starve!' is not a good reason against becoming a philosopher, as long as we know that

there is no chance that everyone *will* become a philosopher. Even where
sufficient others might want to do what I am doing to bring about the bad
consequence – as in the lawn-crossing example – it isn't clear that 'What
if everyone did that?' really shows that an action is wrong. Is it wrong
for me to cross the lawn because I might set a bad example to others,
and thus increase the chances that everyone will do it? What if it is late
at night and no one else is around? Is it wrong because my imprint on
the grass will make a causal contribution, even if only a small one, to the
grass wearing out? Suppose that I have studied the amount of traffic this
lawn can bear, and I find that it can withstand ten people walking across
it per day without showing any signs of wear at all. I also know that no
more than six people do walk across it each day. So as long as I only do it
when fewer than ten people are crossing it each day, and I do it when no
one else is looking, and so do not influence others to cross it, my stroll
over the lawn will have no harmful consequences at all. Am I still wrong
to do it because it would be bad if everyone did it?

Here consequentialists and non-consequentialists differ. An act-
utilitarian who judges every act in accordance with its consequences
would say that if you could really be sure that walking across the grass
would have no harmful consequences at all, it would not be wrong to
do it. A rule-utilitarian could say that because the best rule for everyone
to observe in these circumstances would be 'Do not cross the lawn', it
would be wrong for me to cross it, even if my crossing would have no
bad consequences. A Kantian, too, could reject lawn crossing because
Kant said that if I cannot will the maxim of my action to be a universal
law, then it must be wrong. The difficult question for the rule-utilitarians
and Kantians, however, is how to formulate the rule or maxim that must
be universalized. It is true that 'Cross the lawn whenever it is convenient to you to do so' would, if widely observed, damage the lawn; and
because I value the unspoilt law, I could not will it to be a universal
law. What about 'Cross the lawn whenever crossing it will not set a bad
example and will not damage the grass'? If we are allowed to make
our rules or maxims as specific as that, then, as David Lyons showed in
his book *Forms and Limits of Utilitarianism,* rule-utilitarianism becomes
indistinguishable from act-utilitarianism – that is, rule-utilitarians will
approve of just those actions of which an act-utilitarian would approve,
and they will disapprove of those of which an act-utilitarian would
disapprove. R. M. Hare made a similar claim in respect of Kant's
appeal to the idea of universal law, arguing that this principle leads
utilitarianism.

In *Ideal Code, Real World*, Brad Hooker argues for a version of rule-utilitarianism that provides a barrier against making rules too complicated. He holds that we act wrongly if we act contrary to a rule that would be part of the set of rules that, if internalized by the overwhelming majority of people, would have the best consequences. If we make rules too specific, people will find them too difficult to internalize, or act on, and the costs of educating people to act on the rules will be too high. Because, on Hooker's view, the code must be publicly known and promoted, it is hard to imagine that a rule like 'Cross the lawn only when you can do it in secret' could be part of the best moral code, for then everyone would know that 'secret' lawn crossings were permitted, and too many people would cross the lawn.

Christopher Kutz examines these issues in his book *Complicity: Ethics and Law for a Collective Age*, and suggests what he calls the Complicity Principle:

I am accountable for what others do when I intentionally participate in the wrong they do or the harm they cause.

This principle is not consequentialist, Kutz says, because it makes me accountable independently of the actual difference I make. As an example of complicity, he considers the emission of chlorofluorocarbons, or CFCs, the gases that damage the ozone layer and enlarge the ozone hole, causing an increase in the rate of skin cancer in many parts of the world. Although in many respects the ozone hole problem was similar to the problem of climate change – individual emissions from many nations were damaging the atmosphere, to the detriment of all – the ozone was being damaged by a much more specific and economically less significant class of gases, used largely in refrigerators and some air-conditioners. International agreement on stopping the use of the gases was therefore far easier to obtain and was achieved by the 1987 Montreal Protocol, which granted developing countries a longer period than the industrialized nations to phase out their use of CFCs. Kutz focuses on an individual driver who uses a CFC-based coolant in his car's air-conditioning. Is he doing anything wrong? Kutz says that although there is no clear victim of the driver's use of CFCs, 'individuals must think of themselves as inclusively accountable for what they do together'. If collectively we cause harm, then – even though we do not deliberately set out to do something together, and the contribution of a single individual may make no difference to the harm done – each one of us is complicit in causing the harm and accountable for it.

It isn't clear, however, that we need a special non-consequentialist complicity principle of the kind that Kutz proposes. Neither the ozone damage nor global warming is like the case of a lawn that could withstand the tread of a few more people without any damage. By the time the dangers of CFCs and of greenhouse gases were known, the threshold for damage had already been crossed. Our emissions of CFCs were, and our emissions of greenhouse gases still are, making the situation worse – and of course the damage is much more serious than ruining a lawn. This suggests that we do not need to depart from consequentialism to show what is wrong with emitting harmful gases into the atmosphere. In *Reasons and Persons*, Derek Parfit points out that we tend to think that we can only be harming others in a serious way if there is someone who has a ground for a serious complaint. That may be a relic of the conditions of our earlier existence when, as mentioned at the beginning of this chapter, if we harmed someone, it was usually obvious that we had done so, and nothing we did was likely to affect a very large number of people. Now our actions can affect millions – perhaps billions. This means that we can inflict harm that is so broadly dispersed that no one individual can plausibly claim to have been seriously affected by it.

Jonathan Glover offers a vivid illustration of how ignoring impercept-ible harms can lead us astray. Glover imagines that in a poor village, 100 people are about to eat lunch. Each has a bowl containing 100 beans. Suddenly, 100 hungry bandits swoop down on the village. Each bandit takes the contents of the bowl of one villager, eats it, and gallops off. Next week, the bandits plan to do it again, but one of them is afflicted by qualms about causing poor peasants to go hungry. These doubts are set to rest by another bandit who proposes that each of them should take no more than one bean from any villager's bowl. Because the loss of one bean cannot make a perceptible difference to any villager – you don't really notice if you are eating 99 or 100 beans – no bandit will have made anyone worse off. So the bandits swoop down on the village, but instead of just grabbing a whole bowl from a villager, each bandit goes to all 100 villagers, taking just one solitary bean from each bowl. The villagers are just as hungry as they were the previous week, but the bandits can all sleep well on their full stomachs, knowing that none of them has harmed anyone.

Glover's example shows the absurdity of disregarding tiny harms. Even if each of us makes no perceptible difference, we are each responsible for a share of the total harms we collectively cause. If, acting together with a billion other affluent people, we each emit twenty tons of carbon dioxide, each of us makes only an imperceptible difference to the climate and so inflicts only an imperceptible harm on anyone. Yet we are still, collectively, inflicting a very great harm on a very large number of people, and we must bear our share of responsibility for that. We can, following Kutz, see the wrongness of what we are doing in terms of a non-consequentialist principle of complicity, but we can also see it, at least in this kind of case, as consistent with a strict application of consequentialism.

Up to this point, we have been assuming that my change of lifestyle, and that of many others acting on a similarly voluntary basis, will over time result in less carbon dioxide in the atmosphere than there would have been if we had not reduced our emissions. That seems obvious, but as we saw earlier, James Hansen has pointed out that if the government adopts a cap and trade scheme for reducing carbon emissions, individual reductions in carbon emissions may have no effect on reducing emissions. Suppose my government commits itself to reduce greenhouse gases by, say, 50 percent by 2050. In order to achieve this, it calculates how much carbon can be emitted each year and auctions permits, which major emitters need to buy in order to continue to run their power stations or factories. If more people install solar panels, and fewer coal-fired power stations are required, power companies will not need to buy so many permits; or if they have already bought them, they will have surplus permits to sell to whoever needs them. The price of permits will fall and with it the cost of carbon-intensive products. Consumers who care more about saving money than about doing what is right will buy more of these products, and, if the emissions trading scheme is well-designed and implemented, emissions will still equal the target the government has set. The savings in emissions caused by my change of lifestyle will not have resulted in fewer emissions overall.

Could there still be benefits in voluntary lifestyle changes that reduce emissions, even under a cap and trade scheme? People who consume less demonstrate that we can live more lightly on the planet. If the target set by the government for cutting greenhouse gas is easily met, that could persuade the government to make its next target more ambitious. When people change their lifestyles, they are expressing their values and encouraging others to reconsider their values as well. That could lead to greater concern for the environment and for all who share the planet with us. Changes in consumption could also reduce the profits of carbon-intensive industries and thus diminish their lobbying power with the government. This might be particularly important with an industry that has a lot of political muscle, such as the beef industry. Cattle and sheep emit high levels of methane, and hence the livestock industry is a major contributor to climate change – in fact, worldwide, livestock contributes more to global warming than all forms of transport combined. Because of this, in 2010 the UN's Food and Agriculture Organization proposed a tax on livestock. Nevertheless, in many countries livestock producers are lobbying to be exempted from carbon trading schemes, and in some countries, at the time of writing, these lobbying efforts appear to be having considerable success. If they do succeed, a voluntary boycott of products from cattle and sheep would be the only way to reduce the large quantity of emissions these industries cause.

For non-consequentialists, the complicity principle is relevant here. If the government's emissions trading scheme does not cut greenhouse gas emissions to a point at which there is no further danger of serious damage to the planet's climate – and at the time of writing, no country has implemented a scheme that will cut greenhouse gases sufficiently to eliminate such risks – then to continue to emit greenhouse gases, even at a level consistent with the government's scheme, is still to participate in a wrongful practice that will harm others. A non-consequentialist could therefore hold that our intentional participation in this practice is wrong, even if cutting one's own emissions to zero would have no impact on the total amount of greenhouse gases put into the atmosphere. This is a kind of 'I'm keeping my hands clean, anyway, even if it makes no difference' approach that is difficult to justify on direct consequentialist grounds, but some successful movements for change have their origins in the actions of those who resist evil without really giving themselves any chance of making a difference. A resolutely non-consequentialist stance can have good consequences. Perhaps our sense that it is objectionable to be complicit in a harmful practice, even if our own actions make no difference, has arisen because it will sometimes have best consequences if people act as if they were non-consequentialists.

One thing on which everyone can agree is that in addition to being responsible for the wrong we do, either individually or collectively, through our emissions, we have an obligation to try to change the policy of our government in whatever way will best slow the rate of climate change. As we have seen, in failing to cut their greenhouse gas emissions, the rich nations are culpably causing harm to others on a vast scale. There is room for diverse opinions on the best method of cutting emissions. It might involve adopting a carbon trading scheme, or a carbon tax, so that everyone has a strong financial incentive for avoiding products that required the emission of greenhouse gases. By putting a price on carbon emissions – which ideally would mean, including in the price of activities that emit carbon the full cost these activities impose on third parties who are harmed by climate change – we create an incentive for finding new ways to discover cost-effective, low-emission forms of energy that will replace the use of fossil fuels simply because they are cheaper. We can also urge governments to fund research and development in such forms of energy. Note, however, that even if we did find a replacement for fossil fuels, that would still leave untouched the problem of methane emissions from cattle and sheep, so these emissions also need to be taxed or brought within the scope of a carbon trading scheme.

Given the gravity of the risks that our planet and its entire population face from climate change over the next century, the level of protest against inaction has, to date, been quite small. There is an urgent need for greater understanding about what is likely to happen if we do not start cutting, deeply and rapidly, our greenhouse gas emissions. In this situation, we should not be passive spectators.

10

The Environment

A river tumbles through forested ravines and rocky gorges towards the sea. The state hydro-electricity commission sees the falling water as untapped energy. Building a dam across one of the gorges would provide three years of employment for a thousand people, and longer-term employment for twenty or thirty. The dam would store enough water to ensure that the state could economically meet its energy needs for the next decade. This would encourage the establishment of energy-intensive industry thus further contributing to employment and economic growth.

The rough terrain of the river valley makes it accessible only to the reasonably fit, but it is nevertheless a favoured spot for bushwalking. The river itself attracts the more daring whitewater rafters. Deep in the sheltered valleys are stands of rare Huon pine, many of the trees being more than a thousand years old. The valleys and gorges are home to many birds and animals, including an endangered species of marsupial mouse that has seldom been found outside the valley. There may be other rare plants and animals as well, but no one knows, for scientists are yet to investigate the region fully.

Should the dam be built? This is one example of a situation in which we must choose between very different sets of values. The description is loosely based on a proposed dam on the Franklin River, in the south-west of Australia's island state, Tasmania. An account of the fate of that proposal can be found in Chapter 11, but I have deliberately altered some details, and this description should be treated as a hypothetical case. Many other examples would have posed the choice between values equally well: logging virgin forests, building a paper mill that will release pollutants into coastal waters, or opening a new mine on the edge of a national park. In this chapter, I shall explore the values that underlie debates about these decisions, and the example I have presented can serve as a point of reference to these debates. I shall focus particularly on the values at issue in controversies about the preservation of wilderness because here the fundamentally different values of the two parties are most apparent. When we are talking about flooding a river valley, the choice before us is starkly clear.

In general terms, we can say that those who favour building the dam are valuing employment and a higher per capita income for the state above the preservation of wilderness, of plants and animals (both common ones and members of endangered species) and of opportunities for outdoor recreational activities. Before we begin to scrutinize the values of those who would have the dam built and those who would not, however, let's look at the roots of our attitudes towards the natural world.

THE WESTERN TRADITION

Western attitudes to nature grew out of a blend of those of the Hebrew people, as represented in the early books of the Bible, and the philosophy of ancient Greece, particularly that of Aristotle. In contrast to some other ancient traditions, for example those of India, both the Hebrew and the Greek traditions put humans at the centre of the moral universe. Indeed, in some respects even that understates the importance that humans have in the Western tradition, because it suggests that other beings have moral significance, even if they are less centrally important. For much of the Western tradition, however, humans are not merely of central moral significance, they constitute the entirety of the morally significant features of this world.

The biblical story of creation in *Genesis* makes very clear the Hebrew view of the special place of human beings in the divine plan:

And God said, Let us make man in our image, after our likeness: and let them have dominion over the fish of the sea, and over the fowl of the air, and over the earth, and over every creeping thing that creepeth upon the earth.

So God created man in his own image, in the image of God created he him; male and female created he them.

And God blessed them, and God said upon them, Be fruitful, and multiply, and replenish the earth, and subdue it; and have dominion over the fish of the sea and over the fowl of the air, and over every living thing that moveth upon the earth.

Today, Christians debate the meaning of this grant of 'dominion'. Those concerned about the environment prefer to interpret it as 'stewardship'; that is, not as a license to do as we will with other living things, but rather as a directive to look after them, on God's behalf, and be answerable to God for the way in which we treat them. There is, however, little justification in the text itself for such an interpretation; and given the example God set when he drowned almost every animal on earth in order to punish human beings for their wickedness, it is no wonder that people should think the flooding of a single river valley is hardly worth worrying about. After the flood there is a repetition of the grant of dominion in more ominous language:

And the fear of you and the dread of you shall be upon every beast of the earth, and upon every fowl of the air, upon all that moveth upon the earth, and upon all the fishes of the sea; into your hands are they delivered.

The implication is clear: to act in a way that causes fear and dread to everything that moves on the earth is not improper; it is, in fact, in accordance with a God-given decree.

The most influential early Christian thinkers had no doubts about how man's dominion was to be understood. 'Doth God care for oxen?' asked Paul, in the course of a discussion of an Old Testament command to rest one's ox on the Sabbath, but it was only a rhetorical question – he took it for granted that the answer must be negative, and the command was to be explained in terms of some benefit to humans. Augustine shared this line of thought. He explained the puzzling stories in the New Testament in which Jesus appears to show indifference to both trees and animals – fatally cursing a fig tree and causing a herd of pigs to drown – as intended to teach us that 'to refrain from the killing of animals and the destroying of plants is the height of superstition'.

When Christianity prevailed in the Roman Empire, it absorbed elements of the ancient Greek attitude to the natural world. The Greek influence was entrenched in Christian philosophy by the greatest of the medieval scholastics, Thomas Aquinas, whose life work was the melding of Christian theology with the thought of Aristotle. Aristotle regarded nature as a hierarchy in which those with less reasoning ability exist for the sake of those with more:

Plants exist for the sake of animals, and brute beasts for the sake of man – domestic animals for his use and food, wild ones (or at any rate most of them) for food and other accessories of life, such as clothing and various tools. Since nature makes nothing purposeless or in vain, it is undeniably true that she has made all animals for the sake of man.

In his own major work, the *Summa Theologica*, Aquinas followed this passage from Aristotle almost word for word, adding that the position accords with God's command, as given in *Genesis*. In his classification of sins, Aquinas has room only for sins against God, ourselves or our neighbours. There is no possibility of sinning against nonhuman animals or against the natural world.

This was the thinking of mainstream Christianity for at least its first eighteen centuries. There were gentler spirits, certainly, like Basil, John Chrysostom and Francis of Assisi, but for most of Christian history they have had no significant impact on the dominant tradition. It is therefore worth emphasising the major features of this dominant Western tradition, because these features can serve as a point of comparison when we discuss different views of the natural environment.

According to the dominant Western tradition, the natural world exists for the benefit of human beings. God gave human beings dominion over the natural world, and God does not care how we treat it. Human beings are the only morally important members of this world. Nature itself is of no intrinsic value, and the destruction of plants and animals cannot be sinful, unless by this destruction we harm human beings.

Harsh as this tradition is, it does not rule out concern for the preservation of nature, as long as that concern can be related to human well-being. One could, within the limits of the dominant Western tradition, oppose the burning of fossil fuels, the destruction of forests and the proliferation of methane-emitting cattle because of the harm to human health and welfare that will occur as a result of climate change. As for arguments about preserving wilderness, there was a time when wilderness seemed to be a wasteland, a useless area that needed clearing in order to render it productive and valuable. Now, however, a different metaphor is more appropriate: the remnants of true wilderness left to us are like islands amidst a sea of human activity that threatens to engulf them. This gives wilderness a scarcity value that provides the basis for a strong argument for preservation, even within the terms of a human-centred ethic. That argument becomes much stronger still when we take a long-term view. We shall now turn to this immensely important aspect of environmental values.

FUTURE GENERATIONS

A virgin forest is the product of all the millions of years that have passed since the beginning of our planet. If it is cut down, another forest may grow up, but the continuity has been broken. The disruption in the natural life cycles of the plants and animals means that the forest will never again be as it would have been had it not been cut. The gains made from cutting the forest – employment, profits for business, export earnings and cheaper cardboard and paper for packaging – are short-term. Even if the forest is not cut but drowned to build a dam to create electricity, it is very likely that the benefits will last for only a few generations, for in time new technology will render such methods of generating power obsolete. Once the forest is cut or drowned, however, the link with the past is gone forever. That is a cost that will be borne by every generation that succeeds us on this planet. It is for that reason that environmentalists are right to speak of wilderness as a 'world heritage'. It is something that we have inherited from our ancestors and that *we* must preserve for our descendents if they are to have it at all.

In many stable, tradition-oriented human societies, the prevailing culture strongly emphasizes preservation. Our culture, on the other hand, has great difficulty in recognizing long-term values. It is notorious that politicians rarely look beyond the next election; but even if they do, they will find their economic advisors telling them that anything to be gained in the future should be discounted to such a degree as to make it easy to disregard the long-term future altogether. Economists have been taught to apply a discount rate to all future goods. In other words, a million dollars in twenty years is not worth a million dollars today, even when we allow for inflation. Economists will discount the value of the million dollars by a certain percentage, usually corresponding to the real long-term interest rates. This makes economic sense, because if I had a thousand dollars today I could invest it so that it would be worth more, in real terms, in twenty years, but the use of a discount rate also means that values gained in the more distant future may count for very little today. Suppose that we believe that in 200 years, people would be prepared to pay a million dollars (that's in today's dollars, not inflated ones) to be able to have an unspoilt valley. Now imagine that today we can profit by cutting down the forest in the valley, which will never regrow. If we apply an annual discount rate of 5 percent, compounded exponentially, how big would that profit have to be to justify the loss of a million dollars in 2210? The answer, surprisingly, is just sixty dollars! That's all that a million dollars in 200 years is worth, at that rate of discount. Obviously, then, if we use a 5 percent discount rate, values gained one thousand years in the future scarcely count at all. This is not because of any uncertainty about whether there will be human beings or other sentient creatures inhabiting this planet at that time, but merely because of the compounding effect of the rate of return on money invested now. From the standpoint of the priceless and timeless values of wilderness, however, applying a discount rate gives us the wrong answer. There are some things that, once lost, no amount of money can regain. Thus, to justify the destruction of an ancient forest on the grounds that it will earn us substantial export income is unsound, even if we could invest that income and increase its value from year to year; for no matter how much we increased its value, it could never buy back the link with the past represented by the forest.

This argument does not show that there can be no justification for cutting any virgin forests, but it does mean that any such justification must take full account of the value of the forests to the generations to come in the more remote future, as well as those in the more immediate future. This value will obviously be related to the particular scenic or biological significance of the forest; but as the proportion of true wilderness on the earth dwindles, every part of it becomes significant, because the opportunities for experiencing wilderness become scarce, and the likelihood of a reasonable selection of the major forms of wilderness being preserved is reduced.

Can we be sure that future generations will appreciate wilderness? Not really; perhaps they will be happier playing electronic games more sophisticated than any we can imagine. Nevertheless, there are several reasons why we should not give this possibility too much weight. First, the trend has been in the opposite direction: the appreciation of wilderness has never been higher than it is today, especially among those nations that have overcome the problems of poverty and hunger and have relatively little wilderness left. Wilderness is valued as something of immense beauty, as a reservoir of scientific knowledge still to be gained, for the recreational opportunities that it provides, and because many people just like to know that something natural is still there, relatively untouched by modern civilization. If, as we all hope, future generations are able to provide for the basic needs of most people, we can expect that for centuries to come, they too will value wilderness for the same reasons that we value it.

Arguments for preservation based on the beauty of wilderness are sometimes treated as if they were of little weight because they are 'merely aesthetic' – even though we go to great lengths to preserve the artistic treasures of earlier human civilizations. It is difficult to imagine any economic gain that we would be prepared to accept as adequate compensation for, for instance, the destruction of all the art in the Louvre. How should we compare the aesthetic value of wilderness with that of the art in the Louvre? Here, perhaps, judgment does become inescapably subjective; so I shall report my own experiences. I have looked at the paintings in the Louvre, and of many of the other great galleries of Europe and the United States. I think I have a reasonable sense of appreciation of the fine arts; yet I have not had, in any museum, experiences that fill my aesthetic senses as they are filled when I hike to a rocky peak and pause there to survey the forested valley below, or if I sit by a stream tumbling over moss-covered boulders set among tall tree ferns growing in the shade of the forest canopy. I do not think I am alone in this – for many people, wilderness is the source of the greatest feelings of aesthetic appreciation, rising to an almost spiritual intensity.

It may nevertheless be true that this appreciation of nature will not be shared by people living a century or two hence. If wilderness can be the source of such deep joy and satisfaction, that would be a great loss. Moreover to some extent, whether future generations value wilderness is up to us; it is, at least, a decision we can influence. By our preservation of areas of wilderness, we provide opportunities for generations to come; and by the books and films we produce, we create a culture that can be handed on to our children and their children. If we feel that a walk in the forest, with senses attuned to the appreciation of such an experience, is a more deeply rewarding way to spend a day than playing electronic games, or if we feel that to carry one's food and shelter in a backpack for a week while hiking through an unspoilt natural environment will do more to develop character than watching television for an equivalent period, then we ought to do what we can to encourage future generations to have a feeling for nature.

Finally, if we preserve intact the amount of wilderness that exists now, future generations will at least have the choice of going to see a world that has not been created by human beings. If we destroy the wilderness, that choice is gone forever. Just as we rightly spend large sums to preserve cities like Venice, even though future generations conceivably may not be interested in such architectural treasures, so we should preserve wilderness even though it is possible that future generations will care little for it. Thus, we will not wrong future generations, as we have been wronged by members of past generations whose thoughtless actions have deprived us of the possibility of seeing such animals as the dodo, Steller's sea cow, or the thylacine, the striped marsupial also known as the 'Tasmanian tiger'. We must take care not to inflict equally irreparable losses on the generations that follow us.

For this reason, too, the efforts to mitigate the greenhouse effect discussed in the previous chapter deserve the highest priority. For if by 'wilderness' we mean that part of our planet that is unaffected by human activity, it is already too late: there is no wilderness left anywhere on our planet. The first popular book to warn of the dangers of climate change was Bill McKibben's *The End of Nature*. In it, McKibben argued: 'By changing the weather, we make every spot on earth man-made and artificial. We have deprived nature of its independence, and that is fatal to its meaning. Nature's independence is its meaning; without it there is nothing but us.' This is a profoundly disturbing thought. Yet McKibben does not develop it in order to suggest that we may as well give up our efforts to reverse the trend. It is true that, as McKibben says, 'we live in a postnatural world'. Nothing can undo that; the climate of our planet is under our influence. We still have, however, much that we value in nature, and it may still be possible to save at least a part of what is left.

Thus, a human-centred ethic can be the basis of powerful arguments for what we may call 'environmental values'. Properly understood, such an ethic does not imply that economic growth is more important than the preservation of wilderness. In the light of our discussion of speciesism in Chapter 3, however, it should also be clear that it is wrong to limit ourselves to a human-centred ethic. We need to consider more fundamental challenges to this traditional Western approach to environmental issues.

IS THERE VALUE BEYOND SENTIENT BEINGS?

Although some debates about significant environmental issues can be conducted by appealing only to the long-term interests of our own species, in any serious exploration of environmental values a central issue will be the question of intrinsic value. We have already seen that it is arbitrary to hold that only human beings are of intrinsic value. If we find value in human conscious experiences, we cannot deny that there is value in at least some experiences of nonhuman beings. How far does this extend? To all, but only, sentient beings? Or beyond the boundary of sentience?

To explore this question, a few remarks on the notion of 'intrinsic value' will be helpful. Something is of intrinsic value if it is good or desirable in itself, in contrast to something having only 'instrumental value' as a means to some other end or purpose. Our own happiness, for example, is of intrinsic value, at least to most of us, in that we desire it for its own sake. Money, on the other hand, is only of instrumental value. We want it because of the things we can buy with it. If we were marooned on a desert island, we would not want it. Happiness, however, would be just as important to us on a desert island as anywhere else.

Now consider again the issue of damming the river described at the beginning of this chapter. If the decision were to be made on the basis of human interests alone, we would balance the economic benefits of the dam against the loss for bushwalkers, scientists and others, now and in the future, who value the preservation of the river in its natural state. We have already seen that because this calculation includes an indefinite number of future generations, the loss of the wild river is a much greater cost than we might at first imagine. Even so, once we broaden the basis of our decision beyond the interests of human beings, we have much more to set against the economic benefits of building the dam. Into the calculations must now go the interests of all the nonhuman animals who live in the area that will be flooded. Most of the animals living in the flooded area will die: either they will be drowned, or they will starve. A few may be able to move to a neighbouring area that is suitable, but wilderness is not full of vacant niches awaiting an occupant. If there is territory that can sustain a native animal, it is most likely already occupied. Neither drowning nor starvation are easy ways to die, and the suffering involved in these deaths should, as we have seen, be given no less weight than we would give to a similar amount of suffering experienced by human beings. This will significantly increase the weight of considerations against building the dam.

What of the fact that the animals will die, apart from the suffering that will occur in the course of dying? As we have seen, one can, without being guilty of arbitrary discrimination on the basis of species, regard the death of a nonhuman 'merely conscious' animal as less significant than the death of a person, because normal humans are capable of foresight and forward planning in ways that merely conscious animals are not. This difference between causing death to a person and to a merely conscious animal does not mean that the deaths of the animals should be treated as being of no account. On the contrary, utilitarians will take into account the loss that death inflicts on the animals – the loss of all their future existence and the experiences that their future lives would have contained. When a proposed dam would flood a valley and kill thousands, perhaps millions, of sentient creatures, these deaths should be given great importance in any assessment of the costs and benefits of building the dam. For those utilitarians who accept the total view discussed in Chapter 4, moreover, if the dam destroys the habitat in which the animals lived, then it is relevant that this loss is a continuing one. If the dam is not built, animals will presumably continue to live in the valley for thousands of years, experiencing their own distinctive pleasures and pains. One might question whether life for animals in a natural environment yields a surplus of pleasure over pain, or of satisfaction over frustration of preferences – and if there will be fish in the dam, the total utilitarian would have to take the pleasures of their existence into account too as offsetting, to some extent, the loss of the pleasures of the forest animals. At this point, the idea of calculating benefits becomes almost absurd; but that does not mean that the loss of future animal lives should be dismissed from our decision making.

That, however, may not be all. Should we also give weight, not only to the suffering and death of individual animals, but to the fact that an entire species may disappear? What of the loss of trees that have stood for thousands of years? How much – if any – weight should we give to the preservation of the animals, the species, the trees and the valley's ecosystem, independently of the interests of human beings – whether economic, recreational or scientific – in their preservation?

Here we have a fundamental moral disagreement: a disagreement about what kinds of beings ought to be considered in our moral deliberations. Let us look at what has been said on behalf of extending ethics beyond sentient beings.

Reverence for Life

The ethical position developed in this book extends the ethic of the dominant Western tradition but in other respects is recognizably of the same type. It draws the boundary of moral consideration around all sentient creatures, but it leaves other living things outside that boundary. The drowning of the ancient forests, the possible loss of an entire species, the destruction of several complex ecosystems, the blockage of the wild river itself and the loss of those rocky gorges are factors to be taken into account only insofar as they adversely affect sentient creatures. Is a more radical break with the traditional position possible? Can some or all of these aspects of the flooding of the valley be shown to have intrinsic value, so that they must be taken into account independently of their effects on human beings or nonhuman animals?

To extend an ethic in a plausible way beyond sentient beings is a difficult task. An ethic based on the interests of sentient creatures is on familiar ground. Sentient creatures have wants and desires. The question: 'What is it like to be a possum drowning?' at least makes sense, even if it is impossible for us to give a more precise answer than 'It must be horrible'. In reaching moral decisions affecting sentient creatures, we can attempt to add up the effects of different actions on all the sentient creatures affected by the alternative actions open to us. This provides us with at least some rough guide to what might be the right thing to do. There is, however, nothing that corresponds to what it is like to be a tree dying because its roots have been flooded. Once we abandon the interests of sentient creatures as our source of value, where do we find value? What is good or bad for nonsentient creatures, and why does it matter?

It might be thought that as long as we limit ourselves to living things, the answer is not too difficult to find. We know what is good or bad for the plants in our garden: water, sunlight and compost are good; extremes of heat or cold are bad. The same applies to plants in any forest or wilderness, so why not regard their flourishing as good in itself, independently of its usefulness to sentient creatures?

One problem here is that without conscious interests to guide us, we have no way of assessing the relative weights to be given to the flourishing of different forms of life. Is a thousand-year-old Huon pine more worthy of preservation than a tussock of grass? Most people will say that it is, but such a judgment seems to have more to do with our feelings of awe for the age, size and beauty of the tree, or with the length of time it would take to replace it, than with our perception of some intrinsic value in the flourishing of an old tree that is not possessed by a young grass tussock.

If we cease talking in terms of sentience, the boundary between living and inanimate natural objects becomes more difficult to defend. Would it really be worse to cut down an old tree than to destroy a beautiful stalactite that has taken even longer to grow? On what grounds could such a judgment be made? Probably the best known defence of an ethic that extends to all living things is that of the remarkable theologian, philosopher, musician, physician and humanitarian, Albert Schweitzer. In 1952, Schweitzer was awarded the Nobel Peace Prize for his humanitarian work in founding a hospital in Gabon and for his ethic of 'reverence for life'. Though that phrase is often quoted, the arguments he offered in support of such a position are less well-known. Here is one of the few passages in which he defended his ethic:

True philosophy must commence with the most immediate and comprehensive facts of consciousness. And this may be formulated as follows: 'I am life which wills to live, and I exist in the midst of life which wills to live' ... Just as in my own will-to-live there is a yearning for more life, and for that mysterious exaltation of the will which is called pleasure, and terror in face of annihilation and that injury to the will-to-live which is called pain; so the same obtains in all the will-to-live around me, equally whether it can express itself to my comprehension or whether it remains unvoiced.

Ethics thus consists in this, that I experience the necessity of practising the same reverence for life toward all will-to-live, as toward my own. Therein I have already the needed fundamental principle of morality. It is good to maintain and cherish life; it is evil to destroy and to check life. A man is really ethical only when he obeys the constraint laid on him to help all life which he is able to succour, and when he goes out of his way to avoid injuring anything living. He does not ask how far this or that life deserves sympathy as valuable in itself, nor how far it is capable of feeling. To him life as such is sacred. He shatters no ice crystal that sparkles in the sun, tears no leaf from its tree, breaks off no flower, and is careful not to crush any insect as he walks. If he works by lamplight on a summer evening he prefers to keep the window shut and to breathe stifling air, rather than to see insect after insect fall on his table with singed and sinking wings.

The American philosopher Paul Taylor defended a similar view in his book *Respect for Nature*, arguing that every living thing is 'pursuing its own good in its own unique way'. Once we see this, he claims, we can see all living things 'as we see ourselves', and therefore 'we are ready to place the same value on their existence as we do on our own'.

It is not clear how we should interpret Schweitzer's position. The reference to the ice crystal is especially puzzling, for an ice crystal is not alive at all. Does Schweitzer perhaps see any form of killing as a kind of vandalism, a pointless destruction of something of value? Putting this possibility aside, however, the problem with the defences offered by both Schweitzer and Taylor for their ethical views is that they use language metaphorically and then argue as if what they had said was literally true. We may often talk about plants 'seeking' water or light so that they can survive, and this way of thinking about plants makes it easier to accept talk of their 'will to live' or of them 'pursuing' their own good. Once we stop to reflect on the fact that plants are not conscious and cannot engage in any intentional behaviour, however, it is clear that all this language is metaphorical; one might just as well say that a river is pursuing its own good and striving to reach the sea, or that the 'good' of a guided missile is to blow up its target. It is misleading of Schweitzer to attempt to sway us towards an ethic of reverence for all life by referring to 'yearning', 'exaltation', 'pleasure' and 'terror'. Plants experience none of these.

Holmes Rolston, an American environmental philosopher, has objected to my comparison – which first appeared in the second edition of this book – between the 'seeking' behaviour of a plant and a guided missile. He argues that when a missile closes in on a target and blows it up, that may be good for the people who launched the missile, but it is not good for the missile itself. The missile was designed and built for a purpose. With plants and other natural organisms, on the other hand, Rolston writes:

Natural selection picks out whatever traits an organism has that are valuable to it, relative to its survival. When natural selection has been at work gathering these traits into an organism, that organism is able to value on the basis of those traits. It is a valuing organism, even if the organism is not a sentient valuer, much less a conscious evaluator. And those traits, though picked out by natural selection, are innate in the organism, that is, stored in its genes. It is difficult to dissociate the idea of value from natural selection.

Rolston fails to explain why natural selection gives rise to valuing in the organism, but human design and manufacture does not. He must be aware that there is something odd about the idea of a valuer that is not sentient or conscious. In defence of that view, he asks what he appears to think is a rhetorical question: 'Why is the organism not valuing what it is making resources of?' But we can build solar-powered machines that turn their solar panels to the sun so as to get the most energy for their batteries. Should we say that these devices are valuing the sunlight they use? If not, does the difference lie in the fact that the plant's means of sending its roots out towards water are encoded in its genes, whereas the machine's means of obtaining sunlight are encoded in its computer programs? Why would that make one a valuer and the other not?

There are important differences between living things and machines designed by humans. Nevertheless, in the case of both plants and machines, it is possible to give a purely physical explanation of what the organism or machine is doing; and in the absence of consciousness, there is no good reason why we should have greater respect for the physical processes that govern the growth and decay of living things than we have for those that govern non-living things. This being so, it is at least not obvious why we should have greater reverence for a tree than for a stalactite, or for a single-celled organism than for a mountain.

Deep Ecology

More than sixty years ago, the American ecologist Aldo Leopold wrote that there was a need for a 'new ethic', an 'ethic dealing with man's relation to land and to the animals and plants which grow upon it'. His proposed 'land ethic' would enlarge 'the boundaries of the community to include soils, waters, plants, and animals, or collectively, the land'. The rise of ecological concern in the 1970s led to a revival of interest in this attitude. The Norwegian philosopher Arne Naess wrote a brief but influential article distinguishing between 'shallow' and 'deep' strands in the ecological movement. Shallow ecological thinking was limited to the traditional moral framework: those who thought in this way were anxious to avoid pollution to our water supply so that we could have safe water to drink, and they sought to preserve wilderness so that people could continue to enjoy walking through it. Deep ecologists, on the other hand, wanted to preserve the integrity of the biosphere for its own sake, irrespective of the possible benefits to humans that might flow from so doing. Subsequently, several other writers have attempted to develop some form of 'deep' environmental theory.

Whereas the reverence for life ethic emphasises individual living organisms, proposals for deep ecology ethics tend to take something larger as the object of value: species, ecological systems, and even the biosphere as a whole. Leopold summed up the basis of his new Land Ethic thus: 'A thing is right when it tends to preserve the integrity, stability and beauty of the biotic community. It is wrong when it tends otherwise.' Subsequently, Arne Naess and George Sessions, an American philosopher involved in the deep ecology movement, set out several principles for a deep ecological ethic, beginning with the following:

1. The well-being and flourishing of human and non-human Life on Earth have value in themselves (synonyms: intrinsic value, inherent value). These values are independent of the usefulness of the non-human world for human purposes.
2. Richness and diversity of life forms contribute to the realization of these values and are also values in themselves.
3. Humans have no right to reduce this richness and diversity except to satisfy vital needs.

Although these principles refer only to life, in the same paper Naess and Sessions say that deep ecology uses the term 'biosphere' in a more comprehensive way, to refer also to non-living things such as rivers (watersheds), landscapes and ecosystems. Two Australians working at the deep end of environmental ethics, Richard Sylvan and Val Plumwood, extended their ethic beyond living things, including in it an obligation 'not to jeopardise the wellbeing of natural objects or systems without good reason'.

In the previous section, I quoted Paul Taylor's remark to the effect that we should be ready, not merely to respect every living thing, but to place the same value on the life of every living thing as we place on our own. This is a common theme among deep ecologists, often extended beyond living things. In *Deep Ecology* Bill Devall and George Sessions defend a form of 'biocentric egalitarianism':

The intuition of biocentric equality is that all things in the biosphere have an equal right to live and blossom and to reach their own individual forms of unfolding and self-realization within the larger Self-realization. This basic intuition is that all organisms and entities in the ecosphere, as parts of the interrelated whole, are equal in intrinsic worth.

If, as this quotation appears to suggest, this biocentric equality rests on a 'basic intuition', it is up against some very strong intuitions that point in the opposite direction – for example, the intuition that the rights to 'live and blossom' of normal adult humans ought to be preferred over that of yeasts, and the rights of gorillas over those of grasses. If, on the other hand, the point is that humans, gorillas, yeasts and grasses are all parts of an interrelated whole, then it can still be asked how this establishes that they are equal in intrinsic worth. Is it because every living thing plays its role in an ecosystem on which all depend for their survival? But, firstly, even if this showed that there is intrinsic worth in micro-organisms and plants as a whole, it says nothing at all about the value of individual micro-organisms or plants, because no individual is necessary for the survival of the ecosystem as a whole. Secondly, the fact that all organisms are part of an interrelated whole does not suggest that they are all of intrinsic worth, let alone of equal intrinsic worth. They may be of worth only because they are needed for the existence of the whole, and the whole may be of worth only because it supports the existence of conscious beings.

The ethics of deep ecology thus fails to yield persuasive answers to questions about the value of the lives of individual living beings. Perhaps, though, this is the wrong kind of question to ask. The science of ecology looks at systems rather than individual organisms. In the same way, ecological ethics might be more plausible if it looks at the level of species and ecosystems rather than individual organisms. Behind many attempts to derive values from ecological ethics at this level lies some form of holism – some sense that the species or ecosystem is not just a collection of individuals but really an entity in its own right. This holism is made explicit in Lawrence Johnson's *A Morally Deep World*. Johnson is quite prepared to talk about the interests of a species, in a sense that is distinct from the sum of the interests of each member of the species, and to argue that the interests of a species or an ecosystem ought to be taken into account, alongside individual interests, in our moral deliberations. In *The Ecological Self*, Freya Mathews contends that any 'self-realizing system' has intrinsic value in that it seeks to maintain or preserve itself. Living organisms are paradigm examples of self-realizing systems, but Mathews, like Johnson, includes in this category species and ecosystems as holistic entities or selves with their own form of realization. She even includes the entire global ecosystem, following James Lovelock in referring to it by the name of the Greek goddess of the earth, Gaia. On this basis, she defends her own form of biocentric egalitarianism.

There is, of course, a real philosophical question about whether a species or an ecosystem can be considered as the sort of individual that can have interests, or a 'self' to be realized; and even if it can, the deep ecology ethic will face problems similar to those we identified in considering the idea of reverence for life. For it is necessary, not merely that trees, species and ecosystems can properly be said to have interests, but that they have morally significant interests. If they are to be regarded as 'selves', it will need to be shown that the survival or realization of that kind of self has moral value, independently of the value it has because of its importance in sustaining conscious life.

We saw in discussing the ethic of reverence for life that one way of establishing that an interest is morally significant is to ask what it is like for the entity affected to have that interest unsatisfied. The same question can be asked about self-realization: what is it like for the self to remain unrealized? Such questions yield intelligible answers when asked of sentient beings but not when asked of trees, species or ecosystems. The fact that, as James Lovelock points out in *Gaia: A New Look at Life on Earth*, the biosphere can respond to events in ways that resemble a self-maintaining system does not in itself show that the biosphere consciously desires to maintain itself. Calling the global ecosystem by the name of a Greek goddess is a cute idea, but it may not be the best way of helping us to think clearly about its nature. Similarly, on a smaller scale, there is nothing that corresponds to what it feels like to be an ecosystem flooded by a dam, because there is no such feeling. In this respect, trees, ecosystems and species are more like rocks than they are like sentient beings; so the divide between sentient and nonsentient creatures is to that extent a firmer basis for a morally important boundary than the divide between living and non-living things, or between holistic entities and any other entities that we might not regard as holistic. (Whatever these other entities could be: even a single atom is, when seen from the appropriate level, a complex system that 'seeks' to maintain itself.)

This rejection of the ethical basis for a deep ecology ethic does not mean that the case for the preservation of wilderness is not strong. All it means is that one kind of argument – the argument from the intrinsic value of the plants, species or ecosystems – is, at best, problematic. Unless it can be placed on some other, firmer, footing, we should confine ourselves to arguments based on the interests of sentient creatures – present and future, human and nonhuman. These arguments are quite sufficient to show that, at least in a society where no one needs to destroy wilderness in order to obtain food for survival or materials for shelter from the elements, the value of preserving the remaining significant areas of wilderness greatly exceeds the economic values gained by its destruction.

DEVELOPING AN ENVIRONMENTAL ETHIC

The broad outlines of a truly environmental ethic are easy to discern. At its most fundamental level, such an ethic fosters consideration for the interests of all sentient creatures, including subsequent generations stretching into the far future. It is accompanied by an aesthetic of appreciation for wild places and unspoilt nature. At a more detailed level, applicable to the lives of dwellers in cities and towns, it discourages large families. (Here, it forms a sharp contrast to some existing ethical beliefs that are relics of an age in which the earth was far more lightly populated; it also offers a counterweight, in practical terms, to the apparently repugnant implication of the 'total' version of utilitarianism discussed in Chapter 4.) An environmental ethic rejects the ideals of a materialist society in which success is gauged by the number of consumer goods one can accumulate. Instead, it judges success in terms of the development of one's abilities and the achievement of real fulfilment and satisfaction. It promotes frugality and re-use, insofar as that is necessary for minimising the impact we have on the planet. Thus, the various 'green consumer' guides and books about things we can do to save our planet – recycling what we use and buying the most environmentally friendly products available – are part of the new ethic that is required.

An environmental ethic leads us to re-assess our notion of extravagance. In a world under environmental pressure, this concept is not confined to chauffeured limousines and Dom Perignon champagne. Timber that has come from a rainforest is extravagant, because the long-term value of the rainforest is far greater than the uses to which the timber is put. Disposable paper products are extravagant if ancient hardwood forests are being converted into woodchips and sold to paper manufacturers. Motor sports are extravagant, because we can enjoy races that do not require the consumption of fossil fuels and the emission of greenhouse gases. Beef is extravagant because of the high methane emissions that are involved in its production, not to mention the waste of most of the food value of the grain and soybeans that are fed to beef cattle.

In Britain during the Second World War, when fuel was scarce, posters asked: 'Is your journey really necessary?' The appeal to national solidarity against a very visible and immediate danger was highly effective. The danger to our environment is harder to see, but the need to cut out unnecessary journeys, and other forms of unnecessary consumption, is just as great. The emphasis on frugality and a simple life does not mean that an environmental ethic frowns on pleasure, but that the pleasures it values do not come from conspicuous consumption. They come, instead, from loving relationships; from being close to children and friends; from conversation; from sports and recreations that are in harmony with our environment instead of harmful to it; from food that is not based on the exploitation of sentient creatures and does not cost the earth; from creative activity and work of all kinds; and (with due care so as not to ruin precisely what is valued) from appreciating the unspoilt places in the world in which we live.

Civil Disobedience, Violence and Terrorism

We have examined a number of ethical issues. We have seen that many accepted practices are open to serious objections. What ought we to do about it? This, too, is an ethical issue. Here are five cases – all ones that actually happened – to consider.

*

Oskar Schindler was a minor German industrialist. During the war, he ran a factory near Cracow, Poland. At a time when Polish Jews were being sent to death camps, he assembled a labour force of Jewish inmates from concentration camps and the ghetto, considerably larger than his factory needed, and used several illegal stratagems, including bribing members of the SS and other officials, to protect them. He spent his own money to buy food on the black market to supplement the inadequate official rations he obtained for his workers. By these methods, he was able to save the lives of about 1,200 people.

*

Dr. Thomas Gennarelli directed a Head Injury Laboratory at the University of Pennsylvania, in Philadelphia. Members of an underground organization called the Animal Liberation Front knew that Gennarelli inflicted head injuries on monkeys there and had been told that the monkeys underwent the experiments without being properly anaesthetised. They also knew that Gennarelli and his collaborators videotaped their experiments to provide a record of what happened during and after the injuries they inflicted. They tried to obtain further information through official channels but were unsuccessful. In May 1984, they broke into the laboratory at night and found thirty-four videotapes. They then systematically destroyed laboratory equipment before leaving with the tapes. The tapes clearly showed conscious monkeys struggling as they were being strapped to an operating table where head injuries were inflicted; they also showed experimenters mocking and laughing at frightened animals about to be used in experiments. When an edited version of the tapes was released to the public, it produced widespread revulsion. Nevertheless, it took a further year of protests, culminating in a sit-in at the headquarters of the government organization that was funding Gennarelli's experiments, before the United States Secretary of Health and Human Services ordered that the experiments stop.

*

In 1986, Joan Andrews entered an abortion clinic in Pensacola, Florida, and damaged a suction abortion apparatus. She refused to be represented in court, on the grounds that 'the true defendants, the pre-born children, received none, and were killed without due process'. Andrews was a supporter of Operation Rescue, an American organization that takes its name, and its authority to act, from the biblical injunction to 'Rescue those who are drawn toward death and hold back those stumbling to the slaughter.' Operation Rescue was, at the time, using civil disobedience to shut down abortion clinics, thus, in its view, 'sparing the lives of unborn babies whom the Rescuers are morally pledged to defend'. Participants blocked the doors of the clinics to prevent physicians and pregnant women seeking abortion from entering. They attempted to dissuade pregnant women from approaching the clinic by 'sidewalk counselling' on the nature of abortion. Gary Leber, then an Operation Rescue director, said that between 1987 and 1989 alone, as a direct result of such 'rescue missions', at least 421 women changed their minds about having abortions, and the children of these women, who would have been killed, are alive today. Charged with the damage she caused to the Pensacola clinic, Andrews, who had been arrested more than 130 times for her anti-abortion activities, refused to sign a statement promising not to continue her protests. She was sentenced to five years in prison. Since serving that sentence, she has continued to protest, was frequently arrested, and has served more time in prison. Meanwhile, Operation Rescue changed its leadership and its strategy, restricting itself to opposing abortion by legal means. Andrews is no longer associated with the organization.

*

In 1976, a young medical practitioner named Bob Brown rafted down the Franklin River in Tasmania's southwest. The wild beauty of the river and the peace of the undisturbed forests around it impressed him deeply. Then, around a bend on the lower reaches of the river, he came across workers for the Hydro-Electric Commission studying the feasibility of building a dam across the river. Brown gave up his medical practice and founded the Tasmanian Wilderness Society, with the object of protecting the state's remaining wilderness areas. Despite vigorous campaigning, the Hydro-Electric Commission recommended the building of the dam, and after some vacillation the State Government, with support from both the business community and the labour unions, decided to go ahead. The Tasmanian Wilderness Society organized a non-violent blockade of the road being built into the dam site. In 1982, Brown, along with many others, was arrested and jailed for four days for trespassing on land controlled by the Hydro-Electric Commission. The blockade turned the dam into a major issue in the Federal election that was then due. The Australian Labor Party, in opposition prior to the election, pledged to explore constitutional means of preventing the dam from going ahead. The election saw the Labor Party elected to office, and legislation passed to stop the dam. Though challenged by the Tasmanian Government, the legislation was upheld by a narrow majority of the High Court of Australia on the grounds that the Tasmanian Southwest was a World Heritage area, and the Federal Government had constitutional powers to uphold the international treaty creating the World Heritage Commission. Today, the Franklin still runs free. Senator Bob Brown leads the Australian Greens in the Australian Senate, where he represents Tasmania.

*

On a snowy March day in 2009, 2,500 activists surrounded the coal-fired Capitol Power Plant in Washington DC and shut it down for a few hours in protest against the government's inadequate response to global warming. It was the largest act of civil disobedience for climate change to have taken place in the United States. In an open letter released before the protest, Bill McKibben and Wendell Berry, two of America's most thoughtful writers on environmental questions, wrote: 'There are moments in a nation's – and a planet's – history when it may be necessary for some to break the law in order to bear witness to an evil, bring it to wider attention, and push for its correction.' They believed that that time had come, they said, in regard to climate change, and they were willing to make sacrifices themselves, 'even if it's only a trip to the jail'. (The protesters stepped over the property line of the plant and invited arrest, but police did not intervene and no one was arrested.) The protest had no noticeable effect on U.S. policy on climate change; but in the days leading up to it, it was announced that the plant would be converted from coal to natural gas, which will reduce its contribution to climate change.

*

Do we have an overriding obligation to obey the law? Oskar Schindler, the members of the Animal Liberation Front who took Gennarelli's video-tapes, Joan Andrews of Operation Rescue, Bob Brown and those who joined him in front of the bulldozers in Tasmania's southwest, and the protesters who blockaded the Capitol Power Plant were all breaking the law. Were they all acting wrongly?

The question cannot be dealt with by invoking the simplistic formula: 'The end never justifies the means.' For all but the strictest adherent of an ethic of rules, the end sometimes does justify the means. Most people think that lying is wrong, other things being equal, yet consider it right to lie in order to avoid causing unnecessary offence or embarrassment – for instance, when a well-meaning relative gives you a hideous vase for your birthday, and when you thank her politely she asks if you really like it. If this relatively trivial end can justify lying, it is even more obvious that some important end – preventing a murder, or saving animals from great suffering – can justify lying. Thus, the principle that the end cannot justify the means is easily breached. The difficult issue is not whether the end can ever justify the means, but which means are justified by which ends?

INDIVIDUAL CONSCIENCE AND THE LAW

There are many people who are opposed to damming wild rivers, to the exploitation of animals, to abortion and to power plants that emit large quantities of greenhouse gases, but they do not break the law in order to stop these activities. No doubt some members of the more conventional conservation, animal liberation and anti-abortion organizations do not commit illegal acts because they do not wish to be fined or imprisoned; but others would be prepared to take the consequences of illegal acts. They refrain only because they respect and obey the moral authority of the law.

Who is right in this ethical disagreement? Are we under any moral obligation to obey the law if the law protects and sanctions things we hold utterly wrong? A clear-cut answer to this question was given by the nineteenth-century American radical, Henry Thoreau. In his essay 'Civil

Disobedience' – perhaps the first use of this now familiar phrase – he wrote:

Must the citizen ever for a moment, or in the least degree, resign his conscience to the legislator? Why has every man a conscience, then? I think we should be men first and subjects afterwards. It is not desirable to cultivate a respect for the law, so much as for the right. The only obligation which I have a right to assume, is to do at any time what I think right.

In similar vein, the American philosopher Robert Paul Wolff wrote:

The defining mark of the state is authority, the right to rule. The primary obliga-tion of man is autonomy, the refusal to be ruled. It would seem, then, that there can be no resolution of the conflict between the autonomy of the individual and the putative authority of the state. Insofar as a man fulfills his obligation to make himself the author of his decisions, he will resist the state's claim to have authority over him.

Thoreau and Wolff resolve the conflict between individual and society in favour of the individual. We should do as our conscience dictates, as we autonomously decide we ought to do, not as the law directs. Anything else would be a denial of our capacity for ethical choice.

Thus stated, the issue looks straightforward and the Thoreau-Wolff answer obviously right. So Oskar Schindler, the Animal Liberation Front, Joan Andrews, Bob Brown, Wendell Berry and Bill McKibben were fully justified in doing what they saw to be right rather than what the state laid down as lawful. Is it that simple? There is a sense in which it is undeniable that, as Thoreau says, we ought to do what we think right or, as Wolff puts it, make ourselves the authors of our decisions. Faced with a choice between doing what we think right and what we think wrong, of course we ought to do what we think right. This, though true, is not much help. What we need to know is, not whether we should do what we decide to be right, but how we should decide what is right.

Think about the difference of opinion between members of groups like the Animal Liberation Front and more law-abiding members of organizations like the Humane Society of the United States or Britain's Royal Society for the Prevention of Cruelty to Animals: ALF members think inflicting pain on animals is, unless justified by extraordinary cir-cumstances, wrong, and if the best way to stop it is by breaking the law then they think that breaking the law is right. HSUS and RSPCA mem-bers – let us assume – also think that inflicting pain on animals is wrong, unless justified by extraordinary circumstances, but they think breaking the law is wrong too, and they think that the wrongness of breaking the law cannot be justified by the goal of stopping the unjustifiable infliction of pain on animals. Now suppose there are people opposed to inflicting pain on animals who are uncertain whether they should join the militant lawbreakers or the more conventional animal welfare group. How does telling these people to do what they think right, or to be the author of their own decisions, resolve their uncertainty? The uncertainty is an uncertainty about what is the right thing to do, not about whether to do what one has decided to be right.

This point can be obscured by talk of 'following one's conscience' irrespective of what the law commands. Some who talk of 'following conscience' mean no more than doing what, on reflection, one thinks right – and this may, as in the case of our imagined HSUS or RSPCA members, depend on what the law commands. Others mean by 'conscience', not something dependent on critical reflective judgment, but a kind of internal voice that tells us that something is wrong and may continue to tell us this despite our careful reflective decision, based on all the relevant ethical considerations, that the action is not wrong. In this sense of 'conscience', an unmarried woman brought up as a strict Roman Catholic to believe that sex outside marriage is always wrong may abandon her religion and come to hold that there is no sound basis for restricting sex to marriage – yet continue to feel guilty when she has sex. She may refer to these guilt feelings as her 'conscience', but if that is her conscience, should she follow it?

To say that we should follow our conscience is unobjectionable – but unhelpful – when 'following conscience' means doing what, on reflection, one thinks right. When 'following conscience' means doing as one's 'internal voice' prompts one to do, however, to follow one's conscience is to abdicate one's responsibility as a rational agent, to fail to take all the relevant factors into account and act on one's best judgment of the rights and wrongs of the situation. The 'internal voice' is more likely to be a product of one's upbringing and education than a source of genuine ethical insight.

Presumably neither Thoreau nor Wolff wishes to suggest that we should always follow our conscience in the 'internal voice' sense. They must mean, if their views are to be at all plausible, that we should follow our judgment about what we ought to do. In this case, the most that can be said for their recommendations is that they remind us that decisions about obeying the law are ethical decisions that the law itself cannot settle for us. We should not assume, without reflection, that if the law prohibits, say, stealing videotapes from laboratories, it is always wrong to do so – any more than we should assume that if the law prohibits hiding Jews from the Nazis, it is wrong to do so. Law and ethics are distinct. On the other hand, this does not mean that the law carries no moral weight. It does not mean that any action that would have been right if it had been legal must be right although it is in fact illegal. That an action is illegal *may* be of ethical, as well as legal, significance. Whether it really is ethically significant is a separate question.

LAW AND ORDER

If we think that a practice is very seriously wrong, and if we have the courage and ability to disrupt this practice by breaking the law, how could the illegality of this action provide an ethical reason against it? To answer a question as specific as this, we should first ask a more general one: why have laws at all?

Human beings are social in nature, but not so social that we do not need to protect ourselves against the risk of being assaulted or killed by our fellow humans. We might try to do this by forming vigilante organizations to prevent assaults and punish those who commit them, but the results would be haphazard and liable to grow into gang warfare. Thus, it is desirable to have, as John Locke said long ago, 'an established, settled, known law', interpreted by an authoritative judge and backed with sufficient power to carry out the judge's decisions.

If people voluntarily refrained from assaulting others, or acting in other ways inimical to a harmonious and happy social existence, we might manage without judges and sanctions. We would still need conventions about such matters as which side of the road one drives on. Even an anarchist utopia would have some settled principles of cooperation. So we would have something rather like law. In reality, not everyone is going to voluntarily refrain from behaviour, like assaults, that others cannot tolerate. Nor is it only the danger of individual acts like assaults that make law necessary. In any society there will be disputes: about how much water farmers may take from the river to irrigate their crops, about the ownership of land, about the custody of a child, about the control of pollution and about the level of taxation. Some settled decision procedure is necessary for resolving such disputes economically and speedily, or else the parties to the dispute are likely to resort to force. Almost any established decision procedure is better than a resort to force; for when force is used, people get hurt and the desire for retaliation is likely to lead to more violence. Moreover, most decision procedures produce results at least as beneficial and just as a resort to force.

So laws and a settled decision procedure to generate them are a good thing. This gives us one important reason for obeying the law. By obeying the law, I can contribute to the respect in which the established decision procedure and the laws are held. By disobeying, I set an example to others that may lead them to disobey too. The effect may multiply and contribute to a decline in law and order. In an extreme case, it may lead to civil war.

A second reason for obedience follows immediately from this first. If law is to be effective, then – given the way humans are – there must be some machinery for detecting and penalizing lawbreakers. This machinery will cost something to maintain and operate, and the cost will have to be met by the community. If I break the law, the community will be put to the expense of enforcement.

These two reasons for obeying the law are neither universally applicable nor conclusive. They are not, for instance, applicable to breaches of the law that remain secret. If, late at night when the streets are deserted, I cross the road against the red light, there is no one to be led into disobedience by my example and no one to enforce the law against me. But this is not the kind of illegality we are interested in.

In the absence of reasons for disobeying the law, these two reasons for obeying the law are sufficient to resolve the issue; but where there are conflicting reasons, we must assess each case on its merits in order to see if the reasons for disobedience outweigh these reasons for obedience. If, for instance, illegal acts were the only way of preventing many painful experiments on animals, of saving significant areas of wilderness, or of bringing about deep cuts in greenhouse gas emissions, the importance of the ends would justify running some risk of contributing to a general decline in obedience to law.

DEMOCRACY

At this point, some will say: the difference between Oskar Schindler's heroic deeds and the indefensible illegal actions of the Animal Liberation Front, Joan Andrews, the opponents of the Franklin dam, and those who commit civil disobedience to spur action on climate change, is that in Nazi Germany, there were no legal channels that Schindler could use to bring about change. All of the others were living in a democracy and could have made use of legal means of stopping what they considered to be wrong. The existence of legal procedures for changing the law makes the use of illegal means unjustifiable.

It is true that in democratic societies there are legal procedures that can be used by those seeking reforms, but this in itself does not show that the use of illegal means is always wrong. Legal channels may exist, but the prospects of using them to bring about change in the foreseeable future may be very poor. While one makes slow and painful progress – or perhaps no progress at all – through these legal channels, the indefensible wrongs one is trying to stop will be continuing. Prior to the successful struggle to save the Franklin River, an earlier campaign had been fought against a proposal by the Tasmanian Hydro-Electric Commission to flood Lake Peddar, a pristine alpine lake situated in a national park. This campaign employed more orthodox political tactics. It failed, and Lake Peddar disappeared under the waters of the dam. Dr. Thomas Gennarelli's laboratory had carried out experiments for several years before the Animal Liberation Front raided it. Without the evidence of the stolen videotapes, it would probably have functioned for many more years. Similarly, Operation Rescue was founded after fourteen years of more conventional political action had failed to reverse the permissive legal situation regarding abortion that has existed in the United States since the Supreme Court declared restrictive abortion laws unconstitutional in 1973. During that period, according to Operation Rescue's Gary Leber, 'twenty-five million Americans' were '"legally" killed'. The climate change protesters believe, on good evidence, that it will soon be too late to stop dangerous and irreversible climate change. When we take the perspectives of those involved in disobedience, it is easy to see why the existence of legal channels for change does not solve the moral dilemma. An extremely slim chance of bringing about change by legal means is not a strong reason against using illegal means if they are more likely to succeed. The most that can follow from the mere existence of legitimate channels is that because we cannot know, until we have tried them, whether using them will lead to the desired change, their existence is a reason for postponing illegal acts until legal means have been tried and have failed.

Here, the upholder of democratic laws can try another tack: if legal means fail to bring about reform, it shows that the proposed reform does not have the approval of the majority of the electorate; and to attempt to implement change by illegal means against the wishes of the majority would be a violation of the central principle of democracy, majority rule.

The protester can challenge this argument on two grounds, one factual and the other philosophical. The factual claim in the democrat's argument is that a reform that cannot be implemented by legal means lacks the approval of the majority of the electorate. Perhaps this would hold in a direct democracy, in which the electorate voted on each issue, but it is certainly not always true of modern representative democracies. There is no way of ensuring that on any given issue a majority of representatives will take the same view as a majority of their constituents. One can be reasonably confident that a majority of those Americans who saw, on television, excerpts from Gennarelli's videotapes would not have supported the experiments. That, however, is not how decisions are made in a democracy. In choosing between representatives – or in choosing between political parties – voters elect to take one 'package deal' in preference to other package deals on offer. It will often happen that in order to vote for policies they favour, voters must go along with other policies they are not keen on. It will also happen that policies voters favour are not offered by any major party. In the case of abortion in the United States, the crucial decision was not made by a majority of voters, but by the Supreme Court. It cannot be overturned by a simple majority of the electors, but only by the Court itself or by the complicated procedure of a constitutional amendment, which can be thwarted by a minority of the electorate.

What if a majority did approve of the wrong that the protesters wish to stop? Would it then be wrong to use illegal means? Here, we have the philosophical claim underlying the democratic argument for obedience, the claim that we ought to accept the majority decision.

The case for majority rule should not be overstated. No sensible democrat would claim that the majority is always right. If 49 percent of the population can be wrong, so can 51 percent. Whether the majority supports the views of the Animal Liberation Front or of Operation Rescue or of the protesters against climate change does not settle the question of whether these views are morally sound. Perhaps the fact that these groups are in a minority – if they are – means that they should reconsider their means. With a majority behind them, they could claim to be acting with democratic principles on their side, using illegal means to overcome flaws in the democratic machinery. Without that majority, all the weight of democratic tradition is against them, and it is they who appear as coercers, trying to force the majority into accepting something against its will. But how much moral weight should we give to democratic principles?

Thoreau, as we might expect, was not impressed by majority decision making. 'All voting,' he wrote, 'is a sort of gaming, like checkers or backgammon, with a slight moral tinge to it, a playing with right and wrong, with moral questions.' In a sense Thoreau was right. If we reject, as we must, the doctrine that the majority is always right, to submit moral issues to the vote is to gamble that what we believe to be right will come out of the ballot with more votes behind it than what we believe to be wrong; and that is a gamble we will often lose.

Nevertheless, we should not be too contemptuous about voting, or even gambling, when the alternative is something worse. Cowboys who agree to play poker to decide matters of honour do better than cowboys who continue to settle such matters in the traditional style of Western movies. A society that decides its controversial issues by ballots does better than one that uses bullets – which, after all, is no more likely to lead to the right conclusion than voting. To some extent, this is a point we have already encountered under the heading 'law and order'. It applies to any society with an established, peaceful method of resolving disputes; but in a democracy, there is a subtle difference that gives added weight to the outcome of the decision procedure. A method of settling disputes in which no one has greater ultimate power than anyone else is a method that can be recommended to all as a fair compromise between competing claims to power. Any other method must give greater power to some than to others and thereby invites opposition from those who have less. That, at least, is true in the egalitarian age in which we live. In a feudal society in which people accept as natural and proper their status as lord or vassal, there is no challenge to the feudal lord and no compromise would be needed. (I am thinking of an ideal feudal system, as I am thinking of an ideal democracy.) In most parts of the world, those times seem to be gone forever. The breakdown of traditional authority created a need for political compromise. Among possible compromises, giving one vote to each person is uniquely acceptable to all. As such, in the absence of any agreed procedure for deciding on some other distribution of power, it offers, in principle, the firmest possible basis for a peaceful method of settling disputes.

To reject majority rule, therefore, is to reject the best possible basis for the peaceful ordering of society in an egalitarian age. Where else should one turn? To a meritocratic franchise, with extra votes for the more intelligent or better educated, as John Stuart Mill once proposed? Could we agree on who merits extra votes? To a benevolent despot? Many would accept that – if they could choose the despot. In practice, the likely outcome of abandoning majority rule is none of these: it is the rule of those who command the greatest force. Those who carry out disobedience on one issue – say, animal rights – should remember that there will be other issues on which they support the law and want it enforced against those who seek to stop a practice of which they approve. Many people in the animal rights movement believe that women should be able to obtain safe and legal abortions, and many people in the anti-abortion movement see nothing wrong with experimenting on animals, nor with slaughtering them for food. These members of the Animal Liberation Front therefore will want the law enforced against Operation Rescue, and vice versa.

So the principle of majority rule does carry substantial moral weight. Disobedience is easier to justify in a dictatorship like Nazi Germany than in a democracy like those of North America, Europe, India, Japan or Australia today. In a democracy, we should be reluctant to take any action that amounts to an attempt to coerce the majority, for such attempts imply the rejection of majority rule, to which there is no acceptable alternative. There may, of course, be cases where the majority decision is so appalling that coercion is justified, whatever the risk. The obligation to obey a genuine majority decision is not absolute. We show our respect for the principle, not by blind obedience to the majority, but by regarding ourselves as justified in disobeying only in extreme circumstances.

DISOBEDIENCE, CIVIL OR OTHERWISE

If we draw together our conclusions on the use of illegal means to achieve laudable ends, we shall find that: (1) there are reasons why we should normally accept the verdict of an established peaceful method of settling disputes; (2) these reasons are particularly strong when the method is democratic and the verdict represents a genuine majority view; but (3) there are still situations in which the use of illegal means can be justified.

We have seen that there are two distinct ways in which one might try to justify the use of illegal means in a society that is broadly democratic. The first is on the grounds that the decision one is objecting to is not a genuine expression of majority opinion. The second is that although the decision is a genuine expression of the majority view, this view is so seriously wrong that action against the majority is justified. It is disobedience on the first ground that best merits the name 'civil disobedience'. Here, the use of illegal means can be regarded as an extension of the use of legal means to secure a genuinely democratic decision. The extension may be necessary because the normal channels for securing reform are not working properly. On some issues, elected representatives are overly influenced by special interest groups with large sums to donate to their re-election campaigns. On others, the public is unaware of what is happening. Perhaps the legitimate interests of a minority are being ignored by prejudiced officials. In all these cases, the standard forms of civil disobedience – passive resistance, marches or sit-ins – are appropriate. The blockade of the Hydro-Electric Commission's road into the site of the proposed Franklin River dam, and the protest at Capitol Power Plant, were cases of civil disobedience in this sense.

In these situations, disobeying the law is not an attempt to coerce the majority. Instead, disobedience attempts to inform the majority, to persuade elected representatives that large numbers of electors feel very strongly about the issue, to draw national attention to an issue previously left to bureaucrats, or to appeal for reconsideration of a decision too hastily made. Civil disobedience is an appropriate means to these ends when legal means have failed, because, although it is illegal, it does not threaten or attempt to coerce the majority (though it will usually impose some extra costs or inconvenience on them). By not resisting the force of the law, by remaining non-violent and by accepting the legal penalty for their actions, those who engage in civil disobedience make manifest both the sincerity of their protest and their respect for the rule of law and the fundamental principles of democracy.

So conceived, civil disobedience can often be justified. The justification does not have to be strong enough to override the obligation to obey a democratic decision, because disobedience is an attempt to restore, rather than frustrate, the process of democratic decision making. Disobedience of this kind could be justified by, for instance, the aim of making the public aware of the loss of irreplaceable wilderness caused by the construction of a dam, or of how animals are treated in the laboratories and factory farms that few people ever see.

The use of illegal means to stop something that is undeniably in accordance with the majority view is harder – but not impossible – to justify. We may think it unlikely that a Nazi-style policy of genocide could ever be approved by a majority vote, but if that were to happen it would be carrying respect for majority rule to absurd lengths to regard oneself as bound to accept the majority decision. To oppose evils of that magnitude, we are justified in using virtually any means likely to be effective.

Genocide is an extreme case. To grant that it justifies the use of illegal means even against a majority concedes very little in terms of practical political action. Yet admitting even one exception to the obligation to abide by democratic decisions raises further questions: where is the line to be drawn between evils like genocide, when the obligation is clearly overridden, and less serious issues, when it is not? Moreover, who is to decide on which side of this imaginary line a particular issue falls? Gary Leber, of Operation Rescue, wrote that in the United States alone, since 1973, 'we've already destroyed four times the number of people that Hitler did'. Ronnie Lee, one of the founders of the Animal Liberation Front in Britain, has also used the Nazi metaphor for what we do to animals, saying: 'Although we are only one species among many on earth, we've set up a *Reich* totally dominating the other animals, even enslaving them.' It is not surprising, then, that these activists consider their disobedience justified; but are they the ones who should be making this decision? If not, who is to decide when an issue is so serious that, even in a democracy, the obligation to obey the law is overridden?

The only answer this question can have is: we must decide for ourselves on which side of the line particular cases fall. There is no other way of deciding, because the society's method of settling issues has already made its decision. The majority cannot be judge in its own case. If we think the majority decision wrong, we must make up our own minds about how gravely it is wrong.

This does not mean that any decision we make on such an issue is subjective or arbitrary. In this book, I have offered arguments about a number of moral issues. If we apply these arguments to the five cases with which this chapter began, they lead to specific conclusions. The racist Nazi policy of murdering Jews was obviously an atrocity, and Oskar Schindler was entirely right to do what he could to save some Jews from falling victim to it. (Given the personal risks he ran, he was also morally heroic to do so.) On the basis of the arguments put forward in Chapter 3 of this book, the experiments that Gennarelli conducted on monkeys were wrong, because they treated sentient creatures as mere things to be used as research tools. To stop such experiments is a desirable goal, and if breaking into Gennarelli's laboratory and stealing his videotapes was the only way to achieve it, that was justifiable. Similarly, for reasons explored in Chapter 10, to drown the Franklin valley in order to generate a relatively small amount of electricity could only have been based on values that took a short-term perspective and were indefensibly human-centred. Civil disobedience was an appropriate means of testifying to the importance of the values that had been overlooked by those who favoured the dam. The same can be said about civil disobedience against climate change – indeed here, given the extent of the disaster likely to occur if greenhouse gases are not cut very sharply over the next few years, the question that might be asked is: why has there, as yet, been so little civil disobedience?

On the other hand, in Chapter 6 we found that the arguments that lie behind Joan Andrews' activities are flawed. The human fetus is not entitled to the same sort of protection as older human beings, and those who think of abortion as morally equivalent to murder are wrong. On this basis, a campaign of civil disobedience against abortion is not justifiable. But it is important to realise that the mistake lies in Andrews' moral reasoning about abortion, not in her moral reasoning about civil disobedience. If abortion really were morally equivalent to murder, we all ought to be out there blocking the doors to the abortion clinics.

This makes life difficult, of course. It is not likely that Andrews will be convinced by the arguments in this book. Her reliance on biblical quotations suggests that her opposition to abortion is fundamentally religious, so there is no easy way of convincing her that her civil disobedience is unjustified. We may regret this, but there is nothing to be done about it. There is no simple moral rule that will enable us to declare when disobedience is justifiable and when it is not, without going into the rights and wrongs of the target of the disobedience. (As we saw, however, Operation Rescue no longer practices civil disobedience, perhaps because it came to the conclusion that those tactics were not helping it to achieve its goal of ending abortion in America.)

When we are convinced that we are trying to stop something that really is a serious moral wrong, we still have other moral questions to ask ourselves. We must balance the magnitude of the evil we are trying to stop against the possibility that our actions will contribute to a decline in respect for law and for democracy. We must also take into account the likelihood that our actions will fail in their objective and provoke a reaction that will reduce the chances of success by other means. (For instance, violent attacks on experimenters enable defenders of research on animals to brand all critics of animal experimentation as terrorists.)

One result of a consequentialist approach to this issue that may at first seem odd is that the more deeply ingrained the habit of obedience to democratic rule, the more easily disobedience can be defended. There is no paradox here, however, merely another instance of the homely truth that young plants need to be cosseted, but well established specimens can take rougher treatment. Thus, on a given issue disobedience might be justifiable in Britain or the United States but not in a country that has recently been through dictatorship and civil war and is seeking to establish a democratic system of government.

Every case differs, and these issues cannot be settled in general terms. When the evils to be stopped are neither utterly horrendous (like genocide) nor relatively harmless (like the design for a new national flag), reasonable people will differ on the justifiability of attempting to thwart the implementation of a considered democratic decision. Where illegal means are used with this aim, an important step has been taken, for disobedience then ceases to be 'civil disobedience' if by that term is meant disobedience that is justified by an appeal to principles that the community itself accepts as the proper way of running its affairs. It may still be best for such obedience to be civil in the other sense of the term, which makes a contrast with the use of violence or the tactics of terrorism.

VIOLENCE AND TERRORISM

As we have seen, civil disobedience intended as a means of attracting publicity or persuading the majority to reconsider is much easier to justify than disobedience intended to coerce the majority. Violence is obviously harder still to defend. Some go so far as to say that the use of violence as a means, particularly violence against people, is never justified, no matter how important the end.

Opposition to the use of violence can be on the basis of an absolute rule or an assessment of its consequences. Pacifists have usually regarded the use of violence as absolutely wrong, irrespective of its consequences. This, like other 'no matter what' prohibitions, assumes the validity of the distinction between acts and omissions. Without this distinction, pacifists who refuse to use violence when it is the only means of preventing greater violence would be responsible for the greater violence they fail to prevent. Suppose we have an opportunity to assassinate a tyrant who is systematically murdering those he suspects of being opposed to his rule. We know that if the tyrant dies he is very likely to be replaced by a popular opposition leader, now in exile, who will restore the rule of law. If we say that violence is always wrong, and refuse to carry out the assassination, mustn't we bear some responsibility for the tyrant's future murders? If the objections made to the acts and omissions distinction in Chapter 7 were sound, those who do not use violence to prevent greater violence have to take responsibility for the violence they could have prevented. Thus, the rejection of the acts and omissions distinction makes a crucial difference to the discussion of violence, for it opens the door to a plausible argument in defence of violence.

Marxists used this argument to rebut attacks on their support for violent revolution. In his classic indictment of the social effects of nineteenth-
century capitalism, *The Condition of the Working Class in England,* Engels
wrote:

If one individual inflicts a bodily injury upon another which leads to the death
of the person attacked we call it manslaughter; on the other hand, if the attacker
knows beforehand that the blow will be fatal we call it murder. Murder has also
been committed if society places hundreds of workers in such a position that they
inevitably come to premature and unnatural ends. Their death is as violent as if
they had been stabbed or shot . . . Murder has been committed if thousands of
workers have been deprived of the necessities of life or if they have been forced
into a situation in which it is impossible for them to survive . . . Murder has been
committed if society knows perfectly well that thousands of workers cannot avoid
being sacrificed so long as these conditions are allowed to continue. Murder of
this sort is just as culpable as the murder committed by an individual. At first sight
it does not appear to be murder at all because responsibility for the death of the
victim cannot be pinned on any individual assailant. Everyone is responsible and
yet no one is responsible, because it appears as if the victim has died from natural
causes. If a worker dies no one places the responsibility for his death on society,
though some would realize that society has failed to take steps to prevent the
victim from dying. But it is murder all the same.

One might object to Engels' use of the term 'murder'. The objection
would resemble the arguments discussed in Chapter 8, when we considered whether our failure to aid the starving makes us murderers. We
saw that there is no intrinsic significance in the distinction between acts
and omissions; but from the point of view of motivation and the appropriateness of blame, most cases of failing to prevent death are not equivalent
to murder. The same would apply to the cases Engels describes. Engels
tries to pin the blame on 'society', but society is not a person or a moral
agent and cannot be held responsible in the way an individual can.

Still, this is nit-picking. Whether or not 'murder' is the right term,
whether or not we are prepared to describe as 'violent' the deaths of
malnourished workers in unhealthy and unsafe factories, Engels' fundamental point stands. These deaths are a wrong of the same order of
magnitude as the deaths of hundreds of people in a terrorist bombing.
It would be one-sided to say that violent revolution is always absolutely
wrong, without taking account of the evils that the revolutionaries are
trying to stop. If violent means had been the only way of changing the
conditions Engels describes, those who opposed the use of violent means
would have been responsible for the continuation of those conditions.

Some of the practices we have been discussing in this book are violent, either directly or by omission. In the case of nonhuman animals, our treatment is often violent by any description. Those who regard the human fetus as a moral subject will obviously consider abortion to be a violent act against it. In the case of humans at or after birth, what are we to say of an avoidable situation in which some countries have infant mortality rates twenty times higher than others, and a person born in one country can expect to live thirty years more than someone born in another country? Is this violence? As we saw in Chapter 9, President Museveni of Uganda has said that by their release of greenhouse gases, the industrialized nations are committing aggression against developing nations in tropical regions. Again, it doesn't really matter what term we use: in their effects, these practices are as terrible as violence.

Absolutist condemnations of violence stand or fall with the distinction between acts and omissions. Therefore they fall. There are, however, strong consequentialist objections to the use of violence. We have been premising our discussion on the assumption that violence might be the only means of changing things for the better. Consequentialists must ask whether violence ever is the only means to an important end or, if not the only means, the swiftest means. They must also ask about the long-term effects of pursuing change by violent means. Could one defend, on consequentialist grounds, a condemnation of violence that is in practice, if not in principle, as all-encompassing as that of the absolute pacifist? One might attempt to do so by emphasizing the hardening effect that the use of violence has: how committing one murder, no matter how 'necessary' or 'justified' it may seem, lessens the resistance to committing further murders. Is it likely that people who have become inured to acting violently will be able to create a better society? This is a question on which the historical record is relevant. The course taken by several revolutions – from the French revolution of 1789 to the Bolshevik revolution in Russia and, perhaps most horrifically of all, the rule of the Khmer Rouge in Cambodia – must shake the belief that a burning desire for social justice provides immunity to the corrupting effects of violence. There are, admittedly, other examples that may be read the other way; but it would take a considerable number of examples to outweigh the legacy of Robespierre, Stalin and Pol Pot.

The consequentialist pacifist can also use another argument – similar to the argument I urged against the suggestion that we should allow starvation to reduce the populations of the poorest nations to the level at which they could feed themselves. Like this policy, violence involves the certainty of causing harm, which is said to be justified by the prospects of future benefits. The future benefits, however, can never be certain; and even in the few cases where violence does bring about desirable ends, we can rarely be sure that the ends could not have been achieved equally soon by non-violent means. What, for instance, was achieved by the thousands of deaths and injuries caused by the decades of IRA bombings in Northern Ireland? Only counter-terrorism by extremist Protestant groups. Or think of the completely pointless death and suffering caused by the Baader-Meinhoff gang in Germany, or the Red Brigade in Italy. What has the cause of the Palestinian people gained from terrorism, other than a less compromising, more ruthless Israel than the one against which they began their struggle so many years – and lives – ago? For all the spectacular operational success that Al Qaeda achieved on September 11, 2001, it seems wildly unlikely that its murder of thousands of Americans will have brought it any closer to achieving an end to American military dominance in the Middle East, let alone coercing the United States into becoming an Islamic state. One may sympathize with the ends for which some – not all! – of these groups were or are fighting, but if the means used involve undeniable harm to innocent people, and hold no promise of gaining their ends, it is wrong to use them. These consequentialist arguments add up to a strong case against the use of violence as a means, particularly when the violence is indiscriminately directed against ordinary members of the public, as terrorist violence typically is. For sound practical reasons, terrorism is never justified.

There are other kinds of violence that cannot be ruled out so convincingly. There is, for instance, the previously mentioned assassination of a murderous tyrant. Here, provided the murderous policies are an expression of the tyrant's personality rather than part of the institutions he commands, the violence is strictly limited, the aim is to end much more widespread violence, there is no other way to stop the more widespread violence, and success from a single violent act may be highly probable, violence is justifiable.

Violence may be limited in a different way. The cases we have been considering have involved violence against people. These are the standard cases that come to mind when we discuss violence, but there are other kinds of violence. Animal Liberation Front members have damaged laboratories, cages and equipment used to confine, hurt or kill animals, but they avoid violent acts against any animal, human or non-human. (Not all militant animal rights organizations have followed this policy – at least two people have been injured by explosive devices left by people claiming to be acting in defence of animals. These actions have been condemned by other groups, including the Animal Liberation Front.)

Damage to property is not as serious a matter as injuring or killing; hence, it may be justified on grounds that would not justify anything that caused harm to sentient beings. This does not mean that violence to property is of no significance. Property means a great deal to some people, and one would need to have strong reasons to justify destroying it. But such reasons *may* exist. The justification might not be anything so epoch-making as transforming society. As in the case of the raid on Gennarelli's laboratory, it might be the specific and short-term goal of saving a number of animals from a painful experiment performed on animals only because of society's speciesist bias. Again, whether such an action would really be justifiable from a consequentialist point of view would depend on the details of the actual situation. Someone lacking expertise could easily be mistaken about the value of an experiment or the degree of suffering it involved. Moreover, will not the result of damaging equipment and liberating one lot of animals simply be that more equipment is bought and more animals are bred? What is to be done with the liberated animals? Will illegal acts mean that the government will resist moves to reform the law relating to animal experiments, arguing that it must not appear to be yielding to violence? All these questions would need to be answered satisfactorily before one could come to a decision in favour of damaging a laboratory.

Violence is not easy to justify, even if it is violence against property rather than against sentient beings or violence against a dictator rather than indiscriminate violence against the general public. Nevertheless, the differences between kinds of violence are important, because only by observing them can we condemn one kind of violence – the terrorist kind – in virtually absolute terms. The differences are blurred by sweeping condemnations of everything that falls under the general heading 'violence'.

12

Why Act Morally?

Previous chapters of this book have discussed what we ought, morally, to do about several practical issues and what means we are justified in adopting to achieve our ethical goals. The nature of our conclusions about these issues – the demands they make on us – raises a further, more fundamental question: why should we act morally?

Take our conclusions about the use of animals for food, or the aid the rich should give the poor. Some readers may accept these conclusions, become vegetarians, and do what they can to reduce absolute poverty. Others may disagree with our conclusions, maintaining that there is nothing wrong with eating animals and that they are under no moral obligation to do anything about reducing absolute poverty. There is also, however, likely to be a third group: readers who find no fault with the ethical arguments of these chapters yet do not change their diets or their contributions to aid for the poor. Of this third group, some may just be weak-willed, but others may want an answer to a further practical question: if the conclusions of ethics require so much of us, they may ask, why should we bother about ethics at all?

UNDERSTANDING THE QUESTION

'Why should I act morally?' is a different type of question from those that we have been discussing up to now. Questions like 'Why should I treat people of different ethnic groups equally?' or 'Why is abortion justifiable?' seek ethical reasons for acting in a certain way. These are questions within ethics. They presuppose the ethical point of view. 'Why should I act morally?' is on another level. It is not a question within ethics, but a question about ethics.

'Why should I act morally?' is therefore a question about something normally presupposed. Such questions are perplexing. Some philosophers have found this particular question so perplexing that they have rejected it as logically improper, as an attempt to ask something that cannot properly be asked.

One ground for this rejection is the claim that our ethical principles are, by definition, the principles we take as overridingly important. This means that whatever principles are overriding for a particular person are necessarily that person's ethical principles, and a person who accepts as an ethical principle that she ought to give her wealth to help the poor must, by definition, have actually decided to give away her wealth. On this definition of ethics, once a person has made an ethical decision no further practical question can arise. Hence, it is impossible to make sense of the question: 'Why should I act morally?'

It might be thought a good reason for accepting the definition of ethics as overriding that it allows us to dismiss as meaningless an otherwise troublesome question. Adopting this definition cannot solve real problems, however, for it leads to correspondingly greater difficulties in establishing any ethical conclusion. Take, for example, the conclusion that the rich ought to aid the poor. Although the argument for this conclusion in Chapter 8 drew on the intuitive appeal of our readiness to rescue the child drowning in the pond, we saw that if that intuition were rejected, it could still rest on the assumption that suffering and death are bad things, even when they are not *your* suffering and death. If we define ethical principles as whatever principles one takes as overriding, then someone could say that her overriding principle is an egoistic one, and the suffering and death of strangers doesn't matter at all. We could not invoke universalizability in order to deny that this could be an ethical principle, because if anything anyone takes as overriding counts as that person's ethical principle, there can be no requirement that one's ethical principles be universalizable. Thus, what we gain by being able to dismiss the question 'Why should I act morally?' we lose by being unable to use the universalizability of ethical judgments – or any other feature of ethics – to argue for particular conclusions about what is morally right. Taking ethics as in some sense necessarily involving a universal point of view seems to me a more natural and less confusing way of discussing these issues.

Other philosophers think that 'Why should I act morally?' must be
rejected for the same reason that we must reject 'Why should I be
rational?' Like the question 'Why should I act morally?', the question
'Why should I be rational?' questions something that we normally presuppose. But to question rationality – not the use of reason in any specific
context, but in general – really is logically improper because in answering
it we can only give reasons for being rational. Thus, the person asking
the question must be seeking reasons and, hence, is herself presupposing rationality. The resulting justification of rationality would have to be
circular – which shows, not that rationality lacks a necessary justification,
but that it needs no justification, because it cannot intelligibly be questioned unless it is already presupposed. (Note that some questions about
whether to use reason to reach a decision are intelligible. For example,
'When deciding whether to trust someone I've just met, should I use my
reason or my instincts?' is an intelligible question, because it questions
the use of reason in a specific context. It is possible that our instincts
will do better than our reason in that context, and if so, the best answer
would be to use your instincts. To say this, however, is itself to give reasons
for not using reason in that context, so the question poses no challenge
to reason as such.)

Is 'Why should I act morally?' like 'Why should I be rational?' in that
it presupposes the very point of view it questions? It would be, if we
interpreted the 'should' as a moral 'should'. Then the question would
ask for moral reasons for being moral. This would be absurd. Once we
have decided that an action is morally obligatory, there is no further
moral question to ask. It is redundant to ask why I should, morally, do
the action that I morally should do.

There is, however, no need to interpret the question as a request for an
ethical justification of ethics. 'Should' need not mean 'should, morally'.
It could simply be a way of asking for reasons for action, without any
specification about the kind of reasons wanted. We sometimes want to
ask a very general practical question from no particular point of view.
Faced with a difficult choice, we ask a close friend for advice. Morally, he
says, we ought to do A, but B would be more in our interests, whereas
etiquette demands C and to do D would be just *so cool!* This answer may
not satisfy us. We want advice on which of these standpoints to adopt.
If it is possible to ask such a question, we must ask it from a position of
neutrality between all these points of view, not of commitment to any
one of them. 'Why should I act morally?' is this sort of question. If it were
not possible to ask practical questions without presupposing a point of

view, we would be unable to say anything intelligible about the most ultimate practical choices. Whether to act according to considerations of ethics, self-interest, etiquette or aesthetics would be a choice 'beyond reason' – in a sense, an arbitrary choice. Before we resign ourselves to this conclusion, we should at least attempt to interpret the question so that the mere asking of it does not commit us to any particular point of view.

We can now formulate the question more precisely. It is a question about the ethical point of view, asked from a position outside it. What is 'the ethical point of view'? I have suggested that a distinguishing feature of ethics is that ethical judgments are universalizable. Ethics requires us to go beyond our own personal point of view to a standpoint like that of the impartial spectator.

Given this conception of ethics, 'Why should I act morally?' is a question that may properly be asked by anyone wondering whether to act only on grounds that would be acceptable from this universal point of view. It is, after all, possible to act – and some people do act – without thinking of anything except one's own interests. The question asks for reasons for going beyond this personal basis of action and acting only on judgments one is prepared to prescribe universally.

REASON AND ETHICS

There is an ancient line of philosophical thought that attempts to demonstrate that to act rationally is to act ethically. The argument is today associated with Kant and is mainly found in the writings of modern Kantians, though it goes back at least as far as the Stoics. The form in which the argument is presented varies, but the variations tend to have a common structure, as follows:

1. Some requirement of universalizability or impartiality is essential to ethics.
2. Reason, whether theoretical or practical, is universally or objectively valid. If, for example, it follows from the premises 'All humans are mortal' and 'Socrates is human' that Socrates is mortal, then this inference must follow universally. It cannot be valid for me and invalid for you.

Therefore:

3. Only a judgment that satisfies the requirement described in (1) as a necessary condition of an ethical judgment will be an objectively

rational judgment in accordance with (2). For I cannot expect any other rational agents to accept as valid for them a judgment that I would not accept if I were in their place; and if two rational agents could not accept one another's judgments, they could not be rational judgments, for the reason given in (2). To say that I would accept the judgment I make, even if I were in someone else's position and they in mine is, however, simply to say that my judgment is one I can prescribe from a universal point of view. Ethics and reason both require us to rise above our own particular point of view and take a perspective from which our own personal identity – the role we happen to occupy – is unimportant. Thus, reason requires us to act on universalizable judgments and, to that extent, to act ethically.

Is this argument valid? I have already argued for the first point, that ethics involves universalizability. The second point also seems undeniable. Reason must be universal. Does the conclusion therefore follow? Here is the flaw in the argument. The conclusion appears to follow directly from the premises; but this move involves a slide from the limited sense in which it is true that a rational judgment must be universally valid, to a stronger sense of 'universally valid' that is equivalent to universalizability.

The difference between these two senses can be seen by considering a non-universalizable imperative, like the purely egoistic: 'Let everyone do what is in *my* interests.' This differs from the imperative of universalizable egoism – 'Let everyone do what is in *her or his own* interests' – because it contains an ineliminable reference to a particular person. It therefore cannot be an ethical imperative. Does it also lack the universality required if it is to be a rational basis for action? Surely not. Every rational agent could accept that the purely egoistic activity of other rational agents is rationally justifiable. Pure egoism could be rationally adopted by everyone.

Let us look at this more closely. It must be conceded that there is a sense in which one purely egoistic rational agent – call him Jack – could not accept the practical judgments of another purely egoistic rational agent – call her Jill. Assuming Jill's interests differ from Jack's, Jill may be acting rationally in urging Jack to do A, while Jack is also acting rationally in deciding against doing A.

This disagreement is, however, compatible with all rational agents accepting pure egoism. Though they accept pure egoism, it points them in different directions because they start from different places. When

Jack adopts pure egoism, it leads him to further his interests; and when Jill adopts pure egoism, it leads her to further her interests. Hence, the disagreement over what to do. On the other hand – and this is the sense in which pure egoism could be accepted as valid by all rational agents – if we were to ask Jill (off the record and promising not to tell Jack) what she thinks it would be rational for Jack to do, she would, if truthful, have to reply that it would be rational for Jack to do what is in his own interests rather than what is in her interests.

So when purely egoistic rational agents oppose one another's acts, it does not indicate disagreement over the rationality of pure egoism. Pure egoism, though not a universalizable principle, could be accepted as a rational basis of action by all rational agents. This shows that the sense in which rational judgments must be universally acceptable is weaker than the sense in which ethical judgments must be. 'Let everyone do what is in *my* interests' could be a valid reason for Jack to do what is in his interests, although it could not be an ethical reasons for him to do it.

A consequence of this conclusion is that rational agents may rationally try to prevent one another doing what they admit the other is rationally justified in doing. There is, unfortunately, nothing paradoxical about this; on most theories of rationality, it is just a fact of everyday life. Salespeople competing for an important sale will accept one another's conduct as rational, though each aims to thwart the other. The same holds of rivals in love, enemy soldiers meeting in battle, or footballers vying for the ball.

Accordingly, this attempted demonstration of a link between reason and ethics fails. Are there other ways of forging this link? The chief obstacle to overcome is the nature of practical reason. Long ago David Hume argued that reason in action applies only to means, not to ends. The ends must be given by our wants and desires. Hume unflinchingly drew out the implications of this view:

'Tis not contrary to reason to prefer the destruction of the whole world to the scratching of my finger. 'Tis not contrary to reason for me to choose my total ruin, to prevent the least uneasiness of an Indian or person wholly unknown to me. 'Tis as little contrary to reason to prefer even my own acknowledged lesser good to my greater, and have a more ardent affection for the former than the latter.

Extreme as it is, Hume's view of practical reason has stood up to criticism remarkably well. His central claim – that in practical reasoning, we start from something we want – is difficult to refute; yet it must be refuted if any argument is to succeed in showing that it is rational for all of us to act ethically irrespective of what we want.

In an attempt to refute Hume, several writers start by asserting that it is rational to take one's *own* future desires into account, whether or not one now happens to desire the satisfaction of those future desires. In *The Possibility of Altruism*, Thomas Nagel argued forcefully that not to take one's own future desires into account in one's practical deliberations would indicate a failure to see oneself as a person existing over time, with the present being merely one time among others in one's life. So it is, on Nagel's view, my conception of myself as a person that makes it rational for me to consider my long-term interests. This holds true even if I have 'a more ardent affection' for something that I acknowledge is not really, all things considered, in my own interest.

Derek Parfit provides a striking illustration of someone who fails to consider his or her interests over time in a way that strikes most of us as obviously irrational. He asks us to imagine someone with a condition he calls 'Future Tuesday Indifference':

This man cares about his own future pleasures or pains, except when they will come on any future Tuesday. This strange attitude does not depend on ignorance or false beliefs. Pain on Tuesdays, this man knows, would be just as painful, and just as much *his* pain, and Tuesdays are just like other days of the week. Even so, given the choice, this man would now prefer agony on any future Tuesday to slight pain on any other future day.

About such a person, Parfit comments:

That some ordeal would be much more painful is a strong reason *not* to prefer it. That this ordeal would be on a future Tuesday is *no* reason to prefer it. So this man's preferences are strongly contrary to reason, and irrational.

He adds that although no one has this attitude, it is similar to the bias many people have towards the near. It would be similarly irrational, he suggests, for anyone to postpone a minute of agony today, knowing that this would mean an hour of the same degree of agony tomorrow. Less extreme departures from a position of temporal neutrality – that is, an attitude of equal concern for all moments of time, putting aside uncertainties about the future – are also, in Parfit's view, irrational.

Whether Nagel's or Parfit's arguments succeed in vindicating the rationality of prudence, or of temporal neutrality, is one question; whether a similar argument can also be used in favour of a form of altruism based on taking the desires of *others* into account is another question altogether. Nagel attempted this analogous argument in *The*

Possibility of Altruism. The role occupied by 'seeing the present as merely one time among others' is, in this argument for altruism, taken by 'seeing oneself as merely one person among others'. The problem is that whereas it would be extremely difficult for most of us to cease conceiving of ourselves as existing over time, with the present merely one time among others that we will live through, the way we see ourselves as a person among others is quite different. Henry Sidgwick's observation on this point seems exactly right:

> It would be contrary to Common Sense to deny that the distinction between any one individual and any other is real and fundamental, and that consequently 'I' am concerned with the quality of my existence as an individual in a sense, fundamentally important, in which I am not concerned with the quality of the existence of other individuals: and this being so, I do not see how it can be proved that this distinction is not to be taken as fundamental in determining the ultimate end of rational action for an individual.

So it is not only Hume's view of practical reason that stands in the way of attempts to show that to act rationally is to act ethically; we might succeed in overthrowing that barrier, only to find our way blocked by the commonsense distinction between self and others. Nagel no longer holds that the argument in *The Possibility of Altruism* succeeds, and Parfit is largely in agreement with Sidgwick about the rationality of acting to further one's own interests, even when this is contrary to the greater interests of others. Largely, but not entirely, because he thinks that it is irrational to act on your own interests where you have only minor interests at stake and others have a great deal at stake. So if you could save yourself one minute of discomfort by doing something that would inflict an agonizing death on a million people, this would, on Parfit's view, be an irrational thing to do, even if it were in your own interests. Still, this is very far from establishing that doing what is impartially good, or what is right, is required by reason.

Hence, even if Hume's view of reason is wrong, the next most defensible view of reason – Sidgwick's, perhaps as modified by Parfit – does not enable us to conclude that reason requires us to act morally.

ETHICS AND SELF-INTEREST

If practical reasoning begins with something wanted, to show that it is rational to act morally would involve showing that by acting morally we will achieve something we want. If, agreeing with Sidgwick rather than Hume, we hold that it is rational to act in our long-term interests irrespective of what we happen to want at the present moment, we could show that it is rational to act morally by showing that it is in our long-term interests to do so. There have been many attempts to argue along these lines ever since Plato, in *The Republic*, portrayed Socrates as arguing that to be virtuous is to have the different elements of one's personality ordered in a harmonious manner, and this is necessary for happiness. We shall look at these arguments shortly; but first it is necessary to assess an objection to this whole approach to 'Why should I act morally?'

People often say that to defend morality by appealing to self-interest is to misunderstand what ethics is all about. F. H. Bradley stated this eloquently:

What answer can we give when the question Why should I be Moral?, in the sense of What will it advantage Me?, is put to us? Here we shall do well, I think, to avoid all praises of the pleasantness of virtue. We may believe that it transcends all possible delights of vice, but it would be well to remember that we desert a moral point of view, that we degrade and prostitute virtue, when to those who do not love her for herself we bring ourselves to recommend her for the sake of her pleasures.

In other words, we can never get people to act morally by providing reasons of self-interest, because if they accept what we say and act on the reasons given, they will only be acting self-interestedly, not morally.

One reply to this objection would be that the substance of the action, what is actually done, is more important than the motive. People might give money to help those in extreme poverty because their friends will think better of them if they do, or they might give the same amount because they think it is their duty. Those helped by the gift will benefit to the same extent either way.

This is true but crude. It can be made more sophisticated if it is combined with an appropriate account of the nature and function of ethics. Ethics is a social practice that has evolved among beings living in social groups, and it promotes ways of living that are in the interests of individuals living in groups. Ethical judgments can do this by praising and encouraging actions in accordance with these values. Ethical judgments are concerned with motives because this is a good indication of the tendency of an action to promote what is considered desirable or undesirable, but also because it is here that praise and blame may be effective in altering the tendency of a person's actions. In this respect, conscientiousness (that is, acting for the sake of doing what is right) is a particularly useful motive. People who are conscientious will, if they accept the values of their society (and if most people did not accept these values, they would not be the values of the society), always tend to promote what the society values. They may have no generous or sympathetic inclinations, but if they think it their duty to help the poor, they will do so. Moreover, those motivated by the desire to do what is right can be relied on to act as they think right in all circumstances, whereas those who act from some other motive, like self-interest, will only do what they think right when they believe it will also be in their interest. Conscientiousness is thus a kind of multipurpose gap-filler that can be used to motivate people towards whatever is valued, even if the natural virtues normally associated with action in accordance with those values (generosity, sympathy, honesty, tolerance, humility, etc.) are lacking. (This needs some qualification: a conscientious mother may provide as well for her children as a mother who loves them, but she cannot love them because it is the right thing to do. Sometimes conscientiousness is a poor substitute for the real thing.)

On this view of ethics, it is still results, not motives, that really matter. Conscientiousness is of value because of its consequences. Yet, unlike, say, benevolence, conscientiousness can be praised and encouraged only for its own sake. To praise a conscientious act for its consequences would be to praise not conscientiousness but something else altogether. If we appeal to sympathy or self-interest as a reason for doing one's duty, then we are not encouraging people to do their duty for its own sake. If conscientiousness is to be encouraged, it must be thought of as good for its own sake.

It is different in the case of an act done from a motive that people act on irrespective of praise and encouragement. The use of ethical language is then unnecessary. We do not normally say that people ought to do, or that it is their duty to do, whatever gives them the greatest pleasure, for most people are sufficiently motivated to do this anyway. So, whereas we praise good acts done for the sake of doing what is right, we withhold our praise when we believe the act was done from some motive like self-interest.

This emphasis on motives and on the moral worth of doing right for its own sake is now embedded in our notion of ethics. To the extent that it is so embedded, we will feel that to provide considerations of self-interest for doing what is right is to empty the action of its moral worth.

My suggestion is that our notion of ethics has become misleading to the extent that moral worth is attributed only to action done because it is right, without any ulterior motive. It is understandable, and from the point of view of society perhaps even desirable, that this attitude should prevail; nevertheless, those who accept this view of ethics, and are led by it to do what is right because it is right, without asking for any further reason, are falling victim to a kind of confidence trick – though not, of course, a consciously perpetrated one.

That this view of ethics is unjustifiable has already been indicated by the failure of the argument discussed earlier in this chapter for a rational justification of ethics. In the history of Western philosophy, no one has urged more strongly than Kant that our ordinary moral consciousness finds moral worth only when duty is done for duty's sake. Yet Kant himself saw that without a rational justification this common conception of ethics would be 'a mere phantom of the brain'. This is indeed the case. If we reject – as in general terms we have done – the Kantian justification of the rationality of ethics but try to retain the Kantian conception of ethics, ethics is left hanging without support. It becomes a closed system, a system that cannot be questioned because its first premise – that only action done because it is right has any moral worth – rules out the only remaining possible justification for accepting this very premise. Morality is, on this view, no more rational an end than any other allegedly self-justifying practice, like etiquette or the kind of religious faith that comes only to those who first set aside all sceptical doubts.

Taken as a view of ethics as a whole, we should abandon this Kantian notion of ethics. This does not mean, however, that we should never do what we see to be right simply because we see it to be right, without further reasons. Here once again, we need to appeal to the distinction Hare has made between intuitive and critical thinking. When I stand back from my day-to-day ethical decisions and ask why I should act ethically, I should seek reasons in the broadest sense and not allow Kantian preconceptions to deter me from considering self-interested reasons for living an ethical life. If my search is successful, it will provide me with reasons for taking up the ethical point of view as a settled policy, a way of living. I would not then ask, in my day-to-day ethical decision making, whether each particular right action is in my interests. Instead, I do it because I see myself as an ethical person. In everyday situations, I will simply assume that doing what is right is in my interests; and once I have decided what is right, I will go ahead and do it, without thinking about further reasons for doing what is right. To deliberate over the ultimate reasons for doing what is right in each case would impossibly complicate my life; it would also be inadvisable because in particular situations I might be too greatly influenced by strong but temporary desires and inclinations and so make decisions I would later regret.

That, at least, is how a justification of ethics in terms of self-interest might work, without defeating its own aim. We can now ask if such a justification exists. I will here put aside one ancient justification that is still significant for many religious believers: the belief that virtue will be rewarded and wickedness will be punished in a life after our bodily death. To rely on such a justification, one would first have to show that we do survive death, in some form, and secondly that we will be rewarded and punished in accordance with the extent to which we have lived an ethical life. I do not know how this could be demonstrated.

In *The Republic*, Plato portrays Socrates as debating with skeptics who ask why they should be just and eventually reaching the conclusion that 'the just man is happy and the unjust man miserable.' Socrates' argument convinces few readers today, however, as he seems to operate with a concept of leading a good life that assumes that to live well is both to do what is right or just and to prosper and be happy. That may have been what it meant to live a good life in ancient Greece, but today we are sharply aware that living ethically is one thing and being prosperous and happy is another – even if we remain open-minded on whether there is a link between them. Many other philosophers have followed Socrates and Plato in trying to show that the good man will be happy: Aristotle, Aquinas, Spinoza, Butler, Hegel and even – for all his strictures against prostituting virtue – Bradley. These philosophers made broad claims about human nature and the conditions under which human beings can be happy. Philosophers are not empirical scientists, of course, and many of the factual claims made by past philosophers lack any sound basis in evidence. But at this point it is relevant to draw on the growing body of modern research in what is sometimes called 'positive psychology' – the part of psychology that explores the sources of happiness.

Here we do find evidence for at least a correlation between some aspects of living ethically and happiness. Americans who give to charity were, in one large survey, 43 percent more likely to say that they were 'very happy' about their lives than those who did not give. Those who did voluntary work for charities were similarly more likely to say that they were happy than those who did not. In a separate study, those who give were 68 percent less likely to have felt 'hopeless' and 34 percent less likely to say that they felt 'so sad that nothing could cheer them up'. Giving blood, another altruistic act, also makes people feel good about themselves. Volunteering actually seems to improve the health of elderly people and help them live longer. Jonathan Haidt, a professor of psychology and author of *The Happiness Hypothesis*, comments: 'At least for older people, it really is more blessed to give than to receive.'

Is this more than just a correlation? Perhaps. In one experiment, researchers gave $100 to each of nineteen female students and gave them the option of donating some of the money to a local food bank for the poor. To ensure that any effects observed came entirely from making the donation, and not, for instance, from having the belief that others would think they were generous, the students were informed that no one, not even the experimenters, would know which students made a donation. While the students were deciding what to do, the researchers were using magnetic resonance imaging, which shows activity in various parts of the brain. The research found that when students donated, the brain's 'reward centres' – the caudate nucleus, nucleus accumbens and insulae – became active. These are the parts of the brain that respond when you eat something sweet or receive money. This is a small-scale experiment and only more research will show whether this is a widespread phenomenon, and whether it is part of the explanation for why those who give are more likely to say that they are happy.

The research cited focuses on giving and helping behaviour. Would something similar apply to living ethically in general? There seems to be little or no research on this broader topic. A. H. Maslow, an American psychologist, asserted that human beings have a need for self-actualization that involves growing towards courage, kindness, knowledge, love, honesty and unselfishness. When we fulfill this need, we feel serene, joyful, filled with zest, sometimes euphoric and generally happy. When we act contrary to our need for self-actualization, we experience anxiety, despair, boredom, shame, emptiness and are generally unable to enjoy ourselves. It would be nice if Maslow should turn out to be right; unfortunately, the data Maslow produced in support of his theory consisted of very limited studies of selected people and cannot be considered anything more than suggestive.

Human nature is so diverse that one may doubt if any generalization about the kind of character that leads to happiness could hold for all human beings. What, for instance, of those we call 'psychopaths'? Psychiatrists use this term as a label for a person who is asocial, impulsive, egocentric, unemotional, lacking in feelings of remorse or shame or guilt, and apparently unable to form deep and enduring personal relationships. Psychopaths are certainly abnormal, but whether it is proper to say that they are mentally ill is another matter. At least on the surface, they do not *suffer* from their condition, and it is not obvious that it is in their interest to be 'cured'. Hervey Cleckley, the author of a classic study of psychopathy entitled *The Mask of Sanity*, notes that since his book was first published he has received countless letters from people desperate for help – but they are from the parents, spouses and other relatives of psychopaths, almost never from the psychopaths themselves. This is not surprising, for although psychopaths are asocial and indifferent to the welfare of others, they have an inflated opinion of their own abilities. When interviewed they say things like:

A lot has happened to me, a lot more will happen. But I enjoy living and I am always looking forward to each day. I like laughing and I've done a lot. I am essentially a clown at heart – but a happy one. I always take the bad with the good.

There is no effective therapy for psychopathy, which may be explained by the fact that psychopaths see nothing wrong with their behaviour and often find it rewarding, at least in the short term. Of course, their impulsive nature and lack of a sense of shame or guilt means that some psychopaths end up in prison, though it is hard to tell how many do not, because those who avoid prison are also more likely to avoid contact with psychiatrists. Studies have shown that a surprisingly large number of psychopaths are able to avoid prison despite grossly anti-social behaviour, probably because of their well-known ability to convince others that they are truly repentant, that what they did will never happen again, and that they deserve another chance.

The existence of psychopaths – or more broadly, of people with psychopathic tendencies – counts against the contention that benevolence, sympathy and feelings of guilt are present in everyone. It also appears to count against attempts to link happiness with the possession of these inclinations. Let us pause before we accept this latter conclusion. Must we accept psychopaths' own evaluations of their happiness? They are, after all, notorious liars. Moreover, even if they are telling the truth as they see it, are they qualified to say that they are really happy when they seem unable to experience the emotional states that play such a large part in the happiness and fulfillment of others? Admittedly, a psychopath could use the same argument against us: how can we say that we are truly happy when we have not experienced the excitement and freedom that comes from complete irresponsibility? We cannot enter into the subjective states of psychopathic people, nor they into ours, so the dispute is not easy to resolve.

Cleckley suggests that the behaviour of psychopaths can be explained as a response to the meaninglessness of their lives. It is characteristic of psychopaths to work for a while at a job and then, just when their ability and charm have taken them to the crest of success, commit some petty and easily detectable crime. A similar pattern occurs in their personal relationships. They live largely in the present and lack any coherent life plan. Sometimes their failure to consider the future consequences of their acts – even to themselves – is breathtaking. Here is an example from a study by R. D. Hare:

One of our subjects, who scored high on the Psychopathy Checklist, said that while walking to a party he decided to buy a case of beer, but realized that he had left his wallet at home six or seven blocks away. Not wanting to walk back, he picked up a heavy piece of wood and robbed the nearest gas station, seriously injuring the attendant.

We can find support here for Thomas Nagel's account of imprudence as an irrational failure to see oneself as a person existing over time, with the present merely one among other times one will live through. Psychopaths have an extreme form of this failure. Cleckley explains their erratic and inadequately motivated behaviour by likening the psychopath's life to that of a child forced to sit through a performance of *King Lear*. Children are restless and misbehave under these conditions because they cannot enjoy the play as adults do. They act to relieve boredom. Similarly, Cleckley says, psychopaths are bored because their emotional poverty means that they cannot take interest in, or gain satisfaction from, what for others are the most important things in life: love, family, success in business or professional life and so on. These things simply do not matter to them. Their unpredictable and anti-social behaviour is an attempt to relieve what would otherwise be a tedious existence. These claims are speculative, and Cleckley admits that it may not be possible to establish them scientifically. They do suggest, however, an aspect of the psychopath's life that undermines the otherwise attractive nature of the psychopath's free-wheeling life. Most reflective people, at some time or other, want their life to have some kind of meaning. Few of us could deliberately choose a way of life that we regarded as utterly meaningless. For this reason, most of us would not choose to live a psychopathic life, however enjoyable it might be.

Yet if we are to reject the psychopath's claim to be living an enjoyable life on the ground that it is a meaningless life, we have to face the question of whether we can find meaning in our own lives. If we are not religious believers, don't we have to accept that life really is meaningless, not just for the psychopath but for all of us? And if this is so, why should we not choose – if it were in our power to choose our personality – the life of a psychopath? Is it true, though, that, religion aside, life is meaningless? Now our pursuit of reasons for acting morally has led us to what is often regarded as the ultimate philosophical question.

HAS LIFE A MEANING?

In what sense does rejection of belief in a god imply rejection of the view that life has any meaning? If this world had been created by some divine being with a particular goal in mind, it could be said to have a meaning, at least for that divine being. If we could know what the divine being's purpose in creating us was, we could then know what the meaning of our life was for our creator. If we accepted our creator's purpose (though why we should do that would need to be explained), we could claim to know the meaning of life.

When we reject belief in a god, we must give up the idea that life on this planet has some preordained meaning. Life *as a whole* has no meaning. Life began, as the best available theories tell us, in a chance combination of molecules; it then evolved through random mutations and natural selection. All this just happened; it did not happen for any overall purpose. Now that it has resulted in the existence of beings that prefer some states of affairs to others, however, it may be possible for particular lives to be meaningful. In this sense, atheists can find meaning in life.

Let us return to the comparison between the life of a psychopath and that of a more normal person. Why should the psychopath's life not be meaningful? We have seen that psychopaths are egocentric to an extreme: neither other people, nor worldly success, nor anything else really matters to them. Why is their own enjoyment of life not sufficient to give meaning to their lives?

Most of us would not be able to find full satisfaction by deliberately setting out to enjoy ourselves without caring about anyone or anything else. The pleasures we obtained in that way would seem empty and soon pall. We seek a meaning for our lives beyond our own pleasures and find fulfilment and happiness in doing what we see to be meaningful. If our life has no meaning other than our own happiness, we are likely to find that when we have obtained what we think we need to be happy, happiness itself still eludes us.

That those who aim at happiness for happiness's sake often fail to find it, whereas others find happiness in pursuing altogether different goals, has been called 'the paradox of hedonism'. It is not, of course, a logical paradox but a claim about the way in which we come to be happy. Like other generalizations on this subject, it lacks empirical confirmation. Yet it matches our everyday observations and is consistent with our nature as evolved, purposive beings. Human beings survive and reproduce themselves through purposive action. We obtain happiness and fulfillment by working towards and achieving our goals. In evolutionary terms, we could say that happiness functions as an internal reward for our achievements. Subjectively, we regard achieving the goal (or progressing towards it) as a reason for happiness. Our own happiness, therefore, is a by-product of aiming at something else and is not to be obtained by setting our sights on happiness alone.

The psychopath's life can now be seen to be meaningless in a way that a normal life is not. It is meaningless because it looks inward to the pleasures of the present moment and not outward to anything more long-term or far-reaching. More normal lives have meaning because they are lived to some larger purpose.

All this is speculative. You may accept or reject it to the extent that it agrees with your own observation and introspection. My next – and final – suggestion is more speculative still. It is that to find an enduring meaning in our lives it is not enough to go beyond psychopaths who have no long-term commitments or life plans; we must also go beyond more prudent egoists who have long-term plans concerned only with their own interests. The prudent egoists may find meaning in their lives for a time, for they have the purpose of furthering their own interests; but what, in the end, does that amount to? When everything in our interests has been achieved, do we just sit back and be happy? Could we be happy in this way? Or would we decide that we had still not quite reached our target, that there was something else we needed before we could sit back and enjoy it all? Most materially successful egoists take the latter route, thus escaping the necessity of admitting that they cannot find happiness in permanent holidaying. People who slave to establish small businesses, telling themselves they would do it only until they had made enough to live comfortably, keep working long after they have passed their original target. Their material 'needs' expand just fast enough to keep ahead of their income.

In recent years, we have had plenty of examples of the insatiable nature of the desire for wealth – and where it leads. For the 1980s, it was summed up in Oliver Stone's movie *Wall Street* starring Michael Douglas as a convincingly unpleasant Gordon Gekko, a financial wheeler-dealer whose manner of operation resembles that of the real-life financier Ivan Boesky who famously pronounced 'Greed is good.' The critical voice in the film is provided by Bud Fox, played by Charlie Sheen. While Gekko attempts his usual takeover and asset-stripping procedure on the airline for which Fox's father works as a mechanic, an angry Fox asks: 'Tell me, Gordon, when does it all end, huh? How many yachts can you water-ski behind? How much is enough?' For Boesky, it seems, $150 million was not enough, because his fortune was at least that when he sought to boost it even further by insider trading, a crime for which he eventually lost his fortune, his reputation and his liberty. With the man who had given the decade its tagline in prison, people began talking about finding fulfilment and satisfaction rather than just accumulating wealth. When economic good times returned in the first decade of the twenty-first century, however, ostentatious spending reached new heights, with the founders of equity firms competing to throw lavish birthday party bashes that cost upwards of $5 million. When the global financial crisis hit in 2007, and Bernard Madoff's Ponzi scheme became the equivalent of Boesky's insider trading, the talk once again turned to finding meaning and fulfilment – and it seems safe to predict that, in time, the cycle will repeat itself.

For anyone seeking to escape this cycle of accumulation and ruin, ethics can provide a more durable alternative. If we are looking for a purpose broader than our own interests, something that will allow us to see our lives as possessing significance beyond the narrow confines of our wealth or even our own pleasurable states of consciousness, one obvious solution is to take up the ethical point of view. The ethical point of view does, as we have seen, require us to go beyond a personal point of view to the standpoint of an impartial spectator. Thus, looking at things ethically is a way of transcending our inward-looking concerns and identifying ourselves with the most objective point of view possible – with, as Sidgwick put it, 'the point of view of the universe'.

The point of view of the universe is a lofty standpoint. In the rarefied air that surrounds it, we may get carried away into talking, as Kant does, of the moral point of view 'inevitably' humbling all who compare their own limited nature with it. I do not want to suggest anything as sweeping as this. Earlier in this chapter, in rejecting Thomas Nagel's argument for the rationality of altruism, I agreed with Sidgwick and Parfit that there is nothing irrational about being concerned with the quality of one's own existence in a way that one is not concerned with the quality of existence of other individuals. Without going back on this, I am now suggesting that rationality, in the broad sense that includes self-awareness and reflection on the nature and point of our own existence, may push us towards concerns broader than the quality of our own existence; but the process is not a necessary one, and those who do not take part in it – or who, in taking part, do not follow it all the way to the ethical point of view – are not irrational or in error. Some people find collecting stamps or following their favourite football team an entirely adequate way of giving purpose to their lives. There is nothing irrational about that; but others again seek something more significant as they become more aware of their situation in the world and more reflective about their purposes. To this third group, the ethical point of view offers a meaning and purpose in life that one does not grow out of. At least, one cannot grow out of the ethical point of view until all ethical tasks have been accomplished. If that utopia were ever achieved, our purposive nature might well leave us dissatisfied, much as egoists might be dissatisfied when they have everything they need to be happy. There is nothing paradoxical about this, for we should not expect evolution to have equipped us, in advance, with the ability to find satisfaction in a situation that has never previously occurred. Nor is this going to be a practical problem in the near future.

I will conclude by making these abstract speculations more personal and concrete. Henry Spira was one of the most effective twentieth-century American activists for animals. (To give just one example, it is due to Spira more than anyone else that the words 'not tested on animals' appear on so many cosmetic products today.) In addition to his many campaigns that saved an immense amount of animal suffering, Spira marched for civil rights in the South, fought against corruption in the National Maritime Union, and taught underprivileged kids in New York high schools. I had the good fortune to count him as my friend, staying with him many times in the sparsely furnished, rent-controlled New York apartment that served as his home and his office. When he had cancer and knew that the end was not far away, I asked him what had driven him to spend his life working for others. He replied:

I guess basically one wants to feel that one's life has amounted to more than just consuming products and generating garbage. I think that one likes to look back and say that one's done the best one can to make this a better place for others. You can look at it from this point of view: what greater motivation can there be than doing whatever one possibly can to reduce pain and suffering?

That answer will not provide everyone with overwhelming reasons for acting morally. It cannot be proven that we are all rationally required to reduce pain and suffering and make the world a better place for others. Ethically indefensible behaviour is not always irrational. We will probably always need the sanctions of the law and social pressure to provide additional reasons against serious violations of ethical standards. On the other hand, those reflective enough to ask why they should act ethically are also those most likely to appreciate the reasons Spira offered for taking the ethical point of view.

Notes, References and Further Reading

PREFACE

For more on the protests against the views expressed in this book, see Peter Singer, "On Being Silenced in Germany", *The New York Review of Books*, August 15, 1991, and Peter Singer, "An Intellectual Autobiography", in Jeffrey Schaler (ed.), *Peter Singer Under Fire* (Chicago, 2009).

The injunction against comparing humans and animals is from *Ethische Grundaussagen* (*Ethical Foundational Statements*) by the Board of the Federal Association Lebenshilfe für geistig Behinderte e.V., published in the journal of the association, *Geistige Behinderung* 29:4 (1990) p. 256.

CHAPTER 1: ABOUT ETHICS

The issues discussed in the first section – relativism, subjectivism and the alleged dependence of ethics on religion – are dealt with in several textbooks. Perhaps the best brief introduction is James Rachels, *The Elements of Moral Philosophy*, 6th ed., edited by Stuart Rachels (New York, 2009). The online *Stanford Encyclopedia of Philosophy* is a useful up-to-date source, here as well as on other topics discussed in this book. See also the articles on these topics by David Wong, James Rachels and Jonathan Berg, respectively, in Peter Singer (ed.), *A Companion to Ethics* (Oxford, 1991). Plato's argument against defining 'good' as 'what the gods approve' is in his *Euthyphro*. Engels' discussion of the Marxist view of morality and his reference to a 'really human morality' are in his *Herr Eugen Dühring's Revolution in Science*, chap. 9. For a discussion of Marx's critique of morality, see Allen Wood, "Marx against morality", in Peter Singer (ed.),

A Companion to Ethics (Oxford, 1991). C. L. Stevenson's emotivist theory is most fully expounded in his *Ethics and Language* (New Haven, 1944). R. M. Hare's basic position is to be found in *The Language of Morals* (Oxford, 1952), *Freedom and Reason* (Oxford, 1963) and *Moral Thinking* (Oxford, 1981). For a summary statement, see Hare's essay "Universal prescriptivism", in P. Singer (ed.), *A Companion to Ethics* (Oxford, 1991). J. L. Mackie's *Ethics: Inventing Right and Wrong* (Harmondsworth, Middlesex, 1977) defends a version of subjectivism. Derek Parfit provides a closely argued defence of objective truth in ethics in his *On What Matters* (Oxford, forthcoming).

The description of chimpanzee behaviour that suggests a sense of justice comes from Frans de Waal, *Chimpanzee Politics*, (Jonathan Cape, London, 1982), pp. 205–7. For a detailed account of recent findings on the evolved nature of our moral intuitions, and a discussion of the significance of these findings for ethics, see Joshua Greene, *The Moral Brain and How to Use It*, Penguin Press, New York, forthcoming.

Mill's essay "On Nature" was first published in John Stuart Mill, *Nature, The Utility of Religion, and Theism*, (London, 1874).

The more important formulations of the universalizability principle referred to in the second section are in Immanuel Kant, *Groundwork of the Metaphysic of Morals*, Section II; R. M. Hare, *Freedom and Reason* and *Moral Thinking*; R. Firth, "Ethical Absolutism and the Ideal Observer", *Philosophy and Phenomenological Research*, vol. 12 (1951–2); J. J. C. Smart and B. Williams, *Utilitarianism, For and Against* (Cambridge, 1973); John Rawls, *A Theory of Justice* (Oxford, 1972; revised edition, 1999); J. P. Sartre, "Existentialism is a Humanism", in W. Kaufmann (ed.), *Existentialism from Dostoevsky to Sartre* (2nd edition, New York, 1975); and Jürgen Habermas, *Legitimation Crisis*, (tr. T. McCarthy, London, 1976) pt. 111, chap. 2–4.

The tentative argument for a form of utilitarianism based on interests or preferences owes most to Hare, although it does not go as far as the argument to be found in his *Moral Thinking*. Sidgwick distinguishes the preference view from the hedonistic view in his *The Methods of Ethics* (7th edition, London, 1907), book I, chap. 9, pp. 109–15. For a useful discussion of consequentialism, see the article by Walter Sinnott-Armstrong in the *Stanford Encyclopedia of Philosophy*, http://plato.stanford.edu/entries/consequentialism.

For the finding that winning lotteries does not lead to greater happiness, see Philip Brickman, Dan Coates and Ronnie Janoff-Bulman, "Lottery winners and accident victims: Is happiness relative?" *Journal of Personality and Social Psychology*, 36 (1978), pp. 917–27.

CHAPTER 2: EQUALITY AND ITS IMPLICATIONS

Rawls's argument that equality can be based on the natural characteristics of human beings is to be found in Sec. 77 of *A Theory of Justice* (Cambridge, MA, 1971; revised edition, 1999).

For a discussion of intelligence and IQ tests, see James Flynn, *What is Intelligence? Beyond the Flynn Effect* (Cambridge, 2009). Arguments in favour of a link between IQ and race can be found in A. R. Jensen, *Genetics and Education* (London, 1972) and *Educability and Group Differences* (London, 1973) and in H. J. Eysenck, *Race, Intelligence and Education* (London, 1971). A variety of objections are collected in K. Richardson and D. Spears (eds.), *Race, Culture and Intelligence* (Harmondsworth, Middlesex, 1972). See also N. J. Block and G. Dworkin, *The IQ Controversy* (New York, 1976); H. J. Eysenck and Leon Kamin, *Intelligence: The Battle for The Mind* (London, 1981); R. C. Lewontin, Steven Rose and Leon Kamin, *Not in Our Genes* (New York, 1984) especially chap. 5; R. J. Herrnstein and C. Murray, *The Bell Curve* (New York, 1994) and the debate between Robert Nichols and James Flynn, with a comment by Jensen, in S. Modgil and C. Modgil, *Arthur Jensen, Consensus and Controversy* (New York, 1987), pp. 213–35 and 374–81. Thomas Jefferson's comment on the irrelevance of intelligence to the issue of rights was made in a letter to Henri Gregoire, 25 February 1809.

The nature and origin of psychological and cognitive differences between the sexes are considered in Eleanor Maccoby and Carol Jacklin, *The Psychology of Sex Differences* (Palo Alto, 1974); Diane Halpern, *Sex Differences in Cognitive Abilities,* (3rd edition, London, 2000); Doreen Kimura, *Sex and Cognition,* (Cambridge, Mass., 2000); and Melissa Hines, *Brain Gender* (New York, 2005). For a critique of some of the science, see Cordelia Fine, *Delusions of Gender* (New York, 2010).

A typical defence of equality of opportunity as the only justifiable form of equality is Danel Bell, "A 'Just' Equality", *Dialogue* (Washington DC, 1975) vol. 8, no. 2. The quotation by Jeffrey Gray is from "Why Should Society Reward Intelligence?" *The Times* (London), September 8, 1972. The dilemmas raised by equal opportunity are acutely set out in James Fishkin, *Justice, Equal Opportunity and the Family* (New Haven, 1983).

For an overview of the issue of affirmative action, see Robert Fullinwider's article "Affirmative Action" in the online *Stanford Encyclopedia of Philosophy,* http://plato.stanford.edu/entries/affirmative-action. See also Robert Fullinwider and Judith Lichtenberg, *Leveling the Playing Field: Justice, Politics, and College Admissions* (Lanham, Maryland, 2004). Evidence that minority students admitted under affirmative action do less well than the class as a whole is presented in Richard Sander, "A Systemic Analysis of Affirmative Action in American Law Schools," *Stanford Law Review*, 57 (2004), pp. 367–484. The argument that affirmative action is bad for minority students can be found in Stephan Thernstrom and Abigail Thernstrom, *America in Black and White: One Nation, Indivisible* (New York, 1997). Affirmative action is defended by two former presidents of Princeton and Harvard Universities in William Bowen and Derek Bok, *The Shape of the River: Long-Term Consequences of Considering Race in College and University Admissions* (Princeton, New Jersey, 1998).

CHAPTER 3: EQUALITY FOR ANIMALS?

For a fuller account of my views on the ethics of how we should treat animals, see *Animal Liberation* (2nd edition reissued with a new preface, New York, 2009). Mary Midgley, *Animals and Why They Matter* (Harmondsworth, Middlesex, 1983) is a readable account of these issues. James Rachels, *Created from Animals* (Oxford, 1990) draws the moral implications of the Darwinian revolution for our thinking about our place among the animals. Richard Ryder charts the history of changing attitudes towards speciesism in *Animal Revolution* (Oxford, 1989). Also recommended: David DeGrazia, *Taking Animals Seriously* (Cambridge, 1996) and the same author's *Animal Rights: A Very Short Introduction* (Oxford, 2001); Paola Cavalieri, *The Animal Question* (New York, 2001) and *The Death of the Animal: A Dialogue* (New York, 2009); and Karen Dawn, *Thanking the Monkey* (New York, 2008). On the psychology of our relations with animals, see Hal Herzog, *Some We Love, Some We Hate, Some We Eat: Why It's So Hard to Think Straight About Animals,* (New York, 2010). Anthologies dealing with animals and ethics include: Tom Regan and Peter Singer (eds.), *Animal Rights and Human Obligations* (2nd edition, Englewood Cliffs, NJ, 1989); Peter Singer (ed.) *In Defense of Animals* (Oxford, 1986) and *In Defense of Animals: The Second Wave* (Oxford, 2006); Susan Armstrong and Richard Botzler (eds.), *The Animal Ethics Reader* (London, 2003); and Cass Sunstein and Martha Nussbaum (eds.), *Animal Rights: Current Debates and New Directions* (New York, 2004).

Bentham's defence of animals is from his *Introduction to the Principles of Morals and Legislation* (1789) chap. XVIII, sec. 1, note.

A more detailed description of modern farming conditions can be found in *Animal Liberation,* chap. 3; in Michael Pollan, *The Omnivore's Dilemma* (New York, 2006), chap. 17; and in Peter Singer and Jim Mason, *The Ethics of What We Eat* (New York, 2006). Similarly, *Animal Liberation,* chap. 2 contains a fuller discussion of the use of animals in research than is possible in this book, but see also Richard Ryder, *Victims of Science* (2nd edition, Fontwell, Sussex, 1983). Details of the Botox experiment can be found at http://www.hsus.org. The experiments by H. F. Harlow on isolating monkeys were originally published in *Journal of Comparative and Physiological Psychology*, 78 (1972), p. 202; *Proceedings of the National Academy of Science*, 54 (1965), p. 90, and *Engineering and Science*, 33 (April 1970), p. 8. On the continuation of Harlow's work, see *Animal Liberation* (2nd edition), pp. 34–5.

Among the objections, the claim that animals are incapable of feeling pain has usually been associated with Descartes. Descartes' view is less clear (and less consistent) than most have assumed. See John Cottingham, "A Brute to the Brutes?: Descartes' Treatment of Animals", *Philosophy*, 53 (1978), p. 551. In *The Unheeded Cry* (Oxford, 1989), Bernard Rollin describes and criticises more recent ideologies that have denied the reality of animal pain. On pain in crustaceans, see Robert Elwood and Mirjam Appel, "Pain experience in hermit crabs?" *Animal Behaviour*, 77 (2009), pp. 1243–46 and Stuart Barr et al., "Nociception or pain in a decapod crustacean?" *Animal Behaviour*, 75 (2008), pp. 745–51.

The source for the anecdote about Benjamin Franklin is his *Autobiography* (New York, 1950), p. 41. The same objection has been more seriously considered by John Benson in "Duty and The Beast", *Philosophy*, 53 (1978), pp. 545–7.

In the section on 'Ethics and Reciprocity', the quotation from Plato's *Republic* is from Book 11, pp. 358–9. Later statements of a similar view include John Rawls, *A Theory of Justice* (Oxford, 1972; revised edition, 1999); J. L. Mackie, *Ethics*, chap. 5; and David Gauthier, *Morals by Agreement* (Oxford, 1986). They exclude animals from the centre of morality, although they soften the impact of this exclusion in various ways (see, for example, *A Theory of Justice*, p. 512, and *Ethics*, pp. 193–5). My discussion of the looser version of the reciprocity view draws on Edward Johnson, *Species and Morality*, PhD Thesis, Princeton University, 1976 (University Microfilms International, Ann Arbor, Michigan, 1981), p. 145.

For an interpretation of the contract view of ethics that is much more favourable to animals, see Mark Rowlands, *Animal Rights: Moral Theory and Practice*, (2nd edition, London, 2009).

In the section 'Differences between humans and animals', Jane Goodall's observations of chimpanzees are engagingly recounted in

In The Shadow of Man (Boston, 1971) and *Through a Window* (London, 1990), and in more scholarly form in *The Chimpanzees of Gombe* (Cambridge, Mass., 1986). For more information on the capacities of the great apes, see Paola Cavalieri and Peter Singer (eds.), *The Great Ape Project* (London, 1993). On the relative moral status of animals and people with profound intellectual disability, see Peter Singer, "Speciesism and Moral Status", and Eva Feder Kittay, "The Personal is Philosophical is Political: A Philosopher and Mother of a Cognitively Disabled Person Sends Notes from the Battlefield", both in Eva Feder Kittay and Licia Carlson, (eds.), *Cognitive Disability and Its Challenge to Moral Philosophy* (Malden, MA, 2010) pp. 331–44 and pp. 393–413.

Of the objections to the argument discussed in the section 'Defending Speciesism' the claim that we should give individuals the moral status that corresponds with the capacities normal for their species was made by Stanley Benn, "Egalitarianism and Equal Consideration of Interests", in J. Pennock and J. Chapman (eds.), *Nomos IX: Equality* (New York, 1967) pp. 62ff.; the argument that we have special duties to humans because we think of ourselves as human was made by John Benson, "Duty and the Beast", *Philosophy*, 53 (1978), and related points are made by Bonnie Steinbock, "Speciesism and the Idea of Equality", *Philosophy*, vol. 53, pp. 255–6 and at greater length by Leslie Pickering Francis and Richard Norman, "Some Animals are More Equal than Others", *Philosophy*, vol. 53 (1978), pp. 518–27. Bernard Williams defends "The Human Prejudice" in an essay with that title, reprinted in Jeffrey Schaler (ed.), *Peter Singer Under Fire* (Chicago, 2009). A fuller response from me can be found in the same volume.

CHAPTER 4: WHAT'S WRONG WITH KILLING?

Andrew Stinson's treatment is described by Robert and Peggy Stinson in *The Long Dying of Baby Andrew* (Boston, 1983).

Joseph Fletcher's article "Indicators of Humanhood: A Tentative Profile of Man" appeared in *The Hastings Center Report*, vol. 2, no. 5 (1972). John Locke's definition of 'person' is taken from his *Essay Concerning Human Understanding*, (1690) bk. II, chap. 27, par. 9.

Aristotle's views on infanticide are in his *Politics*, bk. VII, p. 1335b; Plato's views are in the *Republic*, bk. V, 460c. Support for the claim that our present attitudes to infanticide are largely the effect of the influence of Christianity on our thought can be found in the historical material on infanticide cited in the notes for Chapter 6. (See especially the article by

W. L. Langer, pp. 353–5.) For Aquinas' statement that killing a human being offends against God as killing a slave offends against the master of the slave, see *Summa Theologica*, II, ii, question 64, article 5.

Hare propounds and defends his two-level view of moral reasoning in *Moral Thinking* (Oxford, 1981).

Michael Tooley's "Abortion and Infanticide" was first published in *Philosophy and Public Affairs*, vol. 2 (1972). The passage quoted in the section 'Does a person have a right to life?' on p. 81 is from a revised version in J. Feinberg (ed.), *The Problem of Abortion* (Belmont, 1973), p. 60. His book *Abortion and Infanticide* was published in Oxford in 1983.

For further discussion of respect for autonomy as an objection to killing, see Jonathan Glover, *Causing Death and Saving Lives* (Harmondsworth, Middlesex, 1977), chap. 5., and H. J. McCloskey, "The Right to Life", *Mind*, vol. 84 (1975).

Jeremy Bentham gives his account of what it is for something to be in the interests of an individual in his *Introduction to the Principles of Morals and Legislation*, (1789), chap. 1, pars. II, V.

My discussion of the 'total' and 'prior existence' versions of utilitarianism owes much to Derek Parfit. I originally tried to defend the prior existence view in "A Utilitarian Population Principle" in M. Bayles (ed.), *Ethics and Population* (Cambridge, Mass., 1976) but Parfit's reply, "On Doing the Best for Our Children", in the same volume, persuaded me to change my mind. Parfit's *Reasons and Persons* (Oxford, 1984) is required reading for anyone wishing to pursue this topic in depth. See also his short account of some of the issues in "Overpopulation and the Quality of Life", in Peter Singer (ed.), *Applied Ethics* (Oxford, 1986). Parfit uses the term 'person-affecting' where I use 'prior existence', which seems more suitable as the view has no special reference to persons, as distinct from other sentient creatures.

The distinction between the two versions of utilitarianism appears to have been first noticed by Henry Sidgwick, *The Methods of Ethics* (London, 1907), bk. IV, chap. 1, pp. 414–16. Later discussions include, in addition to those cited previously, J. Narveson, "Moral Problems of Population", *The Monist*, vol. 57 (1973); T. G. Roupas, "The Value of Life", *Philosophy and Public Affairs*, vol. 7 (1978); R. I. Sikora, "Is it Wrong to Prevent the Existence of Future Generations", in B. Barry and R. Sikora (ed.), *Obligations to Future Generations* (Philadelphia, 1978); Jeff McMahan, "Problems of Population Theory", *Ethics*, 92 (1981), pp. 96–127; Melinda Roberts, *Child versus Childmaker: Future Persons and Present Duties in Ethics and the Law*, (Lanham, MD, 1998); Jesper Ryberg and

Torbjorn Tannsjo (eds.), *The Repugnant Conclusion: Essays on Population Ethics* (New York, 2005); Elizabeth Harman, "Can we harm and benefit in creating?" *Philosophical Perspectives* 18 (2004), pp. 89–109; and Caspar Hare, "Voices from another world: Must we respect the interests of people who do not, and will never, exist?" *Ethics*, 117 (2007), pp. 498–523. For an overview, see Jesper Ryberg, "The Repugnant Conclusion" in the online *Stanford Encyclopedia of Philosophy,* http://plato.stanford.edu/entries/repugnant-conclusion/

Mill's famous passage comparing Socrates and the fool appeared in his *Utilitarianism* (first published 1863; J.M. Dent, London, 1960) pp. 8–9.

For a thoughtful in-depth discussion of the entire area covered in this and the next three chapters, see Jeff McMahan, *The Ethics of Killing: Problems at the Margins of Life* (New York, 2001).

CHAPTER 5: TAKING LIFE: ANIMALS

The breakthrough in communicating with a being of another species was announced in R. and B. Gardner, "Teaching Sign Language to a Chimpanzee", *Science,* vol. 165 (1969), pp. 664–72. The information on language use in chimpanzees, gorillas and an orangutan is drawn from the articles by Roger and Deborah Fouts, Francine Patterson and Wendy Gordon, and H. Lyn Miles, in Paola Cavalieri and Peter Singer (eds.), *The Great Ape Project* (London, 1993). For an account of Washoe's life, see Roger Fouts, *Next of Kin* (New York, 1997), and for a discussion of the mental lives of dolphins, see Thomas White, *In Defense of Dolphins,* (Blackwell, Oxford, 2007).

The quotation in the first section of Chapter 5 is from Stuart Hampshire, *Thought and Action* (London, 1959), pp. 98–9. Others who have held related views are Anthony Kenny, in *Will, Freedom and Power* (Oxford, 1975); Donald Davidson, "Thought and Talk" in S. Guttenplan (ed.), *Mind and Language* (Oxford, 1975); and Michael Leahy, *Against Liberation* (London, 1991).

Julia's problem-solving abilities were demonstrated by J. Döhl and B. Rensch; their work is described in Jane Goodall, *The Chimpanzees of Gombe,* p. 31. Frans de Waal reports his observations of chimpanzees in *Chimpanzee Politics* (New York, 1983). Goodall's account of Figan's thoughtful manner of obtaining his banana is taken from p. 107 of *In the Shadow of Man.* The study showing that pigs avoid showing heavier pigs where food is located is by S. Held, M. Mendl, C. Devereux, and R. W. Byrne,

"Foraging pigs alter their behavior in response to exploitation", *Animal Behaviour* 64 (2002), pp. 157–66. Mathias Osvath reported his observations of the stone-throwing chimpanzee Santino in "Spontaneous planning for future stone throwing by a male chimpanzee", *Current Biology*, 19 (2009), pp. R190-1. The remarkable mental powers of scrub jays is demonstrated in Sérgio P.C. Correia, Anthony Dickinson and Nicola S. Clayton, "Western Scrub-Jays Anticipate Future Needs Independently of Their Current Motivational State", *Current Biology*, 17 (2007), pp. 856–61. On this topic generally, see Michael Mendl and Elizabeth S. Paul, "Do animals live in the present? Current evidence and implications for welfare," *Applied Animal Behaviour Science*, 113 (2008), pp. 357–82.

Animal self-awareness and mirror tests are discussed in several essays included in M. Bekoff, C. Allen and G. Burghardt (eds.), *The Cognitive Animal: Empirical and Theoretical Perspectives on Animal Cognition* (Cambridge, Mass., 2002). Irene Pepperberg describes her work with Alex the parrot in *Alex and Me* (New York, 2008). The ability of chickens to exercise self-control was reported in S. M. Abeyesinghe, C. J. Nicol, S. J. Hartnell and C. M. Wathes, "Can domestic fowl, *Gallus gallus domesticus*, show self-control?" *Animal Behavior*, 70 (2005), pp. 1–11. Culum Brown discusses the mental lives of fish in "Not just a pretty face," *New Scientist*, 182 (12 June 2004), p. 42. On novel tool use in an octopus, see Julian K. Finn, Tom Tregenza and Mark Norman, "Defensive tool use in a coconut-carrying octopus", *Current Biology*, 19 (2009), pp. R1069–70.

For more on Gary Varner's understanding of the difference between a person, a near-person and the merely sentient, see his *Personhood and Animals in the Two-Level Utilitarianism of R.M. Hare.* (New York. Forthcoming). Roger Scruton writes about when death is and is not a tragedy in his essay "The Conscientious Carnivore", in *Food for Thought*, edited by Steve Sapontzis (Amherst, NY, 2004), pp. 81–91.

Leslie Stephen's claim that eating bacon is kind to pigs comes from his *Social Rights and Duties* (London, 1896) and is quoted by Henry Salt in "The Logic of the Larder", which appeared in Salt's *The Humanities of Diet* (Manchester, 1914) and has been reprinted in the first edition of T. Regan and P. Singer (eds.), *Animal Rights and Human Obligations* (Englewood Cliffs, NJ, 1976). For more recent re-statements of the argument, see Michael Pollan, *The Omnivore's Dilemma* (New York, 2006) and Hugh Fearnley-Whittingstall, *The River Cottage Meat Book*, (London, 2004). My own earlier discussion of this issue is in chapter 6 of the first edition of *Animal Liberation* (New York, 1975). For a detailed discussion of the issue, arguing against replaceability, see Tatjana Visak, "Killing Happy Animals", a PhD thesis submitted to Utrecht University, 2010.

The example of the two women comes from Derek Parfit, "Rights, Interests and Possible People", in S. Gorovitz et al. (eds.), *Moral Problems in Medicine* (Englewood Cliffs, NJ, 1976); a variation expressed in terms of a choice between two different medical programs can be found in Parfit's *Reasons and Persons* (Oxford, 1984), p. 367. James Rachels' distinction between a biological and a biographical life comes from his *The End of Life* (Oxford, 1987). Hart's discussion of this topic in his review of the first edition of this book was titled "Death and Utility" and appeared in *The New York Review of Books*, May 15, 1980.

Arthur Schopenhauer argues for his pessimistic view of existence in *The World as Will and Idea*, (first published 1818, trans. R. B. Haldane and J. Kemp, London, 1896), bk. IV, secs. 56–9, pp. 397–420. A more recent defence is David Benatar's *Better Never to Have Been: The Harm of Coming into Existence* (Oxford, 2006).

Henry Sidgwick's argument for desirable consciousness, or pleasure, as the ultimate good, can be found in *The Methods of Ethics*, bk. III, chap. 14.

The original presentation of the non-identity problem, which lies behind my climate change scenario and Parfit's "Depletion" example on which it is based, is Derek Parfit, *Reasons and Persons* (Oxford, 1984), pp. 351–74. For an overview of the problem and further references see Melinda Roberts, "The Nonidentity Problem", in the online *Stanford Encyclopedia of Philosophy*, http://plato.stanford.edu/entries/nonidentity-problem.

On the ethics of hunting, see Gary Varner, *In Nature's Interests* (New York, 1998), chap. 5. Steven Davis claims that those who eat grass-fed beef are responsible for fewer animal deaths than vegans in "The Least Harm Principle May Require that Humans Consume A Diet Containing Large Herbivores, Not A Vegan Diet", *Journal of Agricultural and Environmental Ethics*, 16 (2003), pp. 387–94. The error in his calculations is revealed by Gaverick Matheny, "Least Harm: A Defense of Vegetarianism from Steven Davis's Omnivorous Proposal", *Journal of Agricultural and Environmental Ethics*, 16 (2003), pp. 505–11.

CHAPTER 6: TAKING LIFE: THE EMBRYO AND FETUS

The full text of the decision of the U.S. Supreme Court in *Roe v. Wade* is available online; some key sections are reprinted in J. Feinberg (ed.), *The*

Problem of Abortion. For the number of frozen embryos in the United States, see Pam Belluck, "From Stem Cell Opponents, an Embryo Crusade", *The New York Times,* June 2, 2005.

The government committee referred to in the "Quickening" section of Chapter 6 – the Wolfenden Committee – issued the *Report of the Committee on Homosexual Offences and Prostitution,* Command Paper 247 (London, 1957). The quotation is from p. 24. J. S. Mill's 'very simple principle' is stated in the introductory chapter of *On Liberty* (3rd edition, London, 1864). Edwin Schur's *Crimes Without Victims* was published in Englewood Cliffs, NJ, in 1965. Judith Jarvis Thomson's "A Defense of Abortion" appeared in *Philosophy and Public Affairs,* 1 (1971) and has been reprinted in Peter Singer (ed.), *Applied Ethics.*

My account of the development of fetal sentience draws on research carried out by Susan Taiwa at the Centre for Human Bioethics, Monash University, and published as "When is the capacity for sentience acquired during human fetal development?" *Journal of Maternal-Fetal Medicine,* 1 (1992), pp. 153–65. An earlier expert opinion came from the British Government advisory group on fetal research, chaired by Sir John Peel, published as *The Use of Fetuses and Fetal Materials for Research* (London, 1972). See also Clifford Grobstein, *Science and The Unborn* (New York, 1988).

Paul Ramsey uses the genetic uniqueness of the fetus as an argument against abortion in "The Morality of Abortion", in D. H. Labby (ed.), *Life or Death: Ethics and Options* (London, 1968) and reprinted in J. Rachels (ed.), *Moral Problems* (2nd edition, New York, 1975), p. 40. President George W. Bush's speech on the use of embryos to obtain stem cells is here: http://georgewbush-whitehouse.archives.gov/news/releases/2001/08/20010809-2.html.

Don Marquis's argument against abortion was published as "Why abortion is immoral", *Journal of Philosophy,* 86 (1989), pp. 183–202; see also Alistair Norcross, "Killing, Abortion and Contraception: A Reply to Marquis", *Journal of Philosophy,* 87 (1990), pp. 268–77. The quotation about totipotency is from Don Marquis, "Singer on Abortion and Infanticide", in Jeffrey Schaler (ed.), *Peter Singer Under Fire* (Open Court, 2009), p. 151.

On the possibility of creating new human beings from various kinds of cells, see Agata Sagan and Peter Singer, "The Moral Status of Stem Cells", *Metaphilosophy,* vol. 38, no. 2–3 (April 2007), pp. 264–84. The passage quoted from Patrick Lee and Robert George is from their essay "Human-Embryo Liberation: A Reply to Peter Singer", *National Review*

Online (25 January 2006), http://www.nationalreview.com/comment/
lee_george200601250829.asp. See also Patrick Lee and Robert George,
Body-Self Dualism in Contemporary Ethics and Politics, (Cambridge University
Press, Cambridge, 2008), pp. 81–94.

I owe my speculations about the identity of the splitting embryo
to Helga Kuhse, with whom I co-authored "Individuals, humans and
persons: the issue of moral status", in P. Singer, H. Kuhse, S. Buckle,
K. Dawson and P. Kasimba (eds.), *Embryo Experimentation* (Cambridge,
1990). We were both indebted to a remarkable book by a Roman Catholic
theologian that challenges the view that conception marks the beginning
of the human individual: Norman Ford, *When Did I Begin?* (Cambridge,
1988). For the discussion about mourning the loss of "Mary," see David
Oderberg, "Modal Properties, Moral Status, and Identity", *Philosophy &
Public Affairs*, 26 (1997), pp. 270–1. The argument about potentiality in
the context of IVF was first published in Peter Singer and Karen Dawson,
"IVF technology and the argument from potential", *Philosophy and Public
Affairs*, 17 (1988) and is reprinted in *Embryo Experimentation*. Stephen
Buckle takes a different approach in "Arguing from Potential", *Bioethics*,
2 (1988), also reprinted in *Embryo Experimentation*. See also Reginald Wil-
liams, "Abortion, Potential, and Value", *Utilitas*, 20 (2008), pp. 169–84.

The quotation from John Noonan is from his "An almost absolute
value in history," in John Noonan (ed.), *The Morality of Abortion* (Cambridge, Mass., 1970), pp. 56–7. On the percentage of embryos that
become babies, see United States Department of Human Services, Cen-
ters for Disease Control and Prevention, Assisted Reproductive Technology (ART) Report: National Summary, 2007, available at http://apps
.nccd.cdc.gov/ART/NSR.aspx?SelectedYear=2007. Note that to obtain
the probability of any individual embryo surviving, it is necessary to divide
the pregnancy success rates by the average number of embryos used per
cycle (because most pregnancies result in only one child). British figures
can be found on the Web site of the Human Fertilisation and Embryology
Authority, http://www.hfea.gov.uk/ivf-figures-2006.html#1276. For the
Australian state of Victoria, see Victorian Assisted Reproductive Treatment Authority, *Annual Report, 2009*, available at http://www.varta.org
.au/www/257/1003057/displayarticle/1003573.html.

Bentham's reassuring comment on infanticide is from his *Theory of
Legislation* (1802), p. 264 and is quoted by E. Westermarck, *The Origin
and Development of Moral Ideas* (London, 1924), I, p. 413n. In the final part
of *Abortion and Infanticide*, Michael Tooley discusses the available evidence
on the development in the infant of the sense of being a continuing self.

On this topic, see also Alison Gopnik, *The Philosophical Baby* (New York, 2009).

For historical material on the prevalence of infanticide, see Maria Piers, *Infanticide* (New York, 1978) and W. L. Langer, "Infanticide: A Historical Survey", *History of Childhood Quarterly*, vol. 1 (1974). An older, but still valuable survey is in Edward Westermarck, *The Origin and Development of Moral Ideas, 1*, pp. 394–413. An interesting study of the use of infanticide as a form of family planning is Thomas C. Smith, *Nakahara: Family Farming and Population in a Japanese Village, 1717–1830*. References for Plato and Aristotle's views on this topic were given in the notes to Chapter 4. For Seneca, see *De Ira, 1*, 15, cited by Westermarck, *The Origin and Development of Moral Ideas, I*, p. 419. Marvin Kohl (ed.), *Infanticide and the Value of Life* (Buffalo, NY, 1978) is a collection of essays on infanticide. A powerful argument on public policy grounds for birth as the place to draw the line can be found (by readers of German) in Norbert Hoerster, "Kindestötung und das Lebensrecht von Personen", *Analyse & Kritik*, 12 (1990), pp. 226–44.

Articles with some affinity with the position I have taken include Michael Tooley, "Abortion and Infanticide," *Philosophy and Public Affairs*, vol. 2 (1972); Mary Anne Warren, "The Moral and Legal Status of Abortion", *The Monist*, vol. 57 (1973); and R. M. Hare, "Abortion and the Golden Rule", *Philosophy and Public Affairs*, vol. 4 (1975).

CHAPTER 7: TAKING LIFE: HUMANS

Details of the Linares case are from the *New York Times*, 27 April 1989, and the *Hastings Center Report*, July/August 1989. For more detailed information and references regarding the entire topic of life and death decisions for infants, see: Helga Kuhse and Peter Singer, *Should the Baby Live?* (Oxford, 1985); Nufffield Council on Bioethics, "Critical Care Decisions in Fetal and Neonatal Medicine" (2006), http://www.nuffieldbioethics.org/go/ourwork/neonatal/publication_406.html; John D. Lantos and William Meadow, *Neonatal Bioethics: The Moral Challenges of Medical Innovation* (Baltimore: Johns Hopkins University Press, 2006); and Geoffrey Miller, *Extreme Prematurity: Practices, Bioethics and the Law* (Cambridge, New York: Cambridge University Press, 2007).

The numbers of patients in a persistent vegetative state and the duration of these states are reported in "USA: Right to live, or right to die?" *The Lancet*, vol. 337 (January 12, 1991). See also Nancy Frazier O'Brien, "No easy answers seen for questions about persistent vegetative state",

Catholic News Service 9/20/2007 www.catholic.org. On the Schiavo case, see William Yardley and Maria Newman, "Schiavo Dies Nearly Two Weeks After Removal of Feeding Tube", *The New York Times*, March 31, 2005; and Timothy Williams, "Schiavo's Brain Was Severely Deteriorated, Autopsy Says", *The New York Times*, June 15, 2005.

The case of Diane is cited from Timothy E. Quill, "Death and Dignity: A Case of Individualized Decision Making", *The New England Journal of Medicine*, 324(10), pp. 691–4 (March 7, 1991). Betty Rollins describes the death of her mother in *Last Wish* (Penguin, 1987) – the passage quoted is from pp. 149–50. On the death of Janet Adkins, see *New York Times*, 14 December 1990; for Jack Kevorkian's own account, see J. Kevorkian, *Prescription: Medicide* (Prometheus Books, Buffalo, NY, 1991). For more discussion of physician-assisted suicide and voluntary euthanasia, see Margaret Pabst Battin, *The Least Worst Death*, (New York, 1994); J. M. Dieterle, "Physician-Assisted Suicide: A New Look at the Arguments," *Bioethics*, 21 (2007), pp. 127–39; and Michael Gill, "Is the Legalization of Physician-Assisted Suicide Compatible with Good End-of-Life Care?" *Journal of Applied Philosophy*, 26 (2009), pp. 28–42.

My account of events at Memorial Medical Center in New Orleans is based on Sheri Fink, "The Deadly Choices at Memorial," *The New York Times Sunday Magazine*, August 30, 2009.

An official statement of the position of the Roman Catholic Church on euthanasia and the doctrine of double effect can be found in its *Declaration on Euthanasia*, published by the Sacred Congregation for the Doctrine of the Faith (Vatican City, 1980). Other useful discussions are Jonathan Glover, *Causing Death and Saving Lives*, chap. 14 and 15; D. Humphrey and A. Wickett, *The Right to Die: Understanding Euthanasia* (New York, 1986); and Helga Kuhse, "Euthanasia", in P. Singer (ed.), *A Companion to Ethics* (Oxford, 1991).

On the issues around the treatment of severely disabled infants, see C. Gill, "Health Professionals, Disability and Assisted Suicide: An Examination of Relevant Empirical Evidence and Reply to Batavia", *Psychology, Public Policy & Law*, 6:2 (2000), pp. 526–45; A. Batavia, "The Relevance of Data on Physicians and Disability on the Right to Assisted Suicide: Can Empirical Studies Resolve the Issue?" *Psychology, Public Policy and Law*, 6:2 (2000), pp. 546–58; and Eva Feder Kittay, "At the Margins of Moral Personhood", *Ethics*, 116 (2005), pp. 100–31. See also the following essays, and my responses, all of which are in Jeffrey Schaler (ed.), *Peter Singer Under Fire* (Chicago, 2009); Harry J. Gensler, "Singer's Unsanctity of Human Life: A Critique"; Harriet McBryde Johnson, "Unspeakable

Conversations, or, How I Spent One Day as a Token Cripple at Princeton University", and Stephen Drake, "Not Dead Yet!"

The distinction between active and passive euthanasia is succinctly criticized by James Rachels, "Active and Passive Euthanasia", *New England Journal of Medicine*, 292 (1975), pp. 78–80, reprinted in Peter Singer (ed.), *Applied Ethics*. See also Rachels' *The End of Life*; Helga Kuhse and Peter Singer, *Should the Baby Live?*, chap. 4; and Helga Kuhse, *The Sanctity-of-Life Doctrine in Medicine – A Critique* (Oxford, 1987), chap. 2. An account of the Baby Doe case is given in chapter 1 of the same book. The survey of American paediatricians was published as: Loretta M. Kopelman, Thomas G. Irons and Arthur E. Kopelman, "Neonatologists Judge the 'Baby Doe' Regulations", *The New England Journal of Medicine*, 318 (March 17, 1988), pp. 677–83. The British legal cases concerning such decisions are described in Derek Morgan, "Letting babies die legally", *Institute of Medical Ethics Bulletin*, May 1989, pp. 13–18; and in "Withholding of life-saving treatment", *The Lancet*, 336 (1991), p. 1121. Arthur Clough's poem is included in *The New Oxford Book of English Verse*, edited by Helen Gardner (Oxford, 1978). Sir Gustav Nossal's essay cited in the "Active and passive euthanasia" section of Chapter 7 is "The Right to Die: Do we Need New Legislation?" in Parliament of Victoria, Social Development Committee, *First Report on Inquiry into Options for Dying with Dignity*, p. 104. On the doctrine of double effect and the distinction between ordinary and extraordinary means of treatment, see Helga Kuhse, "Euthanasia", in Peter Singer (ed.), *A Companion to Ethics* (Oxford, 1991) and for a fuller account, the same author's *The Sanctity-of-Life Doctrine in Medicine – A Critique*, (Oxford, 1987) chap. 3–4. For Pope John Paul II's decision on the withdrawal of feeding tubes, see "Speech of John Paul II to the Participants at the International Congress, 'Life Sustaining Treatments and Vegetative State: Scientific Advances and Ethical Dilemmas'", March 20, 2004, available at http://www.vegetativestate.org/discorso_papa.htm. See also the previously mentioned *Declaration on Euthanasia* published by the Sacred Congregation for the Doctrine of the Faith, Vatican City, 1980.

The survey of Australian paediatricians and obstetricians was published as P. Singer, H. Kuhse and C. Singer, "The treatment of newborn infants with major handicaps", *Medical Journal of Australia*, 17 September 1983. The testimony of the Roman Catholic bishop, Lawrence Casey, in the Quinlan case is cited in the judgment, "In the Matter of Karen Quinlan, An Alleged Incompetent", reprinted in B. Steinbock (ed.), *Killing and Letting Die* (Englewood Cliffs, NJ, 1980). John Lorber describes his practice of passive euthanasia for selected cases of spina bifida in "Early Results of Selective Treatment of Spina Bifida Cystica", *British Medical Journal*, 27 October 1973, pp. 201–4. The statistics for survival of untreated spina bifida infants come from the articles by Lorber and G. K. and E. D. Smith, cited previously. Different doctors report different figures. Lorber's objection to active euthanasia is from p. 204 of the same article. For further discussion of the treatment of infants with spina bifida, see Helga Kuhse and Peter Singer, *Should the Baby Live?*, chap. 3.

The argument that Nazi crimes developed out of the euthanasia programme is quoted from Leo Alexander, "Medical Science under Dictatorship", *New England Journal of Medicine*, vol. 241 (14 July 1949), pp. 39–47. Gitta Sereny, *Into that Darkness: From Mercy Killing to Mass Murder* (London, 1974) makes a similar claim in tracing the career of Franz Stangl from the euthanasia centres to the death camp at Treblinka; but in so doing she reveals how different the Nazi 'euthanasia' programme was from what is now advocated (see especially pp. 51–5). For an example of a survey showing that people regularly evaluate some health states as worse than death, see G. W. Torrance, "Utility approach to measuring health-related quality of life", *Journal of Chronic Diseases*, 40:6 (1987).

On euthanasia among the Eskimo (and the rarity of homicide outside such special circumstances), see E. Westermarck, *The Origin and Development of Moral Ideas*, vol. 1, pp. 329–34, 387, n.1 and 392, nn.1–3.

CHAPTER 8: RICH AND POOR

For a more detailed discussion of the obligations of the affluent to the poor, see Peter Singer, *The Life You Can Save* (New York, 2009). Other valuable books on this topic are Peter Unger, *Living High and Letting Die* (New York, 1996); William Aiken and Hugh LaFollette (eds.), *World Hunger and Moral Obligation* (Upper Saddle River, NJ, 1996); Thomas Pogge, *World Hunger and Human Rights* (Cambridge, 2002); Deen Chatterjee (ed.), *The Ethics of Assistance* (Cambridge, 2004); Garrett Cullity, *The Moral Demands of Affluence* (Oxford, 2005); and Thomas Pogge (ed.), *Freedom from Poverty as a Human Right* (Oxford, 2007). For a discussion of the causes of poverty, see Paul Collier, *The Bottom Billion* (New York, 2007).

The report of the World Bank's research team on poverty was published as: Deepa Narayan with Raj Patel, Kai Schafft, Anne Rademacher and Sarah Koch-Schulte, *Voices of the Poor: Can Anyone Hear Us?* (New York,

2000). For UNICEf's latest figures on child mortality, see www.childinfo
.org/mortality.html.

For figures on how much aid each nation gives, see http://www.oecd.
org/countrylist/0,3349,en_2649_34447_1783495_1_1_1_1,00.html.

On the difference that an identifiable victim makes on our willingness to help, see Paul Slovic, "Psychic Numbing", *Judgment and Decision
Making*, 2 (2007), pp. 79–95. On the difference – or lack of it – between
killing and allowing to die, see (in addition to the previous references to
active and passive euthanasia) Jonathan Glover, *Causing Death and Saving
Lives*, chap. 7; Richard Trammel, "Saving Life and Taking Life", *Journal
of Philosophy*, vol. 72 (1975); John Harris, "The Marxist Conception of
Violence", *Philosophy and Public Affairs*, vol. 3 (1974); John Haris, *Violence
and Responsibility* (London, 1980); and S. Kagan, *The Limits of Morality*
(Oxford, 1989).

John Locke's view of rights is developed in his *Second Treatise on Civil
Government* (1690), and Robert Nozick's in *Anarchy, State and Utopia* (New
York, 1974). For Narveson's defence of this position and my response,
see Jeffrey Schaler (ed.), *Peter Singer Under Fire* (Chicago, 2009). Thomas
Aquinas' very different view is quoted from *Summa Theologica*, II, ii, ques-
tion 66, article 7. Thomas Pogge argues that we are responsible for
causing or maintaining poverty in his *World Hunger and Human Rights*
(Cambridge, 2002).

On the effectiveness of aid, see www.GiveWell.org and my discussion
in *The Life You Can Save* (New York, 2009), chap. 6.

Garrett Hardin proposed his 'lifeboat ethic' in "Living on a Lifeboat",
Bioscience, October 1974, another version of which has been reprinted
in W. Aiken and H. La Follette (eds.), *World Hunger and Moral Obligation*
(Englewood Cliffs, 1977). Hardin elaborates on the argument in *The
Limits of Altruism* (Bloomington, Indiana, 1977). An earlier argument
against aid was voiced by W. and P. Paddock in their mistitled *Famine
1975!* (Boston, 1967), but pride of place in the history of this view
must go to Thomas Malthus for *An Essay on the Principle of Population*
(London, 1798). A discussion of the population issue, and of how much
grain we waste by feeding it to animals, is in Peter Singer, *The Life You
Can Save*, chap. 7. UN estimates of the drop in fertility rates can be
found in United Nations, *World Population Prospects: The 2006 Revision*,
Department of Economic and Social Affairs, Population Division (New
York, 2007). On the slowing of the pace of fertility decline, see John
Bongaarts, "Fertility Transitions in Developing Countries: Progress or
Stagnation?" Population Council, New York, Poverty, Gender, and Youth
Working Paper no. 7, 2008.

On the actions of the Salwen family, see Kevin and Hannah Salwen, *The Power of Half: One Family's Decision to Stop Taking and Start Giving Back* (New York, 2010). On Zell Kravinsky, see Ian Parker, "The Gift", *The New Yorker*, August 2, 2004. Susan Wolf's article "Moral Saints" appeared in *Journal of Philosophy*, 79 (1982), pp. 419–39. For a discussion of whether a position like that defended here sets too high a standard, see the "Symposium on Impartiality and Ethical Theory", *Ethics* 101:4 (July 1991). For a forceful defence of impartialist ethics against this objection, see S. Kagan, *The Limits of Morality* (Oxford, Clarendon Press, 1989). See also Peter Singer, *The Life You Can Save*, chap. 9–10.

CHAPTER 9: CLIMATE CHANGE

The basic documents for assessing climate change are the Assessment Reports of the Intergovernmental Panel on Climate Change. At the time of writing, the most recent of these documents is the *Fourth Assessment Report*, released in 2007. The reports are available at www.ipcc.ch. Tim Flannery's *The Weather Makers* (New York, 2001) is a fine broad introduction to the topic, as is the same author's briefer *Now or Never* (New York, 2009). The literature on ethical aspects of climate change includes: Stephen Gardiner, *A Perfect Moral Storm* (Oxford, 2011); James Garvey, *The Ethics of Climate Change*, (New York, 2008); and Jeremy Moss (ed.), *Climate Change and Social Justice* (Melbourne, 2009). A useful collection is: Stephen Gardiner, Simon Caney, Dale Jamieson and Henry Shue, eds., *Climate Ethics* (New York, 2010).

The figure on the number of deaths already caused by global warming comes from World Health Organization, *The Global Burden of Disease*, 2004, Annex, p.8, http://www.who.int/healthinfo/global_burden_disease/GlobalHealthRisks_report_annex.pdf.

On the disappearance of the Sunderbans: Somini Sengupta, "Sea's Rise in India Buries Islands and a Way of Life", *New York Times*, 11 April 2007. The predictions regarding the likely future impact of climate change are drawn from the Intergovernmental Panel on Climate Change (IPCC), "Summary for Policymakers", in IPCC, *Climate Change 2007: Impacts, Adaptation and Vulnerability. Contribution of Working Group II to the Fourth Assessment Report of the Intergovernmental Panel on Climate Change* (Cambridge, 2007 and online at www.ipcc.ch), pp. 1–22. For the Brazilian proposal, see:

http://unfccc.int/methods_and_science/other_methodological_issues/items/1038.php For figures on historical responsibility for climate change, see: Niklas Höhne et al., *Summary report of the ad hoc group for the modeling and assessment of contributions to climate change (MATCH)*, November 2008, http://unfccc.int/files/methods_and_science/other_methodological_issues/application/pdf/match_summary_report_.pdf; see also Michel den Elzen et al., "Analysing countries' contribution to climate change: scientific and policy-related choices", *Environmental Science & Policy*, 8 (2005), pp. 614–636. The Chinese document referred to in the text is: Chinese Academy of Sciences, Chinese Academy of Social Sciences, Development Research Center of the State Council, National Climate Center, Tsinghua University, *Carbon Equity: Perspective from Chinese Academic Community*, December 10, 2009.

The United Nations Framework Convention on Climate Change can be found at http://www.unfccc.int/resource/conv/conv.html.
The suggestion that we should not exceed 350 ppm of CO_2 in the atmosphere was made in James Hansen, et al., "Target Atmospheric CO_2: Where Should Humanity Aim?" *Open Atmosphere Science Journal*, 2 (2008), pp. 217–31. Hansen argues against a cap and trade scheme in his "Cap and Fade," *The New York Times*, December 7, 2009; Paul Krugman responds in his "Building a Green Economy," *New York Times Sunday Magazine*, April 5, 2010.

For the approach taken by the German Advisory Council on Global Change, see WBGU, *Solving the Climate Dilemma: The Budget Approach* (Berlin, 2009). available at http://www.wbgu.de/wbgu_sn2009_en.html. The quote from Angela Merkel is from her speech at the symposium "Global Sustainability" given in Potsdam, October 9, 2007, available in German as 'Rede von Bundeskanzlerin Dr. Angela Merkel beim Symposium "Global Sustainability" am 9. Oktober 2007 in Potsdam," Bundesregierung, *Bulletin* 104-1 10.10.2007, http://www.bundesregierung.de/nn_1514/Content/DE/Bulletin/2007/10/104-1-bk-klima.html. For Henry Shue's distinction, see his "Subsistence Emissions and Luxury Emissions", *Law and Policy*, 15 (1993), pp. 39–59. For China's defence of something like this view in 2007, see Xinhua news agency, "China urges accommodation to 'emissions of subsistence'" *China Daily*, 2007–08–02.

President Museveni's remarks are from his speech at the African Union summit, Addis Ababa, Ethiopia, February 2007, as reported in Andrew Revkin, "Poor Nations to Bear Brunt as World Warms", *New York Times*, 1 April 2007.

The UN Food and Agriculture Organization's proposal for a tax on meat was included in its report, *Livestock in the Balance: The State of Food and Agriculture, 2009* (Rome, 2010), p. 74.

The quotation from President George W. Bush is reported in Edmund Andrews, "Bush Angers Europe by Eroding Pact on Warming", *New York Times* April 1, 2001, and that from his spokesperson, Ari Fleisher, is from the White House press briefing of May 7, 2001.

On issues about individual responsibility for actions to which we contribute, the following are relevant: David Lyons, *Forms and Limits of Utilitarianism* (Oxford, 1965); R. M. Hare, "Could Kant have been a Utilitarian?" *Utilitas*, 5 (1993), pp. 1–16; Brad Hooker, *Ideal Code, Real World* (Oxford, 2000); David Schwartz, *Consuming Choices* (Lanham, Md, 2010); Derek Parfit, *Reasons and Persons*, (Oxford, 1984), chap.3; Christopher Kutz, *Complicity: Ethics and Law for a Collective Age*, (Cambridge, 2000); and Jonathan Glover, "It makes no difference whether or not I do it", *Proceedings of the Aristotelian Society*, Supplementary Volume XLIX (1975).

CHAPTER 10: THE ENVIRONMENT

On the proposal to dam the Franklin River in Southwest Tasmania, see James McQueen, *The Franklin: Not Just a River* (Ringwood, Victoria, 1983).

The first Bible quotation is from *Genesis* 1:24–28 and the second from *Genesis* 9:1–3. For attempts to soften the message of these passages see, for instance, Robin Attfield, *The Ethics of Environmental Concern* (Oxford, 1983) and Andrew Linzey, *Christianity and the Rights of Animals* (London, 1987). The quotation from Paul comes from *Corinthians* 9:9–10, and that from Augustine is from *The Catholic and Manichean Ways of Life*, translated by D. A. Gallagher and I. J. Gallagher (Catholic University Press, Boston, 1966), p. 102. For the cursing of the fig tree, see *Mark* 11:12–22 and for the drowning of the pigs, *Mark* 5:1–13. The passage from Aristotle is to be found in *Politics* (J. M. Dent and Sons, London, 1916), p. 16; for the views of Aquinas see *Summa Theologica*, II, ii, question 64, article 1; I, ii, question 72, article 4.

For details on the alternative Christian thinkers, see Keith Thomas, *Man and the Natural World* (Allen Lane, London, 1983), pp. 246–7, and Attfield, *The Ethics of Environmental Concern* (London, 1929), pp. 246–7.

The quotations from Bill McKibben's *The End of Nature* (New York, 1989) are from pp. 58 and 60. See also the same author's *Eaarth*, (New York, 2010).

Albert Schweitzer's most complete statement of his ethical stance is *Civilization and Ethics* (Part II of *The Philosophy of Civilization*), tr. C.T.

Campion, (2nd edition, London, 1929). The quotation is from pp. 246–7. The quotations from Paul Taylor's *Respect for Nature*, (Princeton, 1986) are from pp. 45 and 128. For a critique of Taylor, see Gerald Paske, "The Life Principle: a (metaethical) rejection", *Journal of Applied Philosophy*, 6 (1989).

Holmes Rolston's objection to what I wrote in the 2nd edition of this book can be found in his "Respect for Life: Counting what Singer Finds of no Account", in Dale Jamieson (ed.), *Singer and Critics* (Oxford, 1999), pp. 247–68; see also my response in the same volume.

A. Leopold's proposal for a 'land ethic' can be found in his *A Sand County Almanac, with Essays on Conservation from Round River* (New York, 1970; first published 1949, 1953); the passages quoted are from pp. 238 and 262. The classic text for the distinction between shallow and deep ecology is Arne Naess, "The Shallow and the Deep, Long-Range Ecology Movement", *Inquiry*, 16 (1973), pp. 95–100. For other works on deep ecology, see, for example: Arne Naess and George Sessions, "Basic Principles of Deep Ecology", *Ecophilosophy*, 6 (1984); W. Devall and G. Sessions, *Deep Ecology: Living As If Nature Mattered* (Salt Lake City, 1985) (The passage quoted in the "Deep ecology" section of Chapter 10 is from p. 67); Lawrence Johnson, *A Morally Deep World* (Cambridge, 1990); Freya Mathews, *The Ecological Self* (London, 1991); Val Plumwood, "Ecofeminism: an Overview and Discussion of Positions and Arguments: Critical Review", *Australasian Journal of Philosophy*, 64 (Supplement, 1986); and Richard Sylvan, "Three Essays Upon Deeper Environmental Ethics", *Discussion Papers in Environmental Philosophy*, 13 (1986) (Published by the Australian National University, Canberra). James Lovelock, *Gaia: A New Look at Life on Earth* was published in Oxford in 1979. Christopher Stone's *Earth and Other Ethics* (New York, 1987) is a tentative exploration of ways in which nonsentient beings might be included in an ethical framework.

The original *Green Consumer Guide* was by John Elkington and Julia Hailes (London, 1988). Adaptations have since been published in several other countries, as have many similar guides. On the environmental extravagance of animal production, see the references given for Chapter 8. For an excellent introduction to environmental ethics, see Dale Jamieson, *Ethics and the Environment* (Cambridge, 2008). Dale Jamieson (ed.), *A Companion to Environmental Philosophy* (Oxford, 2001) is a comprehensive collection of essays. See also the article "Environmental Ethics" by Andrew Brennan in the online *Stanford Encyclopedia of Philosophy*.

CHAPTER 11: CIVIL DISOBEDIENCE, VIOLENCE AND TERRORISM

The story of Oskar Schindler is brilliantly told by Thomas Kenneally in *Schindler's Ark* (London, 1982). The case of Joan Andrews and the work of Operation Rescue is described by Bernard Nathanson, "Operation Rescue: Domestic Terrorism or Legitimate Civil Rights Protest?" *Hastings Center Report*, November/December 1989, pp. 28–32. The biblical passage quoted is from *Proverbs* 24:11. The claim by Gary Leber about the number of children saved is in his essay "We must rescue them", *Hastings Center Report*, November/December 1989, pp. 26–7. On Gennarelli's experiments and the events surrounding them, see Lori Gruen and Peter Singer, *Animal Liberation: A Graphic Guide* (Camden Press, London, 1987). On the Animal Liberation Front, see also Philip Windeatt, "They clearly now see the link: militant voices", in Peter Singer (ed.), *In Defence of Animals* (Blackwell, Oxford, 1986). The blockade of the Franklin River is vividly described by a participant in James McQueen, *The Franklin: Not Just a River* (Ringwood, Victoria, 1983). On the unsuccessful earlier campaign to save Lake Peddar, see Kevin Kiernan, "I Saw My Temple Ransacked", in Cassandra Pybus and Richard Flanagan (eds.), *The Rest of the World is Watching* (Sydney, 1990). On the Capitol Power Plant protest, see Bryan Walsh, "Despite Snow – and Irony – A Climate Protest Persists", *Time*, March 3, 2009.

Henry Thoreau's "Civil Disobedience" has been reprinted in several places, among them H. A. Bedau (ed.), *Civil Disobedience: Theory and Practice* (New York, 1969); the passage quoted is on p. 28 of this collection. The quotation immediately following is from p. 18 of R. P. Wolff's *In Defense of Anarchism* (New York, 1970). On the nature of conscience, see A. Campbell Garnett, "Conscience and Conscientiousness", in J. Feinberg (ed.), *Moral Concepts* (Oxford, 1969).

John Locke argued for the importance of settled law in his *Second Treatise on Civil Government* (1690), especially sections 124–6.

On the many attempts to reform the law on animal experimentation, see Richard Ryder, *Victims of Science* (London, 1975). For a defence of civil disobedience in this context, see Pelle Strindlund, "Butchers Knives into Pruning Hooks: Civil Disobedience for Animals", in Peter Singer, *In Defense of Animals: The Second Wave* (Oxford, 2006).

Mill's proposal for multiple votes for the better educated occurs in chapter 8 of his *Representative Government*. The quotation from Engels' *Condition of the Working Class in England* (tr. and ed. W. Henderson and

W. Chaloner, Oxford, 1958), p. 108, I owe to John Harris, "The Marxist Conception of Violence", *Philosophy and Public Affairs,* vol. 3 (1974), which argues persuasively for regarding passive violence as a genuine form of violence. See also Harris's book, *Violence and Responsibility* (London, 1980) and Ted Honderich, *Three Essays on Political Violence* (Oxford, 1976). Dave Foreman and Bill Haywood, *Ecodefense: A Field Guide to Monkeywrenching* is now in its 3rd edition (Chico, CA, 1993).

The relevance of democracy to the justification of disobedience to the law is more fully treated in my *Democracy and Disobedience* (Oxford, 1973). J. G. Murphy (ed.), *Civil Disobedience and Violence* (Belmont, 1971) is still a useful collection. H. A. Bedau has also edited another anthology, in addition to the one referred to previously: *Civil Disobedience in Focus* (London, 1991). For more recent discussion of civil disobedience see Kimberley Brownlee, "Civil Disobedience", in the online *Stanford Encyclopedia of Philosophy.*

Readings on terrorism can be found in Tony Coady and Michael O'Keefe (eds.), *Terrorism and Justice: Moral Argument in a Threatened World* (Melbourne 2002), and in Igor Primoratz (ed.), *Terrorism: The Philosophical Issues* (New York, 2004). Primoratz is also the author of the article on terrorism in the online *Stanford Encyclopedia of Philosophy.*

CHAPTER 12: WHY ACT MORALLY?

For attempts to reject the title of this chapter as an improper question, see S. Toulmin, *The Place of Reason in Ethics* (Cambridge, 1961), p. 162; J. Hospers, *Human Conduct* (London, 1963), p. 194; and M.G. Singer, *Generalization in Ethics* (London, 1963), pp. 319–27. D. H. Monro defines ethical judgments as overriding in *Empiricism and Ethics* (Cambridge, 1967), see for instance p. 127. R. M. Hare's prescriptivist view of ethics implies that a commitment to act is involved in accepting a moral judgment, but because only universalizable judgments count as moral judgments, this view does not have the consequence that whatever judgment we take to be overriding is necessarily our moral judgment. Hare's view therefore allows us to give sense to our question. On this general issue of the definition of moral terms and the consequences of different definitions, see my "The Triviality of the Debate over 'Is-Ought' and the Definition of 'Moral'", *American Philosophical Quarterly,* vol. 10 (1973).

The argument discussed in the second section is a distillation of such sources as: Marcus Aurelius, *Meditations,* bk. IV, par. 4; I. Kant, *Groundwork of the Metaphysic of Morals;* H. J. Paton, *The Categorical Imperative* (London,

1963), pp. 245–6; J. Hospers, *Human Conduct* (London, 1963), pp. 584–93; and D. Gauthier, *Practical Reasoning* (Oxford, 1963), p. 118. For a distinct defence of a Kantian view that would require separate discussion, see Christine Korsgaard, *The Sources of Normativity* (Cambridge, 1996).

Hume defends his view of practical reason in *A Treatise of Human Nature*, bk. II, pt. iii, sec. 3. Thomas Nagel's objections to it are in *The Possibility of Altruism* (Oxford, 1970). Nagel restated his position in *The View from Nowhere* (New York, 1986). Sidgwick's observation on the rationality of egoism is on p. 498 of *The Methods of Ethics* (7th ed., London, 1907). Parfit's account of the person with Future Tuesday Indifference is quoted from Derek Parfit, *On What Matters*, (Oxford, forthcoming), but he first discussed this possible attitude in his *Reasons and Persons* (Oxford, 1984), p. 124. Sharon Street responds to Parfit in "In Defense of Future Tuesday Indifference: Ideally Coherent Eccentrics and the Contingency of What Matters," *Philosophical Issues*, 19 (2009), pp. 273–298. For Parfit's modification of Sigwick's position on the rationality of doing what is in one's own interests, see *On What Matters*, Ch. 6.

Bradley's insistence on loving virtue for her own sake comes from his *Ethical Studies* (Oxford, 1876, reprinted 1962), pp. 61–3. The same position can be found in Kant's *Groundwork of the Metaphysic of Morals*, chap. 1, and in D. Z. Phillips, "Does it Pay to be Good?" *Proceedings of the Aristotelian Society*, vol. 64 (1964–5). Bradley and Kant are expounding what they take to be 'the common moral consciousness' rather than their own views. Kant himself adheres to the view of the common moral consciousness, but later in *Ethical Studies* Bradley supports a view of morality in which the subjective satisfaction involved in the moral life plays a prominent role.

My account of why we believe that only actions done for the sake of morality have moral worth is similar to Hume's view in his *Enquiry Concerning the Principles of Morals*. Socrates' conclusion that 'the just man is happy' can be found in Plato, *The Republic*, 354a.

The first survey mentioned in regards to charitable giving is from the Social Capital Community Benchmark Survey, and the second is from the University of Michigan's Panel Study of Income Dynamics. I owe the references to Arthur Brooks, "Why Giving Makes You Happy," *New York Sun*, December 28, 2007. Other studies are described in Jonathan Haidt, *The Happiness Hypothesis* (New York, 2006), chap. 8. The brain imaging study is reported in William T. Harbaugh, Ulrich Mayr, and Daniel Burghart, "Neural Responses to Taxation and Voluntary Giving

Reveal Motives for Charitable Donations," *Science*, 316 (June 15, 2007), pp. 1622–25.

Maslow presents some very sketchy data in support of his theory of personality in "Psychological Data and Value Theory" in A. H. Maslow (ed.), *New Knowledge in Human Values* (New York, 1959); see also A. H. Maslow, *Motivation and Personality* (New York, 1954).

On psychopaths, see H. Cleckley, *The Mask of Sanity* (5th ed., St Louis, 1976). The remark about requests for help coming from relatives, not the psychopaths themselves, is on p. viii. The quotation from a happy psychopath is from W. and J. McCord, *Psychopathy and Delinquency* (New York, 1956), p. 6. On the ability of psychopaths to avoid prison, see R. D. Hare, *Psychopathy* (New York, 1970), pp. 111–12. The example of the psychopath who forgot his wallet comes from R. D. Hare, *Without Conscience: The Disturbing World of Psychopaths among Us*, (New York, 1993), pp. 58–9. I was directed to it by Heidi Maibom, "Moral Unreason: The Case of Psychopathy", *Mind & Language*, 20 (2005), pp. 237–57.

The 'paradox of hedonism' is discussed by F. H. Bradley in the third essay of his *Ethical Studies*; for a psychotherapist's account, see Viktor Frankl, *The Will to Meaning* (London, 1971), pp. 33–4.

On the relation between self-interest and ethics, see the concluding chapter of Sidgwick's *Methods of Ethics* and the discussion in Derek Parfit's *On What Matters*, Ch. 6.

For details on the birthday parties that cost in excess of $5 million, see Andrew Ross Sorkin, "In Defense of Schwarzman", *The New York Times*, July 29, 2007.

Index